CISTERCIAN STUDIES SERIES: NUMBER TWO HUNDRED SIXTY-ONE

Gregory the Great

Moral Reflections on the Book of Job

Volume 6

Books 28–35

CISTERCIAN STUDIES SERIES: NUMBER TWO HUNDRED SIXTY-ONE

Moral Reflections on the Book of Job

Volume 6

Books 28–35

Gregory the Great

Translated by

Brian Kerns, OCSO

Introduction by

Mark DelCogliano

Afterword by Brian Kerns, OCSO

Comprehensive Index to Volumes 1–6

Cistercian Publications
www.cistercianpublications.org

LITURGICAL PRESS
Collegeville, Minnesota
www.litpress.org

A Cistercian Publications title published by Liturgical Press

Cistercian Publications
Editorial Offices
161 Grosvenor Street
Athens, Ohio 45701
www.cistercianpublications.org

A translation of the critical edition by Marcus Adriaen, *Moralia in Iob*, in Corpus Christianorum, Series Latina 143, 143A, 143B.

Biblical quotations are translated by Brian Kerns, OCSO.

© 2022 by Order of Saint Benedict, Collegeville, Minnesota. All rights reserved. No part of this book may be used or reproduced in any manner whatsoever, except brief quotations in reviews, without written permission of Liturgical Press, Saint John's Abbey, PO Box 7500, Collegeville, MN 56321-7500. Printed in the United States of America.

ISBN 978-0-87907-261-2 (Volume 6)

1	2	3	4	5	6	7	8	9

Library of Congress Cataloging-in-Publication Data

Gregory I, Pope, approximately 540–604.
    [Moralia in Iob. Selections. English]
    Gregory the Great : moral reflections on the Book of Job, vol. 1, preface and books 1-5 / translated by Brian Kerns, OCSO ; introduction by Mark DelCogliano.
        pages cm. — (Cistercian studies series ; number two hundred forty-nine)
    Includes index.
    ISBN 978-0-87907-149-3 (hardcover) — ISBN 978-0-87907-249-0 (pbk.) — ISBN 978-0-87907-754-9 (ebook)
    1. Bible. Job I-V, 2—Commentaries—Early works to 1800. I. Kerns, Brian, translator. II. DelCogliano, Mark, writer of introduction. III. Title.

BS1415.53.G7413   2014
223'.107—dc23   2014015314

I dedicate the six volumes of this work
to the late +Dom John Eudes Bamberger
(1926–2001)
who was always a great inspiration to me,
and whose encouragement in this work never flagged. (BK)

Contents

List of Abbreviations ix

Introduction 1
Mark DelCogliano

Book 28 (Job 38:1–38:11) 9

Book 29 (Job 38:12–38:33) 59

Book 30 (Job 38:34–39:8) 129

Book 31 (Job 39:9–39:32) 205

Book 32 (Job 39:34–40:14) 301

Book 33 (Job 40:15–41:12) 359

Book 34 (Job 41:13–41:25) 439

Book 35 (Job 42:2–42:16) 491

Afterword 539
Brian Kerns

Comprehensive Scriptural Index 543

Abbreviations

Publications: Books and Series

CS   Cistercian Studies series. Kalamazoo, MI, and Collegeville, MN: Cistercian Publications.

De doc chr   *De Doctrina Christiana*, Augustine

LXX   Septuagint

Introduction

Mark DelCogliano

The last of the six parts of Gregory the Great's *Moralia in Job* accomplishes what so many patristic and early medieval authors could not: it brings a monumental verse-by-verse commentary project to its long-desired conclusion, reaching the last verse of the last chapter of the biblical book. Gregory's achievement is all the more impressive given that the object of his study was the lengthy biblical book of Job, with its many chapters of obscure, arcane, and theologically dense poetry. If this last part had been cursorily written in a mad dash to finish the undertaking in the early days of his papacy, one might have been inclined to forgive Gregory.[1] But it is nothing of the sort. In it there are no signs of weariness, no taking of shortcuts, no half-hearted efforts.[2] The capstone of this literary cathedral was set with as much sense of purpose, vigor, and meticulousness as the cornerstone had been.

Part 6 resembles the previous five parts in many ways. Like parts 4 and 5, part 6 was probably originally dictated by Gregory, unlike parts 1–3, which were originally delivered orally.[3] The number of verses covered in the sixth part (145) is on par with that of parts 2 (179), 4 (173), and 5 (165), each of which, like part 6, for the most

---

[1] On the dating, see CS 249:8–11.

[2] Book 35 opens with, "Since this is the last book of this work, and the most difficult passages have already been treated, so that those that are left are less obscure, we are now free to speak more leniently and more casually" (35.I.1). This sentence is followed by a metaphor involving a ship taking down its sails as it floats gently into the harbor. Even if Gregory felt that verses discussed in Book 35 (Job 42:1-17, the prose epilogue) were easier to interpret than the preceding poetry, he does not give them short shrift.

[3] On these different compositional methods, see CS 249:9; CS 259:2.

1

part dispensed with historical interpretations in favor of the typical or moral interpretations (and sometimes both).[4] Similar to all the parts except part 3, part 6 contains the many digressions, excurses, and mini-treatises in which Gregory elaborated at great length on topics of especial interest to himself and his readers. Part 6, however, differs from the 5 preceding parts in one significant way: whereas the first 5 parts contain 5 or 6 books each, part 6 contains 8 books, making the verses-to-books ratio for part 6 on par with part 1, where, however, many verses were subjected to a threefold interpretation.[5] This is another indication, I think, of the unflagging industry with which Gregory completed this project. And so, rather than limping to the finish line, he did not merely maintain his stamina but had a burst of energy when that finish line came into view.

Gregory's renewed energy may have been due to what he had to interpret in part 6. There are two discrete literary units discussed in part 6.[6] The first—and most important in Gregory's eyes—is the climax of the biblical book, when the Lord appears to Job in a whirlwind and finally speaks to him. Here the Lord delivers two speeches to Job, to each of which Job briefly responds (Job 38:1–42:6). It takes Gregory four books (28–31) to comment on the first speech of the Lord (Job 38:1–39:32),[7] whereas the next three books (32–34) are devoted to Job's response to the first speech (Job 39:33-35),[8] the Lord's second speech (Job 40:1–41:25),[9] and Job's response to it

---

[4] See CS 258:1–2. In part 1 Gregory commented on only 84 verses because he attempted to interpret many verses in three ways (historical, typical, and moral); part 3 dealt with 324 verses because Gregory never had the opportunity to revise and expand his originally spoken remarks.

[5] The part 1 verses-to-books ratio is 16::8; part 2, 35::8; part 3, 54::0; part 4, 28::8; part 5, 33::0; and part 6, 18::1.

[6] Gregory does not however identify them as clearly as he did in the case of the speeches of Elihu that were the subject of part 5; see CS 260:1–2.

[7] This is the Vulgate versification; it is 38:1–40:2 in English translations based on the Hebrew text.

[8] 40:3-5 in English translations based on the Hebrew text.

[9] 40:6–41:34 in English translations based on the Hebrew text.

(Job 42:1-6). Book 35 covers the denouement of the book, the prose epilogue in which the Lord rebukes Job's friends and restores Job's fortunes (Job 40:7-17).[10] The chief purpose of the Lord's speeches, according to Gregory, was to keep Job from pride.[11] At this point in the narrative Job had remained virtuous through many trials but was in danger of pride precisely because of his perseverance in virtue. Accordingly, the Lord's speeches to Job for the most part take the form of elaborate rhetorical interrogations of him for the purpose of comparing him to the Lord. In the course of this questioning the Lord makes it bluntly obvious that Job falls infinitely short of the almighty God. In this way Job comes to know the truth of who he is, in all his inadequacy, and—thus humbled—he is protected from pride.[12]

Gregory's interpretation of the Lord's speeches as the thwarting of pride is not surprising given his economy of vice and sin. Following the teaching of Scripture, he understood pride as *the beginning of all sin* (Sir 10:15).[13] He thus viewed pride as the cause of Adam's sin in Paradise, the primordial font of all vice, as it were, the disastrous effects of which were only undone by God's humility in the incarnation.[14] And just as pride is the beginning of all sin for all humanity corporately, so too is it for every human being individually. This is clearly seen in Gregory's enumeration of what he calls the "seven principal vices," which became the basis for the Western tradition of the seven deadly sins. This enumeration appears in part 6, in Book 31, near the end of Gregory's interpretation of the Lord's first speech to Job. In the course of his interpretation of Job 39:25 (*He hears the urging of the captains and the roars of the army*), Gregory teaches that pride is "the queen of the vices, and once she has taken over the vanquished heart completely, she soon hands it

---

[10] See n. 2 above.
[11] See *Moralia* 28.Preface.
[12] See *Moralia* 30.I.1.
[13] See *Moralia* 14.XVI.19; 31.XLV.87.
[14] See *Moralia* 31.I.1.

over to the seven principal vices, who are as it were her captains, to be destroyed."[15] And then what follows each of these captains is a different army—"oppressive multitudes of vices."[16] Gregory lists these seven principal vices (*septem principalia vitia*) as vainglory (*inanis gloria*), envy (*invidia*), anger (*ira*), sorrow (*tristia*), avarice (*avaritia*), gluttony (*ventris ingluvies*), and lust (*luxuria*).[17] Each of these vices is the source of a whole army of other vices—the Latin word *principalia* is cognate with *principium*, "beginning" or "source" or "origin." In 31.XLV.88 Gregory lists the members of each army. For example, "from avarice are born treachery, dishonesty, deception, perjury, disorder, violence, and hardness of heart against mercy." There is no reason to think that any of these lists is exhaustive but rather that Gregory means them to be representative. So Gregory's scheme of seven principal vices is an aetiology of sin that traces each sin back to one of the seven principal vices, and these in turn are traced back to pride, *the beginning of all sin.*

At the same time, the order of Gregory's list is also intentional and important. For he remarks that pride gives birth to vainglory, vainglory to envy, envy to anger, and so on.[18] There is a chain of cause and effect wherein an effect in turn becomes a cause. Five of these vices (vainglory, envy, anger, sorrow, and avarice) are rational and spiritual, in the sense that they primarily afflict the mind and soul (today we might call these psychological), and two (gluttony and lust) are carnal, since they are primarily experienced in the body. Gregory describes at length how this cascading of vices works.[19] Thus he envisions a person's descent into vice not merely as the soldier of Christ losing the spiritual battle against the forces of vice led by pride, the queen of vice, but also as a human being's degradation from innate rationality and spirituality into subhuman, bestial carnality.

---

[15] *Moralia* 31.XLV.87.
[16] *Moralia* 31.XLV.87.
[17] See *Moralia* 31.XLV.87.
[18] *Moralia* 31.XLV.89.
[19] *Moralia* 31.XLV.90.

The mini-treatise on the seven principal vices in Book 31 is a good example of something stated in the introduction to part 1: Gregory "recapitulates the best of patristic theology and monastic spirituality; transforms these in the light of his own experience as a pastor, ascetic, and contemplative; and bequeaths his resultant vision of the Christian life to the Middle Ages and beyond."[20] Gregory was not the first to enumerate a list of principal vices, but he was adapting an earlier monastic list of the eight principal thoughts or vices that was originally drawn up by Evagrius of Pontus (+399), who was systematizing the teachings of the Egyptian desert fathers. This list in turn was popularized by John Cassian (+435), whose *Institutes* and *Conferences* became seminal documents of Western monasticism.[21] Gregory's list differs from theirs in significant ways. Whereas their list has eight vices, his has only seven, eliminating pride, which as we have seen precedes the seven principal vices in Gregory's aetiology of sin. Gregory puts pride in a category of its own as the beginning of all sin. Having eliminated pride, Gregory also reverses the order of the list. Yet in spite of these different orders, Gregory agrees with the monastic theoreticians in considering pride the most dangerous and destructive of all the vices; he just highlights this fact differently.

In terms of the individual vices on each of the lists, there is for the most part conceptual overlap, although Gregory combines some of the vices on the monastic list. But there is one exception: there is no parallel to envy in the enumerations of Evagrius and Cassian. Rather, Gregory adds envy to the lists he inherited. With this addition Gregory is thus innovative but at the same time also traditional. Envy was not unknown to the monastic theologians, and before Evagrius, Origen had recognized envy as one of the chief sins.[22] Indeed, since

---

[20] CS 249:1.
[21] Evagrius, *Praktikos* 6–14; John Cassian, *Institutes*, Books 5–12. Their lists are identical: gluttony, fornication, avarice, sorrow, anger, acedia, vainglory, and pride.
[22] E.g. Evagrius, *To Eulogios* 17.18; *On the Vices opposed to the Virtues* 8. In the latter, Evagrius adds jealousy as the ninth principal thought to the eight. See

the days of the apostles envy had been seen as a hindrance to the Christian life.[23] Perhaps Gregory was inspired to add envy because of Wisdom 2:24, *By the envy of the devil death has entered the world.* Though pride was the motive for Adam's primordial sin, Gregory teaches, on the basis of this verse, that the devil's tempting of Adam was motivated by envy.[24] It may be for this reason that envy has an importance for Gregory that it did not have for Evagrius and Cassian.

In the West, Gregory's list of the seven principal vices soon eclipsed those of Evagrius and Cassian. There are innumerable appropriations of Gregory's list of vices, but only a few are mentioned briefly here to illustrate his bequeathing of ideas to subsequent generations. The seven deadly sins became central to Catholic teaching and preaching in the Middle Ages, especially in the context of confessional practices. They were the subject of endless commentary, and many treatises were devoted to them.[25] Thomas Aquinas (+1274) himself defended Gregory's enumeration, though he preferred to call them "seven capital vices."[26] In fact, the seven deadly sins remain part of official Catholic teaching today, though they are not emphasized as they once were.[27]

The seven principal vices also fired the imaginations of writers and artists. Dante Alighieri (+1321), in *Purgatorio*, the second book of his *Commedia Divina*, imagines the geography of purgatory as an island mountain of seven terraces, each of which corresponds to one of the seven deadly sins. While Dante and Vergil ascend this mountain as they journey to Paradise, they encounter souls being punished for the vice that corresponds to the terrace and see examples of its opposite virtue. The painting entitled "The Seven Deadly Sins and the Four

---

also Cassian, *Conferences* 18.15–16. See also Irénée Hausherr, "L'origine de la théorie orientale des huit péchés capitaux," *Orientalia Christiana Periodica* 3 (1933): 164–75.

[23] See e.g. Rom 13:13; 1 Cor 3:3; 2 Cor 12:20; Gal 5:20-21; 5:26; 1 Tim 6:4; Titus 3:3; Jas 3:14; 3:16; 1 Pet 2:1; *Didache* 5:1.

[24] *Moralia* 5.XLVI.85; 31.I.1.

[25] E.g. William Perrault, *Summa de vitiis*, written around 1236.

[26] *Summa theologicae* Ia–IIae, q. 84, a. 4.

[27] *Catechism of the Catholic Church*, no. 1866.

Last Things," attributed to Hieronymus Bosch (+1516), is notable because it represents each of the seven deadly sins not allegorically, as had been the previous custom, but by depicting human beings in the grip of the vice. Indeed, the exploitation of the seven deadly sins in literature and art continues unabated even to the present day. With the publication of the present volume, the new English translation of the *Moralia* by Br. Brian Kerns, OCSO, is complete: six volumes corresponding to Gregory's original six parts. To continue the metaphor used by Gregory at the beginning of Book 35, our ship having made a long journey across the vast sea of these thirty-five books of the *Moralia* has finally let down its sails and docked in the coastal harbor.[28] I congratulate Br. Brian for his many years of dedication to this project, producing such a high-quality translation, which preserves the complexity of Gregory's Latin without loss of clarity and readability. I have no doubt that his translation—all 2376 pages of it—will remain the standard in English for many generations to come. I remain ever grateful to Dr. Marsha Dutton for her editorial oversight of the project and to Cistercian Publications for their willingness to publish this colossal achievement. It has been a thrill for me to write introductions to each of the six volumes, enabling me *inter alia* to be one of the first to read Br. Brian's fantastic work. I wrote my first introduction in 2014 and this one, the last, in 2021. Seven years separate the first and the last: given Gregory's appreciation for the symbolical resonances of this perfect number, I can't help thinking that the span of years it took to complete this publishing endeavor would at least have made Gregory smile.[29]

               Mark DelCogliano
               St. Paul, Minnesota
               July 29, 2021
               Memorial of Saints Martha, Mary, and Lazarus

---

[28] See n. 2 above.
[29] See Gregory's excursus on the symbolism of the number seven in *Moralia* 35.VIII.15–18.

BOOK 28

PREFACE

After the loss of his possessions, after the death of his heirs, after his bodily wounds, after the words of his wrongly persuading wife, after the insulting words of the comforters, after the spears of so many sufferings that he had courageously received, blessed Job ought to have been praised by the Judge for his great constancy in virtue, if he were to be immediately recalled from this present world. But since he was to receive both gifts already here after his original health was restored to him, so that he might enjoy the use of his restored possessions longer, lest his own victory should defeat him through the sword of pride Almighty God had to upbraid him through strict justice, him whose life he had preserved.

What is worse than that conscious virtue should often kill a soul? While that virtue inflates a soul with self-knowledge, it empties it of the fullness of truth. While pride suggests to a soul that it is capable of receiving the reward itself, it distracts it from the intention of self-improvement. Job was in fact righteous before his trials, but he remained still more righteous after them. God's voice praised him before the trials, but later he grew stronger under the lash. He was unquestionably like a trumpet made flexible from hammered metal, whose elevation for the praise of God was as high as the blows of his chastisement were extensive. But he who was struck down by ulcers stood up by virtues and was to be humiliated. He needed to be humiliated lest the spears of pride should penetrate that most powerful breast, because it was plainly evident that the wounds he received had not overcome it.

It was absolutely necessary that a man be found by comparison with whom he could be defeated. But what about the voice of the Lord, who had said of him, *Have you noticed my servant Job? There is none on earth like him.** By whose comparison then could he be defeated about whom God himself bore witness that he could not be equaled by comparison with any man? What then remained to be done except that the Lord himself in person should relate his own powers to him and ask him, *Can you bring out the morning star in its time, or can you make the evening star rise for the children of men?** And again: *Are the gates of death opened for you, or have you seen the dark doors?** Or at least: *Have you commanded the dawn at your rising, or shown the sunrise its place?** But who can do these things but the Lord?

Nevertheless a man is questioned so that he may know that he cannot do them, inasmuch as the man who made progress in so many virtues and is defeated by comparison with no other person, lest he should extol himself, is defeated by being compared to God. But O, how strongly is he lifted up who is humbled in so awesome a way! O how great is his victory who has lost in the comparison with God! O how much greater than other men is he who is proven to be less than God by God's own testimony! His power is undoubtedly great who by such an interrogation is shown to have no power. But since we have been led to dark questions in our digression, let us come at last to the words of the text:

I. 1. *The Lord answered Job from the whirlwind and said.** I think it is noteworthy that if we were told that the Lord's speech was made to one in health and unimpaired from a tranquil space, it would never be written

*Job 1:8; 2:3

*Job 38:32 Vulg
*Job 38:17
*Job 38:12

*Job 38:1

that the Lord had spoken from a whirlwind. But because he is speaking to one who has undergone trials, the Lord is described as having spoken from a whirlwind. The Lord, you see, speaks to his servants in one way when he draws them to interior compunction, and in another way when he presses them by strict methods not to exalt themselves. The loving sweetness of the Lord is then shown to his servants through a coaxing way of speaking, but his fearful power is displayed through a terrifying speech. The former method persuades the soul to keep making progress, whereas the latter represses ambition. The former teaches the soul what to desire, the latter what to fear. The former says, *Praise God and rejoice, O daughter Zion; behold, I am coming, and I will live in your midst.** The latter says, *The ways of the Lord are in the storm and in the whirlwind.** The Lord coaxes us so that he may come to live in our midst. When however he asserts himself through storm and whirlwind, he obviously terrifies the heart that he touches, and he imposes himself for the taming of pride when he makes himself known in his terrible power.

*Zech 2:10
*Isa 66:15

2. Besides that we must know that God's speech is distinguished into two different types. The Lord either speaks through his own means, or he forms his words for us through an angelic creature. When he speaks through his own means, he teaches his word to the heart without words or syllables, because his power is known in a kind of intimate lightening. The full mind is then lifted up, but the empty mind is weighed down, because there is a kind of weight that fills the whole soul and lifts it up. It is an incorporeal light that both fills the internal spaces and externally surrounds what has been filled. It is a soundless word that both opens the sense of hearing and cannot have a sound. It is what has been written about the coming of the Holy Spirit: *Suddenly* there came a sound from heaven, like that of a violent wind blowing, and it filled the whole house where they were sitting, and there appeared to them tongues as of fire distributed and settling on each one of them.* The Lord appeared through fire, but through his own means he spoke an internal word. God was neither fire nor sound, but through what he displayed externally he expressed his internal work. Since he both set the disciples on fire with zeal and taught them the word internally, he revealed the tongues of fire externally.

*Acts 2:2-3

The elements were consequently applied to signify the action, so that the senses of the body might perceive fire and sound, while hearts were taught by invisible fire and soundless voice. Externally then fire appeared, while the Spirit gave knowledge internally. So also the eunuch of Queen Candace drove a carriage on the road while he read the prophet Isaiah, whose book he held without understanding it when the Spirit spoke in Philip's heart and said, *Follow this carriage.** And when Cornelius sent the God-fearing soldiers to fetch Peter, Peter undoubtedly heard the Spirit in his mind say, *Behold, three men are looking for you; get up then and go down; go ahead with them.**

*Acts 8:29

*Acts 10:19

To the Spirit of God it is like speaking a few words to us when he suggests what needs to be done with a hidden urge; he makes the unknowing heart of a person suddenly aware of what is hidden without the noise and slowness of words. Our sense of hearing does not all at once comprehend all the words that are spoken to it, because it has to perceive the meanings of words, particles, and syllables; our sense of sight, however, wherever it is directed, apprehends the whole scene immediately and together. God's speaking to us that happens internally is seen rather than heard, because since it is inserted in us without the delay required by words, it enlightens the darkness of our ignorance with a sudden light. So when Baruch, the son of Neriah, was asked to repeat some words of Jeremiah the prophet that he had heard, he said, *His mouth spoke as though reading, and I wrote it down.** The one who reads out loud is paying attention to one person while he speaks to another, because he speaks out what he sees. The prophets of God, therefore, because they see his words in their heart rather than hearing them, are like readers when they speak. *Jer 36:18

3. When, however, it is through an angel that God reveals his will, sometimes he displays it by words, sometimes by objects, sometimes by words and objects together, sometimes by images in the heart shown to the eyes, sometimes by images temporarily fashioned out of the air for the sake of bodily eyes, sometimes by heavenly beings, sometimes by earthly, sometimes by heavenly and earthly beings together. Sometimes on the other hand he even speaks through an angel to human hearts in such a way that even the angel himself is presented to the mind's eye.

4. God speaks through an angel when no image is seen but the words of heavenly speech are heard, such as when the Lord said, *Father, glorify your Son, so that your Son may also glorify you.** The response was immediate: *I have glorified, and I will again glorify.** Nor did God, who outside of time by the power of his intimate stirring cries out, send forth that voice in time by his own nature; that voice in fact was defined by time and composed of human words; no, he spoke from heaven, yet his will was to be heard by human beings, so he formed the words by the service of rational creatures. *John 17:1
*John 12:28

5. Sometimes God speaks through the angels about things without words, when they predict the future by forming an image out of created elements, such as when

Ezekiel, without hearing any words, saw the form of amber in the midst of fire; such is the case when he saw only an appearance of what would happen at the end. Amber indeed is an alloy of gold and silver, where silver is certainly the more dominant appearance, and the brightness of gold is softened. What does the amber signify but the Mediator between God and the human race? He composed himself out of the divine and the human nature, making the human nature more glorious with the divine and softening the divine nature for our eyes with the human. In that the humanity shone with so many miracles by virtue of the divinity, he improved silver with gold; in that God could be known through flesh and that through flesh he endured so much adversity, it was as if gold were softened by silver. This mystery is rightly revealed in the midst of fire, because the mystery of the incarnation is accompanied by the flames of the coming Judgment. It is written, *The Father judges no one but has given all judgment to the Son.**

*John 5:22

6. God sometimes speaks through angels with words and objects together, when he suggests by means of certain gestures what he says by means of words. Adam could not see the Lord in his divine nature after his sin, but he heard the angel speak words of reproach, as it is written: *When he heard the voice of the Lord God walking in paradise during the afternoon breeze, he hid himself among the trees of paradise.** How is it that after the sin of humankind in Paradise, the Lord no longer stands but walks, unless it is because he wants to show that when guilt intrudes he is shoved out of man's heart? How is it that during the afternoon breeze the cold draft of guilt chilled the sinful soul, unless it was because the ardent light of truth had deserted it? The Lord then walked and scolded Adam, so that he might make known to blinded souls their wickedness not only

*Gen 3:8

by means of words, but also of actions, inasmuch as the sinful human being would hear through words what it had done, and through the Lord's walking would understand the inconstancy of its own changeability when it lost the state of eternity; by the cold air he would notice that the warmth of love had been cast out, leaving him chilled; by the setting of the sun he would know how close he was to darkness.

7. Sometimes God speaks through angels by means of images seen with the eyes of the heart, as when Jacob saw in his sleep a ladder lowered from heaven,* and Peter saw when rapt in ecstasy a sheet full of reptiles and four-legged beasts* (unless he saw these things with incorporeal eyes he would not have been in ecstasy), and Paul saw a Macedonian in a nocturnal vision, who asked him to cross to Macedonia.* Sometimes God speaks through angels with images temporarily fashioned from air in front of bodily eyes, as when Abraham was able to see not only three men but even to welcome them into an earthly dwelling, and not only to welcome them but even to place food before them for them to eat.* Unless the angels who were reporting news to us internally made temporary bodies out of the air, they would certainly not appear to our external sight, nor when Abraham prepared food, unless it was for our sakes that they put on something solid from the heavenly nature. Nor should we wonder why those who were received there are sometimes called angels and sometimes the Lord, since by the word *angels* is expressed the fact that they exercised an external ministry, and by the word *Lord* the one who was their internal master, so that by this presiding power and by the office of ministry the relationship is made clear.

8. Sometimes God speaks through angels with the nature of heaven, as, when the Lord was baptized, we

*Gen 28:12

*Acts 10:10-12

*Acts 16:9

*Gen 18:2-8

read that a voice spoke from the cloud: *This is my beloved Son in whom I am well pleased.** Sometimes God speaks through angels with earthly nature, as when he corrected Balaam and formed human words in an ass's mouth. Sometimes God speaks through angels with heavenly and earthly nature together, as when he spoke to Moses the words of his mission on the mountain, and he added fire to the bush, joining the higher element to the lower. This action only happened then because something was signified by the joining together. When God spoke to Moses through the burning bush, what else was signified except that he would become the leader of his people, he who perceived the flame of the law and nevertheless would not avoid the thorn of sin. Or else it meant that he who would receive the sins of our flesh in the fire of his divinity like the thorns of a bush would arise from that people and save the unconsumed nature of our humanity in the very flame of divinity.

*Matt 3:17

9. Sometimes however God infuses the power of his inspiration into human hearts through angels by means of their hidden presence. That is why Zechariah said, *The angel who spoke in me said to me.** Since he said that the angel spoke to him but nevertheless in him, he clearly showed that the one who expressed words to him was not outside him by his bodily form. That is why he added a little later, *Then I saw the angel who spoke to me go out.** They often do not appear externally, but since they are angelic spirits, they make God's will known to the senses of prophets and also lift them up to the high places; whatever is going to happen on earth they display as present in the original causes. The human heart is weighed down with the very burden of corruptible flesh, and it experiences this very corpulence as an obstacle against its penetrating inwards; it lies heavily outside, having no hand to lift it internally.

*Zech 1:14

*Zech 2:3

So it happens, as has been said, that the delicate nature of angelic power appears to the prophets' senses as it is, and as their minds are touched by the slenderness of the spirit they are lifted; no longer do they lie below, sluggish and torpid, but their minds are filled with internal inspiration and they ascend to the heights; there, as if from a kind of mountain peak, they see what is going to happen to them inside. But lest anyone should suppose from the cited words of Zechariah that either the Father, the Son, or the Holy Spirit is intended by the word *angel*, if we consider the text of Holy Scripture carefully, we will quickly correct our impression, since that text never mentions either the Father or the Holy Spirit, and never calls the Son an angel except for the sake of the preaching of his incarnation. So it is clear and apparent that in the cited words of Zechariah a real angel, that is a creature, is meant: *The angel who spoke in me went out.* He quickly adds, *and another angel went to meet him and told him, "Run over and tell that young man, 'Jerusalem will be inhabited, but without any walls.'"** The angel who is sent is therefore not God, since he is given words to say by another angel.

*Zech 2:3-4

But since in the Creator's sight the angelic ministries are arranged and distinguished by positions of hierarchy, so that even while seeing their maker and rejoicing in a common enjoyment of the blessed state, some of them minister to others for the arrangement of dignity, and one angel sends another to the prophet. So one sees the other rejoicing in God together with himself; he then teaches and directs him, because he is higher, both through his superior knowledge and intellectual power and through the superabundant grace by which he attains a peak of power.

10. These few points have been mentioned to show how God speaks in various ways to people. So when

God is said to have answered blessed Job from the whirlwind, we are in doubt as to whether he spoke of himself, or whether he spoke through an angel. There could of course be disturbances in the air caused by an angel, and even the words spoken to Job that follow could have been delivered by an angel. Again, the angel could have caused the air in the whirlwind to be expelled externally. On the other hand, the Lord could have made the power of his declaration resound in Job's heart without words, so we may believe that Job himself, who was full of God, put the sayings of the Lord that follow, which he had already heard wordlessly, into words. So it follows:

II. 11. *Who is this person wrapping up statements in unskillful sentences?** Just as we already said in an earlier part, such a question is the first rebuke, when someone asks: "Who is this?" Elihu also asked in arrogance: "Who is this?" We are not speaking of anyone specific, but of someone whom we do not know. For God to know means approbation, and not to know means disapprobation. That is why he says to certain ones of whom he disapproves: *I do not know where you come from. Get away from me, all you evildoers.** Accordingly, what does it mean to ask this arrogant person, "Who is this?" but to say openly, "I do not know any arrogant people"? In other words, I disapprove of their way of life in my professional wisdom. Since they are inflated with human praise, they are empty of the true honor of eternal retribution. However, since he said *statements* and did not qualify them, we certainly accept good ones, which on the other hand he says are wrapped up in unskillful sentences, because they are modified by arrogant words.

The trouble with unskillful words is that we wrongly think what is right; that is, we bend the heavenly gift towards an appetite for earthly praise. Just as it often

*Job 38:2

*Luke 13:27

happens that we say good things badly and bad things well, so in the arrogant case of Elihu he spoke out what was right in a wrong way, because he made humble statements to defend God in a way that was not humble. In so doing he serves as a cogent example of those who are zealous for vainglory inside the catholic church. These latter think themselves to be more skillful than anyone else, so they are convicted of unskillfulness by divine judgment, just as the apostle said: *The one who thinks he knows something does not yet know in the way he should know.** The primordial folly of the angel was the pride in his heart, so true wisdom for the human being is constituted by humility in his or her own estimation. Whoever abandons humility by thinking great thoughts becomes a fool by the very act by which he loses self-knowledge. So Elihu both proclaimed declarations and wrapped up words in unskillful sentences, because he knew the right words to say about God, and yet his stupid pride made his own words look foolish. Having disdained Elihu, the Lord turned his words to the teaching of Job:

*1 Cor 8:2

III. 12. *Gird up your loins like a man.** Holy Scripture is accustomed to call a man anyone who unquestionably follows the ways of the Lord with robust, not dissolute, footsteps. So also the psalmist says, *Act like a man and strengthen your heart.** Paul too says, *Lift up your listless hands and your wobbly knees.** So Wisdom speaks in the Book of Proverbs: *To you I cry out, O men.** It is as if he said openly, "I do not speak to women, but to men, because those with unstable minds can never receive my words."

*Job 38:3

*Ps 30:25
*Heb 12:12

*Prov 8:4

To gird up one's loins, however, means to restrain lust, whether in act or in thought. The pleasure of the flesh is in the loins. That is why the holy preachers are told, *Let your loins be girt and your lamps burning.** The loins signify lust, and the lamps the clear light of good

*Luke 12:35

works. They are ordered therefore to gird their loins and to hold their lamps. It is as if they clearly heard, "First restrain the lust that is in you, and then give a good example to others of your good works." But since we know that blessed Job was endowed with such chastity, why is he told after having undergone so many trials, *Gird up your loins like a man*? It means of course to restrain lust with courage. Why then unless lust of the flesh by which we ruin chastity is something other than lust of the heart, by which we boast of chastity? So he is told, *Gird up your loins like a man*, so that the one who had already won the battle against the lust of corruption might now restrain the lust of pride, lest in his pride for the sake of patience or chastity, his lust might show up worse inwardly in God's eyes the more he seemed patient and chaste in the eyes of people. That is why Moses was right to say, *Circumcise the foreskin of your hearts*,* that is, after you put an end to lust of the flesh, cut off as well superfluous thoughts from the heart. The next verse:

*Deut 10:16

IV. 13. *I will ask you, and you answer me.** The Creator customarily interrogates us in three ways: Either he strikes us with severe trials and shows us how much patience we have or do not have, or he orders us to do things that we refuse to do and so reveals to us our obedience or disobedience, or he reveals things hidden from us and hides others, and in this way he makes known to us a yardstick to measure our humility. He interrogates us with trials when he strikes with affliction the mind already completely subject to him through tranquility, just as the same Job is praised by the Judge's attestation, he who is nevertheless allowed to receive the blows of the striker so that his patience might the more truly show up the more harshly it has been interrogated. He questions us, you see, by ordering us to do things that are hard, just as Abraham was ordered to leave his own land, to

*Job 38:3

go to a place he did not know, and to take his only son to a mountain to sacrifice, the one he had received as a comfort in his old age. And when he answered the question well, obedient to the command, he was told, *Now I know that you fear God.** Or, as it is elsewhere written, *The Lord your God tries you, so that he may know if you love him.** For God to try us means to question us with peremptory orders. For him to know means that he makes us know our obedience. God questions us by revealing certain things to us and keeping others hidden, as when the psalmist says, *His eyelids question the sons of men.** When our eyelids are open we see; when they are closed we do not see. What do we take God's eyelids to be if not his judgments? These judgments are in one sense closed to human beings and in another sense opened, so that people who do not know themselves may be awakened to themselves. This happens when people understand certain things intellectually while they are by no means able to know others, so they quietly ask their own hearts if God's judgments, though closed, do not stimulate them, or when open do not fill them with pride.

Paul was certainly tried by such questioning, he who after having received interior wisdom, after the open gates of Paradise, after going up to the third heaven, after the mysteries of heavenly words, still said, *I do not suppose that I have already attained the prize,** and, *I am the least of the apostles and I am not worthy to be called an apostle,** and, *Not that we are sufficient of ourselves to think anything of ourselves, but our sufficiency is from God.** So when Paul was questioned by God's open eyelids, he gave the right answer, since he both heard the heavenly secrets and yet remained sublimely humble in his heart. Another time when he discussed God's secret judgments on the rejection of the Jews

*Gen 22:12

*Deut 13:3

*Ps 10:5

*Phil 3:13

*1 Cor 15:9

*2 Cor 3:5

and the calling of the Gentiles and he could not reach an understanding on that subject, it was as though he were questioned by God's closed eyelids. But he still gave the right answer, and he wisely bowed down to God in his own ignorance, saying, *O the deep riches of God's wisdom and knowledge! How mysterious are his judgments and unsearchable his ways! Who has known the mind of the Lord? Who has counseled him?** See how agreeable and right was his answer concerning the hidden mysteries when he was questioned by God's closed eyelids! He knocked at the door of the mystery, but he could not be admitted inside that door through knowledge, so he humbly remained outside the door through confession. What he could not comprehend internally he fearfully praised externally.

*Rom 11:33-34

That is why blessed Job, after having been interrogated by trials, is now also subjected to an examination by words, so that he might consider the things that are above; he does not understand the things that are above at all, so he should return to himself and realize that he is little better than nothing in comparison with the highest reality. So let him hear, *I will ask you, and you answer me.* It is as if he were openly told: "With my own words I am urging you to consider the highest reality, and since you perceive that you do not know the things that are above you, I am telling you about them myself. Then you will give me the right answer when you understand your ignorance." The next verse:

V. 14. *Where were you when I laid the foundation of the earth? Tell me, if you have understanding. Who worked out its measurements, do you know? Who stretched out a line upon it? Upon what were its bases fastened?** See how practically all that concerns the beginning of the world is contained in a historical account. However, it is immediately followed by something that

*Job 38:4-6

seems to be said not about the world, but about the condition of the church. It is said, *Or who has put its cornerstone in place?** The fact that the church was not created at the beginning of the world is proved by what was just quoted; they were not written about the beginning of the world. Certain obscure and strident words, you see, are mixed in with those that are plain and obvious, precisely so that what seems inconsistent with the literal understanding may lead us to a mystical inquiry of what seems to be spoken literally. Just as we know certain matters that are closed by means of certain other matters that are clear, so we are compelled by closed matters to press a higher understanding upon matters we thought were clear.

*Job 38:6

Let him say it then: *Where were you when I laid the foundation of the earth?* In Holy Scripture, then, what else do we take foundations to mean but the preachers? The Lord gave them the first position in Holy Church, so the whole structure of the building that follows rises from them. So also when the priest enters the temple he is ordered to carry the twelve stones on his breast, obviously because our high priest offers himself as a sacrifice for us, and he showed us strong preachers in the very beginning; he carried the twelve stones underneath his head at the very top of his body. The holy apostles accordingly, for the first display or ornamentation, are the stones on the breast, and for the first solidity of the building on the ground are the foundation. So when the prophet David saw Holy Church placed and built upon the sublime minds of the apostles, he said, *Her foundations are on the holy mountains.**

*Ps 86:1

However, when we read in Holy Scripture not the plural, *foundations*, but the singular, *foundation*, nothing else but the Lord is intended, through the power of whose divinity the unstable hearts of our weakness are strengthened. About him Paul said, *No one can lay any other foundation than the one that is there, namely Christ Jesus.** He is the unquestionable foundation of the foundations, because he is both the beginning of the beginners and the constancy of the mature. Since therefore our foundations are those who have borne the burdens of our iniquities, lest blessed Job should be lifted up in pride over the strength of his virtues, in the very beginning of the Lord's speech he is questioned on the mention of the holy preachers, so that the more their coming is foreseen and admired, the lower is Job's self-esteem in comparison with them.

*1 Cor 3:11

That fact is described by the Lord as though it were already past for this reason: whatever is an external future action is internally already done in predestination. That is why he is asked, *Where were you when I laid the foundation of the earth?* It is as if he openly said, "Consider the virtue of the courageous, then take my measure, who created them before the ages, and when you look at their wonders, whom I created in time, weigh again how much you should be subject to me, whom you know to be the Creator of wonders without time." The next verse:

VI. 15. *Tell me, if you have understanding. Who worked out its measurements, do you know? Who stretched out a line upon it?** A measuring line is stretched to partition lands, so that equal dimensions may be held by the very stretching of the line. So when the Lord came in flesh to the church, he measured out plots of land with lines, because he fixed the bounds of the church with the fine lines of hidden judgment. Hidden measuring lines were stretched upon this earth when the holy preachers moved by the Holy Spirit were called to go in various parts of the world but were kept from approaching various other parts. The apostle Paul, you see, neglected to preach in Macedonia, but a Mace-

*Job 38:4-5

donian appeared to him in a vision and said, *Come over to Macedonia and help us.** On the other hand, it is written, *The apostles tried to go to Bithynia, but the Spirit of Jesus did not allow them.** Since therefore the apostles were both called to Macedonia and not allowed to go to Asia, this hidden measuring line was drawn to one place and not drawn to the other. It was drawn to Macedonia, so that Macedonia could be included within the space occupied by Holy Church, but it was drawn outside Asia, so that Asia might be left outside the boundary of Holy Church. There were in fact at that time those living in Asia who could not be collected, because of whom—having now deservedly perished—Asia is now received within the confines of the church by God's gift.

*Acts 16:9

*Acts 16:7

16. Within these boundaries, then, all the chosen ones live, whereas outside them are all the reprobate, even if they might seem to be within the confines of faith. That is why it is written in the Apocalypse, *Leave the exterior court of the temple out, and do not measure it.** What else but the full extent of the present life does the court represent? And rightly are they outside the temple who are designated by the court, and they are not to be measured precisely because the gate that leads to life is narrow, since the breadth of the life lived by depraved people is not allowed entrance to the measured life and rules of the chosen ones. These are the spiritual lines that are stretched out by hidden judgment, when to one who said, *Master, I will follow you wherever you go*, the same Master replied with his own voice, *Foxes have dens, and the birds of the air have nests, but the Son of Man has nowhere to lay his head.** These same lines and measurements were laid out when to another who said, *Lord, let me first go and bury my father*, the same Master said in his own voice, *Let the dead bury their own dead. You go and proclaim the kingdom of God.**

*Rev 11:2

*Matt 8:19-20

*Luke 9:59-60

See how one person promises to follow him and is rejected, whereas another requests a breathing space and is kept. How do we account for this, unless by the fact that the lines of heavenly judgment were stretched out over the hidden spaces of the heart, so that the incomprehensible measuring lines confined one person inside while the other not unjustly remained outside? But if no one knows that God stretches out these measuring lines of hidden judgment, why is Job asked, *Tell me, if you have understanding. Who worked out its measurements, do you know? Who stretched out a line upon it?* Is he questioned for this reason, that he might tell what he knows but could nevertheless overlook? Inasmuch as he assesses the weight of God's mysteries at all solicitously, he knows that the human being's position obviously depends not on human resources but on the Creator's hand, so that when he considers the things the Creator does invisibly, the human being should attribute nothing to his own powers, nor should he any longer dare to do anything of himself when he fears God's hidden judgments, but, carefully weighing the measuring lines from above, which are incomprehensibly taut, he should be all the more humble and fearful the more clearly he sees how everything depends on the power of the Measurer.

VII. 17. *Upon what were its bases fastened?** What else do we take the bases of this earth to mean but the teachers of Holy Church? On the bases, of course, the columns rest, and over the columns the whole weight of the building is erected. It is not unreasonable therefore for the holy teachers to be designated by the word *bases* when they preach what is right and their lives conform to what they preach; by the determined gravity of their behavior they hold up the whole burden of the church, they bear severe temptations from those who

*Job 38:6

are unfaithful, and they show by the example of their works that whatever the faithful fear as difficult in God's commandments is really easy. That is why, as a good type of the church, the meeting tent was designed, and Moses was told, *You will make four columns with their bases covered with silver.** What else do we take the silver to mean but the brilliance of the word of God? It is written, *The words of the Lord are pure like silver refined in an earthen furnace.** So the bases covered with silver hold up the four columns of the tent of meeting, because the preachers of the church, decorated with the word of God so that they might show everyone an example, carry the four evangelists' words in their mouths and in their deeds.

*Exod 26:32

*Ps 11:7

18. The bases could also mean the prophets, who, while they were the first to speak openly about the Lord's incarnation, were like bases of a sort that we see rise from the foundation and hold up the weight of the structure that is built upon them. So when the Lord directed Moses to erect the panels of the meeting tent, he ordered that their bases be cast in silver. What do the panels signify if not the apostles, whose preaching grew by being spread throughout the world, and what do the silver bases mean if not the prophets? Strong though molten, the bases hold up the panels placed upon them, and the lives of the apostles are based upon their teaching and made firm by their authority; that is why each two bases are connected and hold up each two panels, because as long as the holy prophets agree in their words about the Mediator's incarnation, they undoubtedly build up the preachers of the church who were to follow, so that since they do not disagree themselves, they fix the apostles more firmly in place.

Nor is it without reason that the bases for the panels signify the prophets, since it is ordered that they be made of silver. The brightness of silver is indeed kept by use; without being used it turns black. So also the words of the prophets before the Mediator's coming were not used for spiritual understanding, since they could not be seen for their darkness, and they remained black, as it were. But when the Mediator came he rubbed them with the hand of his incarnation before our eyes, and whatever light was hidden in them shone out; he let the knowledge of the ancient patriarchs be utilized, because he illuminated the words with deeds.

So whether it was the prophets or the teachers who followed in the last times, which he signified by the word *bases*, let the Lord say, *Upon what were its bases fastened?* You understand what follows: [upon what] except upon me, who miraculously holds everything together and who principally presents the origin of external goods within? He who attributes to himself what is good is not a solid base, because he is not supported by the foundation, and so he falls by his own weight into the depths.

But since so much has been said about Holy Church's construction, the mind desires to hear by what power the hostile nations have been joined together, in other words by what skill the buildings that are different from this house agree. The next verse:

*Job 38:6

VIII. 19. *Who has laid its cornerstone?** It is already clear to everyone through God's grace that the one whom Holy Scripture calls the cornerstone, the one in fact who receives the Jewish people from one side and the Gentile people from the other, joins them together as in two walls of the one building of the church. He is

*Eph 2:14

the one of whom it is written, *He made them both one.** He showed himself to be the cornerstone, not only in the lower regions, but also in the higher, because he associated the Gentile nations both with the people of Israel on earth and also with the angels in heaven. On the very day of his birth the angels cried out, *Peace on earth to men of good will.** At a king's birth men would never be offered the happiness of peace as a great good if they were not at war.

*Luke 2:14

The prophet says about this stone, *The stone rejected by the builders has become the cornerstone.** King Jechoniah was the type for this stone, him whom Matthew named twice when he enumerated the groups of fourteen generations.* The one he named at the end of the second group he put at the beginning of the third. He is the one, you see, who migrated to Babylon with the people of Israel, he who, since he was led from one place to the other, was not unreasonably included with the second group as a stone for both walls. By the bend of this migration Matthew signifies the cornerstone. So where the line bends from a straightforward direction to move in a different direction it creates a corner. He could then correctly be named twice, since he both displays two sides by means of the two walls and therefore rightly bears his image, he who was born in Judea and gathers the Gentiles as if he came from Jerusalem to Babylon. In himself indeed with the tools of charity he rebuilds the house of faith, which was previously ruined by the animosity of discord. Now since we have spoken of the signifying of Holy Church, let us return and briefly speak about the moral sense. It is fitting, you see, that through the words we know were spoken to blessed Job, we should call back to our hearts the fact that the mind then really understands the word of God when it seeks itself in it. So then he says,

*Ps 117:22

*Matt 1:11-12

IX. 20. *Where were you when I laid the foundation of the earth?* The sinner's soul is dust, since it is superficially puffed up and caught in temptation's trap, so that it is written, *The wicked are not like that, but they are like dust that the wind drives away from the face*

*Ps 1:4 LXX   *of the earth.** Consequently there is nothing against understanding earth to mean the soul of the righteous, of whom it is written, *The earth drinks the rain that often falls upon it and brings forth vegetation useful*
*Heb 6:7   *for those who live upon it; so it receives a blessing.** But faith is the foundation of this earth. The foundation of this earth is laid when fear of God, the first cause of solidity, is inspired in the hidden reaches of the heart. This person does not yet believe that the word he hears is eternal; with faith he is given the foundation for the building of works that will follow. He now believes in eternity but has no fear; he has only contempt for terror at the coming Judgment and boldly gets involved in sins of the flesh and of the spirit; however, when fear of what is coming is suddenly infused into him, the foundations are already laid for the building of a good life to rise.

So when the foundations are laid for fear to prosper, and when the building of virtues is growing high, it is necessary for each one who is making progress to cautiously take the measure of his powers, so that when he is already beginning to grow strong in divine construction, he should ceaselessly look at himself and remember what he has been; indeed he should humbly be aware of the merits he has attained and never attribute to himself what he has become through grace. So now blessed Job is led back to himself by the heavenly voice, and lest he should dare to boast of his virtues, he is reminded of his former life and asked, *Where were you when I laid the foundation of the earth?* It is as if Truth openly told the justified sinner, "Do not attribute to yourself the virtues you received from me. Do not extol yourself against me because of my gift. Remember where I found you when I first laid the foundation of virtue in you. Remember where I found you when I strengthened you with my fear. Consequently, so that I may not destroy in you what I have built, you yourself must not cease to consider what I have found." Whom else has Truth found but criminals or extremists? But after that we can best keep what we are if we never neglect to consider what we have been. Sometimes, however, a clandestine pride is wont to creep up even in solicitous hearts, so that the thought of good deeds, although a fragile and frightened thought, when it quickly grows in virtues, forgetful of its own weakness, never recalls to memory the vices it used to have. That is why almighty God, seeing that our weakness grows even when salutary remedies are applied, imposes a limit on our very progress, so that we may have certain good results from virtues that we never sought and we seek others but cannot have them. The net result is that when our mind cannot have what it desires, we should understand that what we have we do not have of ourselves; then what is there makes us consider what is not there and what is fortunately missing, so it lets us keep humbly the good that is there. So he rightly adds for the benefit of this earth, that is, of the righteous soul,

X. 21. *Tell me, if you have understanding. Who worked out its measurements, do you know? Who stretched out a line upon it?** Who but our Creator has measured out this earth? It is he who by a hidden guidance of internal judgment grants to one person the discourse of wisdom, to another that of knowledge, to another perfect faith, to another the grace of healing, to another the power of good works, to another prophecy, to another discernment of spirits, to another different languages, to another interpretation of speech, inasmuch as this one is proficient in the words of wisdom in one and the same spirit but is not supported by the words of knowledge or doctrine, because he is able to know and to find what cannot be learned by the labor of study;

*Job 38:4-5

that one excels in the words of knowledge but is weak in those of wisdom, because he may be able to explain what he has learned, and yet he has not learned enough to understand by himself anything recondite. This one even commands the elements through faith, but he does not cure bodily ailments through the grace of healing; that one removes diseases by the power of prayer, but he does not bring rain for the thirsty earth by a word. Someone else calls the dead back to the present life by the exercise of power, but he does not have the grace of prophecy and does not know the future. Someone else pays attention to the future as if it were present, and yet he does not busy himself with any doing of signs. Someone else through discernment of spirits subtly sees the minds in their deeds but is ignorant of different kinds of languages. Someone else examines different kinds of languages but does not discern the different hearts whose behavior is similar. Someone else in the single language that he knows prudently interprets and explains the meanings of words, and yet he patiently does without the other gifts he does not have.

22. Accordingly that is how our Creator and Manager arranges everything, so that the one who might wax proud from the gift he possesses should be humbled by the virtue he does not have. That is how everything is arranged, so that when he raises one person through lavish grace, he also lowers him through a different grace bestowed upon another. So anyone may notice that the one he surpasses by one gift is superior by another, and although he thinks himself better in some ways, nevertheless he is inferior in other ways to the one over whom he excels. God so disposes all things that while each gift separately belongs to all, by the mediation of a certain obligation of charity all gifts belong to each, and everyone so possesses in another person what he does not receive himself that he humbly offers to the other for his possession what he receives himself. That is why Peter says, *Just as each person receives grace, so each one administers it to others like good stewards of the manifold grace of God.** *1 Pet 4:10

Then, you see, manifold grace is dispensed rightly when a gift that is received is both thought to be his who does not have it and supposed to be given for his sake to whom it is offered. That is why Paul says, *Serve one another through love.** Then indeed charity frees us from the yoke of sin when it subjects us to one another through love by means of our mutual servitude, when we both believe the other's good to be our own and offer our own to the other to be his own. So Paul again says, *The body is not one member, but many. If the foot says, "I am not a hand, so I do not belong to the body," is it for that reason not part of the body? If the ear should say, "I am not an eye, so I do not belong to the body," is it for that reason not part of the body? If the whole body were an eye, where would be the hearing? If the whole body were an ear, where would be the sense of smell?** And a little later, *But if they were all one member, where would be the body? But now there are indeed many members, still one body.** *Gal 5:13

*1 Cor 12:14-17

*1 Cor 12:19-20

23. What else then is Holy Church but the body of her heavenly Head? In her is one eye looking upwards, one hand doing the right thing, one foot running to obey, one ear understanding the voice of precepts, one nose to smell the stench of evil and the fragrance of good. All these like members of bodies, when they fulfill in turn the duties they have received, make up one body out of themselves; when they perform different actions by charity, they forbid that body to be diverse wherein they are contained. If they all together did one thing, they would not be a body that is formed out of many parts, because such a compact entity would not exist if this concordant diversity of members did not hold it together. Since accordingly the Lord shares among the holy members of the church gifts of virtues, he measures the earth. So Paul says again, *To each one God has assigned a measure of faith.** And again: *From whom the whole body, compacted and connected through every ligament with which it is supplied, according to the measured working of each member, grows harmoniously and is built up in love.**

*Rom 12:3

*Eph 4:16

24. But when with admirable counsel our Creator and Administrator bestows on one person what he denies to another or denies to the first what he bestows on the second, whoever tries to be able to do more than he has been given tries to go beyond the limits imposed upon him. For example, if the one who has only been given the ability to discuss the hidden precepts tries to win fame by miracles, or if the one to whom God only grants the gift of heavenly power to work miracles tries to reveal the secrets of divine law as well, it is not right. He who pays no attention to the limiting unit of measurement imposed upon him puts down his foot over a precipice. And the one who boldly and impatiently starts something he is not able to succeed at frequently loses even the ability he has. Only then do we make good use of our members when we take good care of their distinct services. With the eyes, obviously, we see light, and with the ears we hear voices. However, if any disorderly person applies the eye to voices or the ears to light, both organs are clearly useless to him. If any want to smell odors with their mouth, or to enjoy a taste with their nose, they pervert the exercise of both senses and thereby ruin them. Because both senses are not applied to their proper object, they both lose their own function and are unable to adapt to a different one.

25. So David also forced the foot of his heart to accept the limits he had received from God's bounty, and he said, *I have not walked among the great, nor did I walk among marvels beyond me.** He would in fact walk in wonderful deeds above himself if he wanted to appear great beyond his strength. That person is lifted up in wonders beyond his strength who tries to look qualified in matters where he has insufficient experience. Paul too confined himself within measurable limits in the very breadth of his preaching when he said, *I do not dare say anything except what Christ has wrought through me.** Only then is the limitation we have accepted kept intact when a life has been placed before spiritual people and seen by them. The next verse:

*Ps 130:1

*Rom 15:18

XI. 26. *Who stretched out a line upon it?** A measuring line is stretched over this earth, you see, when the examples of the ancient patriarchs are shown to each chosen soul, so that they may take from them a pattern of life; these souls should consider the patriarchs' lives from the point of view of how they could serve as patterns for their own lives, inasmuch as having observed the track of righteousness, they might neither be wanting or negligent following the least demanding course, nor, tempted by pride, advance beyond the most demanding objective; they should neither try to do less than what suffices nor seize a higher goal than the one they have been given, lest they should either be unable to reach the level they should or abandon that level and fall outside its compass.

*Job 38:4-5

Narrow indeed is the gate that leads to life, and they enter it who in all that they do are carefully confined by the fine line of discretion for its sake. The one, you see, who enlarges his scope by his own will with an untroubled mind loses the entrance of the narrow gate for himself. Accordingly, for the measure of this earth to be followed, a line is stretched over it by God; so that even our smaller works may prosper, or our greater ones be restrained, the fine line of the lives of the holy patriarchs who preceded us is enlarged before us by Holy Scripture—what we must do and how much is shown to us clearly by their discretion.

27. Look! Someone fears either the loss of possessions or some bodily affliction; he fears even more the threats of worldly power; he is not bold enough to defend himself against the force of those who resist the truth. Peter sees such a one in dire straits and in fear and, having displayed the line of his own example, urges him on to more inclusive virtue. Peter was in fact flogged by the leaders of the people, and when on that account he saw himself freed, warned to stop preaching, and forbidden to speak in the future, he by no means stopped at that time. No, he answered forthwith, and said, *We must obey God rather than men.** And again: *We cannot refrain from speaking of what we have seen and heard.** But that person was long feeble and feared present losses; now he contemplates examples of such bold courage that he already follows the line of Peter with the authority of the word; already he fears no adversity, already he disdains the worldly powers that oppose God, even when his body is scourged.

*Acts 5:29

*Acts 4:20

But the more he destroys the power of persecutors by suffering bravely, and the more he yields to no terror in the midst of adversities, the more often he puts himself ahead of the others, even in the opinions he has held when placed among the faithful. He chooses his own counsel and trusts himself rather than others. He unquestionably does not give in to unrighteous taunts but acts with courage; he does not accept advice from others even if it is correct, and he puts his foot forward, out of the beaten track. Peter calls this man back within the accepted boundary, yet later he defies the authority of the leaders with his free voice, and through a humble heart he accepts the advice of Paul about not circumcising Gentiles. In this way Peter takes care to exert his own authority against adversaries, so that nevertheless he does not trust himself in matters where his thinking is incorrect, and so that he might defeat the proud powers with the freedom of courage and should show obedience with humility and meekness in good counsel even to the least of the brethren, he takes his stand sometimes through himself to others, sometimes to himself with others. In Peter's actions therefore certain lines of authority and humility are stretched out before our eyes, so that our minds may not be afraid and so kept from reaching the right measure, or through pride exceed it.

28. We have spoken about the ways in which a line is stretched out lest we should cross over from the courage of one action to the vice of another; let us now speak of how we abandon the line of discretion in the same virtue if we do not know how sometimes to exercise the virtue and sometimes to put it aside. A virtue is not always the same thing; from moment to moment of time the merits of actions often change. So it happens that when we do well, we often do better to cease from that particular action, and for a time it is more praiseworthy to abandon what the mind in a praiseworthy manner held in its own time. If, for example, because of our lesser virtues, by which we make progress but lose nothing when we let them go, we hurt our neighbor, so that much evil threatens his labors, it is essential for us to put aside our progress in virtue lest we should cause detriment to the weaker neighbor's faith, lest our works be no longer virtuous, and lest by chance in other people's hearts the foundations of virtue be destroyed.

29. Paul displayed this line of discretion clearly before the eyes of beholders when he forbade the circumcision of the Gentiles who came to the freedom of faith;* nevertheless, when he passed through Lystra and Iconium, he circumcised Timothy himself, because Timothy was born of a Gentile father.* He saw that unless he showed himself an observer of the literal commandment, he would arouse the fury of the Jews even against those who were then his companions, so he put aside his forceful assertion, and without loss of faith he protected himself and his friends from brutal persecution. He did then what out of love for the faith he forbade to be done, but he turned back what as it were was not faithfully done to the ministry of faith.

*Acts 15:1-2

*Acts 16:3

It often happens that a virtue is lost when it is indiscreetly clung to, but when it is discreetly let go, more of it is kept. It is no wonder if we understand regarding immaterial matters what we see happen in material things. A bow, you see, is intentionally left unstrung so that it may be usefully bent when the time comes. Whoever does not accept the idleness of rest loses the power of striking because of his habitual tension. It so happens sometimes with the exercise of virtue that when it is let pass through discretion, it is kept ready, so that it may strike valiantly after a vice shows itself to the extent that it prudently ceased from striking in the interim. The line of discretion therefore is drawn lightly on this earth when the examples of the ancient patriarchs have been shown to each individual soul and the virtue has been aroused for useful operation and sometimes more usefully restrained.

30. But when for a little while the courage of zeal is put aside from our behavior, there is need for another consideration, lest by chance it is not the counsel of the common good, but fear for oneself or the self-interest of some ambition that causes us to cease from the exercise of virtue. When this takes place we are no longer following a plan, but a sin. So we must be extremely careful that when people accept a job that requires a cessation in the practice of a virtue, they should first examine themselves in the bottom of their heart, lest they should be avariciously desiring to get something for themselves out of this business or timidly making things easy for themselves alone, and for that reason the job should turn out to be crooked, because it does not proceed from a thought of good intention.

That is why Truth rightly says in the gospel, *Your eye is the lamp of your body, so if your eye is simple, your whole body will be full of light, but if your eye is evil, your whole body will be full of darkness.** What else is meant by the eye but the intention of the heart watching over a person's work? Before that intention was fulfilled in action it already contemplated the object of its desire. What else is signified by the word *body* but each action that follows its intention as if it were a gazing eye? Accordingly y*our eye is the lamp of your body*, because the ray of a good intention illuminates the worth of an action. *If your eye is simple, your whole body will be full of light*, because if our intention is pure through the simplicity of our thought, we complete a good work, even if it might seem to be not so good. *But if your eye is evil, your whole body will be full of darkness*, because when we do anything with an evil intention, even if it is correct, even if it seems splendid to people, under the watchful eye of the internal Judge it is darkened. So he rightly adds, *If the light that is in you is darkness, how great is the darkness!**

*Matt 6:22-23

*Matt 6:23

If we darken what we thought we were doing well with an evil intention, how evil must those things be that we were not unaware of being evil even while we were doing them? And if we see nothing in that case, when we hold, as it were, the light of discretion, how blindly do we stumble against the evil that we commit without discretion? We must therefore scrutinize our intention with watchful care in all our works, so that we desire nothing worldly in the things that we do but let our intention fix itself in the solidity of eternity, lest the building of our action should be set down without a foundation, and it should dissolve in a wide open gap of earth. So he also adds correctly at this point,

XII. 31. *Upon what were its bases fastened?** The intentions of each individual soul are its bases. Just as a building is supported by pillars and pillars by bases, so our lives are supported by virtues, and virtues are held up by deep intentions. So we find it written, *No one can lay any other foundation than the one that is there, namely Christ Jesus.** So then the foundation is laid upon its bases when our intentions are made firm in Christ. In vain, consequently, are high buildings erected on top of bases if the bases do not themselves stand on a solid foundation, because naturally however lofty the works may be that we vainly do, if the intentions of our hearts are without the certitude of eternity, the works fail. If they do not seek the rewards of true life, they accumulate for themselves more serious losses in ruins the more buildings without foundations they have built. When they do not aim for the rewards of eternal life, the more virtues they accumulate, the deeper they fall into the pit of vainglory.

*Job 38:6

*1 Cor 3:11

We must not accordingly count on what the bases support but rather on how they are supported, because human hearts are unquestionably examined by God, not on what they do alone, but on what they seek in what they do. So when Paul described the strict Judge, he also spoke of good actions and said, *He will render to each man according to his works, and to those indeed who have the patience of good works he will give glory and immortality.** Once the patience of good works has been mentioned, of course, he has spoken of the whole building of chosen action and diligently searched it out in the same place where the bases of the same building stood, saying, *To those who seek glory, honor, and immortality he will give eternal life.** It is as if he said openly, "And even if any people display the patience of good works, they do not receive glory and immortality if they do not fix the intentions of their heart, that is, the bases of the building, in the foundation, obviously because God does not inhabit the building even of an upright life whose position outside himself he does not himself support."

*Rom 2:6

*Rom 2:7

32. Since therefore the intentions of each chosen soul are supported by the hope of eternity, it is good to hear the Lord's voice ask about this earth, *Upon what were its bases fastened?* It is as if he said openly, "Except on me? Since that is what every righteous soul intends, all that it does in time it undoubtedly constructs in me outside of time." On the other hand, since we are then more securely fitted into the foundation, when we follow God's words even in the external precepts by understanding them in more detail in our internal senses, he rightly adds,

XIII. 33. *Or who has put its cornerstone in place?** There are two ways to understand the cornerstone as used in the sacred writings. The cornerstone then is laid by God when in strict judgment there is nothing to hamper it in the darkness of its ignorance, but it enjoys a certain freedom of movement when in following God's precepts it is enough either to put into practice an external action or to understand something internally by contemplation. Our understanding would never rise to this level unless our Creator himself came to share our nature. He is called the cornerstone in one sense because

*Job 38:6

he unites two peoples in himself, and in another sense because he displays in himself the example of the union of two kinds of life, the active and the contemplative.

The contemplative life, you see, is far different from the active, but when the Redeemer came to be incarnate, he displayed both these lives and united them at the same time in himself. He both worked miracles in the city and spent nights on the mountain in continuous prayer. He showed an example to his faithful ones, so that they should neither neglect devotion to their neighbors for the sake of contemplation nor, on the other hand, being inordinately bound to the care of their neighbors, forsake their attention to contemplation. Rather they should so join both duties in their minds that love of the neighbor does not impede the love of God, nor does the love of God excuse anyone from love of the neighbor because it is transcendent. Since therefore the Mediator of God and humankind has appeared to the human heart that knows not what to do, he who by acting arranged time-bound reality and by contemplation pointed out how all things are suspended, he is right to say, *Or who has put its cornerstone in place?* It is as if the Lord said clearly, "Except me, who have displayed my only Son, whom I have engendered outside of time to save the human race in time, by whose life they should also learn that different aims in life are not at variance." And it is noteworthy that he did not say "laid" but "put," obviously because the Son received a human nature and came from the highest to the lowest place. And since the chosen angels marveled at the mystery of the incarnation, they who were not redeemed by that mystery, he is right to add,

XIV. 34. *When the morning stars praised me in unison.** Because we believe that the nature of rational spirits was created at the beginning of time, it is not

*Job 38:7

illogical for the angels to be called *morning stars*. That being the case, since the earth was invisible and formless, and darkness covered the deep places, the morning stars preceded the coming day of the new world by their existence through the light of wisdom. Nor should we hear the addition of the words *in unison* negligently, because the morning stars along with the evening stars praise the Redeemer's power, since the chosen angels along with redeemed humankind at the end of the world glorify the generosity of heavenly grace. In order that they might incite us to praise the Creator, these angels do as we have said above: with the sunrise through the flesh they cry out, *Glory be to God on high and on earth peace to the people of good will.** praise God in unison, because they apply the voices of their elation to our redemption. They praise God in unison, because while they are seeing us receive redemption, they rejoice that their number is being filled.

*Luke 2:14

Perhaps they are called morning stars because they are often sent out to exhort human beings, and while they foretell the coming of the morning, they make the darkness of the present life vanish from human hearts. See how the angels praise God's power, because the very vision of such great glory fills them. But we the redeemed are still weighed down by the corruption of the flesh: by what power do we praise the gift we receive? How will the tongue be able to speak what our mind is unable to understand? Next:

XV. 35. *And all the sons of God shouted for joy.** The shout of joy means that the joy in the heart is not satisfied by the effectiveness of the mouth, but joy issues forth by whatever means it can, such means that the one who rejoices can neither restrain nor fulfill. And so the angels praise the extent of such great glory that they already see in the highest. So let people shout for joy

*Job 38:7

in the lowest places, although they still experience the inadequacy of speech. The Lord certainly knew what the future held, so he does not so much infer what will happen as proclaim what is done. But how is it that while good people shout for joy at the mystery of their redemption, envy incites evil? The chosen ones make progress, but reprobate sinners are incited to the fury of anger, and they persecute the good things that are being generated, because they do not want to imitate them.

Nevertheless, in the midst of such happenings, the Redeemer does not abandon us. It is written, *God is faithful, and he will not let you be tempted beyond your strength, but he will send along with the temptation a way for you to resist.** Our Creator knows of course when he allows the storm of persecution to rise and when he stills the rising storm. He knows how to still the storm for our protection that he allowed to rise against us for our practice in virtue, so that while the storm fiercely washes over us, it does not drown us. The next verse:

*1 Cor 10:13

XVI. 36. *Who has enclosed the sea within its bounds when it burst forth as though emerging from the womb?** What do we take the sea to mean if not the world, and what the womb if not the conception of thoughts of the flesh? The word *womb* in this passage certainly signifies hidden and malicious thoughts of the flesh. Such a womb does not conceive from the bodily tissue in order to bring forth new offspring, but it conceives material pain to fulfill evil deeds. About this womb of wicked hearts it is elsewhere written, *He conceived sorrow and brought forth iniquity.** Depraved people conceive through this womb when they think evil thoughts. Through this womb they also give birth when they put into practice the evil that they thought.

*Job 38:8

*Ps 7:15

The sea then burst forth as though emerging from the womb when the waves of worldly threats that were conceived by the iniquity of thoughts of the flesh raged for the ruin of Holy Church. But by the power of God this sea is confined within its bounds, because the saints oppose the pride of persecutors like gates of a kind, so that by their miracles and reverence the wrath of persecutors might be cut off. When the princes of the earth were humbled the Lord unquestionably made Holy Church stand through them upon the summit of the world, and the violent attack of the sea subsided when the power of the same church grew. But let us hear what the Lord did with this violent sea. The next verse:

XVII. 37. *When I made a cloud his garment and wrapped him up in darkness as if in swaddling clothes.**   *Job 38:9
The raging sea is dressed in a cloud, because the cruelty of persecutors is clothed in the garment of their own folly. With the darkness of their own unfaithfulness covering them, the persecutors cannot see the transparent light of truth, and they do not know what they are doing, urged on by cruelty, because of the power of their own blindness. As the apostle said, *If they had known, they would never have crucified the Lord of glory.**   *1 Cor 2:8
This cloud not only covers unfaithful people outside the church, but it even darkens some of those who live according to the flesh inside her bounds. That is why the saints who also suffer from the negligence of others figure that they too suffer when they sense that other people are undergoing suffering, and in their prayers they say, *You have placed a cloud in the way, so that no prayer can get beyond it.**   *Lam 3:44

It is as if they said outright, "Against our minds that are accustomed to worldly desires you fling with just judgment the apparitions of the concerns of those desires, and with them you confound us in the very intentions of our prayer, and because you are certainly aware that our minds are given over to base desires, you beat them back, deservedly blinded as they are, from seeing the transparency of your light; so then, when our minds look toward you, they are turned away by the very cloud of their own thoughts; they assiduously desire those worldly thoughts that they have, so they also have to bear them at the time of their prayer, when they do not want them." Since therefore the very depravity of persecutors is confined by a heavenly dispensation to keep it from being freely executed against the saints as much as it desires, after he said, *When I made a cloud his garment,* he added, *and wrapped him up in darkness as if in swaddling clothes.* His feet and arms indeed are confined by swaddling clothes, lest they should be flung here and there with easy-going freedom.

Since accordingly the persecutors of Holy Church are restless with inconstancy of heart and devoted to this world, they think childish, not aged, thoughts, so they are indeed confined by obscurity and darkness, not by the awareness of high Judgment. And lest they should be able to persecute as much as they want, they are said to be wrapped up in swaddling clothes, because, as has been said, their thoughts are childish, but they are confined by God's arrangement, and they do not stretch out their arm where they wish. Even if they thoughtlessly desire to perpetrate all the evil they can, they are by no means allowed to fulfill all their evil desires. The next verse:

*Job 38:10 *I surrounded it with my boundaries.** The Lord surrounds the sea with his boundaries, because he restrains the wrath of persecutors by the arrangement of his judgments, so that the bursting water of mindless agitation might break up on the wide shore of the hidden dispensation. The next verse:

XVIII. 38. *And I set up bars and doors, and I said, "This far shall you come and not advance farther, and*
*Job 38:10-11 *here will break your bursting waves."** What else is

meant by the doors but the holy preachers? What by the bars but the incarnate Lord? He obviously placed these doors to oppose attack from the raging sea just as vigorously as he strengthened them with his own oversight. Because these doors of Holy Church have been strengthened by the force of these bars, they could be battered by the waves, but they could not be broken, so that externally the waters of persecution could be let loose against them, but those waves could never get through to the internal spaces of their hearts. And since the holy teachers by their preaching are indeed open to their followers but by their authority closed to those who resist them, they are not improperly called doors: they are open to the conversion of humble people, but closed to the terror of the proud. Not improperly are they called doors, because they are open for the faithful to enter, but on the other hand they are opposed to the entrance of the treacherous.

Let us consider then what kind of door Peter was, he who received Cornelius, who was searching for faith, but repulsed Simon, who requested a miracle for money. To the first he said, *I found in truth that God is no respecter of persons,** and kindly opened the secrets of the kingdom to him; to the second he said, *May your money accompany you to hell,** and through a sentence of strict condemnation he closed the entrance to the court of heaven. What else are all the apostles but the doors of Holy Church when they hear the voice of their Redeemer say, *Receive the Holy Spirit; whose sins you shall forgive, they are forgiven, and whose sins you shall retain, they are retained*?* It is as if they were told in so many words, "Through you those to whom you open yourselves will come to me, and those to whom you are closed will be repulsed." So when the sea grows stormy the Lord opposes it with bars and doors, because when

*Acts 10:34

*Acts 8:20

*John 20:22-23

storms of persecution rage in the world from bitter and treacherous hearts, God exalts the glory of his only begotten Son and the reverence due his preachers, and when he makes known the mysteries of divine fortitude, the waves of anger break against the impious.

39. It was well said, *This far shall you come and not advance farther.** Because it is unquestionably a measure of hidden judgment both when the storm of persecution springs forth and when it quiets down, lest if it is not raised it does not exercise the chosen ones, or if it does not quiet down it drowns them in the sea. But when knowledge of the faith is extended even to persecutors, the rising of the troubled sea is put down, and there the sea breaks up its waves, because it comes to knowledge of the truth, and it is ashamed of all its wicked deeds. The broken wave is dashed against itself, because wickedness is overcome and is even accused by the thought of its own heart, and it is as though it received the force itself that it started, because it feels the impulse of its own guilt from the depraved actions that it set in motion.

*Job 38:11

That is why Paul told certain people, *But then what good did those things do you which embarrass you now?** It is as if they were told, "Why did the waves of your depraved behavior lift themselves up on high, which, now that they are broken themselves and you are converted, confound you in the same way as before they puffed you up with perverse behavior?" So it was rightly said, *Here will break your bursting waves.* We are told for the second time about this blocking of the sea by doors according to the custom of Holy Scripture, since what is said once is repeated for confirmation.

*Rom 6:21

40. However, in case we ought to take the sea in this passage not to mean the crowd of persecutors specifically, but rather the world in general, the Lord blocked

the sea with doors for the second time, because he both gave the human race laws and precepts at first and later gave them the testament of new grace; he blocked the onslaught of the sea with doors for the second time when those whom he raised for the purpose of administering his own worship he first restrained from the worship of idols by giving them the law, and later kept from carnal understanding by revealed grace. The doors received the sea a second time, because God first forbade the human race the doing of evil, and later he also restrained them from guilty thoughts.

Let us see how the Lord first blocked the surging sea with doors. Here is what is written in the law: *You shall not kill; you shall not commit adultery; you shall not steal; you shall not bear false witness.** Let us see how the Lord blocked this sea with doors the second time. In the Gospel he says, *You have heard that the elders were told, "Do not commit adultery." But I tell you that anyone who looks at a woman lustfully has already committed adultery with her in his heart.** Again he says, *You have heard how it was said, "You shall love your neighbor and hate your enemy," but I tell you: "Love your enemies and do good to those who hate you."** He who first forbade the works of evil later excluded guilty thoughts of the heart, which shows that he twice imposed doors on the raging sea, lest it should be carried across the beach of justice.

*Exod 20:13-16

*Matt 5:27-28

*Matt 5:43-44

41. So when he said, *Who has enclosed the sea within its bounds,* he rightly added the time in the same place, saying, *when it burst forth as though emerging from the womb.** Obviously, since it was then that God presented the human race with the precepts of the law, when the world was still very near its origin, it was as though it issued forth from its own birth towards the project of the life of the flesh. To emerge from the

*Job 38:8

womb of course means to appear in the flesh in the light of the present glory. And he rightly adds, *When I made a cloud his garment.* Unquestionably God did not show himself to the human race at that time by a clear revelation, but while he freed them from the error of bad faith, nevertheless he did not open up his glorious light for them; he hid them away from the darkness, as it were, but he still wrapped them up in a cloud, so that they should leave behind their former depraved actions, even though they did not yet clearly see the future good. So he rightly adds, *And wrapped him up in darkness as if in swaddling clothes.*

God taught primitive peoples, you see, not with the direct preaching of spiritual reality, but with figurative language he confined them to literal precepts, and those whose understanding was still weak he wrapped up in the darkness of his own words as if in swaddling clothes; in this way they were confined to the following of more obvious commandments and matured thereby, lest in their mistaken freedom they should perish by following their own pleasures. As long as it was not yet charity but still fear that confined them to the road of justice, the divine dispensation embraced them while it nursed them. So when the weak people unwillingly accepted the swaddle of precepts, they reached a sounder state of health out of their very bondage. Because fear first restrained the people from sin, they suitably passed on to liberty of spirit later.

Those swaddling clothes of infancy that the Lord gave to beginners, he reproved through the prophet, saying, *I gave them precepts that were not good.** It is as if evil stopped being evil by comparison with what was worse, and as if good was no longer good by comparison with what was better. Just as worse things were said to sinful Judea about Sodom and Samaria—*You have made*

*Ezek 20:25

your sisters look justified by all the abominable things that you have done*—so also the good precepts that were given to a still primitive people were mentioned as being no longer good by comparison with the later precepts of the New Testament that were better. Nor could minds that are accustomed to the habits of life in the flesh be torn away from base pursuits unless they gradually progressed, as led by preaching. That is undoubtedly why when the people were still in Egypt their hidden concupiscence was gently coaxed by kindly and righteous moderation, and having begged their neighbors for gold and silver ornaments, they were told to go. When they were led to Mount Sinai to receive the law, they soon heard, *You shall not covet anything of your neighbor's.**

*Ezek 16:51

*Exod 20:17

That is why the same law specifies that an eye for an eye and a tooth for a tooth must be exacted,* whereas one day, when grace is revealed, those who are struck on one cheek will be ordered to present the other.* Because anger always demands a retribution that is greater than the injury, they learn that evil should not be multiplied in reprisal, but one day they would learn that multiplied evils should be willingly put up with. That is why God forbade certain things to that same primitive people but kept certain things for them in their former use; still, even these he arranged as a figure of a better life. They slaughtered brute animals for idols in Egypt, and God allowed them to keep the practice of slaughtering animals afterwards, but he forbade the worship of idols, so that while they lost something of their former practice, their weak natures might be mollified by the fact that they still had something of that practice. By a wonderful dispensation of his wisdom the Lord allowed them to retain something of the custom of the flesh, which he turned into a more powerful representation of the spirit.

*Exod 21:24

*Matt 5:39

What indeed does the sacrifice of those animals signify but the death of God's only begotten Son? What else does the sacrifice of those animals signify but the killing of our life in the flesh? Where accordingly God condescended to the weakness of a primitive people, there the greater strength of the spirit is announced to them through the foreshadowing forms of allegory. So it was rightfully spoken, *and I wrapped him up in darkness as if in swaddling clothes*, because where he submitted to the weakness of the people's tender condition, there he created a high cloud of spiritual meaning.

42. He girded the extreme deviations of their souls by means of the limit imposed by precepts, so he correctly adds, *I surrounded him with my boundaries.** And since he confined the actions of this human race by sending the Mediator, he fittingly adds, *And I set up bars and doors*. He certainly did set up bars and doors when he sent the Redeemer to combat sins and misbehavior, and he strengthened the preaching of the new life. With the doors closed and the bars set in place, the people are strengthened. God set the bars in place accordingly when he sent his only begotten Son against the unrestrained behavior of the human race, and he strengthened the spiritual precepts that he taught in speeches by putting them into practice.

The Lord's speech continues: *and I said, "This far shall you come and not advance farther, and here will break your bursting waves."* This sea had overflowed those first doors, because the water of human pride had leaped over the bounds of the law that opposed it, but after the world encountered the opposition of the only begotten Son, he broke the attack of its pride, and it could not pass, because it found the way closed and an end to its fury in the Son's might. So the prophet was right to say, *The sea saw him and fled.** It would not be

*Job 38:10

*Ps 113:3

inappropriate either to understand his openly witnessed sufferings by the doors upon which God secretly fastened bars, because he reinforced them with his invisible divinity. Against them the waves of the world rise but fall back broken, because proud people see and despise them, but when they experience their power they become afraid. Whereas the human race first mocked the sufferings of the only begotten Son, it afterwards took fright; it acted like the sea being aroused against the doors that were set up; moved to action by pride, it fell back with its force broken.

But blessed Job has been told all this precisely because he was to be kept from boasting of so many virtues in his heart, lest he should by chance attribute to himself the fact (which he could not ignore) that his standing was high; since we have carefully weighed so many words spoken for his edification, let us also discuss their moral value. So he says,

XIX. 43. *Who has enclosed the sea within its bounds?** *Job 38:8
What else is the sea but our heart, stormy with anger, harsh in quarrels, pompous with the elation of pride, secretive with the deceit of malice? That person understands how much the sea rages who pays attention to the hidden temptations of thoughts he finds in himself. Even if we already abandon what is perverse, even if we already cling to righteous desires, even if we already cast away depraved actions, nevertheless those perverse habits of our old life that we have brought with us are the hidden internal storms that weary us, and did not the enclosures of boundless fear constrain us with respect to Judgment and the terrible thought of eternal torment, all the foundations of our interior building would collapse. If the fierce internal suggestion should break out externally through a deliberate act, the building of our interior life would have been undermined and have fallen to pieces.

We have been conceived in iniquity and brought forth in sin, and we have brought with us to this world a battle against the troubles brought on by inherent corruption: the battle that we only win with a great deal of trouble. So we are rightly told, *when it burst forth as though emerging from the womb.* The womb of evil thoughts is adolescence, about which God told Moses, *The feeling and thought of the human heart is evil from adolescence on.** The evil of corruption that every one of us sucks in from the birth of desires of the flesh we practice until the onset of mature years, and unless the hand of the fear of God represses them very early, guilt quickly devours all the goodness of created nature in the pit. Let no one therefore attribute the victory over his thoughts to himself, since Truth has said, *Who has enclosed the sea within its bounds, when it burst forth as though emerging from the womb?* Because unless God's grace held back the waves of the heart from the very beginning of the thought, the raging sea with storms of temptation would beyond doubt have engulfed the earth of the human mind, so that it might be drenched by salty waves and be made barren; in other words, it might be delighted by fatal pleasures of the flesh and ruined.

The Lord alone therefore closes the gates of the sea, and he opposes the depraved motions of the heart with the closed doors of inspired fear. However, since we are forbidden to follow what we perceive because the pleasures of the body blunt the edge of the mind, we are now free to lift up the eyes of the mind to what is invisible and follow what we are commanded to see. But what do we do? They are not yet clear to our weakened vision. Behold, we are called to love them, but we are restrained from seeing them, because even if we do sometimes glimpse something fleeting and infinitesimal, we are still darkened by an uncertain vision. So it aptly follows,

*Gen 8:21

XX. 44. *When I made a cloud his garment and wrapped him up in darkness as if in swaddling clothes.* This stormy sea that is our heart is obviously dressed in thoughts, because lest it should perceive unalloyed internal quiet, it is darkened by the confusion of its own uneasiness. This sea is wrapped up in darkness as if in swaddling clothes, because it is hindered by its still tender and weak senses from contemplating the highest reality. Let us look at Paul when he is wrapped up in darkness as if in swaddling clothes and says, *We see now obscurely as if through a mirror, but then we shall see him face to face. Now I partly know, but then I shall know even as I am known.** If he did not perceive himself as an infant when it came to understanding heavenly reality, he would by no means have prefaced those words with a comparison of his own age, saying, *When I was a child, I spoke like a child, I understood like a child, I thought like a child.** We then lift ourselves up to youthful strength when we look with strong feelings at the life toward which we tend, but now that the beam of our intention is weakened and turned away from the internal light, our mind is kept bound with swaddling clothes. So it is appropriately added,

*1 Cor 13:12

*1 Cor 13:11

XXI. 45. *I surrounded it with my boundaries.** The Lord surrounds this sea with his boundaries, because he humbles our heart within the measure of its contemplation while it is still in turmoil with distress and worry over its own corruption, so that even if it desires more, it does not rise above the measure given to it. Or at least the Lord surrounds this sea with his boundaries in the sense that when our heart is beset with temptations he calms it with hidden distributions of gifts: here he sees to it that no evil suggestion comes to delight us, there that no evil pleasure forces our consent. Consequently he looks upon the forbidden emotions of the heart; some

*Job 38:10

of these he forbids to go all the way to consent, and others he restrains even from pleasure; he imposes absolute limits upon the raging sea so that its waves never end in an act, but the waters of temptation keep murmuring softly and crashing within the confines of the mind. Since therefore the mind is valiantly restrained when delight in God and the inspiration of virtues jostle it, the words are rightly added,

XXII. 46. *And I set up bars and doors, and I said, "This far shall you come and not advance farther, and here will break your bursting waves."** What do we take the doors to mean in a moral sense but virtues, and what bars but the solidity of love? The raging sea then separates these doors that are working virtues, unless love supports and holds them from the secret place of the mind. All the goodness of virtues is easily scattered when a temptation attacks the heart, unless it is held fast within by the solidity of love. So also Paul, when in his preaching he opposed certain doors of virtues with the sea of temptation, immediately backed up these doors as it were with sturdy bars and said, *Above all these have charity, which is the bond of perfection.**

*Job 38:10-11

*Col 3:14

Charity is called the bond of perfection, because it absolutely ties together all the good that is done lest it be lost. The tempter certainly uproots any good work quickly if he finds it free of the bond of charity. But if the mind is constrained by the love of God and neighbor when the attack of temptation suggests anything unrighteous, love is opposed against it as a barrier, and it repels the waters of evil suggestion with the doors of virtue and the bars of interior love. Accordingly, since the Lord represses the vices that are born in the heart through the fortitude of inspired love, he blocks the onrush of the rising sea through the closed and sealed doors. Even if anger does secretly irritate us, we do not want the heavenly calm to be lost, so we deny the use of the tongue to the troubled mind, lest the tumult heard in the bosom of the heart should be let out even to the sound of the voice.

If lust incites hidden thoughts in us, we do not want the mind to lose its heavenly purity, so we chastise the members that could obey the conceived impure thoughts, lest the stench of the heart should be exhaled even to the corruption of the body. We do not want the mind to be without the kingdom of heaven, so when avarice excites us, we are content with our own possessions and lock ourselves up in the enclosure of frugality, lest the mind should be enlarged with some act of depravity and the fire of internal concupiscence should burn all the way to an external act. Pride puffs itself up, but lest a person lose true greatness by remembering that he is dust, everyone brings himself down from the high level of pride that he has conceived, struggling mightily lest he should allow any suggested thought to burst out with an external act. It is well said then, *And I set up bars and doors, and I said, "This far shall you come and not advance farther, and here will break your bursting waves."*

As long as every chosen one is both tempted to do evil and yet refuses to do the evil that is suggested, it is as though the sea was held back. Even if it crashes against the mind internally with its destructive waves of thought, it does not exceed the established boundary of the good life. The sea indeed lifts itself up in pride, but as long as it is resisted by fixed deliberation in the heart, it falls back broken. So lest blessed Job should attribute to himself that he bravely stands against the storms in his heart, let him hear God's voice say, *Who has enclosed the sea within its bounds when it burst forth as though emerging from the womb?* And what follows. It is as if he were openly told, "It is in vain that you think yourself involved in external good works if you do not consider me who confine the waters of temptation inside you; just as you are able to control the waves externally in your work, it is my power that breaks the waves of temptation in your heart.

BOOK 29

I. 1. The Lord our God Jesus Christ, because he is the power and wisdom of God, was born of the Father before time, or better, because he neither began to be born nor ended, let us say more truly that he was always born. However we cannot say that he is always born, lest he should seem to be imperfect. On the other hand, so that he can be called eternal, let us both say that he is perfect and that he is always born inasmuch as birth belongs to perfection and always belongs to eternity, so that in some way that essence without time can be signified with the use of words that belong to time, although by the very fact that we call something perfect we have deviated greatly from the expression of that very truth, because what has not been made cannot be called perfect. Nevertheless the Lord condescended to the limitations of our language and said, *Be perfect as your heavenly Father is perfect.** *Matt 5:48

Accordingly God could not be known by the human race in that divine birth, so he came in human nature to be seen; he wanted to be seen so he could be imitated. His birth in the flesh seemed to be despised by the wise people in this world. They had only contempt for the weakness of his human nature, judging it unworthy of God. The human creature was all the more indebted to God the more unworthy attachments he assumed for its sake. *The world did not know God through wisdom, so it has pleased God to save those who believe through the foolishness of our preaching.** It is as if he said, "Since the world could never through its own wisdom find God who is wisdom, it pleased God that the world should see God made man *1 Cor 1:21

through human folly, inasmuch as the wisdom of God descended to our folly so that our blindness, illuminated by the clay of God's human flesh, could see the light of heavenly wisdom." Therefore he was born of the Father without time, and he deigned to be born of a mother in time, so that because his birth was included between a beginning and an end, he who arose without a beginning and was not cut short by an end was revealed to the eyes of the human mind as born. So blessed Job is now told,

II. 2. *After your birth did you give orders to the dawn, or did you show the sunrise its place?** You must suppose the words, "as I did." The rise of divinity does not of course have a before and an after. His being is always through eternity since he surrounds all that passes away, and within himself he encloses the course of time. But since the birth of his humanity begins and ends, it accepts from time the fact of having a before and after. But since because he accepted the shadows of our transient nature, he let the light of his eternity shine upon us, through this birth that the Creator really gave himself in time the dayspring knew its place outside of time. Since the dawn or sunrise is turned from darkness into light, the whole church of the chosen is rightly given the name of dawn or sunrise. Since that church is led from the night of unbelief to the light of faith, like the sunrise it opens the day to the splendor of heavenly light and leaves the darkness behind. That is why the question is asked in the Song of Songs, *Who is she who is coming forth like the dawn rising?** Holy Church desires the reward of heavenly life, and she is called the dawn, because when she abandons the darkness of sin she shines with the light of justice.

3. However, we have something more precise that we would consider concerning the quality of dawn or sunrise. Sunrise or dawn, you see, announces the pass-

*Job 38:12

*Song 6:9

ing of the night, but it does not also reveal the full clarity of the day; still, whereas it dismisses the former, it receives the latter and holds a light mixed with darkness. What are we then, all of us who follow truth in this life, if not sunrise or dawn? Do we not already do certain things that belong to the light, and yet do we lack certain remnants of the dark? The prophet definitely tells God, *no one alive is justified in your sight.** Somewhere else it is written, *Actually we all do wrong in many ways.** Paul says for his part, *I see another law in my body, resisting the law of my mind, and making me a captive of the law of sin residing in my body.** Where then the law of sin contends with the law of the mind, it is certainly still daybreak, because the light that has already burst forth has not yet completely taken hold of the passing darkness. It is still dawn, because as long as the law of the flesh strikes at the law of the mind, and the law of the mind strikes at the law of the flesh, there is turn by turn conflict between light and shadow. So again, when Paul said, *Night has faded,* he by no means added, "The day has come," but, *Daylight has approached.** He then who after the passing of the night remarks not yet that day has come, but that day has drawn near, beyond any doubt proves that between the sunrise and the darkness he is still in the area of dawn.

4. Then however will Holy Church be the full day of the chosen when the shadow of sin is no longer mixed with it. Then will she be the full day when she shines forth with the perfect heat of internal light. Then will she be full day when she endures no tempting memory of the evil she has done and she puts far from her even the remaining shades of darkness. So this dawn is rightly displayed while still in its passage, when the Lord says, *Did you show the sunrise its place?* The one to whom her place is shown is obviously called from one place

*Ps 142:2
*Jas 3:2

*Rom 7:23

*Rom 13:12

to another. What then is the place of the dawn if not the perfect brightness of internal vision? And the one who being thus led will then no longer have any darkness in her from the night that had passed. Now, however, the church still suffers the distress of temptation because the intention of her heart hurries her on to another world, so the dawn moves to her place. If the mind did not discern that place, she would remain in the night of this life. But as long as she contends for perfection every day and wants the light to increase every day, she already sees where her place is and seeks the sun for it to glow fully in her.

The dawn considers her place when a holy soul burns for the contemplation of the form of her creator. Dawn was doing all she could to be in possession of her place when David said, *My soul has thirsted for the living God; when shall I come and present myself before God?** Truth was showing the dawn her place when he said through Solomon, *What more does the wise man have than the fool, and what does the poor man have, except that he should go there where there is life?**

*Ps 41:3

*Eccl 6:8

After his own birth the Lord showed that very same place to the patriarchs who preceded his incarnation, because unless they knew through the spirit of prophecy that the king of the heavenly homeland would take flesh, they would not see how desirable and good that same homeland was. Truth made clear to the dawn its place when he petitioned the Father in front of his disciples and said, *Father, I will that where I am those you have given me may be with me.** He showed the dawn its place when he said, *Wherever the body is, there the eagles will gather.** The dawn hurried to reach this place that it had known when Paul said that his desire was to be dissolved and to be with Christ.* He said again, *For me to live is Christ, and to die is gain.** And again,

*John 17:24

*Matt 24:28

*Phil 1:23
*Phil 1:21

We know that if our earthly house where we live now is destroyed, we have a house from God, a building not made by hands, eternal, in heaven.* ⸻ *2 Cor 5:1

So the Lord rightly maintained that after his own birth he showed the dawn its place, because before he knew the blessedness of the future recompense through his own body, he secured it in the understanding of a few. But when he took on himself the weakness of a human birth, he extended the knowledge of the future glory in the love of an uncounted multitude. But when divine mercy completed the mystery of God's work in such a way that anger should accompany it, inasmuch as the hidden worker looked upon some and redeemed them but abandoned and lost others, since we have known how he enlightened the chosen ones through his incarnation, let us now hear how he condemned the reprobate sinners.

III. 5. *Have you held the ends of the earth to shake it or knocked the wicked off it?** The Lord held the ends of the earth, because at the end of the ages he came to the synagogue, which was already abandoned and given over to foreign kings. Moreover he cast the impious people out of it, because they refused belief in the spiritual preaching of faith, and he even drove them away from the glory of the sacrifice of flesh. Or at least he held the ends of the earth in the sense that he chose the few dejected and humble ones he found in Judea. He held the ends of the earth when he abandoned the teachers of the law and raised up the fishermen, and while he held Judea's ends he cast the impious people out of it, because while he strengthened those who were weak in faith, he condemned the strong unfaithful there. ⸻ *Job 38:13

He was also right to add *to shake it*, because at his coming he even shook the hearts of reprobate sinners with a terrible fear. They were surely shaken who said,

You see we are getting nowhere! Look, the whole world has gone after him!* Whatever is shaken is wearily led here and there. Judea was certainly shaken when *Some said he is a good man, while others said he is not; rather he misleads the crowd.** Through others again she said, *If he were not from God he could do nothing.** Finally at the end she cried out through others, *If he were not an evildoer, we would not have handed him over to you.**

*John 12:19

*John 7:12
*John 9:33

*John 18:30

The reprobate sinners were indeed shaken but not knocked down when here they were struck dumb at seeing miracles, there they saw with contempt and ridiculed the shame of weakness. Were they not shaken when they said, *How long will you keep us guessing? If you are the Christ, tell us plainly?** Or at least he struck and held the ends of the earth, because when he terrified the weak hearts of the humble with holy fear, he did not abandon them with strict justice. The multitude of those who believe in God stood the more firmly because it was alarmed from being humbled in itself. Because God holds the one he strikes, the prophet infers, *For whom do I look, if not for the humble and quiet person, the one who quakes at my word?** Because God holds the one he strikes, he instructs us through the testimony of Solomon, who says, *Blessed is the man who is always fearful, but the hard-hearted man sinks down into evil.** Therefore, since the Lord held the ends of Judea through the apostles, and because their merits demanded it he reproved the scribes, Pharisees, and priests for their impiety, let us hear what remains to be said about their condemnation:

*John 10:24

*Isa 66:2

*Prov 28:14

IV. 6. *The seal shall be restored as clay, and it will stand like a garment.** What else but clay did the Lord find the people of Israel to be, whom he discovered given over to the service of the Gentiles to make bricks in Egypt? When he led her to the Promised Land with

*Job 38:14

so many miracles, when he filled the people he led with the knowledge of his own wisdom, when he conferred on her so many secret mysteries through prophecy, what else did he make her but a seal for preserving the mystery? Divine prophecy itself kept closed whatever Truth revealed of himself concerning the end. But when after so many divine secrets, after witnessing so many miracles at the coming of her Redeemer, she loved her land more than the Truth, she said through the chief priests, *If we leave him alone, everyone will believe in him, and the Romans will come and take away our place and nation.** It was as though she returned to those bricks she had left in Egypt; she who had already been made God's seal turned back again to what she had abandoned, and she displayed herself as clay after she had been a seal in the eyes of Truth when she lost the mysteries of the received word through the malice of impiety and chose to know only what was earthly and what soiled.

*John 11:48

7. At which point he rightly adds, *And it will stand like a garment.** Clothes that are crude and unfitting and yet are worn, because they do not well fit the members they cover, are said to stand by themselves. Judea therefore, with regard to knowledge of the truth, even when she seemed to serve, stood like a garment, because she pretended to serve the Lord through external commandments, but she refused to cling to him through understanding and love. As long as she clung to God's precepts through the letter alone and never joined herself through the spirit to the internal senses, it was as though she did not stick to him who had put her on. So he again aptly continues,

*Job 38:14

V. 8. *From the impious people he will take away their light.** Since they refused belief in the truth, they lost knowledge of the law forever. As long as they boast that they have received the law, they are absolutely

*Job 38:15

blinded by showing off their knowledge. In fact it is written, *Let their eyes be darkened lest they see.** And again it is written, *Blind the heart of this people and make their ears heavy.** Elsewhere it is written, *I came into this world for judgment, that those who do not see may see, and that those who see may become blind.** And since by works of the law they set themselves up against the Creator of the law, he is right to continue,

*Ps 68:24

*Isa 6:10

*John 9:39

VI. 9. *And the high arm shall be brought low.** The high arm is indeed brought low when the grace of faith is preached and proud works of the law are condemned and it is said, *By works of the law will no person of flesh be justified.**

*Job 38:15

*Rom 3:20

10. All this, however, can be understood in a different way. Holy Scripture often calls the church earth. The Lord then holds the ends of the earth and shakes them, because the Lord allows his church to be troubled through the coming of Antichrist by a final and most savage persecution, but in allowing it he does not abandon her. The Lord sometimes holds this earth but does not shake it, and sometimes he both holds and shakes it, because he sometimes possesses her in the quiet peace of faith but sometimes commands that she be shaken by the attack of persecution.

11. When he said, *Have you held the ends of the earth to shake it,* he did well to add, *or knocked the wicked off it?* Paul, you see, bears us witness that there are many on earth who *declare their knowledge of God, yet deny him by their actions.** The Lord then shakes the wicked off the earth, because those whom interior vices now possess will later fall in the pit of open unbelief, and from there they will pass into the heap of chaff when they are stirred by the wind of that temptation. Even if they are now hidden in a corner of the yard under the appearance of faith, they will definitely then be thrown

*Titus 1:16

out, away from the heaps of grain, by the winnowing fan of the close scrutiny.

12. So it is rightly added, *The seal shall be restored as clay.* It is as if he said plainly, "Those who now look like a seal in the bosom of the church will then be restored as clay before the eyes of all." That is, they certainly do not deceive human judgment with their profession of religion, but they display openly how worldly their wisdom is. It is customary in Holy Scripture for faith to be called a seal and for wickedness to be called clay. The younger son, you see, having used up his wealth and returned to his father, was given a ring for a present,* and the Gentile people who lost immortality return to God repentant and are defended by the seal of faith. That is why the church is told by her spouse, *Put me as a seal on your heart.** A seal is placed on things then precisely for this reason: lest they be violated by any bold plunderers. The Bridegroom is therefore placed as a seal on the heart when the mystery of faith in him is impressed and committed to the guardianship of our thoughts, so that unfaithful servant, indeed our adversary, when he notices hearts that are sealed with faith, may not presume to violate them with temptation. As for clay, however, the psalmist avows that it signifies the contagion of earthly things where he says, *You have pulled me out of the pit of misery and the clay of impurity.**

*Luke 15:2

*Song 8:6

*Ps 39:3

Since accordingly many people have been found involved in earthly contagion but led to the church and sealed with the sacrament of heavenly faith, yet they do not abandon their evil practices but cover them up now with the veil of faith—rather, when they have found time they show clearly what they are—it is rightly said, *The seal shall be restored as clay.* Those whom we now think to be faithful we will find later to be the enemies of faith, and although they may seem to be sealed as long as they are not tempted, they will beyond any doubt be clay as soon as they are tempted. And he is right to say *restored*, because their sinful life afterwards clearly shows the kind of conscience they could have had before faith. About them the words that follow are aptly spoken: *and it will stand like a garment.*

13. Holy Church is dressed with as many garments, one might say, as she is decorated with the veneration of the faithful, so when the Gentiles have been shown her by the Lord, the prophet says, *As I live, you will be clothed with all these like a garment.** She is now dressed with many as though they were faithful, but only in appearance; as soon as the attack of persecution is raised she will be quickly undressed and free of them. It is of their fate that it is said here, *and it will stand like a garment.* He uses *stand* here to mean remaining in sin. That is why it is written, *Who does not stand in the path of sinners.** Or at least all reprobate sinners are said to stand like a garment, so that they may be shown to be unable to stand, because just as when a garment is put on it is stretched over the body to display its appearance, but when it is taken off the appearance is lost in its folds, so every person who leaves his or her place in Holy Church at that time was formerly as stretched and beautiful as a garment just put on, but afterwards taken off wrinkled and lying thrown down. If however we take *stand* to mean remaining, then all reprobate sinners stand like a garment, because they briefly remain in this life that they love. That is why the prophet says, *Everything will wear out like a garment. You will change them, and they will be changed.**

So these words were introduced veiled in a cloud of allegory, but now we are given clearer words that follow:

VII. 14. *From the impious people he will take away their light.** Nor does God's light enlighten them now

*Isa 49:18

*Ps 1:1

*Ps 101:27
LXX

*Job 38:15

who cover their malice and wickedness with the name of faith. As long as they neglect to live according to the preaching of faith and yet venerate that same faith by appearance alone, they are seeking honor in the present life with the name of religion, and that aspect of faith is their light, which faith kindles for them among people. There are those, however, who really believe in the eternal words they hear, and yet they contradict the very faith they hold by living evil lives. These people also have their light amidst darkness who, while they act perversely, nevertheless think what is right about God, and lest their darkness be complete, they are partly enlightened by the brightness of the light. As long as they love the earth more than heaven and what their eyes see more than what their ears hear, when the blow of persecution falls, they lose the gain they seemed to have from correct belief.

Such things happen with alarming frequency at that time when that head of iniquity is raised against the church in the last persecution, and his power strides forth along with his free sources of strength. Then and there everyone's heart is revealed; there whatever lay hidden will be opened, and those with pious speech and impious hearts whose malice is made public collapse, and they lose the light of faith that they held only surface deep. But when matters stand thus it is necessary that each one of us should return to the secret place of the heart and greatly fear the loss of our action, lest our merits should demand that we run in the number of such people through the strict justice of God's judgments.

15. But let none recklessly comfort themselves and think that they are excluded from such a fate, because they suppose they will not reach that storm or that tempest. O, how many these are who have not seen that time of trial and yet are now caught in the storm of its temptation? Cain did not see the time of Antichrist, but he deserved to be a member of Antichrist. Judas did not know the savageness of his persecution, and yet he succumbed to the law of his cruelty by the persuasion of avarice. Simon lived at a time far distant from that of Antichrist, and yet by perversely desiring the power of miracles for himself, he became a partaker of his pride. In this way the wicked body, in this way the members are joined to their head and members, when they do not know him mentally and yet are united with him by their depraved actions.

Neither had Pergamum known the books or words of Balaam, but by following his wicked teaching she heard the voice of heavenly chastisement: *You have there some people who hold the teaching of Balaam who taught Balac to put a stumbling block before the children of Israel, that they might eat and fornicate.** The knowledge, times, and places of the church of Thyatira were also far distant from Jezebel, but because the guilty life of that church was tied to her, Jezebel was said to be in it and to be part of it because of its sinful practices, since the angel witness said, *I have this against you: you allow the woman Jezebel to call herself a prophetess and to teach and seduce my servants to commit fornication and to eat meat sacrificed to idols.** You see then that because they could be found who were partakers of Jezebel's sinful life by their sinful actions, we are told that Jezebel was found there, obviously because the practices of a sinful body make it one with it, even if place and time cut them off from it.

*Rev 2:14

*Rev 2:20

So it happens that every wicked person who has already died nevertheless remains behind in his sinful imitators, and that very leader of iniquity has already appeared in his workers, he who has not really come yet. That is why John says, *Many Antichrists have already come forth.** All the wicked people are already his members, obviously because they came out at another time and preceded their head by their evil lives. That is why Paul says, *So that he may be revealed in his own time, since the mystery of iniquity is already at work.** It is as if he said, "Then the Antichrist will be fully revealed, since in the hearts of the wicked he is already hidden and works out his secret evil."

*1 John 2:18

*2 Thess 2:6-7

So that I may be silent about more obvious crimes, behold one person who envies her brother quietly in her heart, and when an opportunity is found she tries to trip him up; of whom is she a member if not of the one about whom Scripture has it, *By the envy of the devil death has entered the world?** Another person figures his own merit is great and puts himself ahead of everyone else by the pride of his heart, thinking everyone inferior to himself: of whom again is he a member, if not of him whom Scripture describes: *He sees all that is lofty. He is the king of all the sons of pride?** Somebody else seeks power in this world, not so that she may help others, but lest she should herself be subject to someone else: of whom again is she a member but of him of whom Scripture says, *He said: I will take my seat on the mount of the covenant, at the edge of the north. I will ascend above the tops of the clouds; I will be like the most high?** Only the Most High in fact so dominates all things that he cannot be subject to any. Him the Devil perversely wanted to imitate when he sought his own dominion and refused to be subject to God. So whoever desires his own power, precisely because he hates subjection to one whom divine decree places over him, imitates the Devil.

*Wis 2:24

*Job 41:25 LXX

*Isa 14:13-14

16. There are, besides, many things that declare the fact that there are faithless people present in the very peace of the church. I see indeed some who so accept the person of one who has power that when requested by him they do not hesitate to deny the truth in the cause of a neighbor to favor him. Who is the Truth if not the one who said, *I am the way, the truth, and the life?** Neither did John the Baptist die when questioned about his confession of Christ, but about the truth of justice, but since Christ is the truth, he persevered until death for Christ precisely because it was for the truth. Let us then place before our eyes the fact that someone has been detained and has accepted the person of the one in power and, lest he should suffer injury even by a word, has denied what is true. What, I ask, would he do with painful punishment who has been ashamed of Christ in the blows of words? Behold, after that he is still a Christian in the eyes of men and women, and yet if the Lord resolved to judge him strictly, he is one no longer.

*John 14:6

17. I see others however to whom the duties of exhortation and accusation have been entrusted by dint of the office of magistrate, and when they see something unlawful committed, fearing to lose the favor of some powerful individuals, they do not dare to make an accusation. Whoever this individual may be, what else is he doing but running away when he sees the wolf approach? He runs away because he remains silent; he remains silent because he holds the grace of eternity in contempt and loves worldly honors more. Behold the one who hides himself in front of the powerful inside his own recesses, and just as if from public persecution he gives way to hidden fear. It is rightly said of such people, *They loved honor among people more than the praise of God.** Whoever this person is, accordingly, if he be strictly judged and there was no public persecution, by remaining silent he denied Christ. So even in the peace of the church the temptations of Antichrist are not absent. No one should be terrified of the persecutions

*John 12:43

of the final times alone. Among the wicked, the plots of Antichrist are being laid every day, because in their hearts his mystery is already now being worked out in secret. And if even now many people who belong to the church in appearance alone pretend to be what they are not, when the Judge finally comes it will be revealed what they really are. About them Solomon rightly says, *I saw the impious buried who while they were still alive were in the holy place and were praised in the city as if they had done righteous deeds.** *Eccl 8:10

So after he said about the wicked, *The seal shall be restored as clay, and it will stand like a garment, and from the impious people he will take away their light,** *Job 38:14-15 which was to happen in that final persecution of Antichrist, he forthwith comforts us with the destruction of that same Antichrist and says,

VIII. 18. *And the high arm shall be brought low.** *Job 38:15 And what else do we take the high arm to mean but the proud height of Antichrist, who raises himself above people's reprobate minds with the conceit of worldly honor just like a sinful person, and yet disdains to be considered human but falsely claims to be God over men? That is why the apostle Paul says, *So that he is enthroned in God's temple as if to show himself to be God.* He had already said, as if to make his pride swell more, *He is the Adversary who lifts himself up against all that is called God or is worshiped.** A person too *2 Thess 2:4 can sometimes be called God, according to what Moses is told: *Behold, I have made you God to Pharaoh.** A *Exod 7:1 mere person, however, cannot be worshiped as God.

But since the Antichrist lifts himself up above some people who are saints and above the very power of God himself, through the very glorious name he has usurped he tries to surpass all that is called God and all that is worshiped. Still it is to be noticed how deep the pit of pride is into which he has fallen, he who has not remained within the dimensions of the ruin of his fall. Both the devil and the human being were corrupted from the condition in which they were made because of a proud mind, so that the first said, *I will ascend above the tops of the clouds; I will be like the most high.** The second believed what he heard: *Your eyes will be opened. You will be like gods.** Both of them fell precisely because they wanted to be like God, not through justice, but through power.

*Isa 14:14

*Gen 3:5

The human being, however, has been liberated through grace; once he had perversely desired likeness to God and had fallen, but in the guilt of his sin he recognizes that he is far from a likeness to God, and he cries out, *Lord, who is like you?** The devil however was rightly dismissed in the failure of his crime, but he hardly kept the same measure of self-destruction. The further he fell short of the grace of the Almighty, the more the guilt of his crime accumulated. He fell because he inordinately desired to be like God, and he was finally led to the point where he came as Antichrist. He then who disdained even to look like God—and God whom in his pride he could not have as an equal—being condemned he considered even worse. What we have already said, *He lifts himself up against all that is called God or is worshiped,** clearly shows that by having long since desired to be like God he wanted to lift himself up next to God, but by letting his sin of pride grow, he has already lifted himself up above all that is called God and is worshiped. Since therefore this pride of his is to be struck down at the coming of the strict Judge (as it is written, *The Lord Jesus will slay him with the breath of his mouth and destroy him by the brightness of his coming*),* it is rightly said, *And the high arm shall be brought low.*

*Ps 34:10

*2 Thess 2:4

*2 Thess 2:8

19. All these points, however, which have already been discussed twice, can still be understood in another way. God's words like pigments are there to help us. Just as the more a coloring substance is ground in a cup, the brighter appears its tint, so the more we grind the word of God by explaining it, the more we help our listeners as if to drink. Because our merciful God puts up with people's sins so long, and when he sees that the end is already near he often changes the minds of sinners, he rightly of himself implies the force of such great love and says,

IX. 20. *Have you held the ends of the earth to shake it or knocked the wicked off it?** By the earth he surely means to signify the human being weak in wisdom, to whom was said after sin, *You are dust, and to dust you shall return.** But because the loving Creator does not abandon what he has made, he both puts up with the evil deeds of humans through his patience and finally forgives them through their conversion. When he sees that their minds are harsh and insensitive, sometimes he terrifies them by threats, sometimes by blows, and sometimes by revelations, so that the minds that had hardened with the worst kind of security might soften with salutary fear inasmuch as they returned, even late, and by that very circumstance, that they took so long to do it, were ashamed.

*Job 38:13

*Gen 3:19

The Lord knows in fact that he judges the end of our life, and by that very fact he purifies his chosen ones at the end more carefully. It is written, *The Lord will judge the ends of the earth.** In fact he watches over the ends of our lives the more intensely the more he considers that the beginnings of the next life depend on it. And since he acts thus in his mercy, he has led forth his love to center stage; in his love he receives the conversion of sinners even though late, and he teaches blessed Job justice,

*1 Sam 2:10

asking, *Have you held the ends of the earth to shake it or knocked the wicked off of it?* You should hear underneath that question how God often terrifies the sinners with blows in their last agony, by converting holds them, and even roots out from their hearts evil emotions and thoughts. So the Lord rightly implies to blessed Job how he converts sinners who are near the end. It is as if he said openly, "See the power of my mercy, and repress the pride of your justice." Such are the last ends of people who, even when they are converted through bodily death, are still accompanied by the curse of that ancient sin, as he forthwith implies, saying,

X. 21. *The seal shall be restored as clay, and it will stand like a garment.** The Lord indeed has made the human being whom he created in his own likeness to be like a seal of his power. But this human being will be restored like clay, since although it escapes eternal punishment through conversion, it is condemned to the death of the flesh as payment for the sin of pride that it has committed. The human being was created from clay and received a rational mind; this being was endowed with the similitude of the divine image, but pride in the heart caused it to be inflated, and it forgot that it was formed of the basest elements. So by the wonderful justice of the Creator it was brought about that because the one who received a rational nature grew proud through thought, he should again become earth through death, which he refused to humbly recognize as his being, and since he lost likeness to God by sinning, by dying he returned to the substance of his clay. So it is rightly said, *The seal shall be restored as clay.* And since the spirit is called to leave the body as though taking off the covering of the flesh, about the same clay it is rightly added, *and it will stand like a garment.* For our clay to stand like a garment means that it endures empty and

*Job 38:14

unoccupied until the day of resurrection. But since not even they who are victorious over pride by a humble life escape that penalty of pride, he adds what the special penalty of proud people is and says,

XI. 22. *From the impious people he will take away their light, and the high arm shall be brought low.** Bodily death that restores their light to the chosen ones takes away the light from the reprobate. The light of the proud, you see, is honor in the present life. That light is taken away from them at the time when they are called to the darkness of their reason through bodily death. Then and there will the high arm be brought low, because the high flying heart will be violently uprooted beyond the usual course of nature, and it is scattered by the huge mountain of divine justice that overtakes it, so that it may know in its eternally broken state from the weight of Judgment how perversely it had lifted itself up for a short time. Not one of us however would know what follows after death unless the Creator of our life came all the way to the penalty of our death. Unless in his mercy he himself sought out the lowest, he would never righteously call us back to the highest after we had lost his image. So he rightly adds,

*Job 38:15

XII. 23. *Have you ever entered the deep ocean, or have you walked on the bottom of the abyss?** It is as if he said, "As I have, who have not only sought out the sea, that is, the world, through the human body and soul that I have assumed, but also willingly laid down my life in death and descended even to the bottom of hell, as if it were the bottom of the sea." If of course the sea, as is the custom of God's word, should be understood as the world, there is nothing against understanding the deep ocean as the prison of hell. The Lord made for that deep ocean when he entered the bottom of hell where he was about to free the souls of his chosen ones. That is

*Job 38:16

why the prophet says, *You have made a road out of the deep ocean for the redeemed to pass.** Before the Redeemer's coming this very deep ocean was no road, but a prison, because there were confined the souls even of good people, although not in cells of punishment. This deep place however the Lord made a road, because when he arrived there he allowed his chosen ones to pass over from the prison of hell to heaven, so that it is rightly said in that passage, *for the redeemed to pass.* What however he called a deep ocean he also named with other words the bottom of the abyss. Just as no image of ours can take in the watery abyss, so we have no comprehension or concept with which to penetrate the hidden places of hell. We see people being taken away from here, but where the retribution of punishment causes them to stay according to their merit we do not see.

*Isa 51:10

24. We must weigh carefully however and alertly the fact that he avows himself to have walked on the bottom of the abyss. The ability to walk certainly belongs to the free and not the bound person. The one whom chains bind of course has his feet impeded from walking. Since therefore the Lord has carried no chains of sin, he has walked in hell, and he comes freely to those who are bound. So it is written, *I became like a helpless man, free among the dead.** For the Lord then to walk on the bottom of the abyss means that he finds nothing to keep him in the place of condemnation, as Peter testifies, saying, *The pains of hell were loosed, because it was impossible for him to be held by them.** Or perhaps, since we are led from one place to another by walking, and we are found to be present here and there, the Lord is said to have walked in hell, so that he may be shown to have been present to chosen souls everywhere through the power of his divinity. That is why the spirit of wisdom too is described as mobile,*

*Ps 87:5-6

*Acts 2:24

*Wis 7:22

so that because there is no place where she is absent it is signified that she meets us everywhere. This descent of his the Lord looks upon as the more wonderful the more often he speaks of it to redeemed humankind. Repeating it again, he adds,

XIII. 25. *Are the gates of death opened for you, or have you seen the dark doors?** The gates of death are the hostile powers. When the Lord descended he opened them, because he overwhelmed their power by dying. They are also called dark doors by using other words, because being unseen and hidden they trap unwary minds and open the way to death. The Lord however sees the dark doors, because he looks upon and subdues the deceptive malice of unclean spirits. Unless in fact he stopped them by looking at them without our knowing it, neither would our mind know anything about their traps, but it would be caught in them and perish. But we too see these dark doors when we are enlightened by the rays of heavenly light. That is why the prophet says, *The Lord is my helper, and I will see my enemies.** Accordingly he sees our enemies, he who by his gift makes them visible to us. Or at least the Lord saw the dark doors at that time when he penetrated the prison of hell and knocked down the cruel spirits, condemning the wardens of death by dying. Here he spoke not yet in the future tense but still in the past tense, precisely because what he was going to do in act he had surely already done by predestination. However, because the church grew after his death and resurrection and has spread to all the nations, he rightly adds,

*Job 38:17

*Ps 117:7

XIV. 26. *Have you considered the extent of the earth?** When he sought out the tight places of death he enlarged his faith among the Gentiles and extended Holy Church in the uncounted hearts of the faithful. To him the prophet says, *Enlarge the area of your tent, and*

*Job 38:18

stretch out the canvas of your dwelling; do not scrimp; pull your cords and secure your pegs. You will be enlarged to the right and to the left, and the nations will inherit your seed.* This extent of territory would certainly not happen unless he first both disdained the life we know by dying and revealed the life we do not know by rising. In his death he surely both opened the eyes of our mind and exposed the kind of life that would follow. That is why he follows this order in the gospel and tells his disciples, *So Christ had to suffer and rise from the dead on the third day; conversion and forgiveness of sins had to be preached in his name to all the nations.**

*Isa 54:2-3

*Luke 24:46-47

Only a few people from the Israelites believed even when he preached, but innumerable people of the Gentiles followed the way of life at his death. He put up with the proud while he was yet alive and able to suffer, but then he died to this suffering life and laid them low. Samson expressed this very truth in himself long before, because he killed few people while he lived, but when he died, in destroying the temple he killed an uncounted number of his enemies, because of course the Lord destroyed the elation of a few proud people while he was alive, but many when the temple of his body was destroyed, and the chosen people of the Gentiles whom he received while alive all died at his death. Rightly therefore, after he showed that he had penetrated hell, he quickly added that the extent of the earth must be considered. It is as if he told a person who had been scourged, "You go through what I have borne and weigh what I have bought and do not complain about the blows, as long as you do not know the rewards of retribution that await you." So among these words of the Creator I find the reward of labor, if we lift our eyes for a moment away from the common public good and notice what he brings about in each one of us in a hidden manner. So he says,

XV. 27. *Have you ever entered the deep ocean?** The deep ocean is certainly the human mind, and God enters its depths when it is troubled to the point of penitential lamentation on account of its deep thoughts through its self-knowledge. When its memory recalls the wickedness of its former life, the soul is deeply moved and shaken to confusion. God penetrates the deep ocean when he even changes the desperate hearts. If of course he enters the ocean when he humiliates the worldly heart, he enters the deep ocean when he does not disdain to enter even minds distraught by crimes. So he is rightly hesitant when he adds, *or have you walked on the bottom of the abyss?* What then is the abyss if not the human heart? As long as it cannot understand itself, it hides itself in all that is just like a dark abyss. So the prophet was right to say, *The abyss uttered its voice from its deep imagination.** While the human mind does not penetrate into itself by comparison with itself, since it cannot comprehend the power of the divine nature, it praises it all the more humbly.

*Job 38:16

*Hab 3:10

28. For God then to walk on the bottom of the abyss means that he even converts the hearts of the most wicked people, and he admirably reforms the hopeless minds by touching them with traces of his visitation. So when anyone is seized by compunction after the most heinous crimes, what else but God do they see walking on the bottom of the abyss? It is as though God were walking on the abyss when he penetrates into the darkness of the heart and tramples on the invisible waves of vices. We often weep, you see, over past sins and are hard pressed by other present ones, so that sometimes we are harassed by pride, sometimes by anger, sometimes by lust, sometimes by avarice that tempts us. But when the Lord represses all these in our heart by fear of his secret visitation, what else does he do but imprint his footsteps on the abyss? We see these footsteps in our mind when in some way we consider the gifts that his fear places in the way against the attacks of these vices. The prophet had seen these footsteps when he said, *They saw your tracks, O God, the footsteps of my God, of my King in his holy place.**   *Ps 67:25

The one who sees the inordinate emotions of his soul repressed by the memory in himself of God's judgments sees the footsteps of the Lord walking in himself. Let blessed Job therefore be asked, *Have you ever entered the deep ocean, or have you walked on the bottom of the abyss?* Behind this you hear as I do that with wonderful mercy God tramples upon anger at times, lust at others, avarice at others, and overweening pride at others in the hearts of sinners. It is as if he were told openly, "If you see me alone repress the hidden vices in your heart, you will stop exalting yourself for your own justification." And because God visits us concerning our mind's hidden and unacceptable emotions, and we are led to confess them, he rightly adds,

XVI. 29. *Are the gates of death opened for you?** The gates of death are certainly evil thoughts that we open up to God whenever we confess them with penitential tears. Even when they are not confessed they are seen, but when confessed they are entered. Then indeed he opens up a way for himself in the gates of death when the evil thoughts have been gotten rid of, and he comes to us after confession. And they are called the gates of death precisely because evil thoughts always open up the way to ruin. He again repeats what he has said:

*Job 38:17

30. *Have you seen the dark doors?** The dark doors are hidden evil in the mind; it may be present internally without being visible to someone else. Nevertheless the Lord sees it when with the hidden vision of grace he destroys it. In fact it is written, *The King who sits*

*Job 38:17

on the throne of judgment puts all evils to flight by his glance.* And because all vice narrows the mind, but all virtue enlarges it, after the vices are destroyed he rightly continues, *Have you considered the extent of the earth?** If virtue did not enlarge the mind, Paul would never tell the Corinthians, *You also must be enlarged: do not get married to unbelievers.** But we must carefully study what is said here:

*Prov 20:8

*Job 38:18

*2 Cor 6:13-14

XVII. 31. *Have you considered the extent of the earth?** The extent of good people is interior and is never comprehended unless after careful consideration. Physical poverty often humiliates them, and intense pain makes them suffer, but even so interior courage always makes them grow in the hope of heaven. The apostles were hard pressed externally when they were scourged, but they stood fast internally, and their liberty was unfettered; among themselves they even turned these blows into joy. It is written, *They left the Sanhedrin rejoicing that they had been considered worthy to suffer reproach for the name of Jesus.** Paul too found this liberty to grow in the midst of hardship when he said, *I want you to know, brothers, that my experiences have rather happened to advance the Gospel, so that my chains have been publicized all over the Praetorian Guard.** David obtained this freedom to grow among trials, and he said, *You advanced my cause among troubles.**

*Job 38:18

*Acts 5:41

*Phil 1:12-13

*Ps 4:2

Accordingly this earth, that is, the awareness of the saints, grows when it is hard pressed by external circumstances and adversities in this world. Whenever it is cast out from the security of the present life, it is forced to turn within, to itself, so that it may aim for the hope of heaven. And when it is not allowed to wander aimlessly, it is recalled to its own heart to grow there. We however discern the adversity that good people suffer, but we do not see how much they rejoice internally. We know and consider their greatness sometimes by their words and sometimes by their actions, but we are totally ignorant of the full extent of their greatness. Let then human wisdom learn how foolish it is: *Have you considered the extent of the earth?* It is as if he said, "As I have, who alone have taken into account the hidden joy of the righteous person when he is surrounded by trials, because I alone form things with mercy. Or at least blessed Job is interrogated about whether he had considered the extent of the earth precisely in order that he might be humbled by the example of someone else's greatness. It is as if he were told point blank, "Consider those whom the innumerable evils of the present life are unable to straiten, and stop boasting about the state of your heart in the midst of blows. The next verse:

XVIII. 32. *Tell me, if you know everything, where the light shines on the road and what is the place of darkness, so that you may bring everything to its appointed place and may understand the paths of its house.** Blessed Job is interrogated with harsh questions, so that he may be asked about the road of light and the place of darkness, that he might bring everything to its appointed place and might understand the way to its house. What then do we take the word *light* to mean if not justice, and what is meant by *darkness* but wickedness? That is why certain converts from the wickedness of sin were told, *You were darkness once, but now you are light in the Lord.** And certain ones who remain sinners are mentioned: *Those who sleep, sleep at night.** So Job is asked: *Tell me if you know everything, where the light shines on the road and what is the place of darkness.* It is as if he were asked, "If you think your knowledge is complete, tell me either whose heart now lacking innocence receives it, or whose heart now containing malice perseveres in it." He says, *where*

*Job 38:18-20

*Eph 5:8

*1 Thess 5:7

the light shines on the road, that is, whose mind justice comes to and fills. *What is the place of darkness?*

In other words where does blind wickedness persevere? *So that you may bring everything to its appointed place*: that is, so that you may judge whether the one who is now discerned as wicked ends his life in wickedness or whether the one who is judged righteous finally concludes his life with perfect righteousness. *And so that you may understand the paths to its house*: that is, so that you may consider and discern either that the one who perseveres in good behavior receives an eternal mansion in the kingdom, or whether the one whose evil behavior to the end of his life forces him to be condemned to eternal punishment. *House* of course stands for mansion, and *path* for behavior. Path consequently leads to house, because behavior leads to mansion.

But what person being questioned would say this? What undaunted person could even listen to it? We see in fact many people daily shining with the light of justice, those who are nevertheless blinded by the darkness of their own evil at the end; we also see many who are blinded by the darkness of sin and who are nevertheless suddenly freed by the light of justice near the end of their lives. We know again many people who, once they found the way of justice, kept it intact even to death, and we have seen many who, having once begun a life of sin, kept adding to it without stopping.

33. But who would shine the ray of his mind's eye among these clouds of hidden judgments, so that he might discern by means of some consideration who will keep doing evil, who will persevere in goodness, who will be converted from the basest sins to the highest good, or who will be turned from the highest to the lowest? Such answers are hidden from people's minds, nor is anything known about anyone's end, because the abyss of God's judgments is in no way penetrated by the eye of a human mind. We see instead that the Gentile world, adversary of God that it is, is flooded with the light of justice, while Judea, beloved of old, is now blinded by the night of unbelief. We know also that the thief went over from the cross to the kingdom* and that Judas fell from the honor of an apostle to hell.* Again we know that some fates do not change and that the other thief went on to be punished; we know as well that the apostles received the promised kingdom that they had desired.

*Luke 23:43
*Matt 27:5

Who then could discover on what road light has its dwelling or what is the place of darkness, so he might bring everything to its proper end and understand the paths of his house? I see Paul, who was called from the cruelty of persecution to the grace of the apostolate,* and yet he so feared the hidden judgments that he worried about becoming a reprobate himself even after his call. He said, *I chastise my body and force it into subjection, lest while preaching to others I should ever chance to become reprobate.** He also said elsewhere, *I do not suppose that I have already attained the prize. I seek one thing: that forgetful of what is behind, I may stretch forward to what is ahead and follow to the prize of the upward call of Christ. I keep following in order to grasp it, as I have been grasped.** And it certainly had been already said of him by the Lord's voice, *He is a vessel whom I have chosen.** Yet he still chastised his body and worried lest he become reprobate.

*Acts 9:1-6

*1 Cor 9:27

*Phil 3:12-14

*Acts 9:15

34. Woe to us wretches who have as yet heard no voice of the Lord concerning his choice of us and who now languish in inactivity as if it were security. We ought indeed, we surely ought, to have security in hope, but also fear in conduct, so that hope might encourage us to fight, and fear might sting our listlessness. That is why the prophet spoke righteously: *Those who fear the*

Lord should hope in the Lord.* It is as if he said plainly, "He presumes on hope in vain who refuses to fear God in his actions." But why is blessed Job questioned with such intense questions about something that no human being is unaware of, so that he should understand the end of both the righteous and the wicked, unless it is because he cannot know someone else's end, but has recourse to his own? Because just like other people's end, he does not know his own, and because he does not know it he fears it, and because he fears it he should be humbled. Having been humbled already, he should not extol himself because of his works, and not being proud he should persist in the stronghold of grace.

*Ps 113:11

So let it be said to him, *Tell me, if you know everything, where the light shines on the road and what is the place of darkness, so that you may bring everything to its appointed place.** It is as if he said, "Just as you do not know anything about those who are converted from evil to good, or from good return to evildoing, so you do not even know yourself; neither do you understand what your merits demand should be done with you. And just as you in no way understand someone else's end, neither can you foreknow your own. You do know how far you have progressed already, but you do not yet know what I secretly think of you. You already consider your own righteous acts, but you do not know how strictly I have weighed them myself." Woe also to the praiseworthy life of people if it should be judged without reference to personal concern, because strictly examined in the Judge's presence under the aspect where it is considered pleasing, it is dismissed. So the prophet is right to say to God, *Do not enter into judgment with your servant, because no one alive is justified in your sight.**

*Job 38:18-19

*Ps 142:2

Solomon too speaks rightly: *The righteous and the wise as well as their works are in God's hand, and yet*

*Eccl 9:1

*Prov 20:24

*a person does not know whether he be worthy of love or hate, but everything remains uncertain for the future.** So Solomon again says, *What man could understand his own path?** And yet anyone knows by the testimony of his conscience whether he does good or evil. Still we are told that no one knows his or her own path, precisely because, even if we know when we are doing right, by examining ourselves strictly we do not know where we are headed. Therefore, after anyone has become terrified from this very consideration concerning his own goal, he or she returns to the examination about their beginning, and lest they be asked why they do not know where they are headed, they remember as well that they do not even know by what beginning they have arrived at their present position. So he goes on:

XIX. 35. *Did you know then that you were going to be born, or did you realize how many days you were going to have?** It is as if he told him openly, it is no wonder that you do not understand your end, when you do not comprehend your beginning. And when you do not know from what beginning you got this far, there is nothing surprising in the fact that you do not know what end takes you away. Accordingly, if it was my lot to produce your physical presence out of hiding through a beginning, it will also be my lot to recall your physical presence back to hiding. Why then do you want to know anything about the arrangement of your life, when you are held in the Maker's hand without knowing yourself? Therefore there is all the more reason that you should not extol yourself in your actions, when you are enclosed in the bosom of eternity and know neither by what process you got here nor when or how you will be led away from here.

*Job 38:21

36. But these words can also be understood differently: *Did you know then that you were going to be* born, or did you realize how many days you were going to have?* You should hear unspoken the words, "As I did, because I knew I was going to be born, since even before my human birth I always lived essentially in the divine nature." People however begin to be at that time when they are born in their mother's womb. Conception itself, you see, is also called birth, according to what is written: *That which has been born in her is of the Holy Spirit.** People do not know they are going to be born, precisely because they do not pre-exist their creation. God however always existed without any beginning, and he knew beforehand about himself that he would have a beginning in the Virgin's womb. Because he foreknew, he arranged; because he arranged, he allowed absolutely nothing in the human form that he did not will. Let a man be convinced then when he complains about trials why he suffers them, he who could not know his birth beforehand, when God even foreknew and arranged his birth and prepared himself to suffer trials among men. It goes on:

*Job 38:21

*Matt 1:20

XX. 37. *Have you ever entered the treasuries of the snow or seen the treasuries of hail that I have prepared against the enemy for the day of battle and war?** What else should we understand by snow and hail but the cold hard hearts of depraved people? It is the custom of Holy Scripture to characterize love by heat and malice by cold. It is written, *Just as a cistern has made its waters icy cold, so he has made his malice frigid.** And again: *Wickedness will spread far and wide, and the love of many will grow cold.** So in the cold snow or in the hard hail what could be more suitably expressed than the lives of depraved people, which both grow numbly cold and through hard malice strike blows? Nevertheless the Lord puts up with their lives, because he makes use of them to put his righteous people to the test. So he

*Job 38:22-23

*Jer 6:7

*Matt 24:12

rightly added the words, *that I have prepared against the enemy for the day of battle and war.*

When our adversary the Devil tries to tempt us, you see, he makes use of the behavior of depraved people against us as his weapons. Through them he harshly tortures us but—with them unknowing—chastens us. They become in his hands a whip to scourge our sins, and while their lives are such as to put us on trial, we are liberated from eternal death. So it happens that the life of the chosen ones even profits from the lost life of reprobate sinners, and while the perdition of sinners brings about our advantage, it happens by a wonderful dispensation that as far as God's chosen ones are concerned, not everything perishes that perishes.

38. The words can also be understood in another way, so that since they are added to the previous words, they are not out of tune with the exposition of those words. Since that exposition indicated the possibility of good people converting to bad or bad people to good, the following verse immediately added, *Have you ever entered the treasuries of the snow or seen the treasuries of hail that I have prepared against the enemy for the day of battle and war?** In snow and hail, frozen and hard, we understand, as we said, the hearts of depraved people. But since almighty God chose his saints from such as these, and he knows how many chosen ones he has still living out their lives placed among the lives of the depraved, he suitably declares that he has treasuries of snow and hail.

*Job 38:22-23

The word *treasury* comes from the Greek θεσεως, which means "position." God is concerned about many people who remain long in a frozen life, those whom he produces at will in public and displays shining with the brightness of justice through heavenly grace. It is written, *Wash me, and I shall be whiter than snow.**

*Ps 50:9

He hid them long in the bosom of his foreknowledge, prepared for the day of war and battle, but when he suddenly led them out he struck the opposing breasts of their adversaries with their words and accusations as if they were some kind of hailstones. That is why it is said elsewhere, *From the brightness in front of him hailstones and coals of fire broke through the clouds.** They break through the clouds from the brightness, because the holy preachers run out over the whole extent of the earth with glorious miracles. They are also called hailstones and fiery coals, because they strike with correction, and they ignite with the flame of charity.

*Ps 17:13

The very untrammeled reproaches of the saints are advantageously expressed by the nature of hail, since hail falls and strikes as solidified water. The holy ones strike the hearts of listeners with fear, and their encouragements wash over them. The prophet describes how they strike thus: *They will speak of the might of your terrible acts, and they will announce your greatness.** He also follows up and adds how they pour out encouragement: *They will proclaim the memory of your abundant sweetness and pour out your justice.** There are then treasuries of snow and hail, because those who are frozen with the numbness of iniquity are often raised up by heavenly grace and shine in Holy Church with the light of justice and beat against the depraved knowledge of adversaries with the repeated blows of their teaching.

*Ps 144:6

*Ps 144:7

That is why the Lord follows up with the words, *that I have prepared against the enemy for the day of battle and war.* Saul had indeed been snow or hail through frozen insensibility, but he became snow or hail against the breasts of adversaries by either the brightness of justice or the strict corrections of his eloquence. O what a rich treasure he possessed in snow and hail, when the Lord already saw him secretly living among depraved people as his chosen one! O how many were the adversaries whose breasts were to be struck by this hailstone picked up by the hand of the Lord, through which he knocked down so many resisting hearts!

39. Let no one then extol himself on the strength of his works, and let no one despair about those they see still frozen, since they do not see God's treasuries of snow and hail. Who would believe that he would move ahead to the grace of apostleship at the stoning of Stephen, he who at Stephen's death even guarded the clothing of all those who were stoning him? If then we have recourse to these gifts or secret judgments, we will never lose hope for anyone, nor will we prefer ourselves to them in our hearts, over whom we temporarily hold authority, because even if we now see how far we have excelled, we do not know if those who have just begun will outrun us. So blessed Job is rightly asked, *Have you ever entered the treasuries of the snow or seen the treasuries of hail that I have prepared against the enemy for the day of battle and war?** It is as if he were told frankly, "You must not prefer yourself to anyone on account of your works, because concerning those whom you see still frozen in guilt, you do not know what workers for justice and defenders of true faith I am going to make of them." But since the coming of the Mediator is in question, the Lord rightly adds,

*Job 38:22-23

XXI. 40. *By what path is the light shed?** He is himself the way who said, *I am the way, the truth, and the life.** Accordingly he is the way or path by which light is shed, because the whole Gentile world has been illuminated by his presence. And he suitably used the verb *shed*, because through the voices of the apostles the light of preaching shone, not in a narrow or confined way, but in a widespread arc. Once the light of conversion has been received, you see, the power of

*Job 38:24

*John 14:6

love burns bright within, so that either the evil that has been done is anxiously mourned, or the good to come is most ardently desired. So he befittingly adds,

XXII. 41. *The heat is distributed upon the earth.** After the light is shed, the heat is distributed upon the earth, because justice is preached openly, and the heart is anxious to seek God, and it grows through the practice of virtue, so that this one shines through wise discourses, that one through the teaching of knowledge, this one grows strong with the grace of healing, that one with the practice of virtue; while each person receives the gifts of the Holy Spirit in different ways, necessarily joined each to each, they are all unanimously aroused. But after the light is said to be shed we may suitably understand that heat signifies persecution, since the light of preaching has enlightened the hearers, so that the heat of persecution has been forthwith enkindled in the hearts of unbelievers. The Lord's sermon, you see, bears us witness that heat signifies persecution, when he speaks of the seed being thrown upon the rocky ground. He said, *When the sun rose they were all scorched, and having no roots they withered.** When he later explained his words he called the heat persecution.

*Job 38:24

*Matt 13:6

So the light being shed, heat was distributed upon the earth, because the lives of the faithful became bright, and the cruelty of unbelievers was inflamed. The heat was distributed upon the earth, because first at Jerusalem, then at Damascus, then in other far-off regions persecution raged. It is written, moreover, *On that very day a great persecution started in the church at Jerusalem, and they were all scattered throughout the regions of Judea and Samaria.** It is also written, *Still breathing threats and murder against the Lord's disciples, Saul approached the high priest and asked him for letters to the synagogues at Damascus, so that if he*

*Acts 8:1

found there any belonging to this way, he might bring men and women bound to Jerusalem.* Since accordingly persecution raged now here, now there, those who had known the light of truth were in a way like those who panted as the heat was burning and distributed.

42. But since we have heard from the words related above how blessed Job was questioned about hidden judgments, we must examine more closely what was said about the light that was shed and the heat that was distributed. He is interrogated yet again by intense scrutiny, so that he might at least learn that he does not know, and he is asked, *By what path is the light shed and the heat distributed upon the earth?** What does the word *light* mean if not righteousness? Of this it is written, *The people who walked in darkness have seen a great light.** Everything that is shed is not thrown out continuously but with certain pauses, and that is why the light is said to be shed, because although we already see a certain amount as it is, we do not yet see of the light what is going to be seen. The light that was shed had held Peter's heart, and this light had shone with such brilliance of faith and miracles, and yet when he would impose the burden of circumcision on the converted Gentiles, he did not know the right thing to say.* Light then is shed in this life, because it is not held continually for the understanding of everything. As long as we understand one thing just as it is and not something else, it is as though light were shed and we saw only partly,* while we remain partly in the dark. Then, however, the light will no longer be shed over us when our mind being completely taken up to God will radiate light.

43. And since we do not know by what means this very light enters the human heart, it is rightly asked in the interrogation, *By what path is the light shed?* It is as if he said plainly, "Tell me by what sequence of acts

*Acts 9:1-2

*Job 38:24

*Isa 9:2

*Gal 2:11-15

*1 Cor 13:9-10

I instill my righteousness in the hidden recesses of the heart when my approach is not seen, and yet I invisibly change the visible works of human beings when I illuminate one and the same mind with one virtue here and another there, and yet because of the light shed I allow another part of that mind to remain in the darkness of temptation." Let the unknowing person be questioned as to the path by which light is shed as if he were clearly told, "While I soften the hardened hearts, while I bend what is rigid, while I smooth out what is rough, while I warm what is cold, while I strengthen what is weak, while I make firm what is inconstant, while I steady what is wavering, see, if you can, how I come without a body and by what movements I enlighten everything." In truth we see all these things done, because we do not know how they are accomplished internally. Truth has shown us in the Gospel that this road of light is invisible to us, since he has said, *you hear its voice, but you do not know where it comes from or where it goes.**

*John 3:8

44. But since after the light was shed the temptations from the hidden enemy against the enlightened mind quickly increased, it is rightly added, *the heat is distributed upon the earth.* The wily enemy of course exerts himself to incite with sinful desires the minds of those whom he sees shining with the light of righteousness, so that it often happens that they feel themselves attacked by more temptations than when they did not see the rays of internal light. That is why after the Israelites were called they complained against Moses about their increased labor, and they said, *May the Lord see and judge how you have brought us into bad odor with Pharaoh and his servants and given them a sword to kill us with.** In fact from those who wanted to leave Egypt Pharaoh had withheld straw, and yet he demanded the same amount of work from them. It is as though the

*Exod 5:21

mind murmured against the law, because after knowing the law, the mind experiences more acute attacks of temptations, and when it sees that it has to work still harder, since it displeases its adversary it is sad, because Pharaoh sees how bad it smells. So after the light, heat follows, because after the illumination of the divine gift the battle of temptation grows hot.

45. But the heat is also said to be distributed, because not all individuals are troubled by all vices, but certain ones by certain vices close to it and touching it. The ancient enemy of course first looks over the sprinkling that has reached each one, and then he sets his ambush of temptations accordingly. One person, you see, is characterized by a happy disposition, another by a sad, another by a fearful, another by a proud. But that is how the hidden adversary can easily trap us; he uses deceptions that are adapted to our dispositions or sprinklings. Since then pleasure is adapted to a happy disposition, he proposes lust to a happy disposition; since sadness easily falls into wrath, he offers sad people the cup of discord; because timid people are afraid of punishment, he tempts the fearful with extreme dread; since he sees proud people honored by praise, he coaxes them to do whatever he wants by means of ingratiating support. He lies in wait for every single person then with vices adapted to his or her disposition. Nor would he easily trap anyone if he proposed bribes to the lustful, or pleasures of the flesh to the avaricious, or the boast of abstinence to the gluttonous, or if he should nudge those who fast with satisfaction of the stomach, or if he wanted to trap the meek with eagerness for battle or those prone to anger with fear or dread. So then in the heat of temptation the devil slyly lies in wait for everyone and lays traps adapted to their moral behavior, and, it is rightly said, *the heat is distributed upon the earth.*

46. However, it was first asked, *By what path is the light shed?* Then it was immediately added, *the heat is distributed upon the earth.* Obviously we are shown that by the same path that light is shed heat is also distributed. The grace of the Holy Spirit is lofty and incomprehensible; his light illuminates our senses, and it even modifies the Adversary's temptations in its dispensation, so that they do not come too many at a time, and they only touch the soul already enlightened by God in the measure that they can be borne; their touch does torment us with its heat, but their burning does not completely consume us, as Paul bears us witness, saying, *God is faithful, and he will not let you be tempted beyond your strength, but he will send along with the temptation a way for you to resist.** The sly imposter distributes the heat in one way, and the merciful Creator in another. The former distributes it to consume the fuel quickly; the latter makes it tolerable. And since we are worn out by temptation, we are instructed not only internally by God's spirit, but also externally by the word of preaching, so after mentioning the distributed heat, the Lord goes on to say,

*1 Cor 10:13

XXIII. 47. *Who arranged the course of the most violent rain?** If, as we have said above, that persecution in the land of Judea is meant by the use of the words *distributed heat*, since the very harshness of that persecution did not by any fear prevent the holy preachers, who were helped by God's gift, from the exercise of their ministry, the words were suitably added, *Who arranged the course of the most violent rain?* It is as if he answered, "Who else but me? Once the heat was distributed, you see, it was up to me to have set a course for the most violent rain and to have strengthened the attack of preaching against those severe trials of temptation, so that the more the power of preaching grew,

*Job 38:25

the more the cruel persecution opposed it; in this way the drops of rain kept pouring in on the dry hearts of the hearers, so that they irrigated the dryness of unbelief more thoroughly, and even if the heat of hostility grew still more intense against them, nevertheless the voice of grace in them was not silenced." Paul both withstood and irrigated this heat of persecution when he said, *I labor even to the point of chains like an evildoer, but the word of God is not chained.** *2 Tim 2:9

About this rain it is said elsewhere, *I will order the clouds not to send down rain upon her.** *Isa 5:6 About this course of the rain that is followed in the hearts of the chosen ones the psalmist avows, *His word runs swiftly.** *Ps 147:15 We often have rain that does not follow a course, because the preaching does reach the ears, but when internal grace is not present, it does not reach the hearts of those who hear. About the words of this preaching for the sake of the chosen ones it is said, *Your arrows have indeed penetrated them.** *Ps 76:18 God's arrows do indeed penetrate when the words of his preaching descend from the ears to the heart. And since this happens only by means of God's gift, the Lord testifies that he has given the course of the rain.

48. But I think it is noteworthy that he does not call this rain simply violent but rather most violent. Violent rain is a great force, but the most violent rain is the immense power of preaching. It was certainly a violent rain when holy preachers urged people to trust in eternity, but it was the most violent rain when they argued that material security should be abandoned for the sake of hope, that all visible comforts should be despised for the sake of the invisible, and that present pain and torture should be endured for the sake of joys that they heard about. But along with the faith they had come to know, while savage waves of persecution rolled over them, so many chosen ones abandoned their possessions and forgot the desires of the flesh; for the sake of spiritual joy they allowed their bodily members to be tortured: what else did the Lord do in all this but plot a course for the most violent rain, and through the words of the body irrigate the invisible ground of the heart even to the point of following the highest precepts? So he fittingly added,

XXIV. 49. *A way for the sound of thunder.** What do we take thunder to mean if not the preaching of heavenly terror? When they hear this terror, human hearts quake. However, thunder sometimes means the incarnate Lord himself, because he is foretold by the agreement in prophecy of the ancient patriarchs that has come down to us as a message, as if the clouds united and let it rain down. He visibly appeared among us, and there was a terrifying sound above us, so that the holy apostles themselves who were born of his grace were called *Boanerges*, that is sons of thunder.* Sometimes, however, as has been said, thunder is taken to mean his very preaching, through which the terror of heavenly Judgment is heard. But any old preacher can speak words in our hearing but cannot open our hearts, and only almighty God offers invisible welcome through internal grace to the words of preachers in the hearts of those who listen; preaching then is heard in vain by the listener's ear and is forbidden entrance to the interior by the deaf heart, but the Lord proclaims that it is he who shows the way to the sound of thunder, who gives words to the preacher and compunction to hearts through terror.

  The famous preacher Paul, while he gave utterance to heavenly mysteries inspired by terror, knowing that he did not know the way of himself, warned his disciples in these words: *At the same time pray for us, that God may open up for us an entrance for the word and*

*Job 38:25

*Mark 3:27

for speaking of the mystery of Christ.* He then spoke of mysteries, but he prayed for the Lord to open an entrance for these mysteries in the hearts of listeners; he indeed had thunder already, but he wanted a way to be given him from on high. John knew that he was unable to give this way himself, and he said, *You do not need anyone to teach you, but his anointing teaches you everything.** Actually Paul expressed clearly who it was who would give this way and said, *Neither the planter nor the waterer amounts to anything, but only God who makes the plant grow.** Now that we know the way, let us hear what this thunder and rain does:

*Col 4:3

*1 John 2:27

*1 Cor 3:7

XXV. 50. *So that it may rain on the ground in the desert where there is no man and where no mortal being exists.** For the word of God to rain on the ground in the desert where there is no man means that he preaches to the Gentiles. Because the Gentiles had no worship of divinity and showed no kind of good works, they were obviously deserted. There was no legislator there, nor was there anyone who sought God by reason, so it was as though there was no human being in that land, and, occupied only by wild beasts, it existed without the presence of a mortal being. Someone has said about this desert land, *He has made a path in the desert.** The psalmist also bears witness to this preaching offered to the Gentile world and says, *He made rivers flow in the desert.** We must take notice, however, that after the heat was distributed upon the earth the most violent rain was given a course,* so that it might rain on the desert after the harsh persecution raged in Judea, when not only would Judea not accept the faith, but the Jews fought against it even with swords, so that any preacher sent to Israel turned aside to call the Gentiles to faith.

*Job 38:26

*Isa 43:19

*Ps 106:33

*Job 38:24-25

The sequel found the holy apostles telling the Jewish persecutors whom they were abandoning, *We were bound to speak the word of God to you (Jews) first, but since you reject it and show yourselves unworthy of eternal life, we will now go to the Gentiles.** So the heat was distributed, and the land that was deserted without a human being upon it received rain, because the faithful people of the land of Judea were scattered by the persecution, while the land that was long abandoned and a stranger to the light of reason, as it were—the Gentile world, in fact—was bedewed by drops of water from preaching. This Gentile world still had to be discovered by the preachers, as we learn from the following: *So that he might fill the waste and desolate land.** We are shown, however, what the rain caused the land to produce when he immediately adds,

*Acts 13:46

*Job 38:27

XXVI. 51. *And so that it might produce green plants.** The Gentile country, you see, long remained a wasteland, and there was no open road for God's word to reach it. At the coming of our Redeemer, in fact, such was the calling of grace that Gentiles received that there was no previously existing road of prophecy. And the Gentile country is rightly called desolate, obviously deprived of rational counsel and desolate of good works. The Lord then provided a course for the most violent rain and a road for the sound of thunder, so that there might be rain in the desert that would fill the waste and desolate land and produce green plants; that is, he brought to external preaching internal inspiration, so that the dry hearts of Gentiles might grow green, the wasteland might lie open, the empty country be filled, and the fruitless sprout.

*Job 38:27

52. In Holy Scripture, you see, the word *plant* is sometimes taken as the freshness of worldly honor, sometimes as devil's food, sometimes as the support of preachers, sometimes as good works, and sometimes as the knowledge and doctrine of eternal life. It is taken as the freshness of worldly honor when the prophet says, *Let it wither like a plant in the morning; in the morning let it bloom and wither.** To bloom and wither in the morning means that the distinction of worldly honor in the prosperity of this present life quickly withers. A plant is taken as devil's food when the Lord says of the devil, *The mountains bear plants for him.** It is as if he said, "Proud and presumptuous people display their wicked thoughts and actions, and in so doing they feed the devil with their own iniquities." Plants as the support of preachers are mentioned when it is said, *He produces grass and plants on the mountains for the use of human beings.** On the mountains indeed is where plants are produced as food for the use of human beings, when the great ones of this world who are called to the knowledge of faith distribute transitory provisions to holy preachers on the journey of this life.

  Plants signify good works as when it is written, *Let the earth bring forth green plants.** Although we hold that this happened in the creation of the world historically, nevertheless we not unsuitably take earth to mean the church, which brought forth green plants in the sense that she performed works that were fruitful in mercy for the word of God. Sometimes we take green plants to signify the knowledge and doctrine of eternal freshness, as when Jeremiah says, *The wild asses stood by the banks breathing hard like dragons, and their eyes fell, because there was no grass.** By these words was prophesied the proud and most wicked persecution by the Jews. The wild asses themselves are so named for the pride of the mind and the dragons for poisonous thoughts. They stand by the banks, because they do not trust in God but rather in the highest powers of this world, and they say, *We have no king but Caesar.** They breathe hard like dragons, because they have swelled up with

*Ps 89:6

*Job 40:15 Vulg

*Ps 146:8

*Gen 1:11

*Jer 14:6

*John 19:15

the air of self-glorification, and they pant with evil pride. Their eyes fell, obviously because they lost hope in their goal. They loved the things of time and neglected the expectation of eternal life; they even lost temporal gains, precisely because they had preferred them to God. They said, *If we leave him alone, everyone will believe in him, and the Romans will come and take away our place and nation.** They were afraid that they would lose their place unless the Lord was killed, and yet when he was dead they still lost it. But Jeremiah added the reason this happened to the miserable people: *because there was no grass.** In other words it was because their hearts were without the knowledge of eternity, and no food of fresh internal teaching fed them.

*John 11:48

*Jer 14:6

So in this passage what do we take the green plants to mean but the knowledge of holy teaching or befitting works? The land that is a desert then receives rain so that green plants may be produced on it, because as long as the Gentile country received the rain of holy preaching, it brought forth both the works of life and the words of teaching. This freshness is promised to the desert country by the prophet's voice saying, *In the lairs where dragons formerly lived will arise fresh reeds and rushes.** What is signified by the reeds but writers, and what by the rushes that always grow close to the sources of water but the weak and tender hearers of sacred doctrine? The green reeds and rushes then sprout in dragons' dens, because in those peoples possessed by the malice of the ancient enemy both the knowledge of educated people and obedient listeners are gathered together.

*Isa 35:7

53. If, however, we carefully examine what is said about the Gentile country in a general way, we will see how it happens to individuals within the bosom of Holy Church. There are, you see, many people who are radically insensitive to the word of God. They are counted under the name of faith certainly, and they hear the words of life with their ears, but they do not allow them to penetrate to their deep interior hearts. What else are these people but desert land? This land obviously has no human in it, because its mind lacks the use of reason. No mortal creature lives in this land, because if the people ever become aware of any thoughts about the use of reason, they do not keep them. Evil desires find a place in their hearts, but if upright thoughts ever arise, they fly away as if repelled. But when the merciful God deigns to plot a course for his rain and a road for his thunder to be heard, those who have been struck by compunction through internal grace open the ears of their hearts to the words of life.

The pathless land is then filled, because when it opens its ear to the word, it is filled with mystery. It brings forth green plants, because it has been filled with the grace of compunction, and it not only freely receives the word of preaching but even gives it back copiously, so that what it could not hear before it now desires to speak; formerly it did not listen, and it dried up internally, but now it speaks holy words, and by its own freshness it nourishes any people who hunger. That is why the prophet rightly says, *Send forth your spirit, and you will renew the face of the earth.** In this way, yes, precisely so is the face of the earth changed by the power of renewal, when the mind that was dry so long is drenched by the coming of grace, and after its long period of dryness it is dressed in the freshness of knowledge as if by the sprouting of green plants. This grace of our Creator is even now highly recommended to us when the Lord adds,

*Ps 103:30

XXVII. 54. *Who is the father of rain? Who has brought forth the dewdrops?** It is as if he said, "If not I? I freely spray drops of knowledge on the dry earth of the

*Job 38:28

human heart." About this rain it is elsewhere said, *You, O God, collect the rain you will to give your inheritance.** The Lord indeed collects the rain he wills to give his inheritance, because he offers it to us, not for our merits, but for the sake of the gift of his kindness. And that is why in this passage he is called the father of the rain, since the heavenly preaching is brought forth for us, not for our merit, but because of his favor. These dewdrops are the holy preachers who fill the fields of our hearts that are drying out among the evils of the present life as if in the darkness of the drying night with the grace of heavenly abundance. About these drops stiff-necked Judea is told, *Therefore the drops of rain were forbidden to fall, and there was no late rain.**

*Ps 67:10

*Jer 3:3

The dewdrops are themselves like drops of rain. When by some arrangement they lower the rate of preaching, it is as though they were giving a light spray of dew. When on the other hand they speak with the power that comes to them from above and prevail, it is as though they were pouring down an abundantly flowing rain. Paul sprinkled dew when he told the Corinthians, *I determined to know nothing among you but Jesus Christ and him crucified.** Later he poured down rain and said, *Our mouth is open toward you Corinthians, and our heart is wide.** That is why Moses knew he was going to speak harsh words to the strong and soft words to the weak and said, *My word will be awaited like rain, and let my words come down like the dew.**

*1 Cor 2:2

*2 Cor 6:11

*Deut 32:2

But pay attention now: we have heard by what favor the Gentiles have been called; let us hear by what severity Judea is rejected. We have heard how he cultivates the desert, and how he inundates the dry land; let us now hear how he projects what is as it were seen internally. Neither does he gather the chosen ones in such a way that he does not also judge reprobate sinners, nor does he pardon the sins of any in such a way that he does not strike others down. It is indeed written, *Both mercy and anger are his.** So it is likewise here: after he has mentioned so many gifts of grace, he does not hide the judgments of his wrath. He goes on to say,

*Sir 5:7

XXVIII. 55. *From whose womb has ice come forth, and who gave birth to the frozen air in the heavens?** What else do we take the ice or frozen air to mean but the frozen hearts of the Jews, constrained by the paralysis of unbelief? They once were secure through receiving the law, through keeping the commandments, through the ministry of sacrifice, through the mysteries of prophecy, by such means within the bosom of grace, as if they were inside the womb of the Creator. But because at the Lord's coming they were constrained by the cold rigor of unbelief, they lost the heat of faith and charity, and they were cast out of the secret bosom of grace as if they were ice, to leave the Creator's womb. He said, *and who gave birth to the frozen air in the heavens?* And what else do the heavens mean here but the sublime life of the saints? To that heaven it is said, *Listen, you heavens, and I will speak.** He did not speak to a creature without senses, but to a rational creature. It was about this heaven that the Lord said, *Heaven is my throne.** About that throne it is elsewhere written, *The soul of the righteous is the seat of wisdom.** Since therefore God is wisdom, if heaven is God's throne, and the soul of the righteous is the seat of wisdom, the soul of the righteous must be heaven. Abraham was heaven, Isaac was heaven, and Jacob was heaven. But since the priests of the Jews were the persecutors of the Lord, those who were frozen with the paralysis of unbelief went forth away from the offspring of those patriarchs, and like ice they left heaven, because the frozen and unbelieving people went forth from the sublime race of

*Job 38:29

*Deut 32:1

*Isa 66:1
*Prov 12:23

the saints. Since Caiaphas was a son of Abraham, you see, what else does it mean but that ice came forth out of heaven? That is the ice the Lord says he brought forth, precisely because he naturally created the Jews good, and by righteous judgment he lets them go out frozen by their own malice. The Lord is Creator of nature, not of guilt. He brought them forth by natural creation and allowed them to live evil lives by putting up with them patiently. Since the hearts of the Jews were once tender and permeable by faith, but later obdurate and obstinate in unbelief, he rightly added,

XXIX. 56. *The water hardened just like a stone.** I remember that I have often taught that water should be taken as people. Stone however, because of its hardness, sometimes means the Gentile people. The Gentiles in fact worshiped stones,* and the prophet says of them, *Let those who make them and all those who trust in them become like them.** That is why when John saw the Jews exalting themselves for the pedigree of their birth, while he foresaw that the Gentiles would become the seed of Abraham by the knowledge of faith, he said, *Do not presume to say within yourselves, "We have Abraham for our father." I tell you God can raise up children of Abraham out of these stones.** He obviously calls the Gentiles stones for the hardness of their unbelief. So since Judea believed in God first, while all the Gentiles remained obstinate in their unbelief, but afterward the hearts of the Gentiles were softened for faith while the unbelief of the Jews was hardened, it was well said, *The water hardened just like a stone.* It is as if he said, "The soft hearts of the Jews that were permeable by faith were turned into the unfeeling hearts of Gentiles."

When God's mercy called the Gentiles, his anger rejected the Jews. So it happened that just as long ago the Gentile world had been obdurate against the reception of

*Job 38:30

*Ezek 20:32

*Ps 113:16

*Matt 3:9

faith, so later when the Gentiles received the faith, the people of Judea hardened with the lassitude of unbelief. That is why the apostle Paul tells the same Gentiles, *Just as you once did not believe in God, but now have received mercy because of their unbelief, so they in turn did not believe in your mercy, so that they too might receive mercy. God has, you see, enclosed everything in unbelief, so that he might have mercy on all.** This statement of his is first about the calling of the Jews and rejection of the Gentiles, but later he seriously considers the calling of the Gentiles and rejection of the Jews and reflects that he cannot understand the hidden judgments of God. He goes on to exclaim, *O the deep riches of God's wisdom and knowledge! How mysterious are his judgment and unsearchable his ways!** So here again, when the Lord says about the unbelief of the Jews, *The water hardened just like a stone*, he wants to show how hidden his judgments are about their rejection, and he rightly adds,

*Rom 11:30-32

*Rom 11:33

XXX. 57. *And the surface of the abyss is frozen.** Because of a certain veil of ignorance that has been thrown over the eye of the human mind, the incomprehensibility of divine Judgment can by no means be penetrated. It is in fact written, *Your judgments are many and deep.** No one then desires to search into the reasons that one person is rejected while another is chosen or that one person is chosen while another is rejected, because the surface of the abyss is frozen. Paul is our witness: *How mysterious are his judgments and unsearchable his ways!**

*Job 38:30

*Ps 35:7

*Rom 11:33

58. Now concerning what was said—*From whose womb has ice come forth, and who gave birth to the frozen air in the heavens?**—there is nothing wrong with understanding Satan in the ice and frozen air. He indeed came forth in a way from God's womb as ice,

*Job 38:29

because he is frozen with the numbness of malice, and he came out of the heat of God's secrets as the master of iniquity. Ice itself is born of heaven, because he is the one who is going to freeze the hearts of reprobate sinners, so he was allowed to fall from the highest to the lowest. Although he was created in heaven, he fell like ice and froze the minds of his followers in the ice of guilt. The text goes on to explain what he did to human beings when he came down to earth: *The water hardened just like a stone.* Waters signify people, and the stone signifies Satan's hardness. When Satan came down to the lowest place, water was hardened to the likeness of stone, because human beings who imitated his malice lost the soft bosom of love. His lying counsel could not be detected by the deceived human beings, so the text continues, *And the surface of the abyss is frozen.* In fact one thing lurked inside him while he presented something else outside. He transfigures himself like an angel of light, and by the cunning art of deception he often proposes praiseworthy acts, so that he may draw us to what is forbidden. The surface of the abyss is frozen, because while his brand of persuasion shows us good like solid ice on top, his malice lurks deeper unseen.

59. We can however understand all this in a different way, if we search the moral sense. Almighty God, you see, forms human minds in the fear of him, and so he conceives them, and when he brings them forth for open virtues, he bears them, but if they grow proud of the virtues they have received, he abandons them. And we have often known certain people experiencing compunction by the consideration of their own sins to grow warm by the dread of divine terror, and from the beginning of dread to move all the way to the summit of virtue. But when they grow proud on account of these same virtues that they received, they are caught in the snare of vainglory and return to their former lethargy. The Lord is right then to cast out such as these and say, *From whose womb has ice come forth?* It is as if ice came out of God's womb, you see, when those who first grew warm internally froze because of the gift of virtues, and there insensitively desire external honors where they ought to burn more ardently for internal love. So when one excels in signs, another in knowledge, another in prophecy, and another in mighty works, and they desire to please people with these gifts, all that previously burned hot internally, in love with praise externally grows numb externally.

Consequently it is as though ice came out of the womb when after benefiting from the gifts, we are separated from the inner warmth of heavenly love. Are they not frozen who with the virtues they receive seek human praise? Nevertheless, when the Judge comes they remind him of the gifts they received and say, *Lord, Lord, did we not prophesy in your name? Did we not cast out demons in your name? Did we not work many miracles in your name?** But the Lord shows how he rids himself of this ice and says, *I never knew you. Get away from me, you evildoers.** The Lord now holds this ice in the womb, because he puts up with it in the bosom of the church. But later he openly casts it out, when he repels such people from sharing in the heavenly secrets in the final public Judgment. So what in fact is brought about by these words except that blessed Job is humbled concerning the sublimity of his virtues, lest he should become proud and freeze because he had warmed through living well and should consequently be rejected by the womb of divinity and expelled therefrom, if within the bosom of his heart he should proudly extol himself.

60. And because the just judgment of God allows proud minds that have received virtues to go out and

*Matt 7:22

*Luke 13:27

sin, the Lord rightly adds the words, *and who gave birth to the frozen air in the heavens?** He often offers the knowledge of the sacred word, but when the one who receives that knowledge is extolled by it, he is blinded by that very sacred word through the wrath of the strict Judge, so that through it he goes after public applause, and he no longer sees what is within; he who could be warm by remaining within goes out and freezes, and, hardened, he sinks to the lowest place, he who formerly was teachable in the knowledge of God and stood watered in the highest place. Is not Holy Scripture heaven? Does it not begin the day of understanding for us? Does the Sun of justice not shine on us? When the night of the present life holds us fast, do the stars of the commandments not light up for us?

*Job 38:29

But since there must be heresies so that those who are approved may come to light, the proud mind being repelled by the healthy intellect, by the punishment of the strict Judge ice is born from heaven, while Holy Scripture itself warms the hearts of the chosen ones, and those who want knowledge in their pride are cast out frozen. They go wrong indeed precisely where they should have corrected those who were going wrong, and while they were themselves hardened against the heavenly understanding of the shining word, they would seduce others; they fell to the lowest place and became ice, and now they confine others. The Lord himself maintains that it is he who gives birth to ice, not because he himself forms depraved minds to sin, but because he does not free them from sin, since it is written, *I will harden Pharaoh's heart.** Because he refuses to soften it in mercy, he straightforwardly announces that he strictly hardens it.

*Exod 4:21

61. But since when the beginning virtue of fear of God is lost, the image of the virtue is retained because of human applause, the Lord rightly adds, *The water hardened just like a stone, and the surface of the abyss is frozen.* Water then hardens to ice on the surface but remains liquid deep down. And what do we take the waters to mean if not the unstable hearts of reprobate sinners? When they intentionally abandon virtue, they display their strength in good works like hypocrites, and when they fall away to vice within while they pretend to imitate saints or courageous people outside, *The water hardened just like a stone, and the surface of the abyss is frozen.* Their unstable and inconstant awareness is thus hidden from people by an assumed appearance of holiness. Although they seem repulsive to themselves internally, they clothe themselves before the eyes of strangers with a kind of lively charm.

62. But lest anyone should wish to take these words of the Lord in good part, we ought to build on them in such a way even for seekers that we are less likely to be judged neglectful of truths that should be searched out. In an earlier verse it was asked, *Who is the father of rain? Who has brought forth the dewdrops?** Then it was immediately added, *From whose womb has ice come forth, and who gave birth to the frozen air in the heavens?** If then the following sentence is joined to the preceding ones without a jarring sense, the way is certainly clear for us to take the words in good part without any obstacle or contradiction.

When seed is sown on the ground after it rains, you see, it is bound to be more fruitful. But on the other hand if the rain waters the ground excessively, it channels rich growth to the plant's stalk. However, if the seed thrown upon the soil after the rain is pressed down by ice, it is kept from appearing too soon above the ground, and below the root grows stronger, so that it is forced to multiply to the extent that it cannot rise, because

*Job 38:28

*Job 38:29

a too-early appearance is restrained, and the lateness of its birth makes for a more abundant fruit. How is it then that the Lord first intimates that he is father of the rain, then tells us that ice proceeds from his womb, and finally proclaims that he brings forth the ice from heaven himself? Is it not because in a wonderful way he prepares the earth of our heart to receive the seed of the word? Does he not first water us with the rain of hidden grace, and later, lest we grow excessively proud of the virtues we have conceived, does he not restrain us with the discipline of the internal plan, so that what he waters with the rain of received grace, he also restricts with rigorous discipline? Otherwise the plant conceives and brings forth before it should, or more virtues than necessary, in which case the fruits would turn into grass.

It often happens, you see, that a good work set in motion by beginners is displayed before it ought to be and deprived of the completed grain; likewise virtues often abound more than necessary, and they are lost. So it happens that the Lord either denies the premature wishes of his chosen ones or, on the other hand, when they are expressed at the right time but immoderately, he checks them lest they be satisfied before or more than they ought to be, and they should fall into the trap of pride because of the greatness of their success. When the heart suffers compunction after sin, the earth that was dry is wet again by the rainfall, and when after abandoning wickedness it determines to do good works, it is as though it were seeded after rainfall. Many people, you see, when they conceive holy desires, already desire ardently to occupy themselves with sublime virtues, so that not only does guilt not sully their actions, but it does not even touch their thoughts. And they are indeed still resident bodily, but they no longer want to experience any communication with the present life. They desire to follow internal stability of mind in their intention, but they are beaten back by the temptations they meet with, obviously so that they may remember their weakness and not be elated by the virtues they receive. And when this happens by a wonderful subduing action of discipline, what else is it but ice from heaven forming on top of an inundated earth? What else is it but ice produced from God's womb, when an arrangement proceeds from internal mystery, and our wills are reined in even from good desires?

63. Let us see what ice of discipline formed on the watered ground restrains Paul when he says, *The willing is close to me, but the doing of a good work I cannot find in me.** When he asserts that he has the will power already through the inspiration of grace, he shows us the seeds that lie hidden in him. But when he does not find the power to perfect a good work, he undeniably indicates how firm the ice of the heavenly dispensation is that restrains him. Had not this ice restrained the hearts of those to whom he said, *So that you do not perform what you would*?* It is as if he said outright, "The seeds hidden in your hearts already want to produce fruit, but they are restrained by the ice of heavenly moderation, so that they may go forth more fruitfully later, the more patiently they bear the present burden of restraint imposed by God's judgment."

*Rom 7:18

*Gal 5:17

64. Since human hearts are often unable to let themselves go practice those virtues they want to practice, for the very reason that they shrink from the perfection of their intention, they are worn out by the pinpricks of temptation; nevertheless they resist those tempting thoughts and compose themselves in a certain rigorous lifestyle through their daily practice, so he follows up, *The water hardened just like a stone.** Even if the flow of thoughts provokes us internally, still they do not force us to finally consent to do something evil. The mind,

*Job 38:30

however, has developed a custom of living well, and it is under a certain duress to hide externally whatever is yielding internally to the temptation's urging. So the Lord rightly adds, *And the surface of the abyss is frozen.** Even if the evil thought gets as far as suggestion, it still does not reach so far as consent, because holy deliberation is rigorous enough to block the soul's unstable movements. *Job 38:30

65. Ice or frozen air can also mean the adversity of the present life, because while it constricts the saints with its severity, it makes them stronger. While almighty God lets us be tried by distress, he also draws us on to the state of a better life by the intermediary of harsh experience; by an admirable plan he lets ice and frozen air settle on the fruit that is coming, so that all the chosen ones may put up with contrary winds and frost in this life as if it were winter, and afterwards, as if in the brightness of summer, might display the fruits they conceived here. That is why the Bridegroom's voice is addressed to every soul hastening to those green fields of eternity after the tornadoes of this world: *Arise and run, my friend, my beautiful one, come; winter is already passing, and the rain is over and gone.** *Song 2:10-11 So then we are free if only prosperity is present to us, but we are hardened for virtue better through adversity, so it is rightly added, *The water hardened just like a stone.** *Job 38:30 In other words, the minds that flow smoothly through prosperity are hardened when hindered by adversity; just like a stone conducted by the water, when any unstable people receive from above the ability to endure, they imitate the passion of their Redeemer. Just like a stone he had endured the water, but that former impatient persecutor who was later called Paul said, *I supply in my flesh what is missing from the passion of Christ.** *Col 1:24

66. Since when we are brought low by adversity we more skillfully guard our internal gifts, the Lord rightly adds, *And the surface of the abyss is frozen.** Joy usually opens the hidden places of the mind, and by opening them loses them. Adversity on the other hand, while it humbles us externally, makes us more careful internally. And so after ice and frozen air hardens the surface of the abyss, our mind is fortified by its very adversities for the purpose of keeping safe the deep gifts it has received. Isaiah had frozen the surface of his abyss when he said, *My secret is my own; my secret belongs to me.** Paul had hardened the surface of his abyss when, tired out from all his adversities and dangers, under some pretense or other he spoke of himself and said, *I heard secret words that people are not free to utter.** And again, *I forbear, lest anyone should suppose me to be anything else but what they see in me or hear from me.** Accordingly the one who suffered external hardship was afraid to reveal his secrets, lest he should by chance let praises run out, so what else did he do but cover the abyss of his secrets with a frozen surface? The next verse:

*Job 38:30

*Isa 24:16

*2 Cor 12:4

*2 Cor 12:6

XXXI. 67. *Will you be able to join the shining stars of the Pleiades, or can you break the circuit of Arcturus?** The stars of the Pleiades are απο του πλειστου in Greek. They are called so to indicate plurality. They were created close to one another and yet distinct, so that they might be together; still they cannot be joined, inasmuch as (granted) they are joined by closeness, but separated in physical contact. Arcturus so illuminates the nocturnal hours that its position at the axis of the heavens allows it to turn in different directions, but it never sets. Nor does it move outside its orbit, but it is stationary; it will never fall, but it turns toward all the parts of the world. How is it then that the human being, made out of earth and placed upon the earth, is questioned about the administration of the heavens if he can join the Pleiades that he sees created and almost joined

*Job 38:31

together, if he can break the circuit of Arcturus that he can nevertheless see almost gone by its own rapid movement? Or is it that in these dispositions people consider the Creator's power and remembers their own inadequacy? Do they ponder his inestimable power in his government of these heavenly dispositions, whose majesty they still cannot see?

68. But why do we speak thus, we who are spurred on by the goad of reason, so that we may understand these pregnant words by the use of mystical senses? What else are the shining Pleiades, seven in number, but the heralds of all the saints? Do they not light up the darkness of the present life for us with the light of the grace of the seven spirits? Those who were sent at various times to prophesy from the beginning of the world to its end: were they not joined together in one sense and separated in another? As we said above, the stars of the Pleiades were joined by being close together, and separated by not touching. They are located in the same place, yet they focus rays of light individually. In the same way all the saints who appear at various different times to preach are divided because of their formal appearance but joined because of the intention of their mind. They shine together because they preach the same thing, but they do not touch one another because they are divided by differences in time.

69. How different were the times when Abel, Isaiah, and John appeared! They were in fact divided by time but not by preaching. Abel, you see, signified the passion of our Redeemer, and he offered a lamb as a sacrifice, and Isaiah spoke of the passion: *Like a lamb he stood mute before the shearer, and he did not open his mouth.** See how different were the times when they were sent, and yet they concurred on the innocence of our Redeemer! John pointed out the same lamb as Isaiah

*Isa 53:7

foresaw, and Abel spoke of it by offering in sacrifice; the one whom John pointed out and Isaiah spoke of was the same one whom Abel signified and held in his hands.

70. So since we have said that the stars of the Pleiades sing together about the Redeemer's humanity, we will now show how they indicate the unity of the Trinity by shedding light together. David, Isaiah, and Paul appeared in this world at different times, but not one of them thought differently from the others, because even if they did not know each other's faces, they learned the same thing by divine knowledge. David, for example, so that he might show the triune God as Creator of all, said, *May God, our God, bless us; may God bless us.** And lest he should be thought to have spoken of three gods because of having named God three times, he immediately maintained the unity of the same Trinity by adding, *And let all the ends of the earth fear him.** He who added not *them* but *him* certainly maintained that the three were one. Isaiah too, beginning the praise of the united Trinity, repeated the words of the Seraphim and said, *Holy, holy, holy.** And lest by using the word *holy* three times he should seem to break the unity of the divine nature, he added, *The Lord God of hosts.** Accordingly he said not *lords* and *gods*, but *the Lord God*, and in so saying he showed that he is one in existence whom he had called *holy* three times.

Paul too, so that he might demonstrate the working of the Holy Trinity, said, *From him, through him, and in him are all things.** He also, so that he might indicate the unity of the same Trinity, added forthwith. *To him be glory, forever and ever, amen.** He therefore who added not *to them*, but *to him*, qualified him as one divine nature according to three persons, to whom he had referred above three times. It is as if then the Pleiades were located in the same place, since they together thought of

*Ps 66:7-8

*Ps 66:8

*Isa 6:3

*Isa 6:3

*Rom 11:36

*Rom 11:36

one God, and yet they do not touch one another, since, as has been said, through the different times of this world they are distributed.

71. This truth is what the prophet Ezekiel briefly described when he said he saw different types of animals and then said, *The wings of each one touched the others.** The wings of each one of the animals indeed touched the others, because no matter how different their actions may be, the voices and the powers of the saints accompany one another in the very same single sense. Although one may be a man by doing all things rationally, another bold in suffering may be a lion by not fearing any worldly adversity, another through abstinence may be a calf by offering himself as a living sacrifice, and another by rapidly taking flight in high contemplation may be an eagle, nevertheless their wings still touch in flight; yes, they are joined together by unanimity in confession of voice and power. It is only by means of divine power that those who are sent at various times can be joined together in the preaching of the faith and that those who have been endowed with various powers can be united in their bright intention, so the Lord rightly says, *Will you be able to join the shining stars of the Pleiades?* It is as if he added, "As I can, who alone fulfill all things, and who by fulfilling in the sense of unifying, join together the minds of the chosen ones."

*Ezek 1:9

72. Arcturus on the other hand illuminates the nocturnal hours through its orbit, and it never sets, so it does not signify the individual lives of the saints, but rather the whole united church; she indeed suffers weariness, but she is not caused to lose her proper status. She suffers the orbit of labor, but she does not hurry to her setting along with the spaces of time. Nor is Arcturus led at night time to the end of the heavens, but night ends while it is still revolving. Holy Church, you see, is being shaken by many tribulations, while the darkness of the present life is nearing its end. While the church is still continuing, night ends, because while she stands fast in safety, this mortal life speeds on. But there is in Arcturus something we may possibly look at more carefully. There are seven stars that revolve in Arcturus; sometimes three of them are positioned on high while four are inclined below, and sometimes four are lifted up on high while three incline below.

Holy Church too displays at times the knowledge of the holy Trinity to unbelievers, and sometimes preaches four virtues to the faithful, that is prudence, fortitude, justice, and temperance; in this way, as though rotating in her preaching, she changes in a way the appearance of her state. She strips certain ones of confidence in their own acts, those who boast of those acts, and in this way she exalts faith in the Trinity. What else happens but that Arcturus lifts up three stars and inclines four stars downward? And when she forbids certain ones who have no good works to presume on faith alone, but orders them to work more zealously on what has been commanded, what else happens but that she raises four stars upward, and lets three stars go downward?

Let us see how three are lifted up and four go downward: see how Paul speaks out against those who boast of works against faith: If Abraham was justified by works, he has praise, but not from God. What then does the Scripture say? *Abraham believed God, and it was credited to him as justice.** Let us see how four are lifted up and three decline: see how James speaks out against those who boast of faith against works: *Just as the body is dead without the spirit, so faith without works is dead.** So Arcturus moves on, because it rotates thus in the troubles of this life.

*Rom 4:2-3

*Jas 2:26

But the Lord sometimes varies its rotation, because he changes the church's labors to rest, and then he joins

Pleiades more closely together when he does away with the orbit of Arcturus; then indeed all the saints are joined together even by visible appearance when Holy Church is released at the end of the world from all the labors she now endures. So let the Lord say, *Will you be able to join the shining stars of the Pleiades, or can you break the circuit of Arcturus?** You should hear him say quietly, "As I do, because I then unite the saints' lives even by visible appearance, when I do away with the orbit of the universal church." And who is there who does not know that this is due to God's power alone? But so that the human being may know what he or she is, let him or her carefully remember what only God can do.

*Job 38:31

73. We still have something else to learn from the Pleiades stars and Arcturus. Pleiades rises of course from the east, but Arcturus from the northern region. Pleiades shows us by what path Arcturus turns in its orbit, and when the light of day is already near, the lineup of Pleiades' stars is stretched out. By Arcturus consequently in its rising from the cold region may be signifying the law; Pleiades however in its rising from the east may signify the grace of the New Testament. The law as it were had come from the north, and the law overawed those subject to it with all its rigid severity; like a frozen region it commanded some people to be stoned for their sins and others to be punished by sword thrust. As though it were a stranger to the sun of charity, it rather nipped the seeds of its commandments with cold than fertilized them with warmth. Peter was so shaken by the weight of its oppression that he said, *Why do you tempt God by placing a yoke on the disciples' neck that neither our fathers nor we are able to bear?**

*Acts 15:10

Nor is it remarkable that the Old Testament is indicated by the seven stars of Arcturus, since the seventh day stands out in the veneration of the law, and the devotion of the offering of sacrifices was extended through an entire week.* Pleiades on the other hand, which, as I said above, also has seven stars, clearly signifies the grace of the New Testament, just as we all clearly observe that the Holy Spirit illuminates his faithful with that light of the seven gifts. Whatever way Arcturus turns it shows the Pleiades, because whatever the Old Testament says, it announces the works of the New Testament. The mystery of prophecy, you see, hides behind the literal text. Arcturus as it were turns and shows itself, because while it inclines toward spiritual understanding, the light of sevenfold grace is signified and opened through it. And as the light of day draws near, the lineup of its stars is extended, because after Truth made itself known to us, he freed the literal precepts from carnal observance.

*Num 29:12-34

74. Our Redeemer, however, came in the flesh and joined Pleiades together, because he had all the operations of the sevenfold Spirit together, remaining in himself. Isaiah said of him, *A shoot will sprout from Jesse's root, from which a flower will bloom, and the spirit of the Lord will rest upon him: a spirit of wisdom and of understanding, a spirit of counsel and of fortitude, a spirit of knowledge and of piety, and he will be full of the spirit of fear of the Lord.** Zechariah added: *Seven eyes on one stone.** And again: *Seven candles on the golden candelabra.** No human being ever had all the operations of the Holy Spirit at once except the Mediator of God and mankind; the same Spirit belongs to him, and he proceeded from the Father before the ages.

*Isa 11:1-3 Vulg
*Zech 3:9
*Zech 4:2

Zechariah then was right to say, *Seven eyes on one stone*. For this stone to have seven eyes means to possess at once in operation all the power of the Spirit of sevenfold grace. But according to the distribution of the Holy Spirit one receives prophecy, another knowledge, another virtues, another different tongues, another the interpretation of tongues; no one, however, is able to receive all the gifts of the Holy Spirit at once. Our Creator nevertheless took on himself all the shortcomings of our nature, and he taught us that he has all the virtues of the Holy Spirit at once through the power of his divinity. Accordingly there is no doubt that he joined the shining Pleiades together. But while he joins the Pleiades together he also stops the orbit of Arcturus, because while he made known to us that he became man himself, and that he possesses all the operations of the Holy Spirit, he put an end to all struggle with the letter in the Old Testament, so all the faithful can now understand with the freedom of the spirit what they formerly served in fear among so many distinctions.

So let blessed Job hear the words, *Will you be able to join the shining stars of the Pleiades?** It is as if he said freely, "You can have, granted, the light of certain virtues, but are you able to practice at the same time all the operations of the Holy Spirit? Behold me then joining Pleiades together with all the virtues and stop boasting of a few." Let him hear the words, *Or can you break the circuit of Arcturus?** It is as if he were clearly told, "Even if you already know what is right yourself, can you do away with the struggle of crude intelligence in other people's hearts also by means of your own resources? Consider me then who correct the stupidity of carnal people, when I reveal myself through the foolishness of the flesh, so that you may all the more humble what you think is the fortitude of your own virtues the less you detect the traces of my shortcomings." So since in the very mystery of the Lord's incarnation the light of truth is shown to some people, while the hearts of others are darkened by the stumbling block, the Lord rightly adds,

*Job 38:31

*Job 38:31

XXXII. 75. *Can you bring out the morning star in its time, or can you make the evening star rise for the children of men?** The Father certainly produced the morning star at the proper time, since it is written, *But when the fullness of time came, God sent his Son, born of a woman, born under the law, that he might redeem those who were under the law.** He who was born of the virgin was like the morning star when he appeared in the darkness of our night, because when the darkness of sin fled, God announced the eternal morning to us. He pointed out himself as the morning star, because he rose from the dead in the morning, and he pushed away the black shadow of our mortal nature with the brightness of his light. He is rightly called by John, *The brilliant morning star.** He appeared alive after death and became our morning star, because while he showed himself an example of resurrection for us, he pointed out the light that follows.

*Job 38:32

*Gal 4:4-5

*Rev 22:16

The Lord however makes the evening star rise upon the sons of earth, because he allows Antichrist to take command of the unfaithful hearts of the Jews, since their merits demand it. They indeed are justly subjugated to this evening star by the Lord for the reason that they themselves desired of their own volition to be sons of earth. In fact they wanted to find earthly things and not heavenly, so they were blinded and kept from seeing the light of our morning star, and since they demanded to have the evening star rule over them, they are drowned in the eternal night of condemnation that follows. That is why the Lord says in the gospel, *I have come in my Father's name, and you did not receive me. If someone else comes in his own name, him you will receive.** Paul says for his part, *Because they did not receive the love of truth, so that they might be saved, God will send them one who does wrong, so that they might believe*

*John 5:43

a lie, and that those who did not believe the truth but consented to iniquity might be judged.* So the evening star would never rise over them if they had wanted to be sons of heaven. But since their desire is for visible things, having lost the light of the heart, their way is darkened under the leadership of night.

*2 Thess 2:10-12

76. If we discuss the moral sense of this passage we find that it happens every day that the morning star really does rise for the chosen ones, and the evening star rules over reprobate sinners with God's permission. One and the same word of God is in the mouth of the preacher, and when the former hear it joyfully and the latter enviously, they trade the light of the morning star for the darkness of the evening star. When the chosen humbly accept the words of holy preaching, it is as though they opened the eyes of their heart to the star's light, and when the reprobate sinners envy the one who is speaking well, not seeking a condition of salvation but rather the boasting of pride, the evening of their iniquity suddenly falls, and they close their eyes in the sleep of death. It happens through a hidden judgment therefore that the one who is a morning star for the chosen becomes an evening star for the reprobate sinner who is listening, because holy exhortation by means of which good people return to life causes bad people to become worse and to die in sin.

So Paul was right to say, *We are the sweet odor of Christ toward God for those who are being saved, and for those who are perishing; for the last indeed an odor of death leading to death, but for the first an odor of life leading to life.** The fact is that he saw his words as both a morning star and an evening star for those who heard them, and he knew that some would be rescued from iniquity while others contrariwise would fall asleep in iniquity. And since it is a question of hidden judgments

*2 Cor 2:15-16

of God, which cannot be understood by human beings in this life, he was right to add, *But who is qualified for these matters?** It is as if he said, "We may indeed be qualified to consider that they happen, but we are unqualified for the investigation into why they happen." So here again the Lord had said that the morning star is produced for some, whereas the evening star rises for others, and lest the human person should presume to investigate God's hidden judgments, he quickly adds,

*2 Cor 2:16

XXXIII. 77. *Do you really know the workings of heaven, and do you make known its purpose on earth?** To know the workings of heaven means to see the hidden predestination of heavenly dispositions. To make known its purpose on earth means to reveal the causes of such secrets to human hearts. To make known the heavenly purpose on earth obviously means to examine the mysteries of heavenly judgments by consideration or to reveal them by speech. No one lodged in this life can do that. So that we may leave small details behind and come to important matters, who could understand what the purpose of hidden things might be when a righteous person is often not only without vindication in judgment but even punished, while his evil adversary is not only unpunished but even goes away victorious? Who could understand why one person lives by setting traps to kill his neighbors, while someone else dies who could have profited the lives of many? One person attains the pinnacle of power when he is eager for nothing but to do harm; another only desires to defend those who have been injured, and yet he suffers oppression and defeat himself. One wants a life of retirement, and instead is involved in numerous business affairs; someone else desires involvement in business but is forced to retire.

*Job 38:33

One person begins badly, and all his life long until the end he grows worse; another begins well and keeps making progress and adding to his merits over a long period of time. On the other hand one lives badly and is left alone that he might correct himself, while another seems to live well, but his life goes on, and he reaches the point where he breaks down and acts perversely. One is born into an erroneous system of belief and dies in the same erroneous system; another is born in the correct system of catholic faith and ends his life in the same correct catholic faith. On the other hand someone else leaves his mother's womb a catholic, but near the end of his life he is sucked in by the whirlwind of error; another however ends his life in catholic devotion who had been born an unbeliever with his mother's milk and whose life had increased the poison of error. One both wills and is able to desire the loftiness of a good life; another neither wills nor can; another wills but cannot; another can but does not want it.

Who could inquire into these secrets of heavenly judgments? Who could understand the delicate balance of hidden equity? No one in fact reaches the knowledge of these places of hidden judgments. Let the human person be told then to know that he does not know; let him know that he does not know, so that he may be afraid; let him be afraid so that he may be humbled; let him be humbled so that he may not be presumptuous; let him not be presumptuous, so that he may request his Maker's help. The one who trusted in himself is dead, but by desiring and asking his Maker's help he may live.

So let the righteous person hear, the one who already really knows himself but still does not know the things that are above him. *Do you really know the workings of heaven, and do you make known its purpose on earth?**   *Job 38:33
In other words, "Do you comprehend the secret order of heavenly judgments, or are you able to reveal them to human ears? Blessed Job then is questioned about the

investigation into incomprehensible judgments, and it is as if he were told outright, "You must suffer everything, and you ought to put up with your sufferings to the same extent as, being ignorant of heavenly secrets, you do not know the reason for your sufferings."

BOOK 30

I. 1. Blessed Job is interrogated by the Lord about whether he had made such things as no human being could possibly make, so when Job realized that he could not do those works, he would take refuge in God, who alone as he then understood had the power to do them. Job would then look better in the eyes of his Judge if he truly knew his own inadequacy. That this work is done wonderfully by the Lord is not unknown, but the knowledge is demanded of Job by God's voice addressing him:

2. *Will you lift up your voice in a cloud, and will a burst of water then cover you?** The Lord indeed lifts up his voice in a cloud when through the mouths of his preachers he delivers an exhortation to the darkened hearts of unbelievers. A burst of water covers him when the crowd of resisting people threatens the right actions of his members. That situation is in fact what is written: *The word of the Lord came to Jeremiah, and he said: Go and stand in the court of the house of the Lord; speak out against all the cities of Judah from which they come up to worship in the house of the Lord; speak to them all the words that I have commanded you to speak.** And a little later: *The priests and the prophets and all the people heard Jeremiah speaking these words in the house of the Lord. And when Jeremiah had finished speaking, the priests and the prophets and all the people took hold of him and said: You will surely die! Why have you prophesied in the name of the Lord?** See how the Lord raised his voice in the cloud, because the prophet directly censured the dark minds of proud people. See

*Job 38:34

*Jer 26:1-2

*Jer 26:7-9

how a burst of water covers him forthwith, because God himself in Jeremiah suffered all that happened when the people were aroused and incited on account of his words of censure, words that he himself commanded.

The Lord himself also lifted up his voice in the cloud when he even showed himself present by the body he had assumed, and he even did much preaching against his adversaries, although it was with words veiled in riddles. In the cloud he lifted up his voice, because he made his truth heard as if through darkness by the unbelievers who would not follow. That is why it is rightly written in the Books of Kings, *A cloud filled the house of the Lord, and the priests could not perform their ministry because of the cloud.** When the high priests of the Jews hear the divine mysteries uttered through parables, since their actions deserve it, it is as though the priests in the house of the Lord could not perform their ministry because of the cloud. Even in the Old Testament they disdained the project of investigating mystical understanding amidst the gloomy darkness of allegory, covered as they were by the veil of the letter, so that they lost the ministry they owed their faith to because of the cloud. To them even then the Lord projected the voice of his teaching in the cloud when he himself spoke truths that were obvious. What is more obvious than the words, *I and the Father are one*?* What is more obvious than to say, *Before Abraham came to be, I am*?* But the darkness of unbelief had filled the minds of those who were listening, and it was as though a cloud lay in the path of the rays of the sun and hid them.

3. At this lifting up of his voice the waters forthwith burst out and covered him, because the crowd of people quickly rose up with hostility against him. It is written, *Consequently the Jews wanted to kill him, because not only did he violate the Sabbath, but he called God his Father, making himself God's equal.** The prophet cries

*1 Kgs 8:10-11

*John 10:30

*John 8:58

*John 5:18

out about this outburst of waters, *They surrounded me like water all day long; all together they surrounded me.** And again, *Save me O God, for the waters have risen over my head.** He suffered these waters indeed in himself up to his death, but in his own followers he suffered them even after the ascension. Hear what he cries out against their leaders: *Saul, Saul, why do you persecute me?** See how he had already ascended to heaven, and yet Saul is still persecuting him with the burst of unfaithful waters, and still more stormy waters have reached others. It is he who speaks what is right through good people, he who is tortured by the suffering of others. Therefore the Lord wanted to show how wonderful the union of love is by which he himself preaches to unworthy listeners through the mouths of his saints, so he said, *Will you lift up your voice in a cloud?* However, he also wanted to show that it was he who suffered all the adversity that his saints suffered, so he added, *And will a burst of water then cover you?** You should hear underneath, "like me? None of the wicked in fact understood that it was I who spoke through the preaching of the saints, or that I suffered through the death of the saints." The Lord in fact tells what people suffer so that he might mitigate the pain of afflicted humankind. It is as if he said, "Weigh things with my precision, and impartially moderate the result with your standard. Your wounds hurt you much less than it pains me to suffer what is human."

*Ps 87:18
*Ps 68:2

*Acts 9:4

*Job 38:34

4. However, we can study these words with still more precision if among our heavenly gifts we carefully weigh our hearts. We are already faithful, we already believe what we hear to be from heaven, and we already love what we believe. But when we are hard pressed by certain superfluous concerns, our mind is darkened by the confusion that has resulted, and when even though we are in such a state the Lord makes his presence felt in a wonderful way, it is as though he lifted up his voice in the cloud. When he speaks of himself to our darkened minds, it is as though the One who is not seen was heard in the cloud. Lofty indeed are the truths we learn from him, and yet we still do not see him by whom we are instructed by secret inspiration. He offers our hearts a speaking voice, but he hides his form, as if he formed words in a cloud. But look now: we hear God's words within, as he speaks to us of himself, and we already realize by what continuous zeal we should be attached to his love. Yet we still are caused to fall away from the peak of internal consideration to our customary state by that changeability of our mortal nature, and we are tempted by the unfortunately assiduous importunity of sins that threaten us. So when God slips his fine perceptions into our darkened minds, he lifts up his voice in a cloud.

5. When however our understanding is oppressed by God on account of temptation from our sinful habits, it is as if God were covered in his voice by a burst of water. We send as much water over him in fact as, after being inspired by his grace, we set the illicit thoughts whirling around in our hearts. God, however, does not abandon us when we are oppressed, but he quickly returns to the mind; he disperses the clouds of temptation, and he sends down the rain of compunction; he brings back the sun of fine understanding; he shows us how much he loves us in that not even when he rejects us does he abandon us, so that hardly has human awareness been so instructed than it is ashamed of admitting temptations into it when its Redeemer does not stop loving the one that strays.

This evil God himself endures in us; this evil he bears in the unfaithful every day through his preachers, and yet he is not dissuaded by our weakness from continuing to inspire us internally with his gift. His words are publicly despised, and yet he is not put off by any evil actions of the unbelievers from the generous infusion of his grace. Rather, when depraved people disdain preaching, he adds miracles that can be venerated. So after the voice has sounded and after the burst of water in rain, it is rightfully added,

II. 6. *Do you send bolts of lightning, and do they go, and return to tell you, "Here we are?"** Bolts of lightning to be sure come from the clouds, just as wonderful works are shown by the holy preachers, and preachers, as I have often said, are usually called clouds for the very reason that they shine with miracles and rain down words. After they have been unmoved by the preaching, you see, the human hearts are troubled by the very flashing of the miracles, as we have learned from the prophet's witness: *You will multiply lightning flashes and rout them.** It is as if he said, "As long as they do not listen to the words of your preaching, they are troubled by the miracles wrought by your preachers. That is why it is said elsewhere, *Your arrows will fly like the light in the flashing of lightning from your armor.**

*Job 38:35

*Ps 17:15

*Hab 3:11

For God's arrows to fly like the light means that his words resound with open truth. But since people often deride the words of truth even when they are understood, miracles are often added. That is why the prophet adds, *in the flashing of lightning from your armor.** Lightning from his armor of course means the brightness of miracles. We are protected by armor while we destroy adversaries with arrows. Armor together with arrows means preaching backed up by miracles. The holy preachers then attack their adversaries with words like so many arrows while they protect themselves with armor, that is, with miracles. So then the preachers must be heard as much as the sound of arrows striking, and they are to be revered as much as the armor of miracles glows

*Hab 3:11

brightly. That is why blessed Job is asked, *Do you send bolts of lightning, and do they go, and return to tell you, "Here we are?"** You should hear the words "as I do" underneath.

*Job 38:35

The bolts of lightning go forth when the preachers glow with miracles, and the listeners' hearts are transfixed with heavenly reverence. Returning, they say, "Here we are," when they attribute not to themselves but to God's power whatever they realize that they have done powerfully. What does it mean then to tell God, "Here we are?" In this phrase there is a certain act of worship declared. So for the returning holy preachers to say, "Here we are" means that they return thanks and praise to him from whom they know they have received victory in battle, lest they should attribute to themselves what they did. They could go indeed striking with lightning, but they cannot return with pride.

7. Let us see then how the lightning bolt goes: Peter says to a certain lame person, *I have no silver or gold, but what I have I give you. In the name of Jesus Christ of Nazareth arise and walk! And taking him by the right hand he pulled him up. And forthwith his feet and ankles were made firm, and he stood up and walked.** But when a crowd of Jews had gathered on account of this deed, see how the lightning returns when Peter says, *Men of Israel, why are you wondering about this, and why are you staring at us as if we had some power or craft to make this man walk? No, it was the God of Abraham, the God of Isaac, and the God of Jacob, the God of our fathers who glorified his Son Jesus.** And a little later: *We are his witnesses. It is by faith in his name that this man is whole whom you see and know. Faith in his name has given full health to this man in the sight of you all.** The lightning went forth when Peter worked the miracle; it returned when he attributed the deed not

*Acts 3:6-8

*Acts 3:12-13

*Acts 3:15-16

to himself but to the Creator. When the holy preachers display miracles, bolts of lightning go forth, but they return and say, "Here we are," when in the deed they hurry back to the Creator's power.

8. However, it can be understood in still another way. The saints, as we said above, are sent like lightning, and they go when they leave the hidden place of contemplation for the public arena. They are sent and they go when they spread out from the secret place of interior observation into the spaciousness of the active life. But they return and tell God, "Here we are," because they always run back to the bosom of contemplation after completing their external works, so that they might renew the flame of their zeal there and be rekindled as it were by the touch of heavenly glory. They would quickly freeze in those very good works externally unless they kept going back with anxious attention to the fire of contemplation. That is why Solomon wisely says, *To that place from which they flow the rivers return, so that they may flow out again.** In this text they are surely called rivers who in the other one are called lightning. As rivers they irrigate the hearts of listeners; as lightning they ignite them. About them it is written elsewhere, *The rivers have lifted up, O Lord, the rivers have lifted up their voices.** And again: *His lightning has illuminated the world.**

*Eccl 1:7

*Ps 92:3
*Ps 96:4

The rivers then return to the place from which they flow, because the saints—even when they leave the presence of the Creator whose glory they mean to look upon mentally, because for our sake they come forth to exercise the ministry of the active life—nevertheless never cease to return to the holy quest of contemplation; as they preach externally they root themselves in material words for our ears, while their mind always returns quietly to the contemplation of the fountain of light. Of them it is well said, *So that they may flow out again.** Unless their mind always returned anxiously to the contemplation of God, you see, internal blindness would surely dry up even their external words of preaching. But as long as they never stop thirsting to see God, it is as though their interior river kept rising internally to flow again externally, inasmuch as they take in internally the love by which they flow out to us by preaching.

*Eccl 1:7

So let the Lord rightly say, *Do you send bolts of lightning, and do they go, and return to tell you, "Here we are?"** You should hear underneath, "As I do, who whenever I wish prepare my preachers for the ministry of the active life after the grace of contemplation, and I always call them back from external good works to the internal peak of contemplation, so that at one time they are ordered to go out and practice good works, and at another they are called back to the familiar observation of contemplation in my presence." So they return and say, "Here we are," because however little contemplation may be seen in their external actions, nevertheless through their ardent desire by which their mind is continuously on fire they manifest their presence in worship before God. For them to say, "Here we are," then, means that they manifest their presence by love. The next verse:

*Job 38:35

III. 9. *Who has put wisdom inside the human internal organs, or who has given intelligence to the rooster?** Who else are meant by the word for rooster in this passage but the same holy preachers mentioned again in another way, who in the darkness of the present life zealously foretell the coming light by preaching, and as it were by singing? They say, *Night has faded, and daylight has approached.** They shake off the slumber of our lethargy and cry out, *It is time now for us to*

*Job 38:36

*Rom 13:12

rise from sleep.* And again: *Arise you just and sin no more.** About this rooster it is elsewhere said, *There are three creatures that walk high, and a fourth that walks happily: The lion is the strongest beast and fears the encounter of none; the rooster girds up its loins; as for the ram, no king resists him.** The lion mentioned in this passage is of course the one about which it is written, *The Lion of the tribe of Judah has won,** and he is called the strongest beast, because in him *the weakness of God is stronger than men.** He fears the encounter of none, and he says, *The prince of this world is coming, and over me he has no power.**

*Rom 13:11
*1 Cor 15:34

*Prov 30:29-31

*Rev 5:5

*1 Cor 1:25

*John 14:30

The rooster girds up its loins, and the holy preachers in the darkness of this world foretell the true morning. They gird up their loins, because they restrain their members from the flux of lust. Lust is obviously resident in the loins, which is why the Lord tells them, *Let your loins be girt.** *As for the ram, no king resists him.* Who do we take the ram to mean here but the first order of priests within the church? Of them it is written, *Bring the Lord the sons of rams.** By their example they lead the people on the march, as if they were a flock of sheep following them. Against them no king has enough power to resist when they live spiritually and rightly, and whatever persecutor meets them, he cannot contradict their intention. They know how both to run eagerly towards him whom they desire and to reach him by dying. The lion therefore goes first, the rooster second, and the ram third. The first to appear was Christ, then the holy preaching apostles followed, and then finally followed the spiritual fathers set over the churches, obviously the leaders of the flocks, because they were the teachers of the peoples that followed.

*Luke 12:35

*Ps 28:1

10. But we will affirm these truths better if we continue our exposition of the other words in the same passage. Because after these three the Antichrist will also appear, the wise man added the fourth at this point and said, *The one who appeared as a fool was later lifted up to the heights. If he had understood he would of course have put his hand over his mouth.** He certainly will be lifted up to the heights when he lies, saying he is God. But the one lifted up to the heights will appear as a fool, because in his very elevation he will fall because of the coming of the true Judge. If he had understood, he would have put his hand over his mouth. In other words, if he had foreseen his punishment when he took it upon himself to act with pride, the one who had once been created right would not have lifted himself up in such a self-display of pride.

*Prov 30:32

But what was said above—*And a fourth that begins happily*—would not move the proud. He rightly said of course that three are high steppers, and the fourth was happy. In fact not everything that is happy steps high, and certainly in this life not everything that steps high is happy. All three, you see, the lion, the rooster, and the ram, step high but not happily here, because they suffer wars of persecution. The fourth however steps happily but not high, because Antichrist steps in his deception. During the brief time of the present life he will prosper by his very deception, just as it is written of him in the Book of Daniel in the person of King Antiochus, *Power was given him against the daily sacrifice because of sin, and truth will be cast down to the earth, and he will act and prosper.** So in saying *he will prosper,* Daniel repeats Solomon's *fourth that walks happily.* According to this testimony then, in Solomon's words, *the rooster girds up its loins,* we do well to take the rooster to mean the holy preachers.

*Dan 8:12

Consequently God refers everything to himself when he says, *Who has put wisdom inside the human internal organs, or who has given intelligence to the rooster?* It is as if he asked, "Who has infused the grace of heavenly wisdom into the heart of the wise human being?" Or "Who but I have given understanding to those holy preachers, for them to know when or to whom they should foretell the coming morning? They know what they should do and when, precisely because they know inwardly that I revealed it." It is however noteworthy that wisdom inspired by God is placed inside the human internal organs, because as far as the number of the chosen is concerned, not only the words but also the senses are given to expect an answer, so that the consciousness lives according to what the tongue speaks, and his light shines all the brighter externally the more truly it burns in the heart.

11. But the next addition is a subject of great labor: *or who has given intelligence to the rooster?* It requires a still more detailed exposition. The intelligence of teachers must be very fine, indeed, the deeper it has to penetrate the invisible when it has nothing material to discuss when, although it speaks through the body's voice, it transcends all that belongs to the body. This intelligence indeed would in no way correspond to the highest reality unless the Creator of the highest himself supplied it to the crowing rooster, that is, to the preaching teacher. The rooster then received intelligence too, so that he might first discern the hours of the nocturnal period and then finally lift up his voice of waking. So then every holy preacher first considers the quality of life in those who are listening and then finally composes a fitting sermon to preach for their instruction. The act of judging the quality of sins, you see, is like discerning the hours of the night; the act of correcting dark actions with words capable of censure is like discerning the hours of the night. Intelligence then is given to the rooster from on high, and to the teacher of truth the virtue of discernment is provided by God, so that he might know to whom, what, when, and where he should teach.

12. One and the same exhortation, you see, is not suitable for everyone, because an equal quality of behavior does not bind everyone. What is profitable for some people often constitutes a block for others. Even the grass that nourishes some animals often kills others. A slight whistle that quiets horses excites puppies. A remedy applied to one disease relieves it but makes another worse; the bread that nourishes the life of the strong takes away the life of infants. The lessons of teachers then should be composed with the quality of the audience in mind, so that it should be suitable for each one's own profit and yet never be wanting to the artistry of common edification. What else in fact are the attentive minds of listeners but the close plucking of strings on a lyre? The skilled player does not want to compose a song with the strings out of tune; the strings give back a harmonious song, because they are plucked with one finger, but not with one action. So every teacher wants to edify all his listeners with one virtue of charity, so he should touch their hearts with one teaching, but not with one same exhortation.

13. Men have to be exhorted in one way, women in another; young people in one way, elders in another; the poor in one way, the rich in another; the happy in one way, the sad in another; subjects in one way, magistrates in another; slaves in one way, lords in another; the wise of this world in one way, the dull-witted in another; brazen people in one way, modest people in another; bold people in one way, retiring people in another; impatient people in one way, patient people in another; generous people in one way, envious people in another; simple people in one way, crude people in another; the healthy in one way, sick people in another. Those who fear the lash and therefore live blamelessly should be corrected in one way, and those who act wickedly so obdurately that they cannot even be corrected with the lash should be corrected in another; those who are too quiet in one way, those who are long-winded and easy-going in another; the fearful in one way, the bold in another; slow people in one way, rash people in another; the meek in one way, those prone to anger in another; the humble in one way, the proud in another; obstinate people in one way, inconstant people in another; gluttonous people in one way, abstemious people in another.

Those who already give away their goods in mercy should be corrected in one way, those who aim to steal the goods of others but will not give away their own should be corrected in another way; those who neither steal the goods of others nor give away their own should be corrected in one way, but those who both give away their own goods and do not stop taking those of others should be corrected in another way; those who argue with others should be corrected in one way, but the peaceable in another; those who sow discord should be corrected in one way, peacemakers in another; those who do not correctly understand the words of the holy law should be corrected in one way, those who in fact understand it rightly but do not speak of it humbly should be corrected in another way; those who are able to preach well but are afraid of it because of their humble mien should be corrected in one way; those whom immaturity or youth prevents from preaching but whom rashness impels to it should be admonished in another.

Those who desire worldly goods and are prosperous should be corrected in one way, and those who likewise desire worldly goods but are worn out by labor and adversity should be corrected in another; those who are bound with marriage vows should be corrected in one way, and those free of the ties of marriage in another; those who have had experience of carnal union should be corrected in one way, and those without experience in another; those who deplore sinful acts should be corrected in one way, and those who deplore sinful thoughts in another; those who mourn for what they have done but do not forsake it should be corrected in one way, and those who abandon it but do not mourn for it should be corrected otherwise; those who even boast about their unlawful deeds should be corrected in one way, but those who accuse their own wickedness but do not avoid it in another; those who overcome sudden desires should be corrected in one way, but those who are bound by sinful habits should be corrected in another; those who commit little sins frequently should be corrected in one way, while those who avoid little sins but are sometimes tripped up by grave ones should be corrected otherwise.

Those who do not even begin any good work should be corrected in one way, while those who never finish the good they have started should be otherwise corrected; those who do evil secretly and good publicly should be corrected in one way, while those who hide the good they do but allow evil reports of their public acts to be circulated should be otherwise corrected. Actually we should determine in detail what the structure of our exhortation should be, but for fear of a lengthy discourse we hold back. But by God's authority our soul longs to accomplish something along that line, as long as some time remains of this laborious life.

14. We do have in fact some other points we should consider concerning the understanding of that rooster, because in the deeper hours of the night more courageous and productive songs can be sung, but when the period of the morning draws near only very slight and small voices can be heard. So then what the intelligence of this rooster suggests to us in those smaller voices the aforesaid discretion of the preachers opens up to us. When they preach to minds that are still wicked, you see, they impress upon them with loud and high-pitched voices the terror inspired by the eternal Judge, obviously because they are crying out as it were in the deep darkness of the night. But when they know that the light of truth is already present in the hearts of their listeners, they change their loud cries into light sounds of sweetness. They do not then make heard the terrible sounds of punishment so much as the soft sound of rewards. Even then their voices sing faintly, because the morning draws near, and they preach subtle truths about mysteries so that their followers may hear the fainter sounds of heaven, precisely because they are drawing near to the light of truth.

Those whom the rooster's loud cry aroused from slumber, now awake, a lower pitch delights, inasmuch as anyone who has been corrected is free to think subtly and sweetly about the kingdom who previously feared adversity from the Judgment. That is what Moses expressed so well when he was ordered to have two trumpets sounded aloud to gather the army. It is written, *Make yourself two trumpets out of beaten silver.** And a little later, *When the blare of the trumpets is sounded, you will break camp.** The army is summoned, you see, by the two trumpets, and there are also two precepts of charity by which the people are called to gird on faith. The trumpets are ordered to be made of silver precisely for the reason that the words of preaching may be as clear as the brightness of light, and that the minds of listeners may not be obscured by any darkness of their own. The trumpets are to be made of beaten silver, because it is necessary that those who preach about the

*Num 10:2

*Num 10:5

next life should grow through the blows of present tribulations. So it is well said, *When the blare of the trumpets is sounded, you will break camp.* Obviously, when the words of preaching are spoken clearly and in detail, the hearts of the listeners are incited ardently to join battle against temptations.

15. There is still something else that we must carefully notice in the rooster, and that is that when he is already going to sing out, he first shakes his wings, and striking himself, he makes himself more alert. This we will quickly notice if we watchfully look at the lives of the holy preachers. The latter, when they are moved to words of preaching, first occupy themselves with holy actions, lest their own works should be found half-hearted when their words are arousing others. They shake themselves out in public through awesome deeds, and then they make others anxious to be doing what is good. First they strike themselves with the wings of thought, because whatever in themselves hangs limp and useless they find by means of careful investigation, and they correct it with strict attention. First they take care to punish themselves with tears, and then they denounce punishable faults in others. First they make noise with their wings so that they may sing their song, because before they offer words of exhortation, they let their whole speech resound in works; in this way, watching over themselves perfectly, they may call those who are still sleeping to watchfulness.

16. But where does the teacher get this supreme intelligence by which he both watches over himself perfectly and calls those who are still sleeping to watchfulness with insistence and volume, so that he may first shake off the darkness of sin carefully and then discreetly reveal the light of preaching, for it to be on time for each one in his or her own way, and at the same time show itself to all those who follow? By whom is the teacher taught to aim at so great and so subtle an attainment, if not internally by him by whom he was created? Since accordingly the praise of such intelligence does not belong to the preacher's attainment but to the Creator's power, rightly does the very Creator say, *or who has given intelligence to the rooster?* It is as if he said, "Who but me has miraculously instructed the minds of teachers, which I have wonderfully created out of nothing, to understand things that are hidden?" So that he might show that he is not only the inspiration of intelligence in the words of preachers but also the Creator of speech, he adds, *Who has explained the reason for the heavens?** Since however by these words he would show us his own form, he subtracts them and forthwith adds the following:

*Job 38:37

IV. 17. *Who will put the chorus of heaven to sleep?** In this life we are weak, so the Lord has not revealed the form of his majesty but has spoken with the voice of his preachers, so that the tongue of flesh might assail the heart that is still flesh, and that we might perceive what we are not accustomed to all the more easily the oftener we hear it by the sound of a voice that we are accustomed to. However, after the flesh returns to dust through death, and the dust is quickened through resurrection, we will not then want to hear words about God, because we will see only God who fills all things, finally the very form and word of God. So loud will he sound to us then that he will even penetrate our minds with the power of inner illumination.

*Job 38:37

After voices have been uttered, lifted up, and fallen, it is as though a kind of eternal sound of preaching became the very image of internal preaching. That is why the Lord now asks blessed Job, *Who has explained the reason for the heavens? Who will put the chorus of heaven to sleep?** What else do we take the reason for the heavens to be but the heavenly power of hidden things? What else is the heavenly chorus but the harmonious speech of preachers? Our Creator therefore, when he begins to describe the reason for heaven, puts the heavenly choir to sleep, because when he is ready to reveal his own form to us, he actually takes away the words of preachers. That is why the Lord has Jeremiah say, *No longer will a person teach his neighbor, or an individual his brother, saying, "Know the Lord," because they will all know me from the least of them to the greatest, says the Lord.** So Paul says, *Prophecies will pass away, tongues will cease, and knowledge will disappear.**

    Or at least the reason for heaven is the very life-giving power that forms the angelic spirits. Just as God is the cause of causes, and just as he is the life of the living, so also he is the reason for rational creatures. So then God explains the reason for heaven when he shows himself to us just as he presides over the chosen spirits. He describes the reason for heaven when the darkness of our minds is wiped out and he reveals himself in a clear vision. That is why the Lord says in the gospels, *The hour is now coming when I will no longer speak to you in parables, but I will speak plainly to you of the Father.** He claims that he declares the truth about the Father openly, because through his openly declared majesty he clearly shows both how his birth makes him no different from the Father who generated him and how the Spirit who proceeds is coeternal with them both. We will then see clearly how the one generated is not later in time than the one who generated him, and how the one who comes next proceeds and does not precede those who introduce him. We will clearly see then both how one God is divisible into three, and how the three are indivisibly one. The tongue then of

*Job 38:37

*Jer 31:34

*1 Cor 13:8

*John 16:25

the God who proclaims is the glory that is seen of the one who raises. The heavenly choir then sleeps, because when he who rewards works appears for Judgment, the words of exhortation will have already ceased. So it is fitting that the very time of resurrection is added when the Lord forthwith says,

V. 18. *When the dust was poured out upon the earth and the clods congealed.** In its own way, what still lay in the future the Lord's speech described as already past, so that he obviously preserved in himself what he says elsewhere: *He made the future things.** Accordingly the dust was then poured out upon the earth when it was changed into solid members. And the clods congealed, because of course solid bodies arose out of the collected dust. But after we have said how these words of the Lord are to be understood of the future, we will now indicate as well what they have to say about the present.

*Job 38:38

*Isa 45:11

19. *Who has explained the reason for the heavens? Who will put the chorus of heaven to sleep?** The Lord explains the reason for the heavens when he now states the lofty secrets and thereby illuminates the minds of his chosen ones. However, he puts the heavenly choir to sleep when he hides the harmonious hymns of angels and even that joy of the virtues of heaven from the hearts of reprobate sinners by righteous Judgment. Although in itself internally the heavenly choir is awake, in that very ignorance of reprobate sinners it sleeps externally. So the reason for the heavenly secret is explained, and yet the heavenly choir is allowed to sleep, because for some people the knowledge of heavenly retribution stands open through inspiration, and for others the meaning of the sweetness of internal praise is hidden.

*Job 38:37

20. The reason for heaven is announced, because the retribution of the highest is ceaselessly opened to the minds of the chosen ones, so that they may never stop making progress in transcending the visible and in penetrating the invisible. All that is visible, you see, fixes reprobate sinners in this life and drives the chosen ones toward the next life, because while they look upon the good that has been done, they are further aroused to seek him who has done it, and the more they consider him to surpass the good he has created, the more preeminently they love him. The good speaks to them internally, and the invisible tongue of compunction is heard in silence. The more perfectly their attention is turned away from the din of external desires, the more fully they hear the interior tongue. For them accordingly the heavenly choir is not asleep, because their mind knows with the ready ear of love what the sweetness of heavenly praise is. They hear internally what they desire.

By the very desire of divinity they are instructed about the rewards of heavenly goods. They bear the present life reluctantly—not only adversity, but also comfort, because all the objects of sensation are loathsome to them as long as they are still held back from what their inner ear hears. All that is ready to hand they esteem as unbearable, because it is not the object they long for. Their minds are endlessly weary of the very efforts required by day-to-day labors and kept suspended from concentration on that heavenly good, while in the ear of the heart that choir is bursting forth into companionship with daily expectancy of the heavenly citizens. This choir of heavenly praise had burst forth in the ear of him who said, *I will enter the region of the wonderful temple and go all the way to the house of God with the voice of exultation and confession and the sound of feasting.** Consequently the one who had heard the interior voice of exultation and confession and the sound of a city feasting, what else had aroused him but the choir of heaven?

*Ps 41:5

21. The heavenly choir, however, sleeps for reprobate sinners, because it is never noticed in their hearts by the voice of compunction. They have no eagerness, you see, to take into account that desirable familiarity with the heavenly citizens, and they do not look upon those festivals of internal solemnity with any ray of ardor, and they are not lifted up by any wing of contemplation in their inner parts. They serve only what is visible, and therefore they hear nothing internally of heavenly sweetness. As I have said above, the ear of their heart is rendered deaf because of the tumult of worldly anxiety that presses. Since therefore, by the dispensation of secret judgment, what is open to others is closed to them and what is revealed to others is hidden from them, let it be rightly said, *Who has explained the reason for the heavens? Who will put the chorus of heaven to sleep?** But when our Redeemer appeared through the mystery of the divine plan, he made it known to us and bestowed mercy on the unworthy and shut out those who seemed to be worthy, upon which the Lord fittingly added,

*Job 38:37

VI. 22. *When the dust was poured out upon the earth and the clods congealed.** What else do we take the dust to mean but sinners who are not grounded by any weight of reason and are swept away by any gust of temptation? About them it is written, *Not so are the wicked, not so; they are like dust driven by the wind from the face of the earth.** The dust therefore has its base on the earth, when sinners are called to the church and grounded in the principle of faith that is received, so that those whom the wind of temptation formerly swept up when they were unsettled and on the move afterwards became immovable by temptation and stayed put; they persevered in clinging to God, so that they held fast to the fixed weight of a good life.

*Job 38:38

*Ps 1:4

Clods, however, are congealed from dust mixed with moisture. On this earth accordingly clods are put together, because sinners are called and infused with the grace of the Holy Spirit, being united with those grouped together by charity. These clods were put together on the earth when people were united who at first thought differently, being different clouds of dust, but later they received the grace of the Holy Spirit; so they came together in that most peaceful harmony and unanimity, so that the witness of Holy Scripture testifies that they were first three thousand and then five thousand and says, *There was in them one heart and one soul.** Every day the Lord collects these clods on earth from the one element of dust but divisible into different clods, because while preserving the unity of the mystery the Lord collects the faithful peoples in the church according to different codes of behavior and different languages. Even then the Lord planned these clods, when he commanded fifties and hundreds to be seated to eat the bread and fish.*

*Acts 4:32

*Mark 6:40-41

23. However, if we pay attention to these clods in the church from the point of view of different merits, perhaps we can discern more detail to distinguish them. Preachers belong to one class, you see, and listeners to another; rulers to one and subjects to another; married people to one and single people to another; penitents to one and virgins to another. It is as if one earth brought forth different and distinguished forms of clods. Although faith and charity are one, different merits of good works are shown. Those people signified these clods who for the Tent of Meeting offered with the same eagerness different kinds of gifts, as it is written: *Whatever was needed for worship or for vestments, both men and women offered: bracelets, earrings, rings, armlets; all the gold ornaments were taken off and offered to*

the Lord, as were blue, purple, and scarlet cloth twice dipped, linen and goats' hair.*

*Exod 35:21-23

24. Men as well as women offer gifts to adorn the Tent of Meeting. To perform the worship of Holy Church, sublime deeds of the strong and the uttermost actions of the weak are also counted. What else do bracelets that are fastened onto the wrist signify but the works of hard-working leaders? What do earrings mean but the obedience of subjects? What rings but the seal of mysteries? Teachers often seal up, you see, what they consider their listeners cannot understand. What else do armlets signify but the ornaments of the first activity? What else do the gold ornaments offered to the Lord signify but the understanding of divinity? The more that understanding is detached from the affection of lower objects, the more it is lifted up to the only eternal objects that are worth loving. What else does blue cloth signify but the hope of heaven? What purple but the blood and tolerance of passions shown for the sake of the love of the eternal kingdom? What scarlet cloth twice dipped but charity, which is dipped twice to signify perfection, because it is adorned with love of God and neighbor? What else does linen signify but spotless incorruption of the flesh? What does the goat hair signify, with which the rough blanket is stitched, but the harsh suffering of penitents?

So whereas some people courageously exercise the teaching office with bracelets and rings, others show devout obedience and righteous works with earrings and armlets; others again show the outstanding and fine intelligence of God with the offering of gold ornaments, while still others never stop hoping for, believing in, and loving the words of heaven through blue, purple, and scarlet cloth, even when they do not even know them yet with the aid of finer intelligence; others offer up the uncorrupted flesh through the linen; still others bitterly deplore through goat-hair garments what they have freely allowed to happen. So it is as though from one earth uncountable clods have been made, because from one same act of worship the different deeds of the faithful have come forth. Naturally these clods would never form and come out of the dust unless the dust were first watered and then congealed when the dampness dried; similarly, unless the grace of the Holy Spirit first entered certain sinners, the bond of charity would not hold them captive for the works of faith.

So when the Lord spoke of the order of heaven or put the heavenly choir to sleep, it becomes clear. He says, *When the dust was poured out upon the earth and the clods congealed.* It is as if he said, "Then for the first time vocation and discretion became clear, and I revealed spiritual mysteries to some, not without mercy, and not without justice did I close them to others, since I rejected the latter but united the former with the concord of charity within the church." And because Holy Church was rejected by the faithless Jews, she occupied herself with carrying off the Gentiles. The Gentiles were to be converted in the church's body, and this was to be brought about not indeed with her own strength, but with the Lord's, so he is right to add,

VII. 25. *Are you going to kill prey for the lioness, or will you satisfy her offspring's appetite?** This is that very lioness Job had spoken of when he saw proud Judea missing as the church was preaching: *Sons of hawkers have not trodden her ground, nor has the lioness passed through her territory.** The Lord then killed prey for the lioness so that he might satisfy her offspring's appetite, because he seized innumerable Gentiles to fill the church's ranks, and he satisfied the pleading of the apostles' hunger

*Job 38:39

*Job 28:8

with the loot of souls. The lioness's brood, in fact, were so-called for the sake of the pliability of their minds and their fearfulness and weakness; the doors being locked after the Lord's passion, they stayed, just as it was written of them: *The day after the Sabbath when it was late, the doors were closed where the disciples were for fear of the Jews, and Jesus came and stood in their midst.** So concerning these same lion cubs it is also added here conveniently,

*John 20:19

VIII. 26. *When they lie down in caves and hide in places of ambush.** When the holy apostles, you see, were not rising up against the devil's members with voices of untrammeled preaching, and they were not yet confirmed by the outpouring of the Holy Spirit after the Lord's passion, they were still as it were lying in ambush in caves against their adversaries. Behind closed doors, as it were in hidden caves of a sort, the lion cubs that were to take over the world lay down, so that they might later on take upon themselves the task of snatching the prey of souls, though certain it is that at the time they were even hiding in dread of the attack of the world against themselves. Behind those closed doors these lion cubs lay in ambush in search of the death of our death, so that they might kill our guilt and take away all the life of sin in us. To the first of these, that hungry lion cub, but already strong, when he was shown the sheet of the Gentile world as if it were a scene of prey, it was said, *Slaughter and eat.** These lion cubs were told when they were still weak to lie down in caves, when the Lord's voice said, *Stay in the city until you are clothed with power from on high.** Are they not rightly called lion cubs who, being leaders in the church, tear their adversaries in their mouths, that is the world?

*Job 38:40

*Acts 10:13

*Luke 24:49

27. We know in fact that this is what the holy apostles did, and we see it done even now by the holy teachers. Even if they are the fathers of the people that followed, yet they are the sons of the preceding ones. So they are not wrongly called lion cubs. Or at least, even though they are the teachers of some of the faithful, they boast of being disciples of the universal church. The Lord then killed prey for the lioness, because by virtue of his own inspiration he snatches the lives of evildoers from the wrong road, and he satisfies the appetites of the lion cubs, because he fulfills the holy desires of the teachers with the conversion of many people. The Lord continues speaking of these cubs: *When they lie down in caves and hide in places of ambush*.

In fact not all times are convenient for teaching. The power of the word is often lost if it is broached at the wrong time. The action of a gentle word is often facilitated by the chance of a convenient time. Accordingly he knows how to speak the truth who also knows how to be silent effectively. What good is it to correct an angry person at the moment he or she is inflamed, when the mind is estranged and the person is unable either to hear anyone else speak or even to control the self? The one who corrects an angry person in a scolding fashion is like the one who inflicts blows on a drunken person who cannot feel them. In order for the heart of the listener to be able to perceive a teaching, one should carefully consider a time that would be suitable for the person. The Lord therefore rightly says about these lion cubs, *When they lie down in caves and hide in places of ambush*.

Accordingly, when the holy teachers discern that a position is to be taken and yet keep silence in their thoughts, it is as though they were hiding in ambush and concealing themselves in caves, because they are really hiding in their hearts. But when they have found a convenient time they quickly bound forth and hold back nothing that should be said; they grasp the proud heads with the bite of bitter incrimination. So whether it be by the apostles themselves or by the teachers who assume their place, the Lord daily catches prey for this lioness, and through those he captures, he never stops catching new prey. For this purpose indeed the righteous also seize the sinners in this world, and through their conversion other worldly people are also seized. So the very Gentile world is captured by the holy apostles' mouths, so that even the Gentiles themselves suffer with as great a hunger for others as they know the apostles first conceived for them. Therefore he rightly adds,

IX. 28. *Who finds the raven its food, when its nestlings cry out to God, flying aimlessly because they have no food?** What is meant by the use of the word *raven* and by its nestlings if not the Gentile world that is black from its sins? About the Gentile world the prophet says, *He gives the beasts their food and young ravens that cry out to him.** Yes, beasts get their food, when the minds that were once irrational are satisfied with the fodder of Holy Scripture. To the young ravens or sons of Gentiles food is given when their desires are fulfilled by fellowship with us. That raven was food when Holy Church went to search for it, but now it is fed, because by itself it goes in search of others to convert.

*Job 38:41

*Ps 146:9

29. Its nestlings are obviously preachers whom it sends forth, but they do not presume on their own merits; rather they depend on the Redeemer's power. So he is right to say, *when its nestlings cry out to God.* They know they can do nothing by their own power. Although they hunger for the profit of souls with faithful prayers, they long for this to happen by the power of him who works internally at everything. Their true faith enables them to understand that: *Neither the planter nor the waterer amounts to anything, but only God who makes the plant grow.**

*1 Cor 3:7

30. However, that which is said—*flying aimlessly because they have no food?**—signifies nothing else by that aimless flying but the desires of the hungry preachers. While they go around receiving people in the bosom of the church, they are afire with a great ardor, and they desire to gather peoples now here and now there; the very heat of their thoughts is like a kind of aimless flying, and they keep going over to various places as it were by changing direction, while they keep running about to different regions with hungry minds for the purpose of gathering souls in uncountable ways.

31. The young ravens then, or the Gentile children, have learned from the teacher of the Gentiles himself how to go flying aimlessly. He himself indeed was on fire with so vigorous a love that he kept moving constantly from one place to another; he desired to go on from place to place, because he was impelled by the very love that filled him. While he was still far away from the Romans he wrote, *I am always mindful of you in my prayers, earnestly pleading that I might finally find in some way how to make a prosperous journey to you by the will of God. I do desire to see you.** While detained at Ephesus he wrote to the Corinthians, *See, now I am ready to come to you for a third visit.** While he was still staying at Ephesus he told the Galatians, *I only wish I could be with you, so I could change my speech.** At Rome also, while he was kept under guard in prison, because he was not allowed to visit the Philippians in person, he promised to send them a disciple: *I hope in the Lord Jesus to send Timothy to you soon, so that I might be of good heart by knowing how things are with you.** When he was again confined in chains at Ephesus he wrote to the Colossians, *I may be absent in body, but I am with you in spirit.**

*Job 38:41

*Rom 1:9-11

*2 Cor 12:14

*Gal 4:20

*Phil 2:19

*Col 2:5

This is how by means of holy desire he can as it were wander abroad: while the body is held in one place, the spirit is led elsewhere; the feeling of fatherly love is shown to those present and extended to those absent; to specified persons he offers works, and to audiences he expresses wishes; he is efficiently present for those he is with, but not away from those he is not with. We understand his peregrinations better if we consider his words to the Corinthians: *I will come to you when I pass through Macedonia; yes, I will pass through Macedonia, but I mean to spend some time with you, or even stay the winter.** Let us carefully assess this journey plan, I beg of you. By one plan he proposes to remain for a while, by another he announces his departure, and by a third he promises he will change his course. How is it that he is going to so many places with so anxious a mind? Is it not because for all of them he is constrained by the same love?

*1 Cor 16:5-6

Charity of course unites what is divided, and it impels Paul's single heart to be divided for the sake of many. The more closely his heart is united to God, the more widely it scatters through holy desires. Paul therefore wishes by preaching to say everything at once and by loving to see everything at once, because as long as he is in the flesh he wants to live for all, and by transcending the flesh by the mystery of faith he wants to work for the profit of all. Let the young ravens then fly aimlessly; in other words, let the Gentile children imitate their teacher and shake off their mental lethargy; when they fail to find spiritual profit, in other words, food, let them not be silent, but extend their objectives further; let those who are impatient for the advantage of many people be like birds restlessly hungry for their food. Since therefore they do not cease to satisfy the

Gentiles with the food of faith by running about doing the work of preaching, let it be truthfully said, *Who finds the raven its food, when its nestlings cry out to God, flying aimlessly because they have no food?**

*Job 38:41

32. The word *raven* can also signify the Jewish people, whose unbelief renders them black. Their nestlings are said to cry out to God so that the Lord might prepare food for that very raven. The holy apostles of course were born of the Israelite people according to the flesh, so while they poured out prayers to the Lord for their own nation they were like nestlings of ravens, and they were fearful with spiritual understanding for the people who were their parents according to the flesh. Accordingly the raven's nestlings cry out while food is being prepared for the raven, and while the apostles are praying, the people who were long without faith are led to the knowledge of faith, and they are satisfied with the preaching by the children as if by the voice of nestlings.

What we should carefully notice in this verse, however, is that food is first said to be prepared for the raven by means of the cries of the nestlings and later by their aimless flying. Food is made ready for the raven by the cries of the nestlings when the apostles preach the word of God, and Judea listens and is satisfied by spiritual knowledge, first to the extent of three thousand and then of five thousand people. But when they expressed their cruelty against the preachers through the multitude of reprobate sinners and put their own nestlings to death, as it were, those same nestlings were scattered all over the world. That is why when their carnal parents resisted the spiritual preaching, they told them, *We were bound to speak the word of God to you (Jews) first, but since you reject it and show yourselves unworthy of eternal life, we will now go to the Gentiles.** They knew very well that after the Gentile world came to believe, Judea

*Acts 13:46

also would come to the faith. That is why it is written, *Until the full number of Gentiles enters in; then all Israel will be saved.**

*Rom 11:25-26

That is why the holy apostles with all their strength strove both to preach to their first listeners and afterwards to display the example of converted Gentiles to those who are resisting their preaching. They were like hungry nestlings first crying out to this raven for their food and afterwards flying aimlessly to seek it. Wherever the nestlings aimlessly fly, there the raven finds its food; as long as the Jewish people look at the Gentiles converted by the preachers' efforts, they finally sooner or later are embarrassed at the foolishness of their own unbelief. Then they understand the viewpoint of Holy Scripture, when they realize that it was known by the Gentiles before themselves, and after the aimless flying of the nestlings they opened the mouth of their heart to receive the holy word. After the holy apostles had journeyed into the world, the Jewish people finally received that spiritual food from which they had fasted so long under the restriction of unbelief. All this happened under the sole operation of divine power, so that the question was rightly asked, *Who finds the raven its food, when its nestlings cry out to God, flying aimlessly because they have no food?** You should hear underneath the words, "Who but I do this, when I put up with the unfaithful people for the sake of the sons who pray and feed the preachers, and for the sake of those flying aimlessly to other places, I keep those still to be converted one day until the end."

*Job 38:41

33. There is still another way to understand the raven in a moral sense. Having brought forth nestlings, as it is said, the raven only pretends to offer them satisfying food before their feathers grow black, and he lets them suffer hunger until he sees his own likeness in them because of the black color of their wings. They consequently flit back and forth in the nest, and with open mouths they demand the support of food, but when they start to look black he tries just as eagerly to obtain food to offer them as he put off feeding them for so long a time. Every preacher then is a smart raven who cries out in a loud voice and carries about with him the memory of his own sins and the knowledge of his own weakness as if it were a kind of black color. To him certainly disciples are born by faith, but perhaps they do not yet know how to consider their own weakness; perhaps they turn away from the memory of their past sins; they then do not display the humility of blackness that they ought to assume against the boasting of this world. They are like those who open their mouths to receive food when they want to be taught the secrets of heaven.

But their teacher is as much less inclined to give them the food of higher teaching as he knows they are less inclined to weep over their past sins. He waits indeed and warns them that they should first grow dark against the brightness of this world through the lamentations of repentance, and then finally they would receive fitting nourishment of the most refined teaching. The raven looks upon the nestlings opening their mouths, but he is waiting for their bodies to be covered with black wings. And the wise teacher does not administer internal mysteries to the perception of those whom he still does not consider to have cut themselves off from this world. Therefore the less black as it were that the students have become as regards the external culture of the present life, the less they are filled with the internal food of the word, and because they do not empty their bodies of honor, they fast from the spiritual repast.

34. If, however, by the confession of their previous life they utter groans and lamentations as if they were so many black feathers, the thoughtful teacher of contemplation straightway flies like a raven bringing food to its nestlings from the heights and as they open their mouths delivers their meal; from that understanding that he has grasped he doles out to the hungry students in his speech food for them to live by. He feeds them with higher teaching as much more eagerly as he realizes how much more sincerely they darken to the world's brightness by the lamentations of repentance.

35. However, while the nestlings are clothing their wings with the color of black, they show promise of flight themselves, because the more the disciples feel that they have cast off something of themselves and the more they afflict themselves as contemptible, the more they are promised hope of progress towards higher things. Consequently the teacher takes care to nourish them more speedily, those who, through certain indications, he already foresees will be able to profit others. That is why Paul warns Timothy to take great care to nourish them like nestlings growing feathers. He says, *What you have heard from me by many witnesses, recommend to people who are faithful and who are qualified to teach others.** As long as this discretion concerning his teaching is carefully cultivated by the preacher, he is given a more abundant source of preaching by God. As long as he knows how to show compassion for the afflictions of his disciples through charity and as long as he understands through discretion what is a fitting time for teaching, he receives a greater reward for his intelligence, not for his own sake alone, but also for those who will be the beneficiaries of his zealous labors. That is why here too the words are appropriate: *Who finds the raven its food, when its nestlings cry out to God, flying aimlessly because they have no food?** When the nestlings cry out to have sufficient food, food

*2 Tim 2:2

*Job 38:41

is gathered for the raven, because as long as good listeners are hungry for the word of God, greater gifts of intelligence are given to the teachers to feed them.

X. 36. *Do you know the time when the ibex gives birth among the rocks, or have you ever watched the does giving birth?** The southern region calls the ibex a bird that inhabits the Nile river, but the eastern and western regions call it a small four-legged animal.[1] The latter customarily give birth among the rocks, since they cannot live anywhere but among the rocks. If they ever gallop away from the mountain heights, they are kept from harm by their own horns. They run of course with their heads down, so that whatever their horns first strike keeps their whole body unaffected by injury from a fall. Does in fact habitually kill snakes when they find them and tear them apart with their teeth. It is said that when they cross a river they place the burden of their heads on the backs of those in front of them, so that as they follow one another, they do not even feel the weight of the burden.

*Job 39:1

How is it then that blessed Job is questioned about how ibexes and does bring forth their young, unless it is because ibexes and deer signify the roles of spiritual teachers? These latter in fact are like ibexes bringing forth their young among the rocks, because the teaching of the fathers has the solidity of the rock, and it is there that they bring forth souls for conversion. They are also like ibexes in that they suffer no loss when they fall, because they are extricated by their horns, so whatever ruin befalls them in time, they are delivered from it by the two Testaments of Holy Scripture and extricated by the action of their horns. It is written about these

---

[1] Gregory seems to be confusing the ibex with the ibis here. The latter is a bird sacred to Egyptians.

Testaments: *They are horns in his hands.** They have recourse to the comfort of the Scriptures who are hit by some loss resulting from a temporal happening. Was Paul not like an ibex stumbling from the adversities of this world, as he righted himself with his own horns and said, *Whatever has been written was written for our instruction, so that we might have hope through the patience and comfort of the Scriptures?**

*Hab 3:4

*Rom 15:4

The sons begotten by the teachers were also called deer and abandoned in the field, as Jeremiah mentions: *The deer brings forth young and leaves them in the field.** They are like deer who, after having put their own evil habits to death, live on after the killing of snakes, as it were, and after the death of vices they are more eagerly zealous for the fountain of life, according to the psalmist: *As the deer longs for springs of water, so my soul longs for you, O God.** While the moments of this time frame are passing like some ever-flowing rivers, those who are fellow-sufferers in charity place their own burdens on one another; they are careful to keep observing what is written: *Bear one another's burdens, and in this way you will fulfill Christ's Law.** Since, however, after the Lord's incarnation spiritual teachers spread out all over the world, those who could prepared listeners' souls for conversion by their preaching, and since this very time the Lord's incarnation was unknown before the prophets' voices were heard, although the future incarnation was itself known beforehand by all the elect, blessed Job is rightly questioned about the time of the ibex's and doe's bringing forth children and asked, *Do you know the time when the ibex gives birth among the rocks, or have you ever watched the does giving birth?** It is as if he were told, "You loftily believe you have accomplished something, because you do not yet foresee that time when spiritual teachers will be sent into the

*Jer 14:5

*Ps 41:2

*Gal 6:2

*Job 39:1

world and bring forth children through the teaching of the ancient patriarchs, and by their labors will bring me the profit of souls. If you could see their fruitfulness as the offspring of ibexes and does, then you would think exceedingly humbly about your own virtue." Whatever great deeds we have done we hold to be very small when we weigh them against the example of greater ones. But their merit grows in the sight of God when they grow smaller in our own estimation through humility.

37. The word *does*, however, can signify teachers, while by the title *ibexes*, which names the smallest of animals, we may understand listeners. So ibexes bring forth their young among the rocks, because they become fruitful for the doing of holy works through the examples of the former patriarchs, so that when by chance they hear precepts that are lofty, in their awareness of their own shortcomings they do not trust their ability to fulfill them; they should then observe the lives of their great predecessors and be inspired by their courage, so that they can bring forth the children of good works. Anyway, let me speak briefly about many subjects, inasmuch as the intelligent reader can understand many things by few: when David himself was attacked by insulting words, and he was unable to observe the virtue of patience, Shimei was accusing him of so many crimes and David's armed soldiers were pleading to avenge him, he said, *What have I to do with you, you sons of Zeruiah? Let him curse. If the Lord has ordered him to curse David, who is there who would dare ask him why he acts in this way?* And a little later: *Let him curse as the Lord has commanded him. Perhaps the Lord will look upon my misery and do good to me in return for today's curses.** By these words he indicates that in return for the sin he committed with Bathsheba his own son rose against him and put him to flight, and he recalled

*2 Sam 16:10-12

to mind the evil he had done and calmly bore the words he heard; he judged the insulting words not so much as abuse, but as a support by which he could be purified and could find mercy. Then indeed we put up with attacks of abuse when we have recourse in the secret mind to the evil deeds we have done. The injuries we suffer do seem light when we take a good look at our own actions and see that what we deserve is worse, and it happens that instead of anger the insults deserve thanks, inasmuch as by the intervention of God's judgment we believe that a greater punishment can be avoided.

38. See how another person profits from present worldly success when joy in the heart works to his advantage and he endures temptation by the feeling of lust, but let him recall the action of Joseph to memory and keep himself in the citadel of chastity. The latter saw himself being persuaded to the loss of modesty by his own mistress, and he said, *See how my master has turned everything over to my care and does not even know what he has in his house; there is nothing that is not in my power or that he has not turned over to me except you his wife. How then can I do such an evil thing as to sin against my master?** By these words it is made clear that he quickly remembered the good that he had attained and rejected the evil that importuned; he remembered the favored position he had received and broke the force of imminent guilt.

*Gen 39:8-9

When a shifty pleasure tempts us in prosperity, this very prosperity itself must be resisted as a thorn of temptation, so that we should be just as ashamed of committing any sin as we remember how we have freely received good things at God's hand, and we should convert the external gifts we have been favored with into the weapons of virtue, so that we may subdue the things that we have perceived in front of us and that entice us. Because pleasure itself arises out of prosperity, it must be struck down by the consideration of that same prosperity, inasmuch as our enemy should die in the very place where it rises. It is absolutely to be taken into consideration that we should not convert into a bad habit the gift we have received, lest an insatiable chasm of depravity should suck us in when life seems to favor us. We incite the inextinguishable anger of the heavenly Judge against ourselves, you see, if we fight against his kindness with his very generosity towards us.

39. Some others seek the sweetness of interior knowledge, but they do not manage to touch its secrets; they look at the life of Daniel for the sake of imitating him, and they lay hold of the very pinnacle of knowledge that they desire. Daniel of course was later called a man of desires[2] by the angel's voice* on account of his longing for internal knowledge, but before that at the royal court he is said to have tamed the desires of the flesh in himself, so that he would touch none of the rich foods* but preferred harsh and bitter foods to the sumptuous and rich, so when he abstained from luxurious external food he could get to the pleasures of internal nourishment. In this way the more avidly he turned to the taste of internal wisdom, the more robustly he refused the external taste of flesh for the sake of that wisdom.

*Dan 9:23; 10:11

*Dan 1:12

If we cut short our pleasure in the flesh, you see, we will soon find in the spirit what will please us. If external wandering is denied to the attentive soul, it is free to seclude itself internally. When the mind cannot be dispersed outside itself on account of its self-discipline, then it can concentrate on what is above itself by moral

---

[2] *Vir desideriorum* according to the Vulgate, but *man greatly beloved*, according to RSV, translating the Hebrew.

progress, because the tree too is forced to grow higher when its branches are prevented from spreading out. And when we obstruct the edges of a spring, we force it to surge up towards the heights. Consequently, when any eager students concentrate on the lives of the saints with a view to imitating them, they are like ibexes bringing forth their young among the rocks. That is why Paul admonished his listeners to be like ibexes bringing forth children among the rocks after he had enumerated the virtues of the ancients, and he said, *Since we have then such an imposing cloud of witnesses, let us cast aside every weight of sin that stands against us and by patience run the race that is set before us*, and again, *you know the outcome of their life, so imitate their faith.**

*Heb 12:1; 13:7

40. However, when we conceive God's precepts in the heart, we do not immediately bring them forth like something already thought out and solid. So blessed Job is not questioned about the bringing forth of ibexes as such, but about the time of birth. Obviously we never comprehend this time as regards ourselves, so still less do we know it in someone else's mind. The seed of heavenly fear is first received in the womb of the heart, and through meditation and study it takes shape so that it remains; after the concentrated attention of thought has been fixed, this seed proceeds to the rational formation of discretion and singular members are in a way formed; then perseverance is engaged and they are confirmed. As though with the solidity of bones they come forth; finally they are strengthened with perfect authority and proceed as though to be born. This growth of divine seed in somebody else's mind no one notices except the Creator. Even if we know by the attestation of certain elements that somebody or other has already conceived the power of heavenly desire, we are totally ignorant of the time of birth.

41. The seed conceived in the mind, however, often cannot reach perfection, because in being born it has anticipated the time of birth. And because it is not yet completely formed in the thought, it comes forth to human eyes like an aborted birth and so dies. The human tongue in fact often praises the good seed while it is still tender, as if it were already strong, and so kills it. The more untimely it bursts forth for favorable recognition, the more quickly it dies. Sometimes, however, our incomplete thought, while not yet strong, is displayed to people too quickly and is lost because contradicted and resisted. Because it wants to be seen as it is before the proper time, it sees to it that it is not. The saints, however, try hard to see that all their good thoughts grow strong in secret, and they form them first within the womb of their minds like the fetus that is going to come forth. So blessed Job is rightly questioned about the time of bringing forth, which obviously is unique for every single person, unless he is unknown by the Creator. The Creator looks upon the deep places of the heart, when our good thoughts are fittingly given birth before they are made known to human beings, and he knows them. It is rightly said therefore, *Do you know the time when the ibex gives birth among the rocks?** It is as though he said openly, "As I do? Because I give life to the fetuses of the chosen ones precisely for this reason: that I produce in time what I have foreknown." So it is rightly added concerning the fetuses brought forth by the chosen ones: *have you ever watched the does giving birth?** To watch the does giving birth of course means to weigh with careful consideration the very labors of the patriarchs who beget spiritual children.

*Job 39:1

*Job 39:1

42. We must, however, carefully observe how attentively these words were spoken and written down. In fact very few people can imagine the immense labor of preaching the patriarchs had to undertake, the intense suffering and effort involved in bringing forth souls in faith and good living, how wary was the attention with which they saw their situation, so that their precepts might be forceful, their attitude to the weak compassionate, their threats terrible, their exhortations mild, the display of their mastery humble, their contempt for worldly riches dominant, their bearing under adversity stern, and yet, even if they did not attribute their strength to themselves, they were still weak; how great was their sorrow over those who had fallen, how great their fear for those who were steadfast, how great the fervor with which they yearned for fresh attainments, how great the fear with which they preserved what they had already attained! Since therefore there are very few people who think about these things, the Lord rightly asks Job,

43. *Have you ever watched the does giving birth?* There is nothing against assuming that the Lord was talking about teachers, even if he specified *does* instead of *deer*, since naturally they were really fathers on account of their rigid discipline, but mothers because of their deep loving-kindness. In fact they endured the labor of holy conception, and they carried children within the womb of charity to be brought forth for God. They labored harder than mothers in bringing forth offspring, and they endured the growing fetus after conception for a longer time than specified months; it was not without great effort, either, that they let their offspring exit the womb. So he continues speaking with fitting concentration:

XI. 44. *Have you counted the months of their conception?** So when the saints take thought about the progress made by their listeners, it is as though they were already carrying conceived offspring in their womb. But because the words that are to be spoken

*Job 39:2

sometimes differ, and they seek a fitting time for their exhortations, it is as though they desired the offspring they want to deliver to be delayed for a great many months. They often refuse to tell their audience the things they understand, because it is not yet time; in that very slowness of speaking out their message either of persuasion or of reproach they are confirmed by a higher counsel. When the lives of children are in question, the tongue does not let go of the mind's counsel before the proper time has arrived, as if the fetus already conceived were still growing in the womb; the heart's decision should be spoken for the instruction of those who listen at the time when it may be spoken profitably, as though it lived through a successful birth. Now people usually do not know when or how counsels are being decided in the teacher's mind, but God does know and rewards with glory both the effective counsel and its proper time; blessed Job is rightly asked, *Have you counted the months of their conception?* You should hear whispered, "As I have? Yes, I have considered not only the fruits of external labors, but even their daily thoughts, and because of all these I reward the holy preachers."

45. As for the months that are full of days, they can also be understood as the multiplication of virtues. The moon too is reborn each month, so there is nothing against the months' signifying a new creation or regeneration, concerning which the apostle Paul wrote, *In Christ Jesus there is neither circumcision nor uncircumcision, but a new creation.** Accordingly the saints, when they get ready to preach, first renew themselves internally with virtues so that they may live in accord with what they teach by speaking. They consider first what they are internally and purify themselves from all the filth of vice. They take care above all that their patience

*Gal 6:15

should shine like the light against all anger; even purity of heart should shine out against lust of the flesh. They should be alight with zeal against lethargy, they should glow red with serene gravity against confused action and precipitation, they should let humility shine brightly against pride and let the rays of authority be trained on fear. Since therefore they have accumulated so many zealous efforts in themselves first, it is as though in the conception of holy preaching they became months full of virtues. The Lord alone counts those months, because no one weighs the good things that are in their hearts except the one who gave them. And since according to the measure of virtues the effect of their fruits follows, the Lord rightly adds,

XII. 46. *Have you known the time when they bring forth?** You should hear underneath the words, "as I have? In fact, while I am counting the months of virtues in the thought, when they are able to prepare what they desire to fulfill, I know while I am looking at the hidden places of the heart the certain future effect in outward deed of what I measure in the internal weight of thought." The next verse:

*Job 39:2

XIII. 47. *They bend over towards the fetus and bring it forth, and they emit a groan.** Yes they groan, because they bend over in communion with light and give birth to souls in their audience, and because they cannot remove us from eternal punishment without tears and sighs. The holy preachers sow now with tears so that they may later reap the standing grain with joy.* Now they are like does bringing forth young with pain, so that they may later be fruitful with spiritual progeny. So that I may mention one among many, I see Paul like some female deer emitting a groan amidst great pain in bringing forth progeny. He writes, *My children, for whom I again suffer the pains of bringing forth until*

*Job 39:3

*Ps 125:5

Christ is formed in you: I only wish I could be with you, so I could change my speech, because I am upset about you.* See how he wants to change his speech in the midst of bringing them forth, so that his preaching voice may become a groan of pain. He changes his speech, because those whom he had already brought forth by his preaching, he again brought forth with a groan by reforming them.

*Gal 4:19-20

What kind of a groan did this female deer emit in giving birth when she was forced to exclaim to those who were backsliding, *O stupid Galatians, who has enthralled you? Are you so stupid as to have begun in the spirit and now to have ended in the flesh?** or surely, *You were running well; who has kept you from following the truth?** What kind of groan was that which this doe uttered in giving birth, when she brought forth the children with so much labor that she had long conceived, and when she realized that those once born had returned to the womb of malice? Let us reflect upon the extent of pain and of labor that she had when she was again forced to arouse what was dead, the conceived seed she had been able to bring forth.

*Gal 3:1, 3

*Gal 5:7

48. But we must above all notice that these does bend over in order that they may give birth, because of course they cannot give birth while standing erect. Unless the holy preachers, you see, descend from that measureless expanse of internal contemplation that they have received to our fragile nature, as though they were bending down with a kind of humble preaching, they would certainly never bring forth children in faith. They could without question not be advantageous to us if they remained in their upright position of loftiness. But let us look at the doe as she bends herself down to bring forth offspring. Accordingly, he says, *I could not speak to you as spiritual beings, but as carnal; as babes in Christ I* *fed you with milk, not solid food.** And he straightway follows up with the reason for this bending over and says, *Because you were not capable of it, nor are you even now capable.**

*1 Cor 3:1-2

*1 Cor 3:2

But let us see, I appeal to you, let us see this female deer bent over for our sakes, let us see him upright as he says, *We do speak of wisdom among those who are perfect,** and again, *If we are out of our minds it is for God.** When, however, he goes out of his mind to God, we absolutely do not understand his ecstasy. So in order that he may profit us, he bends down toward us. That is why he adds in the same passage, *If we are sober, it is for you.** Consequently, if the saints wished to preach to us what they understood when they were intoxicated with heavenly contemplation and did not rather speak of their knowledge as mediated with a certain moderation and normality, who would understand the words flowing out from that heavenly fountain through the narrow opening of intelligence?

*1 Cor 2:6
*2 Cor 5:13

*2 Cor 5:13

These bent-over does are in another place called heavens, about which we read, *O Lord, bend your heavens and come down.** And when the heavens bend down the Lord descends, because the holy teachers draw him down with their preaching, and they fill our hearts with the knowledge of divinity. God of course would never come down to us if his teachers remained inflexible in an unbending quality of contemplation. The heavens therefore bend down so that the Lord may descend, and the does bend over so that we may be born in the new light of faith. These does that bend over are called the breasts of the bride in the Song of Songs, where it is written, *Your breasts are better than wine.** These are the breasts that are held in the receptacle of the chest and that let us drink milk; they cling to the hidden place of heavenly contemplation and nourish us with refined preaching.

*Ps 143:5

*Song 1:1

Accordingly, so that they may draw us away from the eternal moaning and pain, the does now bend over and emit the groans of childbirth. However, because those who are born from the holy preaching of the patriarchs sometimes surpass their teachers in suffering, so that for those who are still living in this present life they may themselves finally end their lives in martyrdom, the Lord fittingly goes on:

XIV. 49. *Their children separate and go out to pasture; they leave them and do not return.** Holy Scripture calls pasture that fodder of eternal freshness where our feeding no longer stagnates with any withering dryness. It is about this pasture that the psalmist speaks: *The Lord is my ruler; I shall want for nothing. He has placed me where there is pasture.** And again: *We are his people, the sheep of his pasture.** Truth himself in fact says about these pastures, *If anyone enters by me, he will be safe; he will come and go and find pasture.** Accordingly they go to the pastures when they leave the body, and they find that food of internal freshness. They leave the pastures and do not return, because they have been received in that place of the contemplation of joy, and they have no further need of hearing words of teaching. They have gone then and do not return anymore, since they have escaped the trials of the present life. No longer do they require words of exhortation from teachers of life.

  Then indeed is fulfilled what has been written: *No longer will a person teach his neighbor, or an individual his brother, saying, "Know the Lord," because they will all know me from the least of them to the greatest, says the Lord.** Then is fulfilled what Truth says in the Gospel: *I will speak plainly to you of the Father.** The Son does speak plainly about the Father, because as I have said earlier, by the very fact that he is the Word he illuminates

*Job 39:4

*Ps 22:1-2
*Ps 94:7

*John 10:9

*Jer 31:34
*John 16:25

us from the nature of divinity. Accordingly, at that time they will not seek the teaching of words as if they were a kind of rivulets running down from the human tongue; no, they will then be inebriated from the very spring of truth. Consequently, since the bending over of female deer has been figuratively demonstrated, and a great deal has been said about the virtues of teachers, the discourse now turns toward the lives of those who desire the secret places of a far-removed way of life. In fact, such a life of retirement is to be sought by divine assistance and not by one's own resources, so the Lord says of such people,

XV. 50. *Who dismisses an unrestrained wild ass, or who frees it from its chains?** You should hear the whisper, "Who but I?" Actually, the wild ass that lives in the desert not unsuitably represents the life of those whose way of life is remote from where crowds of people congregate. The word *unrestrained* is also advisably used, because worldly business really amounts to a kind of slavery that excessively wears out the mind, even if the exertion is freely embraced. When anyone is free from that condition of slavery, he or she desires nothing further from the world. When any are pressed by a desired prosperity or by a feared adversity, they wear a kind of yoke of slavery. But if they once tear the mastery of worldly desires from their necks, they already enjoy a certain liberty even in this life without feeling any desire for happiness or being terrified by any fear of adversity. The Lord saw this heavy yoke of slavery inflicted upon the necks of worldly people when he said, *Come to me, all you who labor and are burdened, and I will give you rest. Take my yoke upon you. Learn from me, that I am meek and humble of heart, and your souls will find rest. My yoke is easy, and my burden light.**

*Job 39:5

*Matt 11:28-30

It is indeed a bitter yoke, as we have said, and a load of harsh slavery to be subject to temporalities, to walk earthly paths, to keep perishable goods, or to stand where there is no room to stand; it means indeed to desire passing things, but not to want to pass on with the passing things. While everything keeps passing against our will, you see—everything that had previously afflicted our mind because of our desire to obtain it—later the fear of losing it depresses us. So the mind freely lets it go so that, having trampled upon worldly desires, it is securely freed from the burden of grasping for worldly goods. *Who frees it from its chains?* Read into it, "except me."

51. Everyone is freed from his or her chains when the interior ropes of carnal desires are cut loose with divine help. Although our loving intention calls us to conversion, the frailty of the flesh still calls us back from following this intention, so that our soul is tied up and impeded with something like chains. We often see in fact many people who desire to be on the road to a holy way of life, but they are afraid either of headlong falls in the present or of future adversity, so they are hindered from following that road. While they are cautiously looking out for certain evil chances, they are incautiously held in the chains of their own sins. They place many obstacles in front of their eyes, and if those happen to them in their lives, they worry about not being able to stand against them. It is about such as these that Solomon says, *The way of sluggish people is like a thicket of thorns.** Although they desire God's road, presentiments of their own fears oppose and jab them, as if they were thorns of a surrounding thicket. Since such fears usually do not impede the chosen ones, however, Solomon straightway adds, *The road followed by the righteous is without a stumbling block.** Whatever adversity the righteous may meet in fact in their way of life does not hold them back, because they get across

*Prov 15:19

*Prov 15:19

obstacles of temporary adversity with the leap of eternal hope and internal contemplation. God accordingly frees the wild ass from its chains when he breaks the knots of weak thoughts for the souls of every one of the elect, and he kindly disposes of every bond that tied up the divided mind. The next verse:

XVI. 52. *To him I gave a home in the wilderness, and I pitched his tent in the land of salt.** What about the word *wilderness* here? Should we take it to refer to the body, or to the heart? But what good would a physical wilderness be if it were not also a wilderness of the heart? The one who lives apart physically while his worldly thoughts and desires are still planted in the troubled way of life of other people is not in the wilderness. On the other hand, anyone who is forced to live among crowds of people physically but at the same time allows no turbulent thoughts concerning worldly cares to stay in his heart is not in the city. Consequently, first the wilderness of the mind is granted to those who are living rightly, so that they may silence the uproar of worldly desires that is beginning to rise internally and that they may quell the complaints that are bursting out internally in the heart through the grace of heavenly love, quieting all the emotions and unstable thoughts revealing themselves awkwardly. They are like flies buzzing around; the chosen ones should brush them away from the eyes of the mind with a serious hand; they should look for a secret place within themselves that they can share with the Lord; there they can speak with him silently through their internal desires when the external noise has ceased.

*Job 39:6

53. About this secret place in the heart it is said elsewhere, *There was silence in heaven for about half an hour.** In fact the church of the chosen ones is called heaven; when they try to get there, that is, to the eternal

*Rev 8:1

heights, through the ascension of contemplation, they silence the noisy thoughts that rise up from the lowest depths, and within themselves they keep a kind of silence with God. Since that very silent contemplation cannot be perfect in this life, it is said to be kept for half an hour. The noisy din of the thoughts forces itself upon the unwilling soul, even when it is bound for the heights, and they violently draw the eye of the heart back to gaze again upon worldly affairs. That is why it is written, *The corruptible body weighs down the soul, and life on earth depresses the mind with many thoughts.** The silence kept is rightly described as lasting not a full hour, but half an hour, because contemplation here below is never perfect, no matter how zealously it is undertaken.

*Wis 9:15

This truth is conveniently expressed by the prophet Ezekiel, who is said to have seen in the man's hand a measuring reed six cubits and a handbreadth long to measure the city built on a mountain.* The church in fact is found on the mountain of the chosen ones, because it is not built upon base desires. What else does the cubit signify but the work, and what else the number six but perfection? Are we not told that the Lord completed all his work on the sixth day? What is the significance of the handbreadth added to the six cubits if not the vigorous contemplation that already signifies the beginning of the eternal Sabbath rest? But because here below contemplation of eternity is never perfect, the measure of seven cubits is not fulfilled. So since the church of the chosen ones fulfills all the work to be done, it makes the city built on the mountain six cubits long. But because here below only the beginning of contemplation is as yet envisaged, only the handbreadth after the seventh cubit is touched.

*Ezek 40:5

54. What we must know, however, is that we never attain the peak of contemplation if we do not stop bearing the oppression of external concerns. We never look at ourselves so that we could know that the ruling rational nature is different from the animal nature that is ruled, so that having recourse to the secret place of silence we could sleep away from any external disturbance. Adam also prefigured by his sleep this silent place of ours, during which a woman quickly emerged from his side. Any in fact who are snatched away to the understanding of what is internal closes his or her eyes to visible reality; then they distinguish in themselves either the elements that should rule in a masculine sense, or on the other hand the weaknesses that may be ruled, so that there should be something in them that can rule as a man, and something else that is ruled as feminine. Accordingly, in this silence of the heart, while we stay awake internally in contemplation, it is as though we were asleep externally. Since then people are far away, that is, strangers to carnal desire, they inhabit this silence of the mind, but the Lord gave this wild ass a home in the wilderness, so that he might not be harassed by the crowd of worldly desires.

55. *I pitched his tent in the land of salt.** Salt water tends to aggravate thirst. As long as the saints pass their lives in the tents of this life, they are stirred up by the daily passion of their desire for the heavenly homeland, but here they are said to pitch their tents in a salty land. They are unceasingly stirred up so that they might be thirsty, and they thirst so that they might be satisfied, as it is written: *Blessed are they who are hungry and thirsty for justice, because they will be satisfied.** The next verse:

*Job 39:6

*Matt 5:6

XVII. 56. *He scorns the crowds in the city.** To scorn the crowds in the city means to avoid the perverse concentration on human activity, so that one is no longer free to imitate the reckless behavior of worldly people,

*Job 39:7

of whom there are many and who practice iniquity in large measure. They desire to enter the narrow gate with the few, rather than following the many who journey along the broad highway that leads to ruin.* They cleverly keep their eyes fixed on their Creator and on what they were created for, and by righteous consideration of the image they have received they disdain the following of the common multitude. That is why the Bridegroom in the Song of Songs speaks up and tells the bride, *If you do not know, O most lovely of women, go out and follow the tracks of the flock; feed your kids.**

*Matt 7:13-14

*Song 1:7 Vulg

She who is beautiful among women knows herself when any chosen soul, even when placed among sinners, remembers that she has been created in the image and likeness of her Creator, and she walks on according to the order of the likeness she has received. If she does not know herself, she goes out, because she has been expelled from the secret place of the heart, and she wanders among external desires. She has gone out, and she follows the tracks of the flock; she has abandoned her interior life, and she is led along the broad highway; she follows the example of the peoples. She no longer feeds lambs, but goats, because it is not harmless thoughts of the mind but bad carnal emotions that she is inclined to feed. Since therefore every temperate chosen one disdains to follow the tracks of the flock, let it be rightly said, *He scorns the crowds in the city.* So he aptly goes on:

Job 39:7

XVIII. 57. *He does not hear the cry of the creditor.** Who else could we suppose this creditor to be but the Devil, who once in Paradise lent the human being a coin of evil persuasion and now daily demands the payment of this debt from every human being? The speech of this creditor is the beginning of evil persuasion. The shout of this creditor is no longer a light but a violent temptation. This creditor speaks softly when he persuades; this creditor shouts when he tempts out loud. Not to listen to the creditor's shouts then certainly means not to consent to the violent emotions of temptation. Obviously we would listen if we did what he persuades us to do. But when we disdain to act perversely it is rightly said, *He does not hear the shouts of the creditor.**

Job 39:7

58. There are some people however who prefer to understand "stomach" here by the word *creditor*. The stomach, you see, demands from us the payment of a kind of debt, because even by nature it expects the daily fruit of human labor to be paid it. Accordingly those people who abstain are in this passage prefigured by the use of the words *wild ass*, because they repress the violent demands of the stomach, so they disdain the violent demands of that shouting creditor. But when they exchange for innumerable vices in the continent person a large number of virtues that have been fought for, why do they only support restraint of the forceful attacks of the stomach here by saying that the cries of the creditor should be disdained? Perhaps they maintain that no one gets the prize in the spiritual battle who does not first win the victory over the urges of the flesh in himself through denying self-indulgence in the stomach?

Nor do we rise to the level of the spiritual struggle and combat if we do not first subdue the enemy already positioned within us: the appetite for food. Obviously, if we do not defeat the enemy that is closest to us, it is certainly a vain attempt to go on to fight an enemy that is farther away. It is useless to wage war against an external enemy in the field, if we have within the city's walls a treacherous citizen. The very mind of the fighter is discredited by its confusion and is driven away from engaging in the spiritual combat when it is run through and beaten by the weak swords of the flesh in the battle against gluttony. Seeing itself beaten by a minor foe, it is ashamed to engage in more serious combat.

59. Some people, however, are unmindful of the order of battle and neglect the subjugation of the appetites; instead they rise up immediately for the spiritual war. Sometimes they do in fact accomplish much that shows great courage, but when the vice of gluttony masters them, they lose all that they had courageously wrought through the allurement of the flesh; when there is no restraint of the stomach, the concupiscence of the flesh destroys all the virtues at once. That is why it is written about the victory of Nebuchadnezzar, *The captain of the cooks destroyed the walls of Jerusalem.*[3]* What does Holy Scripture mean to express here by the walls of Jerusalem if not the virtues of the soul that is tending towards the vision of peace? Whom do we take the captain of the cooks to indicate but the stomach that the cooks serve with the most zealous care? Accordingly the captain of the cooks destroys the walls of Jerusalem; accordingly when there is no restraint upon the stomach it destroys the virtues of the soul.

That is why Paul undermines the forces of the captain of the cooks who attack the walls of Jerusalem and says, *I chastise my body and force it into subjection, lest while preaching to others I should ever chance to become reprobate.** That is also why he said first, *I run, not as though uncertain, and I fight, not as if battering the air.** In fact when we restrain the flesh with the

*2 Kgs 25:10; Jer 52:14

*1 Cor 9:27

*1 Cor 9:26

---

[3] The reference to 2 [4] Kgs 25:8 given in CCSL 143B:1530, lines 40–41, is incorrect. It should be 2 [4] Kgs 25:10 (according to NAB OSV 1976), which agrees with Jer 52:14. Obviously Gregory (and perhaps the codex of the Vulgate or the LXX he was using) mistranslates "of the Chaldeans" as "of the cooks" (Latin *coquorum*). It fits in neatly with Gregory's allegorical interpretation, of course.

very blows of our continence, it is not the air that we batter, but the unclean spirits, and when we bring our interior parts into subjection, we do battle against the external foes who are drawn up against us. That is why the king of Babylon ordered the furnace to be heated and loaded with naphtha, hemp, pitch, and kindling wood.* Nevertheless this fire did not consume the abstaining boys at all, because although the ancient enemy parades numberless desires for food before our gaze to make the fire of bodily craving hotter, the grace of the heavenly Spirit rushes in to good minds, and they remain unhurt by the fire of concupiscence of the flesh, so that even if the flames are heated to the point of temptation in the heart, temptation does not burn there all the way to the point of consent.

*Dan 3:19-20, 46

60. Besides, we must realize that there are five ways for gluttony to tempt us. Sometimes it comes just before a period of indigence; sometimes, however, it does not precede that period but seeks more sumptuous meals; sometimes it wants its meals to be more meticulously prepared; sometimes the quality of the food and the right time coincide, but the quantity of food to be consumed exceeds the measure of satisfaction; sometimes on the other hand one desires only the commonplace, and yet one sins worse by the very fervor of extreme desire. Jonathan indeed deserved the sentence of death from his father's mouth, because by tasting honey he anticipated the mealtime Saul had decreed.* The people who had been led out of Egypt fell down in the desert because they disdained the manna and demanded meat to eat that they felt to be more satisfying. The first sin that Eli's sons committed was that the priest's servant would not accept boiled meat from anyone who offered sacrifice, as was the ancient custom, but demanded raw meat, which he meticulously pulled out.* Jerusalem was told, *This pride*

*1 Sam 14:27

*1 Sam 2:12-17

was the sin of your sister, Sodom, as well as abundance and satiety of bread.* So we are clearly shown the reason that she lost salvation: by the vice of pride she exceeded the measure of moderate refreshment.

*Ezek 16:49

Esau lost the honor of the firstborn because under the intense passion of desire he wanted the base food of lentils that he preferred to the honor of the firstborn that he sold,* having clearly shown his panting desire for the lentils. His vice was not the food but the appetite. Of course we often consume more sumptuous food than that without any sin, and the more common foods we taste not without guilt in our conscience. Here indeed it is Esau we are talking about, the one who lost the rights of the firstborn for the sake of lentils, but Elijah in the desert preserved the strength of his body by eating meat.[4]* So even the ancient enemy knew that it was not the food, but the panting desire for food that was the cause of condemnation, and he subjected the first man to himself not with flesh, but with fruit,* and he tempted the second man* not with flesh, but with bread.* That is why Adam's sin is often committed even when base and common food is eaten. Nor was Adam alone told to avoid the forbidden fruit when he received the order of prohibition. No, when God shows us that any food is bad for our health, he denies us that food by force of decree. And when our desires reach out for what is bad, what else do we do, may I ask, but taste what is forbidden?

*Gen 25:33-34

*1 Kgs 17:6

*Gen 3:1-5
*Christ
*Matt 4:3

61. We must then consume what the needs of nature require us to, not what a longing for eating suggests. But it is a major work of discretion for this overseer to provide the one and refuse the other, or by not providing to tighten the throat and by providing to nourish nature.

---

[4] But Elijah's case clearly mentions a hearth cake, not meat!

This discretion is perhaps implied when it is said, *He does not hear the shouts of the creditor.** The words of this creditor are of course the necessary demands of nature. When its cries go beyond the measure of necessity, they are the instinctive appetite. This wild ass therefore hears the creditor's words, but not his cries, because the discreet, moderate person nourishes the stomach up to the point of temperate satisfaction and restrains his pleasures.

*Job 39:7

62. We must realize, however, that pleasure so hides itself behind necessity that even the perfect can hardly discern it. While necessity, you see, is asking for the debt to be paid, pleasure behind it asks for its desire to be fulfilled. The more it covers itself with the honest name of fulfilling necessity, the more confidently it prods the stomach on. However, it often secretly follows closely behind necessity on its way to eat; sometimes it even shamelessly and freely tries to precede necessity. It is easy to catch pleasure in the act of anticipating its necessity; however, it is difficult to discern when it secretly joins necessity in the act of eating, because it follows the natural appetite that precedes, and walking behind the latter it is only later perceived. At the very time that necessity's debt is paid, pleasure is mixed with the necessity of eating, so we do not know what necessity requires or what, as has been said, pleasure requests. However, we often do discern something, and because we realize that something has been added, in the circumstance that we have been forced to go beyond the limits, it can happen that we are knowingly deceived, and while the mind is being coaxed by necessity, it is deceived by pleasure. Of course it is written, *Do not be concerned about the flesh in your desires.** We are then told to do nothing by desire, but we are allowed necessity.

*Rom 13:14

63. It often happens however that when we allow ourselves what is necessary, we also satisfy our desires.

And sometimes, while we immoderately refuse our desires, we make our suffering from necessity worse. So it is necessary for each one of us to occupy a stronghold of self-control where we put to death not the flesh itself, but its bad habits. It often happens, you see, that when we restrain the flesh too much, our ability to perform good works is also weakened, so that we cannot either pray or preach, because we are in a hurry to stifle the last urges of the vices. We have a helper, however, for our internal intention: that is the exterior man we carry around with us. Even the interior emotions of unruly behavior are there, and their effects support the doing of good works. We often in fact persecute him as the enemy, even the citizen we love, and we cut him down. Often enough we spare the fellow citizen whom we nourish for battle, and he is the enemy. Vices grow proud on the same foods on which the virtues thrive and live. While the virtues are being fed, the vices often grow strong as well. Even when there is boundless continence, it spreads out the force of vice, so that virtue itself weakens and grows weary. So it is needful for our interior man to have a kind of impartial judge to decide between itself and the external man that operates outside us, inasmuch as this exterior person should always suffice to perform a service owed to the internal and never presume to contradict it with a stiff-necked pride; nor should it move to suggest anything by a suppressed whisper, as long as it has that judge standing over it with its raised heel of domination ready to crush it.

So it happens that while we indeed allow the repressed vices to oppose us, we forbid them to walk with us on the same level, and we do not let the vices prevail against any virtue, nor do we let any virtue succumb with the vices in any kind of ruin. In that case pride alone is done away with at bottom, because whatever victory is in question, the continuous battle helps us to tame the pride of thoughts. So it is well that here, since every continent person is equal to the payment of the debt of necessity and can contradict the violence of desires, the Lord's voice speaks: *He does not hear the shouts of the creditor.** The discreet person therefore lifts himself up to the understanding of higher things, because he chastises the incitements of the flesh in himself, so having disdained the creditor's cries, the Lord goes on:

*Job 39:7

XIX. 64. *He looks around at the pasturing ground on his mountains.** The pasturing ground on his mountains is the lofty contemplation of his internal refreshment. The more, you see, that the saints despise themselves externally and cast themselves down, the more they are internally refreshed by contemplation of what has been revealed. That is why it is written, *He arranged the climbing stages of his heart in the valley of tears.** In other words, those whom the valley of humility encloses externally in tears, the ascent of contemplation raises internally. The pasturing ground on his mountains is identified as the lofty virtues of angels. These virtues refresh us here below with their services and help, because there above they grow rich with the dew of internal contemplation. Because by God's bounty they protect us in all our struggles, they are rightly said to look around. We see them waiting on us. They are all around us, by whose defense against our adversaries we are protected on every side. The mountains of pasturing ground can even be taken to mean the lofty declarations of Holy Scripture about which the Psalmist said, *The high mountains are for the deer.** Those, you see, who already know how to make the leap of contemplation ascend the heights of the divine declarations as if they were the highest mountains; feeble-minded people obviously cannot reach those heights, so it is rightly added here, *The*

*Job 39:8

*Ps 83:6-7

*Ps 103:18

*Ps 103:18 — *hedgehog lives among the rocks.** The feeble-minded obviously do not seek high intelligence, because only faith in Christ contents the humble. The next verse:

*Job 39:8 — **XX. 65.** *He searches for all the green plants.** Dried-out plants are doubtless all the things that have been made in time, and with the coming end are dried up from the happiness of the present life as if by the summer sun. They are called green plants that do not wither with any touch of the things of time. So for this wild ass to search for green plants means that any one of the saints, having despised the things of time, desires those that remain forever.

All those words, however, that were spoken about the wild ass can also be understood in a different way. So we shall repeat the above verses with a new exposition, so that we may leave the choice to the reader's judgment. Therefore, after the arrangement of preachers was described using the image of the deer, so that we might show through whom this same virtue of preaching is granted, in the same passage we commemorated the Lord's incarnation, where it was said,

*Job 39:5 — **XXI. 66.** *Who dismisses an unrestrained wild ass?** No one would judge it unworthy for the Lord's incarnation to be signified by such an animal when a signification exists in Holy Scripture already: namely the worm and the beetle. Is it not written, *I am a worm*

*Ps 21:7 — *and no man*?* According to the Septuagint translation

*Hab 2:11 LXX — the prophet says, *The beetle cried out from the tree.** When therefore the Lord is signified by such mean and base creatures as those that have been named, how can it be called insulting to him, since in fact nothing befitting him can be said? He is called a lamb because of his innocence, he is called a lion because of his power, sometimes too he is compared to a serpent on account of death or wisdom. So all these words can be used for him figuratively, because nothing can be essentially believed about any of them.

Actually if any one of them did exist essentially, no other could be mentioned any more. If the lamb could be named with propriety, the lion could no longer be named. If the lion could be named with propriety, he could no longer be signified by the serpent. But we speak of all these things concerning the Lord as broadly figuratively as they are far from being essentially true. The wild ass can therefore signify the incarnate Lord. But the wild ass is an animal of the field. And since the incarnate Lord profited the Gentiles more than the Jews, he assumed the body of an animal, as one who came not to the house, as it were, but instead to the field. The psalmist of course speaks of this field of the Gentiles as follows: *The form of the field is mine.** Accordingly the incarnate Lord is in the form of God equal to the Father, but in the form of a slave less than the Father, by which he is also less than himself.

*Ps 49:12

Let the Father therefore say of the Son according to the form of the slave, *Who dismisses an unrestrained wild ass, or who frees it from its chains?** *Everyone who sins is a slave of sin.** Since the incarnate Lord was made a partaker of our nature, but not of our sin, he is called free and dismissed, because he is not held under the dominion of sin. About him it is written elsewhere, *He is free among the dead.** He is said to be dismissed and free, because receiving our nature, he is in no way held bound by the yoke of iniquity. Although the stain of our guilt did not touch him, nevertheless the passion of our mortal nature did confine him. So after he was called free and dismissed, it is rightly added concerning him,

*Job 39:5
*John 8:34

*Ps 87:6

XXII. 67. *Who frees it from its chains?** His chains were loosed precisely at the time when the frailty of his passion was changed into the glory of the resurrection.

*Job 39:5

The Lord wore some kind of chains that were equal to our sufferings on account of depravity: the frailty of our mortal nature. He freely willed to be bound with these chains even until death, and he miraculously loosed them through the resurrection. The chain of our mortal nature amounted to hunger, thirst, weariness, and being apprehended, flogged, and crucified. But when his death was complete and the veil of the temple was rent asunder, rocks were broken, graves stood open, and the gates of hell were loosed, what else are we shown by so many proofs of such great power except that all those chains of our frailty were loosed, so that he who had come to receive the form of a slave was freed from the chains of hell in that very same form of a slave, and returned to heaven free along with his members? And concerning these very chains of his the apostle Peter bears witness and says, *God raised him up after having done away with the pains of hell, since it was impossible for him to be held by them.** And since, after his death and resurrection, he deigned to call the Gentiles to the grace of faith, after we were told that his chains were loosed, the Lord rightly adds,

*Acts 2:24

XXIII. 68. *To him I gave a home in the wilderness, and I pitched his tent in the land of salt.** Among the Gentiles of course there was no patriarch, nor was there a prophet. In fact there was no one partaking of the use of reason to know God. There was hardly a man. Isaiah speaks about this wilderness: *The desert and the wasteland will rejoice; the wilderness will exult, and it will blossom like the lily.** He also speaks about the church: *He will make his desert a paradise and his wilderness like the Lord's garden.** This same wasteland is renamed land of salt; before it knew the true wisdom of God, it produced salt water; it produced no green freshness of good intelligence, but knew only perver-

*Job 39:6

*Isa 35:1

*Isa 51:3

sity. God then accepted a home in the wilderness and a tent in the salty land when he became incarnate for men; having abandoned Judea, he possessed the hearts of Gentiles. Accordingly the Father's voice was carried to him through the prophet who said, *Ask it of me, and I will give you the nations as an inheritance, and for your possession I will give you the ends of the earth.**

*Ps 2:8

By the fact that he is God, with the Father he gives us all things; by the fact that he is man, he accepts all from the Father, as it is written: *He has given him power to exercise judgment, because he is the Son of man.** Elsewhere it is written, *Jesus knew that the Father entrusted everything in his hands.** Or as he said of himself, *All that the Father gives me will come to me.** But now, if we want to know the difference between home and tent, a home is a permanent habitation, but a tent is used on a journey. He stayed in the Gentiles' hearts as though making use of tents at his coming, but by confirming justice in those hearts he made them home and dwelled there. And because he despised the imitation of their lives to whom he had come, the Lord rightly adds,

*John 5:27
*John 13:3
*John 6:37

XXIV. 69. *He disdained the multitude in the city.** In other words, he despised the behavior of human association. He became a man and lived among humans, but he refused to follow the practices of humans. For this purpose he became man among us: not only that he might redeem us by his blood poured out, but also that he might change us by showing us an example. In association with us therefore he found one way of life at his coming, and taught another by living it. It was the eager goal of all those previously born of the proud race of Adam to desire prosperity in the present life and avoid adversity, to shun insults and attain honors. The Lord became incarnate among them to desire adversity and spurn prosperity, to embrace insults and shun honors.

*Job 39:7

When the Jews wanted to make him a king over them, he fled being made a king.* When however they set out to kill him, he went willingly to the gibbet of the cross.*

*John 6:15
*John 18:4

Accordingly he fled what all people desire, and he desired what all people flee. But while he fled what all people desire and desired what all people flee, he did what all people would wonder at, so that he, the dead one, would rise and by his death raise up others from death. There are in fact two lives for human beings who exist in a body: one before bodily death, the other after the resurrection, one that all people had known by experience, but the other that they did not know, and the human race expected only that one that it knew about. The Lord came in the flesh, and while he lived the one life, he displayed the other. While he received the one life that is known to us, he demonstrated the other that we do not know. By dying he lived out the one life that we live, but by rising he opened up the other life that we seek. He taught us by his own example that this life that we lead before dying should not be loved for its own sake, but rather endured for the sake of that other life. Since therefore he practiced a new way of life among people, and he was no follower of the behavior of Babylon, it is rightly written about him, *He disdained the multitude in the city.**

*Job 39:7

70. Or at least it shows that he deserted the multitude that goes wandering along the spacious highway and chose the few who walk the narrow way. To disdain the multitude in the city means to condemn that part of the human race that enters the broad highway and that is large because of the multitude of iniquity; it does not share the lot of his kingdom.

*Job 39:7

XXV. 71. *He does not hear the shouts of the creditor.** As we have said above, whom else can we take to be the creditor in this passage but the devil? By persuading us to do evil he conferred the hope of immortality, but by deception he exacted the tribute of death. By persuasion he introduced guilt; in his rage he demanded punishment. The speech of this creditor before human death was cunning persuasion; after that death his cry was already violent plunder. Those whom he secretly traps before death, he violently seizes after death to share his punishment. But when the Lord comes to his own death, he does not fear the violent attack of this creditor, since he himself said, *The prince of this world is coming, and over me he has no power.** *John 14:30

So the Lord was right to say, *He does not hear the shouts of the creditor.** The creditor of the human race really does come to him, because he sees that he is a man. But the one he thinks to be a contemptible man of weakness, he senses to be more than a man and strong. Laban certainly typified this creditor when he angrily chased Jacob to demand his idols.* The name *Laban* in fact is interpreted "whitewash." Even the devil is not inappropriately taken to mean "whitewash." Indeed, while he is deservedly dark, he transforms himself into the likeness of an angel of light. Jacob served Laban, that is, Jacob represented the Jewish people who were of the party of reprobate sinners, from whose flesh the incarnate Lord comes. Laban can also represent the present world that furiously persecutes Jacob, because by persecution it tries to kill the chosen ones who are members of our Redeemer. Jacob carried away Laban's daughter, that is, either the world's or the devil's daughter, when Christ joined the Gentile church to himself. Christ also carried that church away from her father's house, because he told her through the prophet, *Forget your own people and your father's house.** *Job 39:7

*Gen 31:22-30

*Ps 44:11

And what else do the idols signify but avarice? Does not Paul say, *Avarice is slavery to idols*?* Laban *Col 3:5

therefore chased Jacob but did not find an idol, because when the devil showed him the riches of the world, he found no trace of worldly concupiscence in our Redeemer.* But by sitting Rachel covered up what Jacob did not have. Rachel is also called a sheep, and she in fact is a figure of the church. The act of sitting means to desire the humility of repentance, since it is written, *Get up after you sit down.** So Rachel covered up the idols by sitting on them, because Holy Church by following Christ in repentance covered up the vices of worldly concupiscence. The prophet says about this covering of vices, *Blessed are they whose sins are forgiven, whose misdeeds are hidden.**

*Matt 4:8-9

*Ps 126:2 LXX

*Ps 31:1

Accordingly Rachel signified us, and we by sitting repress the idols if by repentance we condemn the guilt of avarice. Avarice in fact is usually not committed by those who manfully run along the road of the Lord, to whom it is said, *Act like a man and strengthen your heart.** But it is rather committed by those who, stepping lightly with ladylike steps, grow limp through worldly blandishments. That is why in the same passage* Rachel speaks these words: *It has happened to me according to women's usual experience.** In Jacob's possession therefore no idols were found, because the cunning creditor did not find in our Redeemer anything to reproach. About this creditor our Redeemer who frees the Gentiles from his dominion is told by the prophet, *You have prevailed over his yoke and burden, the rod of his shoulder, and the scepter of his creditor, as on the day of Midian.**

*Ps 30:25

*of Genesis

*Gen 31:35

*Isa 9:4

The Lord really did free the Gentiles and remove their yoke and burden when he freed them by his coming from that slavery of the demonic tyrant. He prevailed over his rod and burden when he blocked the blow that was heavily swung from perverse actions and deflected it from the redeemed human race. He overcame the creditor's scepter when he destroyed the kingdom of the devil in the hearts of the faithful, of that creditor who had been accustomed to exact the punishment owed for the death-dealing perpetration of vices.

73. But let us hear how all this was done. It follows in the same passage: *as on the day of Midian.* I do not think it will be superfluous for us to discuss here a bit more at length that war against the Midianites that the prophet astutely brought up to compare with the Lord's coming. The Book of Judges in fact describes how Gideon took up the fight against Midian. When he gathered a large army for the war, he was directed by the divine oracle to watch how, when they came to the river, the soldiers knelt to drink the water, and to dismiss some of them from the battle. It happened that only three hundred of them stood drinking the water from their hands, and these were kept. These Gideon led to battle, and he armed them not with weapons but with trumpets, torches, and jars. So, as it is written there, they lighted the torches, put them in the jars, held the trumpets in their right hands with the jars in their left, and coming at close quarters with their enemies, they blew the trumpets, broke the jars, and held the torches; the enemy were terrified at the sound of the trumpets and the halo of light and turned to flight.

How is it that such a battle is publicly introduced by the prophet and its victory compared to the coming of the Redeemer? Did the prophet intend to show us that the victory of the battle led by Gideon illustrated the coming of our Redeemer against the Devil? Such actions in fact were mentioned there as transcend the usual order of battle inasmuch as they remain within the mystery of prophecy. What army ever approached a battle with jars and torches? What army opposed weapons without weapons? These proceedings would have seemed ridiculous to us if they had not terrified the enemy. But we have learned from the testimony of victory not to estimate lightly the things Gideon did.

When he arrives at the battle then, it signals the Redeemer's coming, of whom it is said, *Lift up your heads, you gates; let the eternal gates be lifted up, and the King of glory will enter. Who is this King of glory? The Lord strong and mighty, the Lord strong in battle.** He prophesied not only the Redeemer at work, but also his name. The name Gideon is interpreted as "the one who encircles the womb." Our Lord, you see, surrounds all things through the power of his majesty, but through the grace of his plan he comes to the virgin's womb. Who is the one who encircled the womb, who else but almighty God, who redeems us by his plan, embraces all things by his divinity, and assumes humanity inside the womb? And in that womb he both was made flesh and was not enclosed, because within the womb he remained through the material reality of weakness while he was still outside the world through the power of majesty. The name *Midian* is interpreted "belonging to judgment." So that the Redeemer's enemies could be opposed and destroyed, the event belonged not to the disadvantage of the one who opposed but to the judgment of the one who judges justly. That is why they are called "belonging to judgment," because they are estranged from the Redeemer's grace, and they deserve righteous condemnation even by the words behind their name.

74. So against them came Gideon with his army of three hundred prepared for battle. The number one hundred is ordinarily understood as the fullness of perfection. Accordingly, what else does the number one hundred multiplied by three signify but the perfect knowledge of the Trinity? With them in fact our Lord destroys the adversaries of faith. With them he comes

*Ps 23:7-8

down for the war of preaching, that is, with those who are able to know the divine, who know what God is from the Trinity, who perceive perfection. It is noteworthy however that this number of three hundred is contained in the letter Tau, whose figure is the cross. And if we place on the horizontal line of that letter the one who hangs upon the cross, it is no longer the figure of the cross, but the cross itself. Since therefore this number of three hundred is contained in the letter Tau, and through the letter Tau, as we have said, the figure of the cross is shown, it is not improper that in these three hundred soldiers following Gideon those are signified to whom it was said, *If anyone wants to come after me, let him deny himself, take up his cross, and follow me.** *Matt 16:24

As for those who follow the Lord, the more truly they take up the cross, the more completely they control themselves, and they are crucified by compassion and charity towards their neighbors. That is why the prophet Ezekiel says, *The sign of the Tau was on the foreheads of those who were grieving and crying.** Well, at least these three hundred symbolized by the letter Tau signify the fact that the enemy's weapons are turned back by the wood of the cross. The soldiers were brought to the river so that they might drink water, and whoever kneeled down to drink water was excluded from the warlike purpose. The teaching of wisdom is denoted by water, and the standing posture signifies correct action. Those then who are represented as having knelt to drink water were excluded from participation in the battle and war, and they went away, because Christ goes with them to do battle against the enemies of the faith, who, when they drink the water of teaching, do not bend the stability of righteous action. *Ezek 9:4

We are then told that all the soldiers drank water, but not all of them stood without bending the knee, but those who knelt down to drink water are condemned, since, as the apostle bears witness: *It is not the hearers of the law who are righteous in God's sight, but the doers of the law will be justified.** As we have said, laxity of action is signified in the very bending of the knee, so Paul is again right in saying, *Lift up your listless hands and your wobbly knees.** Accordingly those go ahead to war under the leadership of Christ who show by their works what they proclaim with their mouths, who spiritually drink the water of teaching, but not those who are carnally bent over by depraved actions, since it is written, *There is no comely praise in the sinner's mouth.**

*Rom 2:13

*Heb 12:12

*Sir 15:9

75. So they engaged battle with trumpets, with jars, and with torches. And as I have said, this was the order of battle: they blew the trumpets, they put the torches inside the jars, they broke the jars and held out the torches; the enemy were terrified by the glittering light and turned to flight. The blowing of trumpets signifies the sound of preaching, the lamps the brightness of miracles, the jars the fragility of bodies. Such are the warriors our Leader took with him to the battle of preaching; they disdained bodily safety but cut down their enemies by dying; they were victorious over their swords without swords or armor but with patience. Our martyrs followed their Leader to battle armed with trumpets, jars, and torches. By preaching they sounded their trumpets; they broke their jars when they opposed the enemy's swords with their own bodies to be destroyed in their passion; their torches radiated light when after the destruction of their bodies they glittered with miracles. Their enemies soon took to flight when they saw the bodies of the dead martyrs shine out with miracles; they were broken by the light of truth and believed the truth they had fought against. The trumpets sounded so that the jars might break; the jars broke so that the torches might shine out; the torches shone so that the enemy might be put to flight. In other words, the martyrs preached until their bodies were destroyed in death; their bodies were destroyed in death so that they might shine with miracles; they shone with miracles so that their enemies might fall prostrate under the divine light inasmuch as they by no means stood erect to resist God but were subject to him in fear.

76. And it should be noticed that the enemy stood opposite the jars and fled before the torches, because of course the persecutors of Holy Church resisted the preachers of the faith while they were still bodily present, but after the destruction of their bodies the miracles were witnessed, and then the persecutors were put to flight; terrified by fright, they stopped persecuting the faithful. Obviously the preaching of the trumpets led to the broken jars of bodies, and these in turn led to the torches of miracles, which the persecutors saw and feared.

77. There is another thing we should notice about this text: The soldiers held the trumpets in their right hands, but the jars in their left; we are customarily said to consider anything held in the right hand as important but anything held in the left as worthless. It is rightly written there accordingly that they held trumpets in their right hands and jars in their left, because the martyrs of Christ consider the grace of preaching important, but the life of the body of minor value. Whoever then considers the life of the body to be more important than the grace of preaching holds the trumpet in the left hand and the jar in the right. If we are careful to give the grace of preaching pride of place, consequently, and less importance to the body, we certainly hold the trumpet in our right hand and the jar in our left.

That is why the Lord says in the gospel, *People do not light a lamp to put it under a table; no, they put it on* a stand so it can shed light on everything in the house.* We take the table to mean temporary advantage, but the lamp is the light of preaching; to put the lamp underneath the table, then, is to hide the grace of preaching for the sake of temporary advantage, and none of the elect does that. And the gospel is right to add, *on a stand.* The candlestick signifies the bodily state, on top of which the candle is placed, so that careful preaching is given more importance than the body itself. So the prophet was right to say, *You have prevailed over the scepter of his creditor, as on the day of Midian.** [*Matt 5:15] [*Isa 9:4]

But since I have spoken long enough for the purpose of the exposition of the prophet's testimony, let us return to the logical sequence of our work. Therefore, after we were told, *He does not hear the shouts of the creditor,** since the Lord now revealed in the flesh obviously disdained the traps of the ancient enemy, he rightly adds something about his chosen ones, saying, [*Job 39:7]

XXVI. 78. *He looks around at the pasturing ground on his mountains.** We take the mountains to mean all the proud ones in this world whose heart is swollen up higher than the earth. But since the Lord also implants such as these in the body of his church after they have been converted, and changes their former pride, transforming them into his own members, these mountains of pasture are his, because of course he is fed by the conversion of those who were wandering and by the humility of the proud, as he has said himself, *My food is the doing of the will of him who sent me.** He also ordered the apostles when he sent them out to preach, *Do not labor for perishable food, but for the food that remains for eternal life.** [*Job 39:8] [*John 4:34] [*John 6:27]

The prophet also spoke of these mountains: *The Lord will not reject his people, because in his hand are all the ends of the earth, and he looks down at the high moun-*

*tains.*⁵* High mountains indeed are the exalted feelings of proud people. But the Lord is said to look down on them, that is, he changes their iniquity into something better. The one on whom the Lord looks down he converts. That is why it is written, *The Lord turned around and looked at Peter, and Peter remembered the words the Lord had spoken, "Before the cock crows, you will deny me three times." And he went out and wept bitterly.** Solomon says for his part, *The King who sits on the throne of judgment puts all evils to flight by his glance.** The prophet again says about this glance at the mountains, *The mountains will run like wax away from the face of the Lord.** After the hardening of their perversity, you see, they were liquefied out of fear of God, and in their hardened shell first they spread out from him.

*Ps 94:4

*Luke 22:61-62

*Prov 20:8

*Ps 96:5

79. We should also notice that he did not say, "He inspects," but *He looks around at the pasturing ground on his mountains.* The Lord in fact became incarnate in Judea, whose location is surrounded by Gentiles. On this account he looked around at the mountains, because he gathered the proud ones of this world, who were somehow posted all over out of all the Gentile countries. He grazed in these mountains, because he was satisfied by the good works of the converts as though from green pastures. That is why the bride's voice says to him in the Song of Songs, *Where do you graze, and where do you lie down in the middle of the day?** The Lord grazes when he takes delight in our actions. He lies down in the middle of the day when he finds a cool place of good thoughts in the breasts of his chosen ones, away from carnal desires in the ardent hearts of reprobate sinners.

*Song 1:6

---

⁵ The words *The Lord will not reject his people* are not part of the quotation from Ps 94 but are apparently Gregory's introduction to it.

Matthew was a kind of mountain when he grew fat on the profits of the customs office, but about him it is written that after he came to believe, he invited the Lord to his house and organized a great feast. So this mountain provided the grass of a fresh green pasture for this grazing beast, because he fed him externally with a banquet and internally with the food of virtues. And this fact is explained most fully in what follows:

XXVII. 80. *He searches for all the green plants.** He abandons what withers and searches for all the green plants. The human hearts are withering that are ready to perish as planted in the hope of this world and that have no confidence in eternity. They are fresh and green, however, planted in that inheritance about which the apostle Peter spoke: *An incorruptible, unspoiled, and unfading inheritance.** The more firmly anyone plants the root of his thought in his share of the imperishable inheritance, the more truly green he is. Whoever then is worried about withering internally should externally flee the withering desires of this world. Whoever desires to persistently seek his eternal homeland from the Lord should earnestly grow greener in the internal soil of his heart.

81. These words of exposition, however, on the subject of the twofold understanding of the wild ass should be sufficient. It must be left to the reader's judgment what should be further sought. If by chance he should disdain either interpretation, I will myself freely follow my reader's lead, if he understands the text more wisely and more truly, as a disciple follows his teacher, because I properly believe to be given to me whatever I know that I understand better. All of us, you see, who have a great deal of faith and who try to speak fittingly about God, are organs of truth, and it is in the power of the same truth whether I hear it from another or another hears it from me. Truth in fact is in our midst, yet she

*Job 39:8

*1 Pet 1:4

is not the same to all the living or in the same way, and she often touches one person so that he or she hears well what she says through another, but on the other hand she often touches another so that he or she hears correctly what others say.

82. A teacher's words are often given for the sake of the one who listens, and it is often the fault of the listener that something is lacking in the teacher's words. When the teacher preaches with an abundance of words, he should speak without pride, since it is not for his own sake but for the listener's profit that his tongue is eloquent. When however the teacher speaks sparingly, the listener should not grow impatient, lest perchance the teacher's tongue falter, not purposely but for the sake of reproof of the listener. It is then for the listener's sake that a good speech is given even to false teachers, just as even to the Pharisees words of preaching could be supplied, those about whom it is said, *Do what they tell you, but do not imitate their actions.** It is for the sake of reproving the listeners that even good teachers are deprived of speech, just as Ezekiel is told against Israel, *I will make your tongue stick to the roof of your mouth, and you will be mute, not like a man able to chastise, because it is a rebellious house.**

*Matt 23:3

*Ezek 3:26

83. Sometimes words of preaching are granted for the sake of both; sometimes for the sake of both they are withheld. For the sake of both they are given when God's voice comes to Paul at Corinth: *Do not be afraid, but speak out*, and a little later, *I have many people in this city.** For the sake of both preaching is withheld, as when the priest Eli knew about the evil behavior of his sons and did not exert himself to chastise them properly; since the punishment of death lay in the future as well as the accusation of their sinful conduct, God would impose on him the penalty of silence.* In such a case,

*Acts 18:9-10

*1 Sam 3:12-14

consequently, since we do not know for whose sake the words are granted, or for whose sake they are withheld, the only safe procedure is that we should neither pride ourselves on the fact that we have received more on the behalf of some nor mock someone else who has received less; rather, we should put down the foot of humility and walk seriously and constantly, because in this life the better we know that we cannot of ourselves supply the teaching we need, the more truly learned we are. Why then should anyone pride himself on teaching when he does not know either when it is given to a person by hidden judgment or when it is taken away? Although fear may always seem to be far removed from security, for us nevertheless nothing is safer than to be always fearful under hope, lest the incautious mind should by despair cast itself into bad habits or by inordinate pride run away from the gifts. Before the eyes of the strict but loving Judge, the more we humbly tremble under hope, the stronger we stand in his presence.

BOOK 31

I. 1. The Devil envied the healthy man in Paradise and inflicted on him the wound of pride, so that the one who had not received death in creation would deserve it because of his pride. But it belongs to God's power not only to create good out of nothing, but also to recreate good out of the evil that the devil had perpetrated; the medicine for the wound that the devil in his pride had inflicted appeared, and it was God's humility: they who imitated the enemy's pride and fell would rise humiliated by the Creator's example. And so against the pride of the devil there appeared among human beings a humble God made human. The powerful ones of this world, that is the members of the proud devil, believed him contemptible, because they saw that he was humble. The more the wound in their heart swelled up, the more they despised the medicine of meekness. Our medicine was accordingly rejected by the wound of the proud people, so it came at last to the wound of the humble. *God* indeed *chose the weaklings of the world to shame the strong.** *1 Cor 1:27

What the proud rich might later also wonder at was done among the poor. While they* gazed at new powers in them* for whose lives they first showed contempt, afterwards they were dumbfounded at their miracles. So they soon returned to their hearts in fear, and they dreaded the holy miracles of those whose precepts they despised. The strong were then confounded by the weak, because while the lives of the humble rose in veneration, the self-glorification of the proud fell down. Therefore, since blessed Job typifies Holy Church, and almighty

*the rich
*the poor

God foresaw that at the beginning of the newborn church the powerful ones of this world would refuse to accept her easy yoke and would stiffen the neck of their hearts, let him now say,

II. 2. *Will the rhinoceros want to be your slave?** The untamed nature of the rhinoceros is such that even if it should be captured, it can by no means be held. It is said in fact that it is so impatient that it dies there on the spot. Its name is interpreted in the Latin language to mean a horn in the nose. What else does the nose mean but foolishness, and what else is a horn but pride? We have learned from Solomon that the nose usually means foolishness, since he bears us witness: *A gold ring is in her nose, that lovely, foolish woman.** He sees the heretical teaching shine with bright eloquence while it is out of line with the correct understanding of wisdom, and he says, *A gold ring is in her nose*, that is, a handsome, rounded statement is in the feeling of a foolish mind, and a golden ring hangs from its eloquence, but because of the weight of physical tension, like the motion of a pig, it does not raise its head. And he explains this fact with the following phrase, saying, *that lovely, foolish woman*. That is to say, the heretical teaching consists of lovely words but foolish understanding.

Concerning the horn, which is often taken to be pride, we have learned from the prophet's testimony: *I said to the wicked: do not act wickedly, and to the sinners: do not lift up your horn.** What then does this rhinoceros signify but the powerful ones of this world, or even the very powers wielded by the princes who are puffed up by the strong wind of foolish boasting, yes, inflated by false external honors, while inside they are empty and truly miserable? About such as these it is said, *Why are you proud when you are earth and ashes?** At the very beginning of the newborn church,

*Job 39:9

*Prov 11:22

*Ps 74:5

*Sir 10:9

when the power of the rich was waxing strong against her and crying out for her death with the loud voice of cruelty that was so resourceful, in her anxiety at her tortures, when she would succumb to so much persecution, who at that time could have believed that the stout harsh power would subject its own proud neck, tamed by the yoke of holy fear, and bind itself with the reins of meek faith?

Long indeed in her beginnings was the church exposed to the horn of this rhinoceros and struck by it to the point of being virtually killed by it. But God's grace was in control, and the church was strengthened and given life from the dead, and this rhinoceros was finally weary of striking; it then lowered its head and its horn. What human beings therefore found impossible was not hard for God to accomplish; he broke the rigid powers without words, but with miracles. See how we watch the rhinoceros daily serve the church! The powerful ones of this world long confided in their own strength with their foolish pride, but now we see them subject to God.

The Lord was speaking of a kind of untamed rhinoceros when he said, *How hard it is for a rich man to enter the kingdom of heaven!** When he heard the answer, *Then who can be saved?** he immediately added, *With men it is impossible, but with God anything is possible.** It is as if he said, "This rhinoceros cannot be tamed by human powers, but only by miracles can God subdue it." That is why in this place also blessed Job as type of Holy Church is asked, *Will the rhinoceros want to be your slave?** You should hear whispered, "As he is mine? I have long put up with his resistance to the preaching of humans; nevertheless, when I wished it I quickly vanquished him with miracles." It is as if he said more plainly, "Are not those who rear themselves up with foolish pride subdued by your preaching with

*Matt 19:23
*Matt 19:25
*Matt 19:26

*Job 39:9

my help? Consider then through whom you prevail, and whenever you do prevail, avoid the feeling of pride." Well, certainly blessed Job is led to this knowledge for the humbling of his pride, so that the wonderful things wrought by the apostles at a later time, when they subjected the world to God and bent down and tamed the pride of the rulers of this world, might be known. So it happened that the less self-esteem blessed Job possessed, the more he saw gathered many difficult souls to God by others. So let it be said, *Will the rhinoceros want to be your slave?** You should hear whispered, "Just as through those whom I will send he will be my slave?" The next verse:

*Job 39:9

*Job 39:9   **III. 3.** *Will he stay in your stable?** In this passage we not improperly take *stable* to mean Holy Scripture itself, where the holy animals are nourished with the feed of the word, and it is of them that the prophet speaks: *Your animals will dwell there.** That is why the Lord himself was born and found by shepherds in a stable,* since his incarnation is known by the prophets' writings that nourish us. This very rhinoceros we are talking about, obviously excessively proud as he was in the beginning of the newborn church, as he heard the words of the patriarchs, the mysteries of the prophets, and the secret words of the gospels, he ridiculed them; the more he abandoned himself to his own desires and held his ground of despair, the more he held in contempt the idea of staying in the stable of preaching and being fed there.

*Ps 67:11
*Luke 2:16

Paul certainly meant to speak of that ground of the proud when he said, *In despair they gave themselves over to licentious behavior and all kinds of uncleanness and greed.** Every one of them, the more they despair of ever attaining eternal goodness after this life, the more completely they let themselves go in the evils of the present life. Almighty God certainly put up with this rhinoceros

*Eph 4:19

wandering all over the grounds of evil desires for a long time. Yet when he willed it, he quickly tied him up to his own stable so that, benignly restrained, he could receive the food of life, lest in perilous freedom he should lose his life entirely. Behold now, we already see how the powerful ones of this world, even its leaders, freely listen and continually read the preaching of the Lord; nor do they sneak out of the stable, because they know God's commandments, whether by reading or by hearing, and they never transgress them in their lives, but they stay in the enclosed stable for the feed of the word, so that by eating and staying they might grow fat. So when we see all these things as God's actions, what else do we see but this rhinoceros staying in the stable? But after receiving this food of preaching, the rhinoceros should show some fruits of good works, so he rightly adds,

IV. 4. *Will you harness the rhinoceros for plowing with your yoke?** The yoke is the church's law and teaching. Plowing means opening the earth of the human breast with the plowshare of the tongue through the work of preaching. Accordingly, this rhinoceros, which was once rigidly proud, is even now held and harnessed in the yoke of faith; he is led out of the stable to plow, because he wants to make others know the preaching that fed him. We know that this rhinoceros is certainly an earthly prince, and we also know how harsh and cruel he was at first against the Lord, and now we see how the Lord has arranged matters and how he has humbled the rhinoceros and brought him low. This rhinoceros was not merely bound but harnessed for plowing, obviously because the yoke of discipline not only bound him and kept him from doing evil, but also put him to work in the preaching of the holy faith. See then, it is just as I said above, when we see the very magistrates of human government and the leaders fear God in their actions, what else do we

*Job 39:10

see but men harnessed to a yoke? And when we now see them preach, by the laws they keep promulgating, that very faith they fought and persecuted so long, what else are they doing but laboring and sweating at the plow?

5. We are able to see this rhinoceros, this prince of the earth bound with the reins of faith, in such a way that he both carries his horn through worldly power and bears the yoke of faith through the love of God. This rhinoceros would be very greatly to be feared if he were not bound. He is indeed equipped with a horn, yet he is bound. There is something in his bonds for the humble to love and something in his horn for the proud to fear. Bound with ropes, he serves the piety of the meek, but supported by the horn of worldly power, he wields the domination of that power. He is often seized by obsessive wrath to the point of striking, but he is restrained by the fear of God. Yes indeed, his power is sometimes irritated, and he is infuriated, but when he remembers the eternal Judge, the upraised horn bends itself down. I have often seen it myself, how this rhinoceros was severely aroused to the point of striking, and, as though with elevated horn, he threatened the minor beasts with death, exile, and condemnation and his subjects with extreme fear. But quickly making the sign of the cross on his forehead, he extinguished all the fire of wrath in himself; changed in mind, he rid himself of threats, and because he could not proceed to the execution of his designs he owned himself bound. Not only does he calm his own anger, but he promptly makes his subjects know all that is right and himself demonstrates the veneration of Holy Church for all to know deeply by the example of his own humility. So blessed Job is asked, *Will you harness the rhinoceros for plowing with your yoke?** It is as if he asked straightforwardly, "Are you going to point out to the powerful ones of this world, those who

*Job 39:10

trust in their own foolish pride, the way to the work of preaching, and will you bind them with the chains of discipline?" You should hear whispered, "As I did when I wished? Yes, after first suffering persecution from my enemies, I later made them defenders of the true faith." The next verse:

V. 6. *Will he break up the clods in the valleys after you?** The clods on the surface of cultivated ground usually press down the scattered seed and suffocate it when it sprouts. These clods signify those who through their callousness and destructive lives neither receive in themselves the seed of the word nor allow others to bear fruit from the seed they have received. Every holy preacher, you see, who comes into the world had first plowed the soft ground of the valleys by preaching the Gospel to the poor; the church however was unable to break the callousness of certain proud individuals, so she was distressed, and she left them strewn over the ground like clods left over from her work. There are many people of perverse mind, you see, who having confided in the unbelief of the princes of the earth, oppressed the growing church with the evil burden of their way of life; either by their own damnable examples or by threats or by coaxing, they for a long time ruined as many people as they could, lest the earth of the hearts of those who listened to preaching should be cultivated and reach the point of bearing fruit from the seed.

*Job 39:10

But finally Almighty God subdued this rhinoceros with his yoke, and through it he straightaway dissolved the callousness of the clods. He quickly subjugated the earthly princes to his faith and dissolved the hard hearts of persecutors, so that the broken-up clods could no longer as it were obdurately block the church but would resolutely let the seed of the word that they had received germinate. That is why he now asks, *Will he plow the*

*Job 39:10 *valleys after you?** It is as if he said, "As he does after me? After I enter the mind of any proud person in power, not only do I render him subject to me, but I even urge him to subdue the enemies of the faith, so that when the powers of this world are bound to the yoke of fear of me, not only will they remain faithful to me, but they will also zealously dissolve the hardness of other hearts for my sake."

7. We are speaking these things about those who are without faith, but we see the same thing in many of those who are enrolled as nominally faithful. There are many, you see, who have a place among humble brethren, but they hold only to the words of faith without abandoning the growth of pride; when they persecute whoever they can with violent attacks, when they never accept the seed of the word themselves while others are bearing fruit, when instead they close the ears of their hearts to the voice of the one who exhorts, what else are they but hardened clods lying in plowed valleys? They are the more wicked in that they neither bring forth the fruit of humility themselves nor, what is worse, do they refrain from persecuting those who are humbly bringing forth fruit. Holy Church sometimes, for the sake of softening their hard texture, since her own power is not enough, seeks the assistance of this rhinoceros, that is, of the earthly ruler, so that he should himself dissolve the remaining clods, which the humility of the churches bears as if in fields in the valleys. The rhinoceros tramples upon the clods with his foot and reduces them, because the lowliness of the church cannot resist the boldness and power of the wicked, so the power and reverence of the prince breaks them up. Since this victory is brought about by divine power alone, so that the head of the earthly kingdom is bowed to the advancement of the heavenly kingdom, it is rightly asked in the present instance, *Will he plow the valleys after you?** However, in order that blessed Job should continue in his humble sentiments concerning his own virtues, the divine voice continues to speak about the powers of this world in the name of the rhinoceros, making known their wonders.

VI. 8. *Will you trust his great power and abandon your labors to him?** The Lord affirms that he has confidence in the rhinoceros's strength, because he has bent the powers he has temporarily granted to the earthly principate to the ritual of his own worship, so that from the power the ruler has received, which had long ago caused him to exalt himself against God, he might now offer more reverent worship to God. Because he is the world's most powerful, therefore he prevails more for the world's Creator. Because he was feared by the subjects himself, the more he points out who has the power and should be feared, the more easily he persuades. So let him ask, *Will you trust his great power?** It is as if he said, "As I do, who see the powers of the princes of the earth ready to serve at my worship? The more I already foresee that I will bend even the powers of the great ones of this world to myself, the less esteem I have for anything you do at present." So he rightly asks, *Will you abandon your labors to him?** The Lord then abandoned his own labors to this rhinoceros, because when this earthly prince was converted, he entrusted them to the church that he had redeemed by his death, because obviously in her hand with immense solicitude the peace of the faith was to be committed and protected. The next verse:

VII. 9. *Do you not trust him to return the seed to you and gather it to your threshing floor?** What do we take the seed to mean if not the word of preaching? As in the Gospel, Truth has said, *The sower went out to sow.** And as the prophet said, *Blessed are you who sow seed over all the waters.** What other threshing floor is there that

*Job 39:10

*Job 39:11

*Job 39:11

*Job 39:11

*Job 39:12

*Matt 13:3

*Isa 32:20

we should understand by the Precursor's voice: *He will clean out his threshing floor*?* Accordingly, who would believe at the beginning of the newborn church, when the untamed princes of the earth raged against her with so many threats and tortures, that this rhinoceros would return the seed to God, that is, would recompense the word of preaching he had received with works? Who among the weak ones of that time could have believed that he would assemble his threshing floor?

*Matt 3:12

Behold even now how he promulgates laws for the sake of the church, he who raged for so long a time against her with all kinds of torture! Behold how whatever nations he could capture he leads by persuasion to the grace of faith and points out eternal life to them whom he preserved in the present life after they were captured! Why is this? Obviously he now assembles a threshing floor that at one time with proud horn he scattered and emptied. Let blessed Job therefore hear what the Gentile princes are doing, and let him by no means extol himself in his own sight on account of his pride at his own excellent virtue. Let the king and the powerful one hear how the more powerful kings of the world obey God with such admirable devotion. They do not betray their power as if it were special to the vice of pride, as they see exemplified in others, because even if the Lord does not see any like him, he does foresee many through whom he would blunt his pride.

10. Since therefore the princes of the earth would prostrate themselves before God with great humility, evil persons who long raged against the church while they lived in open infidelity now turn to other lying arguments. Because they see them venerate a religious way of life, they take up the cultivation of religion themselves and afflict the lives of good people, wearing contemptible clothes and behaving wickedly. They are in fact lovers of the world, showing off in themselves the things that people venerate, and they join those who actually despise them, not mentally, but only in the clothes they wear. Being lovers of present honors but unable to gain them, they virtually follow those who despise those honors. Whatever feelings they harbor against good people they would fain show if a convenient time for wickedness were at hand. But even these proofs of wickedness redound to the advantage of the chosen ones. Holy Church, you see, cannot pass the time of pilgrimage without the labor of temptation, and even if she has no public external foes, she has to put up with internal false brethren. Her battlefront is always present against wrongdoing, and even in peacetime she is at war; it can even happen that she is more grievously afflicted when she is not attacked by blows from the outside, but rather by the behavior of her own people. So at either one time or the other she is always at war. When she is persecuted by the princes, she is afraid lest good people should lose what they are, and when the princes are converted she still suffers because bad people pretend to be good when they are not so. So almighty God says the rhinoceros is bound with a yoke, and immediately adds the hypocrisy of depraved people, saying,

VIII. 11. *An ostrich's wing is like the wings of herons and falcons.** Everybody knows of course that herons and falcons surpass all other birds by the speed of their flight. An ostrich's wing has indeed a similarity to theirs, but it does not have their speed; in fact an ostrich cannot lift itself from the earth, and it lifts its wings only with an appearance of flight; never does it suspend itself off the ground in flight. All the hypocrites resemble the ostrich; they pretend to live like good people, and they can imitate the appearance of holiness, but in truth they do not act holy. They have indeed the

*Job 39:13

appearance of wings for flight, but they actually crawl on the ground; they stretch out the wings of holiness for appearance's sake, but they are weighed down by the burden of worldly anxiety, so that there is no way for them to be lifted above the earth. The Lord reproved the ostentation of the Pharisees and as it were reproached the ostrich's wing, whose action was different from its outward appearance, as he said: *Woe to you hypocrites, because you have become like whitewashed tombs that appear splendid to peoples' eyes but are full of dead people's bones inside and all kinds of filth. So too you yourselves present an external appearance of righteousness to people, but within you are full of avarice and unrighteousness.** He might have said, "You seem to be lifted up by a kind of wing, but the weight of life pulls you down to the depths."

*Matt 23:27-28

The prophet speaks about this weight: *Sons of men, how long will your hearts be heavy?** The Lord promises that he will change the hypocrisy of this ostrich when he says through the prophet, *The beasts of the field, dragons and ostriches will glorify me.** What else are we to understand by the word *dragons* but openly malicious minds that always creep upon the ground with base thoughts? What else is meant by the word *ostriches* but those who pretend to live good lives, who present the appearance of holiness of life as if it were a wing in flight, but who do not behave that way in their actions? So the Lord affirms that he is glorified by the dragon or ostrich, because he often changes those who are openly bad and falsely good from their intimate thoughts to his own worship. Or at least the beasts of the field, the dragons and ostriches, glorify the Lord when the Gentiles exalt the faith they have in him, after they have been longtime members of the devil in this world. The prophet reproaches the Gentiles by name for the

*Ps 4:3

*Isa 43:20

malice of dragons, and he also mentions the hypocrisy of ostriches by name. It is as though the Gentiles had received wings but could not fly, since they both had rational nature and did not know how to act rationally.

12. There is still something about the ostrich that we should attentively consider concerning the falcon and the heron. The falcon and the heron, as you know, have smaller bodies, but they are equipped with more intricate wings, and that is why they fly away swiftly, because they have less girth to weigh them down and more power to rise. Ostriches on the other hand are endowed with smaller wings and heavier bodies. So even if they should wish to fly, their meager wings could not hold up the heaviness of their bodies in the air. The heron and the falcon then rightly signify the place and person of the elect, who as long as they live the present life cannot be without some slight contagion of guilt. But since there is very little in their makeup to hinder them, the virtue of good behavior supplies much that can lift them up to heaven.

However, even if the hypocrite does a little that may be uplifting, he perpetrates a great deal that is heavy. It is not that the hypocrite does no good, but since he lowers esteem for it, he commits many perverse actions. The small wings of the ostrich then do not lift its body, because the many depraved actions of the hypocrite outweigh the little good that he does. The ostrich's wing does have a similar color to the wings of herons and falcons, but it does not have anything like their strength. The falcon's and heron's wings are well-defined and solid, and they can move the air in flight by their weight and power; the ostrich, however, has lax wings that cannot even begin to fly, and they are grounded by the very air they should have moved. What then do we see in this state of things but that the virtues of the elect are solid enough to fly, so that they move against the wind of human favor? But the hypocrites, however righteous their actions may seem to be, cannot fly, obviously because the air of human praise is stronger than the shaky wing of virtue.

13. But see here, when we are looking at a usage that is one and the same for the good and the evil alike, and when we see its agreed form in both the elect and the reprobate sinners, how is it that our intelligence supplies us with the ability to distinguish the elect from reprobate sinners and true people from false? We will understand more quickly if we commit these pure words of our Teacher to memory: *By their fruits you will know them.** What the imagination shows us, you see, we cannot weigh, but only the action that follows. So now, after he introduced the image of the ostrich, he straightway adds what it does, saying,

*Matt 7:16

IX. 14. *It leaves its eggs on the ground.* What else do eggs signify but the still tender offspring that must be protected and raised a long time for life and flight? The eggs are of course themselves unaware of this, but when they are warmed they are changed into living winged creatures. So also the listeners are little children, and it is certain that they would remain cold and unresponsive unless they were warmed by the solicitous exhortations of their teacher. Accordingly, lest they should grow numb if left alone in their unresponsive state, they must be warmed by the insistent voices of their teachers, until they are able both to live intelligently and to fly in contemplation. The hypocrites on the other hand do not stop speaking what is right, even though they are always doing what is evil. They bring forth children by speaking well about faith and daily life, but they cannot nurse them by living right. So we are rightly told about this ostrich: *It leaves its eggs on the ground.**

*Job 39:14

Hypocrites neglect the care of their children, because they get involved in external activities out of interior love, and the more these latter excite them, the less they are tormented by the absence of their offspring. To say that the ostrich has left its eggs on the ground means that the sons born through conversion were by no means laid in a nest of exhortation separated from worldly actions. To have left its eggs on the ground means to offer the children no example of heavenly life. Because hypocrites entertain no warmth from the entrails of charity, they never grieve for the insensitivity of the offspring they have begotten, that is, they do not grieve for the coldness of their eggs. The more freely they become involved in worldly actions, the more negligently they let those they have begotten perform worldly actions. But because God's heavenly care does not abandon the abandoned children of hypocrites (in fact, he even foreknows some of them by his intimate choice), and he warms them with the glance of generous grace, he again adds,

X. 15. *Do you perhaps warm them with dust?** It is as if he said, "As I do? Yes, I warm the eggs in the dust, and with the fire of my love I ignite the little souls left in the midst of sinners." What else then is the dust if not sinners? That is why that enemy himself is satisfied with the loss of this sinner, as the prophet declares: *The dust is the serpent's bread.** What else is meant by the dust but the very instability of the wicked? David speaks of this: *Not so are the wicked, not so; they are like dust driven by the wind from the face of the earth.** The Lord then warms the eggs left in the dust, because with the fire of his love he ignites the little souls deprived of the solicitude of his preachers, even when they are left in the midst of sinners.

That is why we see many individuals living among people whose lethargic way of life those individuals do

*Job 39:14

*Isa 65:25

*Ps 1:4

not share. That is why we see many people who do not flee from the crowds of evildoers and yet are on fire with a heavenly flame. That is why we see many people who, so to speak, are on fire in a cold place. That is why some individuals who are placed in the tepid atmosphere of worldly people are on fire with the desires of heavenly hope, so that even among cold hearts they are hot. Does it not mean that almighty God knows where the eggs have been left, and that even in the dust he can warm them and rid them of their former insensibility and coldness? He animates them with the sense of a vital breath, so that they may never lie down in torpid weakness, but turn to life and to flight and hover in contemplation of heavenly things—in other words, fly.

We must take notice, however, that by these words not only is the perverse behavior of hypocrites reproved, but even that of good teachers is checked if by chance pride should creep in. When in fact the Lord says of himself that he warms the eggs left in the dust, he certainly indicates openly that it is he who works internally through the words of teachers, and that without the words of any human being he warms those he wills who are lying in cold dust. It is as if he openly told teachers, "So that you may know that I am the one who works through your speeches, see how I speak to people's hearts without your help, whenever I will it." So after having humbled the thoughts of teachers, the Lord's words turn to the depiction of hypocrites, and how foolish is their lethargy, still using the behavior of the ostrich as a clearer indication. So he goes on:

XI. 16. *She forgets that a foot could trample them, or a beast of the field destroy them.** What do we take the foot to mean but the passing of an action? What is the field if not this present world? Does not the Lord say in the gospel, *The field is the world*?* What else

*Job 39:15

*Matt 13:38

do the beasts mean but the ancient enemy who seizes plunder in this world and is daily glutted by the death of human beings? About this field the Lord promises through the prophet, *No evil beast will pass through her gates.** The ostrich then abandons her eggs, forgetting that a foot could trample them, obviously because after hypocrites have begotten children through conversation they abandon them, and they absolutely do not care if they are left without solicitous exhortation and the guidance of discipline and go astray through the example of depraved behavior. If they did love the eggs they bring forth, they would certainly worry lest anyone should trample upon them by showing off perverse behavior.

*Isa 35:9

Paul feared such a trampling foot against his fragile disciples whom he had laid as eggs when he said, *Many people walk as I have often told you, and now tell you tearfully, as enemies of the cross of Christ.** And again: *Be on the lookout for dogs and for evildoers.** And again: *I enjoin upon you, brothers, in the name of our Lord Jesus Christ, that you withdraw yourselves from any brother who acts disorderly, not according to the tradition he received from us.** John was worried about this foot for the sake of Gaius, and when he had enumerated many of Diotrephes's evil deeds, he added, *Beloved, let us not imitate evil, but good.**

*Phil 3:18
*Phil 3:2

*2 Thess 3:6

*3 John 11

The leader of the synagogue himself worried about his frail flock and said, *When you enter the land the Lord your God will give you, be careful of wishing to imitate the abominations of those nations.** What the beast of the field ruins is forgotten, obviously because the devil rages in this world and seizes the children begotten in good living, and the hypocrite absolutely does not care. Paul was worried about this beast of the field on account of the eggs he had laid, and he said, *I am worried lest as the serpent cunningly seduced Eve, so your understanding might be*

*Deut 18:9

seduced away from the chastity that is in Christ Jesus.* Peter was worried about this beast of the field for the sake of the disciples, and he said, *Your adversary, like a roaring lion, goes around looking for someone to devour. Let your faith be strong and resist him.** Real teachers then have inner feelings of fear for the sake of their disciples from the virtue of love; hypocrites on the other hand, the less they are afraid of anything they should fear for their own sakes, the less they fear for those committed to their care. Since they live with hardened hearts, they know no pity or love that they owe to the very sons they have begotten. So he goes on to speak further about the image of the ostrich:

XII. 17. *She is turned against her own sons, as if they were none of hers.** Anyone who is not filled with the grace of charity looks upon his neighbor as a stranger, even if he has himself begotten him for God; all the hypocrites are exactly like this, since all their minds obviously desire the external at all times and they have become insensible to internal realities. In all that they do they seek only themselves, so concerning affection for the neighbor they are softened by no compassion or charity. O how tender were the feelings held by Paul, when he breathed such warm waves of love toward his sons and said, *Now we are alive, if you stand fast in the Lord.** And again: *God is my witness how I long for all of you in the tenderness of Christ.**

To the Romans he wrote, *God is my witness, whom I serve with my spirit in the Gospel of his Son, that I am always mindful of you in my prayers, earnestly pleading that I might finally find in some way how to make a prosperous journey to you by the will of God. I do desire to see you.** To Timothy also: *I give thanks to my God whom I serve, as my fathers did, with a pure conscience; how constantly I remember you in my prayers! Night*

*2 Cor 11:3

*1 Pet 5:8-9

*Job 39:16

*1 Thess 3:8
*Phil 1:8

*Rom 1:9-11

and day I long to see you.* He showed his love for the Thessalonians also in these words: *But we, brethren, deprived of your presence for a brief time, by sight, not by heart, are hurrying all the more to see your face with all our hearts.** While he was hard pressed by many persecutions, but solicitous for the safety of his sons, he added, *I have sent Timothy, our brother, a minister of God for the Gospel of Christ, to strengthen you and to exhort you in your faith, so that no one should be surprised at these trials. You already know that they are our lot.** To the Ephesians he wrote, *I beg you not to falter in these afflictions of mine for your sake. They are your glory.**

*2 Tim 1:3-4

*1 Thess 2:17

*1 Thess 3:2-3

*Eph 3:13

See how the one afflicted by troubles exhorts others, and through his own sufferings he strengthens others. He was not like the ostrich, forgetful of his own children, but he was afraid to a great extent lest his disciples, when they saw that their preacher was subject to so much abuse and persecution, would disdain faith in him, since they saw innumerable insults and contrary feelings militating against that faith. That is why he grieved less for his own torments; rather, he feared greatly for his sons who were tempted on account of his torments. He held his own bodily wounds to be less important, but he worried about the wounds in the hearts of his sons. He suffered tortures from the wounds he had received, but he comforted his sons and cured the wounds in their hearts. Let us consider, then, what kind of love it was when among his own sufferings he feared for others, what kind of love it was when inconvenienced as he was he would seek the safety of his sons. He was concerned to guide the mental state of his neighbors, even when his own dejection was involved.

18. But hypocrites know nothing about these deep feelings of love, because the more their minds are unhinged in external pursuits through worldly concupiscence, the more obdurate their internal selves become through insensibility. Yes, their minds grow cold inside with unfeeling numbness, because outside they grow soft with damnable love. The mind cannot consider itself, because it has no eagerness for thought. In fact it cannot think of itself, because it is not whole with itself. It is unable to be whole with itself, because it is seized by so many concupiscences that it is scattered abroad away from itself by just as many appearances. It lies scattered among the lowest things, with which, if it wanted to gather them, it would rise to the top.

19. That is why the minds of the righteous, through the maintenance of a rule of conduct, are protected from their unstable appetite for all visible forms, and are therefore collected and whole inside themselves. The mind sees well enough how it should behave toward God and neighbor, because it leaves nothing of itself outside itself; as long as it keeps itself apart from all that is external, it is intimately alive and enkindled. The brighter the fire, the more light there is to find out vices. That is why the saints who are collected within themselves have a wonderful penetrating line of vision to find out strange vices, even when they are hidden. So the prophet Ezekiel was right to say, *The likeness of a hand reached out and grasped me by the hair of my head, and the Spirit lifted me up between heaven and earth; the vision of God led me to Jerusalem near the inner gate that faces north where there was a statue of the idol of jealousy to provoke to envy.**

*Ezek 8:3

What else is the hair of the head but the gathered thoughts of the mind that stick together through constraint, lest they be scattered and blow away? So a hand reaches down from above, and the prophet is lifted up by the hair of his head, since our mind gathers itself through guardianship, and the heavenly power draws us up from the depths. The prophet then rightly declares that he is suspended between heaven and earth, because any saint now situated in mortal flesh does not yet reach heaven in any full sense, but he already leaves the lowest places. The vision of God leads him to Jerusalem, obviously because anyone who is making his way through the eagerness of charity contemplates the church as she ought to be; so he again rightly adds that he was led *near the inner gate that faces north.*

Unfortunately, when the saints look at the church through the doorway of internal contemplation, they find more that is wrongly done than what is right inside her. They turn their eyes as it were to the region of the north, that is, to the left of the sun, because they are inflamed by the sparks of charity against the cold air of the vices. Here it is rightly added that *there was a statue of the idol of jealousy to provoke to envy.* When they consider within Holy Church a group of those who are only surface-deep faithful perpetrating robbery and other crimes, what else do they see but an idol in Jerusalem? That idol is named *Jealousy*, because heavenly envy is instigated by it against us, so that the more dearly the Redeemer loves us, the more strictly he strikes the criminals.

20. Hypocrites accordingly do not gather up the thoughts of their minds, so they are not held by the hair of their heads. And if they do not know their own, when will they find out the crimes committed against themselves? So they are lethargic concerning heaven, for the sake of which they should burn with desire. Instead they anxiously burn with desire for earthly things, toward which they had once been admirably indifferent. Having put aside concern for their sons, they often gird themselves against danger with immense labor, cross the sea, approach judgment, assault princes, break into palaces, meddle in the wrangling crowds of people, and defend their worldly patrimony with laborious surveillance. If by chance you should ask them why they behave this way when they have abandoned the world, they would immediately respond that they fear God, and that is why they weary themselves with such constant attention to defend their patrimony. So the Lord rightly adds more words about the foolish labor of this ostrich:

XIII. 21. *She labored in vain, since no fear forced her.** *They shook from fear, when there was nothing to fear.** Behold, the divine voice orders us, *If anyone takes away your robe and wants to enter into judgment with you, give him your coat as well.** And again: *When someone takes what is yours, do not ask for it back.** The apostle Paul in his turn wanted his followers to disdain external possessions, so that they might be able to keep internal ones, so he admonished them, *Now indeed, it is a failure on your part, when you enter into judgment with one another; why do you not instead suffer wrong? Why do you not let yourself be defrauded?** Nevertheless the hypocrite, having copied the externals of a holy life, would abandon the custody of his own sons and try to defend worldly possessions even with loud arguments. By his own example he fears not to lose the hearts of those he has begotten; instead he fears the loss of his earthly patrimony as if through neglect. The disciple falls into error; nevertheless the hypocrite's heart is wounded by no sorrow. He watches those committed to his care fall into a deep chasm, and as if deaf he walks away. But if he perceives that he has incurred the loss of any worldly item, however small, he is quickly inflamed to anger and revenge in the depths of his heart. Patience is quickly broken; cries of anguish of heart are quickly unleashed in vocal outbursts. While he calmly endures the loss of souls, he rushes in to fend

*Job 39:16
*Ps 13:5

*Matt 5:40
*Luke 6:30

*1 Cor 6:7

off the loss of worldly goods even with a troubled mind, and he displays to all those who are present, with his troubled mind as witness, what he really loves.

There indeed is a great power of defense where there is massive energy of love. The more we love worldly possessions, the more violently we fear being deprived of them. Whatever be the attitude with which we possess anything in this world, we do not learn what it is except when we lose it. Painless of course is the loss of whatever we possess without love. Whatever we have with ardent love, we sigh deeply over when it is gone. Who is there who does not know that the Lord created earthly objects for our use but created human souls for himself? That person is convicted of loving himself more than God who is careless about the things of God but protects his own. Hypocrites are accordingly not afraid of losing the things of God—that is, human souls—but they do fear the loss of their own belongings, which are obviously things that are passing away along with the world, and they are going to reason with the strict Judge about them. It is as if they found it pleasant, when it is a case of desired—that is, rational—goods that are lost, that someone should preserve incomprehensible goods that were unsought. We who wish to possess anything in this world hear Truth cry out, *Unless a man renounce all his possessions, he cannot be my disciple.** *Luke 14:33

22. Why then would perfect Christians fight to defend worldly goods that they are ordered not to have? So when we lose our own possessions, if we are perfect followers of God, we are relieved of an immense burden for the journey of this life. However, if some necessity imposes concern for worldly goods upon us on this same journey and someone seizes them from us, it is simply to be endured; certain people, however, while preserving charity, are to be prevented, not only because they should not take away our concerns, but because they would be taking what does not belong to them and consequently losing themselves. We ought in fact to fear for the thieves more than to be eager for the protection of irrational things. When we die, in any case, we lose things that have not been stolen. We are of course one with the thieves in the present state of the world, even if they should be eager for correction after they have taken what we have. Naturally everybody knows that we ought to love less the things we make use of and love more the person that we are. If then we are speaking about thieves for their advantage, we already win for ourselves not only worldly goods but also those that are eternal.

23. In this matter we must carefully examine the result, lest greed for possessions should creep in through the concern introduced by necessity, and the prohibition instigated by zeal be intensified by an excessive accusation, and finally burst out with a shameful argument riddled with hate. When peace with a neighbor is broken in the heart for the sake of some worldly gain, it is clearly apparent that the worldly gain is loved more than the neighbor. And if we have no deep feelings of love even for the neighbor who is a robber, we treat ourselves worse even than the robber; in fact we do more serious harm to ourselves than the other person could, because we abandon the good behavior of love by our own free will, and what we lose from ourselves is within. What we lose to the robber is of course only external. But the hypocrite is ignorant of this shape of charity, because he loves earthly goods more than heaven, so against the person who steals passing goods he is internally inflamed with inhuman hate.

24. We must realize on the other hand that there are those whom Mother Church nourishes lovingly on her lap and puts up with while she leads them on to maturity and spiritual adulthood; sometimes they behave externally as saints although they are incapable of pursuing the merit of perfection. They in no sense rise to the level of spiritual gifts, and on that account they are slaves to their associates for the purpose of the protection of their worldly possessions, and they are sometimes excessively angry in the defense of those possessions. By no means should it be supposed that they are counted among the hypocrites, because it is one thing to sin through weakness, and something else to sin through malice.

This is the difference between weaklings and hypocrites: that the former are well aware of their weakness, and they prefer to be accused of their faults by everyone to being praised for false holiness. The hypocrites, however, are well aware that they are evildoers, and yet they are proud of the title of holiness in the sight of human judgment. Weaklings are unafraid of depraved people, even if their good actions are displeasing, if only they can please heavenly Judgment. Hypocrites on the other hand never do anything without considering how they can please people by some action. Weaklings, according to the measure of their intelligence, serve God's interests as soldiers even in worldly affairs. Hypocrites use God's interests to serve a worldly aim, because even in those holy actions that they show themselves doing they seek not people's conversion, but the gentle wind of favor.

25. Accordingly, when we see certain people whose way of life is not despicable defending worldly matters excessively or angrily, we ought to reprove their behavior charitably and not let them despair because of our reproof, because often in one and the same person are found certain apparent faults subject to judgment, but equally a certain hidden greatness. In ourselves, on the other hand, greatness often appears on the face, and our reprehensible faults are hidden. So it follows that the pride of our heart should be humbled, whereas the weakness of those others is public knowledge while our weakness is secret. Their courage on the other hand is secret, while ours is noised abroad publicly.

Concerning then those whom we reprove for their obvious weaknesses, it remains for us to venerate and esteem their hidden courage. And if our mind is lifted up on account of their obvious weaknesses, we should consider our hidden weaknesses and impose humility on ourselves. Some people in fact often obey a great many rules of conduct while leaving aside a few, but we put a lot of them aside while keeping a few. So it often happens that because we know the ones we keep, we see other people put those aside, so our mind is quickly lifted up in pride, forgetting how many rules there are that it leaves aside and how very few are those it keeps. It is necessary then that when we reprove others for certain omissions, we should bow the pride of our solicitous thought, because if our soul sees itself placed higher than others, it might be led to a dangerous cliff of singularity and then fall down to utter ruin. But the Lord, still speaking of the figure of the ostrich, elaborates on the theme of the hypocrite's abandoning heavenly gain for earthly profit and the reason, saying,

XIV. 26. *God has deprived her of wisdom, nor did he give her understanding.** It is one thing to deprive and something else not to give. However, he goes back to what he already said: *deprived,* to say "he did not give." It is as if he said, "In saying *deprived* I did not mean he was unjust in taking away wisdom; I meant he was just in not giving it." Accordingly the Lord described the Pharisee's heart as having hardened, not because he made it hard himself, but because the Pharisee's merits demanded that no sensitivity of infused

*Job 39:17

fear should soften his heart any more. But now it is the hypocrite who pretends to be holy, hiding behind the apparition of good works; he is silenced by the peace of Holy Church, and that is why before our eyes he wears the clothes of a religious appearance. However, if any temptation against faith should burst forth, the raging mind of a wolf immediately throws off the garment of sheepskin and displays as much rage against good people as does a persecutor. So he rightly continues,

XV. 27. *When the time has come it lifts up its wings on high and derides both the knight and the horse's mount.** What do we take this ostrich's wings to mean if not the thoughts of this hypocrite that are now silenced and as it were curled up? When the time arrives, it lifts them up on high. When it finds an opportunity, it displays its proud thoughts. To lift up one's wings on high means to display one's thoughts through unbridled pride. Now, however, the hypocrite pretends to be a saint, so he restrains his thoughts inside himself and as it were curls his wings inside his body through humility. It is noteworthy that he did not say, *it derides* "the horse and the rider," but rather *the knight and the horse's mount.* The horse is in fact for each holy soul its body, which it obviously knows how both to restrain from illicit actions with the bridle of continence and to let it run by the prompting of charity in the practice of good works. By the word *knight* the soul of the saint is expressed, which guides well the draft animal that is the body.

*Job 39:18

That is why the apostle John, in his contemplation of the Lord in the Apocalypse, said, *The heavenly army followed him, mounted on white horses.** Yes indeed, he rightly calls the multitude of the saints who have labored in this war of martyrdom "an army," who are said to be mounted on white horses precisely because their bodies shine with the bright light of justice and chastity.

*Rev 19:14

The hypocrite then derides the knight because when his iniquity bursts forth openly, he despises the holiness of the chosen ones; in his pride he calls them fools whom he copied with craftiness when he was silenced by the peace of faith. Who then is the one who mounts this knight if not almighty God, who both in foresight created the things that did not exist and possesses as ruler the things that do exist? Yes, he really mounts the knight, and he possesses the soul of every righteous person, rightly possessing his own members. For this hypocrite to deride means that the knight despises the saints; to deride the one who mounts the knight means to leap forward even to the injury of the Creator.

28. Because in every single fall we always begin again with the lowest place, and with the following increasing sins we go on to greater ones, rightly is this hypocrite's iniquity distinguished by sins that follow, so that he is first called good when he is not, and afterwards he openly despises people who are good; at the very last he is even led to make the leap of insulting the Creator. In fact the soul never stays in the same place to which it has fallen, because having once fallen voluntarily, it is impelled to do worse by the very weight of its iniquity, so that rushing on to deep waters, it always keeps rushing deeper. Let the hypocrite go, then, and let him desire his own praise now; let him later crush the life of his neighbor. Someday he may distinguish himself by mocking his Creator, and the more proud thoughts he keeps thinking, the more deeply he immerses himself in terrible punishments.

O, how many there are that now Holy Church puts up with, who when the time has quickly come an open temptation will reveal. Because for a time their wills do not rise up against her, they twist the bent wings of their thoughts around during the interim. Because this life is commonly led along with the evil as well as the good, the church is now gathered visibly from the number of both, but in God's invisible judgment they are distinguished, and in their very exit the society of the reprobate is separated. But for now there cannot be in her evil without good or good without evil. It is necessary and well for both parts to be joined during the present time, so that the evil can be changed by the example of the good, and the good can be purified by suffering trials from the evil. So also the Lord, after having used the outward form of the ostrich to discourse at length on the reprobation of hypocrites, quickly turns his speech to the lot of the chosen ones, so that those who had heard about the hypocrites should wait for their flight; then they would hear about the chosen ones whom they should love and imitate. The next verse:

29. *Will you teach the horse strength or cover its neck with a neigh?** But perhaps, before we discuss the horse's strength or neigh, we should learn from others—putting aside the moral exposition—how to explain the strength of the rhinoceros and the folly of the ostrich. The word of God, you see, is manna, and whatever the will of the receiver rightly desires, that is tasted forthwith by the mouth of the eater. The word of God is earth, and the more labor is expended in questioning it, the more abundant fruit it brings forth. The understanding of sacred speech must then be agitated by abundant questioning, because it is just like the earth that is often turned over by plowing so that it is prepared to bear more abundant fruit. So let us briefly touch on the various thoughts we have had about the rhinoceros and the ostrich, because we must hurry on to explain those things we are more responsible for.

This rhinoceros (also called monoceros in some Greek manuscripts) is said to have such immense

*Job 39:19

strength that it cannot be captured by any strong hunter; those however who have spent much labor in investigating and describing the natures of animals assert that when a girl who is a virgin is presented and opens her arms to the approaching animal, it forgets all its ferocity and lays its head on her bosom, and in this way those who are trying to capture it suddenly find it as it were helpless. It is also described to be of the color of boxwood. When it attacks elephants in a battle, with its single horn that it bears on its snout, they say it strikes the belly of attacking elephants, so that they are wounded where they are soft, and the rhinoceros easily strikes down its adversaries. This rhinoceros or alternatively monoceros (that is, unicorn) can therefore be understood as the people, because they accepted the law not by doing it but by pride, as having accepted it alone of all peoples, just as the rhinoceros among all other beasts bears a single horn. So the Lord announced his passion when the prophet sang out and said, *Free me from the lion's mouth and deliver my lowliness from the horns of the unicorns.** In fact, just as many unicorns or rather rhinoceroses have dwelled among that people as individuals who have in their foolish pride taken their stand on works of the law against the preaching of truth, so blessed Job, who typifies Holy Church, is now asked,

*Ps 21:22

*Job 39:9

XVI. 30. *Will the rhinoceros want to be your slave?** As if he said more clearly, "Will that people whom you see waxing proud in their foolish exultation in the death of the faithful be inclined to listen to your righteous preaching?" And hear the whispered answer: "As I do, as I watch the single horn extol itself against me? And yet when I wish, I quickly subject it to myself." But we will the more easily understand this if we pass from the genus to the species. Let that Paul be brought before us out of this people as a witness first of pride and then especially of humility. When he unknowingly reared himself up against God as a custodian of the law, he bore his horn before him on his nose. Later he bent down this very nasal horn through humility and said, *Formerly I was a blasphemer, a persecutor, and an abusive person, but I was granted mercy, because I acted in ignorance.** On his nose he bore a horn when he believed he was going to please God with cruelty, as he afterwards accused himself, saying, *I advanced in Judaism more than many of my compatriots in my own tribe, and I emulated to a greater extent the traditions of my forefathers.**

*1 Tim 1:13

*Gal 1:14

All the hunters feared the strength of this rhinoceros, and all the preachers were afraid of Saul's cruelty. It is written, *Still breathing threats and murder against the Lord's disciples, Saul approached the high priest and asked him for letters to the synagogues at Damascus, so that if he found there any belonging to this way, he might bring men and women bound to Jerusalem.** When we take in air with the nose and dismiss it again, it is called breath, and we often perceive by means of odor through the nose what we do not see with the eyes. This rhinoceros then perceived with the nose where he should strike with the horn, because breathing in threats and murder after he had killed those present, he went in search of those who were absent. But behold, every hunter is hidden from him, and every human being—that is, everyone who is rational and wise—is put to flight out of fear of him.

*Acts 9:1-2

To capture this rhinoceros, then, a virgin spreads out her arms to open her breast, that is, the wisdom of God opens up its secret place, itself inviolate in the flesh. It is written that when Paul approached Damascus, in the middle of the day *a light from heaven suddenly shone about him,* and he heard a voice saying, *Saul, Saul, why do you persecute me?* From his prostrate position on the ground he answered, *Who are you, Lord?* And he is forthwith told, *I am Jesus of Nazareth, whom you are persecuting.** The virgin in fact opened her breast to the rhinoceros when the intact Wisdom of God revealed the mystery of his incarnation to Saul by speaking from heaven; the rhinoceros lost his strength because Saul, stretched out on the ground, lost all the weight of pride he had been carrying.

*Acts 9:1-5

Without the light of his eyes he was led by the hand to Ananias, so it is already clear by what ropes this rhinoceros is bound to God, because all at once he is bound by blindness, preaching, and baptism. He even stayed at God's crib, because he did not disdain to graze upon the words of the Gospel. He said, *I went up to Jerusalem with Barnabas along with Titus. I went with a revelation, and I placed before them the Gospel.** He had previously heard while he was fasting, *It is hard for you to kick against the goad.** Afterwards he pressed on by the miraculous power of the presiding Lord, and from the feed of the word he obtained strength and lost the kick of pride.

*Gal 2:1-2

*Acts 9:5

31. God's bonds not only restrained him from ferocity, but, what is more wonderful, they harnessed him to the plow, so that not only did he not attack people with his cruel horn, but he also served up their meal by pulling the plow of preaching. In fact he spoke himself about evangelists as if they were plowers: *The one who plows should plow in hope, and the thresher in hope of sharing the harvest.** Consequently the one who had formerly imposed torments on the people of faith is the same one who afterwards bore stripes willingly for the cause of the faith and who even wrote letters to preach humbly and be subject to contempt for the cause that he had notoriously fought against so long. Without question he is safely bound to labor with the plow for the

*1 Cor 9:10

sake of the crop, he who once lived in the field wrongly free from fear. About him it is rightly said,

XVII. 32. *Will he break up the clods in the valleys after you?** Obviously the Lord had already entered certain minds that believed him to be truly the Redeemer of the human race. However, since they never turned away from their former observance, and since they kept the hard observance of the letter, the famous preacher told them, *If you have yourselves circumcised Christ will be no benefit for you.** Accordingly the one who softened the hardness of the law in the humble minds of the faithful by proving it false did nothing else but break up the clods after the Lord in the valleys. He did not want the furrow cut in the heart by the plow of faith to lose any grains of seed it received by being forced to observe the letter. Concerning this furrow he speaks further and to the point:

*Job 39:10

*Gal 5:2

XVIII. 33. *Will you trust his great power and abandon your labors to him?** God had confidence in the strength of this rhinoceros, because he put up with it when it was more cruelly inducing hardships for him, and he foreknew that it would be tolerating adversity for his sake just as constantly. To the rhinoceros in fact he abandoned the labors that he had undergone in the flesh himself, because he led the convert Paul even to the imitation of his own passion. That is why this same rhinoceros says, *I supply in my flesh what is missing from the passion of Christ.** So he goes on to say,

*Job 39:11

*Col 1:24

XIX. 34. *Do you not entrust to him that he will return the seed to you and assemble your threshing floor?** Let us consider what kind of a man Saul was: that from his youth he remained a helper to those who were stoning, that he destroyed some of the places of the church, that he requested and received letters to destroy others, that no death of the faithful was enough for him,

*Job 39:12

that with some dead he kept panting for the killing of others; beyond question we understand why none of the faithful would believe that God could bend the energy of such pride to bear the yoke of his fear. That is why after Ananias heard the Lord's voice proclaim him converted, he was still afraid and said, *Lord, I have heard about this man from many people: how much evil he has done to your saints in Jerusalem.** Nevertheless he was suddenly changed from an enemy and made a preacher, he carried the name of his Redeemer to all parts of the world, he suffered punishment for the sake of the truth and rejoiced to suffer himself the penalties he had imposed on others; some he called with gentle words, and others he recalled to faith with threats. To the former he promised the kingdom of the heavenly homeland; the latter he threatened with the fire of Gehenna. The latter he corrected with authority; the former he humbly drew to the way of righteousness. On every side he turned himself over to the hand of his own Leader, and he filled God's threshing floor with as much skill as he had formerly emptied it with pride.

*Acts 9:13

35. But neither is it incompatible with Paul that the rhinoceros is of the color of boxwood and that he is said to pierce the elephant's stomach with his horn. Because Paul was accustomed to live according to the rigor of the law, the practice of each virtue, which was harder for others, developed evenly in him. What else in fact does the color of boxwood signify but the pale complexion of abstinence? He is his own witness that he strictly adheres to this practice when he says, *I chastise my body and force it into subjection, lest while preaching to others I should ever chance to become reprobate.** Endowed with the knowledge of the divine law, when he convicts others of greed he strikes elephants in their stomachs with his horn. He had indeed struck elephants

*1 Cor 9:27

in their stomachs when he said, *Many people walk, as I have often told you, and now tell you tearfully, as enemies of the cross of Christ; their end is destruction, their god is their belly, and they boast of their shame.** And again: *Their kind do not serve Christ the Lord, but their own bellies.**

*Phil 3:18-19

*Rom 16:18

This rhinoceros then no longer attacks humans with his horn but beasts when Paul, wielding the power of his teaching, by no means seeks the deaths of humble people but kills the proud cultivators of the stomach. So what we know about Paul's writings remains for us to believe from the deeds of others. Many in fact were converted to the grace of humility from the pride of that people whose hostility the Lord tamed and subjected to the yoke of inspired fear; he actually subjected them to himself by means of the strength of the rhinoceros. But now, since we have heard about God's miraculous power in what was done by his chosen ones, let us listen to his wonderful patience in what he put up with in those whom he condemned.

XX. 36. *An ostrich's wing is like the wings of herons and falcons.** What else are we to understand by the word *ostrich* but the synagogue? It had the wings of the law, but crawling on the ground in its heart, it never lifted itself up above the earth. What else do herons and falcons mean but the ancient patriarchs, who were able to fly by living toward the realities they were able to discern by intelligence? Accordingly the ostrich's wing is similar to those of the herons and falcons, because the voice of the synagogue held the teaching of the patriarchs by speaking of it, but in its life it knew it not. That is why Truth warned the people of the same synagogue against the scribes and Pharisees, saying, *They sit on the seat of Moses. Therefore do what they tell you, but do not imitate their actions.** We could say

*Job 39:13

*Matt 23:2-3

much about the life of the heron, but because it is only the heron's wings we have been led to mention, we are not allowed to speak of its life.

XXI. 37. *It leaves its eggs on the ground. Do you perhaps warm them with dust?** In eggs one thing is seen; another is hoped, and hope cannot be seen. It is Paul who testifies, *Who hopes for what he sees?** What else is meant therefore by the ostrich's eggs but the apostles who were brought forth from the flesh of the synagogue? While they display themselves as the lowly ones who are despised by the world, they teach us the glory of heaven that is to be hoped for. Held by the proud as abject people of no importance, as it were, they have been thrown on the ground like eggs, but the source of their life was hidden inside them, and they flew to heaven on the uplifted wings of hope. The ostrich left those eggs on the ground, because the synagogue disdained to listen to the apostles to whom it had given birth according to the flesh; it left them to the Gentiles, who were to be called. With wonderful power the Lord warmed those eggs left in the dust, because he raised up the living nestlings of the apostles among the Gentiles so long left abject; those whom the synagogue despised as irrational and lifeless are now alive, and they fly with the veneration of the Gentiles through their mastery in teaching. The ostrich left its eggs in the dust, because all those whom the synagogue brought forth by preaching, it kept not at all from earthly desires. When the ancient enemy finds these desires conceived in the heart, he seizes the minds occupied by them and makes them sin. So it goes on,

*Job 39:14

*Rom 8:24

XXII. 38. *She forgets that a foot could trample them, or a beast of the field destroy them.** Then the foot tramples on the eggs, and the beast of the field destroys them when they are left on the ground. Obviously when human hearts desire always to think about earthly things and to

*Job 39:15

perform base acts, the beasts of the field or those belonging to the devil trip them up for their destruction. When they have long been abject because of the vilest thoughts, they are sometimes also ruined by the commission of greater crimes. The synagogue then neglected the eggs it laid, so that they could not leave the earth by living well. But almighty God, although he found her many children dead and cold because of earthly desires, breathed on them the heat of his love. But whereas the synagogue did not give her children life, she later envied them, and by persecution she set out to get rid of those whom she did not remember having given birth to and warmed for the sake of good works. So the Lord goes on to speak pointedly about this ostrich:

39. *She is turned against her own sons, as if they were none of hers.** As if she were not looking at as her own those whom she found living differently from the way she taught them, she hardens her cruel heart and begins to terrorize them; she occupies herself with torturing them. On fire with the torches of envy against those she did not struggle to make live, she now struggles to put them to death, and while she persecutes the members of the Lord, she thinks she is pleasing him by this means. That is why Truth said about these ostrich's eggs, *The hour is coming when anyone who kills you will think he is worshiping God.** Since therefore the synagogue is led by cruelty to persecution, and she thinks she is acting thus by the impulse of the fear of God, the Lord rightly adds,

40. *She labored in vain, since no fear forced her.** It was not fear, then, but cruelty that forced her to labor and pant for persecution. But because vices are often tinted with the color of virtues, their wickedness is much greater because they are not recognized as vices. So the persecution by the synagogue was that much

*Job 39:16

*John 16:2

*Job 39:16

harsher in that she considered herself made more pious by the deaths of the faithful. Consequently she absolutely could not discern what she was doing, because she blocked the light of her intelligence with the blank wall of pride. So the Lord rightly added,

41. *God has deprived her of wisdom, nor did he give her understanding.** The sentence of hidden retribution is exacting. The one who knowingly loses humility unknowingly loses the understanding of truth as well. The wounds the faithful incurred at the Redeemer's coming were much less than those yet to be inflicted on Holy Church at the coming of Antichrist. The synagogue then prepares herself for that time, so that she may harass the lives of the faithful with heaped-up sources of strength. So he again goes on in the same vein:

*Job 39:17

42. *When the time has come it lifts up its wings on high and derides both the knight and the horse's mount.** The ostrich lifts up its wings on high when it already contradicts its Maker, not reverently as previously, but in open rebellion. Changing into members of the devil and believing the man of lies to be God, even as it is extolled on high against the faithful, it boasts of being God's body. It despises not only the humanity of the Lord, but also his divinity, so it equally mocks the knight and the horse's mount. The unity of person having been kept, you see, it is important to understand that the Word of God mounted the knight at that time when he took to himself animated flesh within the womb of the virgin. At that time he mounted the knight when he joined to himself that human soul presiding over its own flesh by creating himself for the divine indwelling. Divinity really received flesh mediated by the soul, and in this way he held the complete knight all at once, because in himself he firmly fixed not only the flesh that is ruled, but also the soul that rules it. Judea accordingly

*Job 39:18

was captured in the trap of seduction by the coming of proud Antichrist, because she had only contempt for our Redeemer when he was humble among people; she derided the knight, because she contradicted his divinity everywhere, and she derided the rider likewise.

But our Redeemer is at once both knight and rider, and when he came into the world he presented strong preachers against the world, and when at the end of the world he endures the deception of Antichrist, he provides his fighters with strength, so that when the ancient enemy weakens in that final freedom of action, which is quickly to end, our faithful people may receive all the power they need to fight against the beaten adversary. So now when it is related how the ostrich lifts up its wings to deride the rider and the knight, in the same place the strong preachers are mentioned, and it is added,

XXIV. 43. *Will you teach the horse strength or cover its neck with a neigh?** In Holy Scripture the word *horse* is sometimes used for the shifty life of depraved people, sometimes for worldly dignity, sometimes for this very present world, sometimes for the preparation of a right intention, and sometimes for a holy preacher. *Job 39:19

Horse signifies the shifty life of the indolent when it is written, *Do not be like a horse or a mule.** And another prophet says, *They have become lovers going after the horse. Every one of them whinnies to his neighbor's wife.** *Ps 31:9

*Jer 5:8

On the other hand, *horse* denotes worldly dignity, as when Solomon says, *I saw slaves on horses and princes walking the earth like slaves.** Of course everyone who sins is a slave of sin, and they are slaves on horses when as sinners they are extolled by honors in the present life. But princes walk like slaves when no honors extol the many who are full of the dignity of virtues; rather, extreme adversity pursues them here below as though *Eccl 10:7

they were dishonorable people. That is why it is said elsewhere, *The riders of horses slept.** That is, those who trusted the honor of the present life closed the eyes of their minds to the light of truth, and their souls died.

*Ps 75:7

Horse also designates this present world, as Jacob declaims: *Let Dan become a snake on the road and a horned serpent¹ on the path to bite the horse's hooves and throw its rider backwards.** Concerning this latter text, we will better explain the significance of the horse if we also describe the context in greater detail. Some authors in fact hold that the Antichrist is to come from the tribe of Dan, because in this passage Dan is described as a snake that bites. So it is not without reason that when the people of Israel received the land by parcels of encampment, to Dan first the northern section was parceled out, signifying that one who had said, *I will ascend above the tops of the clouds; I will be like the most high.** Of Dan also the prophet said, *From Dan was heard a great clamor of horses.**

*Gen 49:17

*Isa 14:13-14
*Jer 8:16

Dan is not only called *snake* but also *horned serpent*. In Greek κερατα means "horn." We are told about a horned serpent in this passage, and the coming of Antichrist is fittingly there proclaimed, because he is armed with the sting of death-dealing preaching and with a powerful horn against the lives of the faithful. Everybody knows that a path is narrower than a road. So Dan becomes a snake on the road, because the wide extent of the present life lets people walk freely who are spared danger and treated with favor, but the snake on the road bites them and consumes them with the

---

¹ The Latin word *cerastes* is a transliteration from the Greek κερατα, which means "horn" or "horned." The patriarch Dan proclaims the arrival of the Antichrist, whose horn of false doctrine is to infect and poison the faithful.

poison of error after it has granted them freedom. But the horned serpent is on the path, and when it finds faithful people who are impelled to undertake the narrow journey of the heavenly precept, not only does it attack them with the wickedness of crafty persuasion, but it also threatens them with fear of its power, and after the benefits of false sweetness it wields the horn of power in the anguish of persecution.

At this point the horse is equivalent to this world, and through pride it foams at the mouth against the course of lost time. And because Antichrist tries to grasp the ends of the earth, this horned serpent is said to bite the horse's hooves. To bite the horse's hooves obviously means to reach the ends of the earth by attack. *And throw its rider backwards.** Whoever is extolled with the world's honors is the horse's rider. And he is said to be thrown backwards, not forward, as Saul was said to be thrown.* To fall forward means that in this life people realize their own sins and mourn over them by repentance. To be thrown backwards where one cannot see means that one suddenly leaves this life without knowing to what punishment he is being led. Since Judea falls into the traps of her own error, and she waits for Antichrist, not Christ, Jacob did well in the passage quoted to turn quickly to the voice of the chosen ones and say, *I wait for your salvation, O Lord.** In other words, "Not like the unfaithful waiting for Antichrist, I faithfully believe in the real Christ, him who is to come to redeem us."

*Gen 49:17

*Acts 9:4

*Gen 49:18

By the word *horse* the preparation of a right intention is understood, as it is written: *The horse is mounted on the day of battle, but the Lord grants salvation.** The soul prepares itself against temptation, but unless it is assisted from on high, it does not fight advantageously.

*Prov 21:31

By the word *horse* every holy preacher is also understood, as the prophet testifies, saying, *You sent your horses into the sea and troubled many waters.** The waters remained settled, of course, as long as human minds lay drugged in the immobility of their vices. But the sea was troubled by God's horses when the holy preachers were sent, and every heart that slumbered in fatal security was moved and shook with salutary fear. Accordingly in this passage the holy preacher is meant by the word *horse* when blessed Job is asked, *Will you teach the horse strength or cover its neck with a neigh?**

*Hab 3:15

*Job 39:19

44. But how is it that the Lord first says he gives the horse strength and later covers its neck with a neigh? The preacher's voice is expressed by the word *neigh*. Every real preacher receives strength first and then the neigh, because he will have rid himself of vices first, and he then receives the voice of preaching for the instruction of others. This horse has strength because it endures adversity resolutely. It can neigh, because it calls us to heaven with encouragement. The Lord vows that he gives both strength and the power to neigh to this horse, because unless both life and speech were united in his preacher, his power would never appear perfect. There is not much advantage in a preacher's being supported by the exercise of an elevated way of living if he is unable to speak and to arouse other people to experience what he experiences. On the other hand, what good is it for him to speak well and to incite others if he displays himself as one who has become slothful by living badly?

Since therefore it is necessary for the preacher to be united, and that both elements be perfectly joined, the Lord administers to his horse a neighing voice along with acting strength and the courage of action along with a neighing voice. And it is noteworthy that the neigh naturally comes from inside and passes the throat, but it is said to cover the neck; in other words it issues forth externally in a circular direction, obviously because the voice of preaching is released from the internal organs but moves in a circle externally. The better to rouse others to live uprightly, the voice binds the preacher's actions to good works, lest his actions should go beyond his works and his life should contradict his words. The horse's neighing is therefore led to cover its neck, because lest he be inclined to act perversely, by his own words even a preacher's life is guarded. That is why a wreath is awarded to those who fight valiantly, so that while they are wearing their badges of strength they can always exert still greater feats and fear to incur the shame of powerlessness, since the reward of courage that they display is already there. That is why Solomon speaks rightly in praise of wisdom to anyone who listens: *You will receive a crown of favor on your head and on your neck a golden wreath.** The next verse: *Prov 1:9

XXV. 45. *Will you rouse him like the locusts?** The word *locusts* sometimes signifies the people of the Jews, sometimes the converted Gentiles, sometimes flattering tongues, but sometimes by the use of comparison the Lord's resurrection or the lives of preachers.

*Job 39:20

That locusts mean the Jewish people, the life of John signifies, of him of whom it is written, *He ate locusts and wild honey.** John of course cries out to him whom his prophetic authority proclaims even by the food he eats. He signifies the Lord by his own person, since he was his forerunner. He came indeed for the sake of our redemption, and since he consumed the sweetness of the unfruitful Gentiles, he ate wild honey. However, since he partly converted the Jewish people in his own body, he took locusts for food. The very quick jumps of the locusts signify the Jews, who immediately drop to the ground. They jumped when they promised to obey the Lord's commands, but they quickly fell to the ground when their evil works denied that they had listened to

*Mark 1:6

them. Let us see in the Jews a kind of leap on the part of locusts: *All the words the Lord has spoken we will heed and do.** Let us notice on the other hand how quickly they fell to the ground: *If only we had died in Egypt instead of coming to this vast desert! If only we had perished and the Lord had not led us into this land!** So they were locusts that leaped through the voice and fell through deeds.

*Exod 24:3

*Num 14:3

46. The word *locusts* also signifies Gentiles. Solomon is our witness: *The almond tree will blossom, locusts will be fattened, and the caper plant will be scattered.** The almond tree naturally blooms before all the other trees. And what else does the almond blossom signify but the beginnings of the church? The church shows forth her first blossoming virtues in the holy preachers, and she anticipated the saints who were to come for the maturing of the fruits of good works; they were in a way the young trees that were to follow. In the church the locust was soon fattened, because the dry sterility of the Gentiles was infused with the fatness of heavenly grace. The caper plant is scattered, because when the Gentiles were called and received the grace of faith, Judea kept her own sterility and lost the good order of right living. That is why Solomon again says, *The locust has no king, but they all emerge troop by troop.** Obviously the abandoned Gentiles long remained strangers to divine guidance, but after a long period of time they were organized against the spiritual adversaries, and they marched for the war of faith.

*Eccl 12:5

*Prov 30:27

47. Again, the word *locust* signifies the flattering tongue, as is testified by the plagues from heaven demonstrated in Egypt; they were once inflicted bodily as punishment for sin, but they were signified spiritually for the evils that daily afflict wicked people. It is written, *A destructive wind swept up the locusts, and they* *went out over the whole land of Egypt. They covered the whole face of the earth and destroyed everything. In this way the grass growing on the ground and all the fruits on the trees were consumed.** Egypt was then afflicted by these plagues; by their means Egypt was struck down by an external blow. Sadly she would count up the loss and ruin she suffered when she neglected the interior life, so that she might witness that what perished externally, though more beloved, was less, and in that way she might sense through the outward appearances the still greater loss that she had suffered internally.

*Exod 10:13-15

What is it then that the locusts symbolically portend when they hurt human fruitfulness more than any other small creatures? Is it not flattering tongues that corrupt the minds of worldly people whenever they see some good being done that they inordinately praise? The fruits of the Egyptians are nothing more than vainglorious acts that the locusts destroy, when flattering tongues incline the hearts of workers to desire transitory praise. The locusts consume the grass whenever flatterers extol the words of speakers with praise. They also devour the fruits on the trees with their empty praise whenever they weaken anyone's courageous character that is already strong enough.

48. The word *locust* also metaphorically signifies the resurrection of our Redeemer. That is why the prophet speaks with his voice and says, *I am shaken off like a locust.** He allowed himself to be held by his persecutors up until his death, but like a locust he shook them off, because by the quick leap of resurrection he escaped their hands.

*Ps 108:23

49. That can also refer to the number of preachers. In them indeed he was shaken off like a locust, because while Judea was raging in their persecution and they were fleeing in every direction, they were in a way leaping as they went. Since however the preacher lifts himself up to the height of perfection, the one who is fortified not only by an active life but also by contemplation, the very perfection of preachers is rightly expressed when as often as they try to lift themselves up in the air, they first lift themselves up on their legs, and then they fly with their wings. That is exactly what the saints do who while they desire heaven first train themselves in the practice of good works of the active life and then finally get themselves into the higher air by flying with the leap of contemplation. They fix their legs and unfold their wings, because they prepare themselves by doing what is right, and they are lifted up for the life on high. Those who remain in this life cannot remain very long in divine contemplation, but they come back to themselves after their feet have leapt like those of locusts, and they turn back to the necessary works of active life from the heights of contemplation; nevertheless, they are not content to remain involved in that active life. But when they jump out to contemplation in their desires, they again seek the air by flying. In this way they pass their lives by ascent and descent just like locusts. They endlessly keep returning to see what is high and return to themselves weighed down by corruptible nature.

50. There is still something else that locusts do and the holy preachers imitate. In the early morning hours, that is, during the lukewarm time of day, locusts hardly lift themselves up from the ground at all, but the more the heat increases, the more actively do they fly. And any holy preacher, as long as he sees that the time of faith is quiet, has a lowly and despicable attitude, and following the locust he hardly lifts himself up off the ground. If however the heat of persecution should be inflamed, the one whose heart is united with heaven quickly shows his elevated state of mind, his wings beat, and he is lifted on high, he who was thought to have lain quietly in the lowest place. So blessed Job is asked by the Lord about this horse, that is, about his preacher, *Will you rouse him like the locusts?** You should hear whispered, "As I do, who awaken and arouse him to higher activity when I allow the fire of persecution and torture to grow fierce, so that stronger virtue might then awaken in him when the fiercer cruelty of the unfaithful begins to mock him."

*Job 39:20

But while the external sufferings of the holy preacher are many while he is tormented by the frightful agitation of persecutors, who is able to see his internal attention when he is unaware of all his external losses? Unless there were salutary wonders that fed him internally, it is beyond doubting that his external tortures would have reached his heart. But the soul was lifted up in the citadel of hope, and that is why the projectiles of external siege terrified him not at all.

Accordingly in this passage the Lord wanted to show how sweetly this horse was already perfumed internally while he suffered so much adversity externally. So he rightly added,

XXVI. 51. *The glory of his nostrils is terror.** In Holy Scripture the word *nostrils* sometimes means foolishness, sometimes the incitement of the ancient enemy, but sometimes intelligence's foreknowledge. Foolishness is meant by the nostrils, for example, as I have explained above by the testimony of Solomon, who said, *A gold ring is in her nose, that lovely, foolish woman.** By the word *nostrils* in the act of exhalation, ambush and the ancient enemy's incitement are also meant, as is written in this very Book of Job when the Lord testifies about him: *Smoke came out of his nostrils.** It is as if he said, "From his perverse incitement there arises in human hearts the darkness of exceedingly wicked thoughts, through which the sight of eyes is darkened."

*Job 39:20

*Prov 11:22

*Job 41:11

Foreknowledge is also meant by nostrils, as the prophet says: *Be quiet about the human creature whose breath is in his nostrils, because he is reputed as most high.** We often know by its smell what we do not see, so that even when they are located far away, some things are known to us by their distinguishing fragrance, and when we breathe through the nose, we often foreknow what we do not see. Our Redeemer's breath is said to be in his nostrils, so his knowledge is obviously meant to be foreknowledge, because whatever he told us that he knew about human nature he of course foreknew before the world came to be by his divinity. The prophet immediately adds the source of the breath in his nostrils and says, *He is reputed as most high.** It is as if he said, "He foreknew that he would be coming from the highest to the lowest," because he came from heaven to the lowest place. The saints also have believed what they heard from him, and they too already foreknow what is to come; as long as they faithfully devote themselves to his commandments, they expect his coming with a sure hope. That is why the horse's nostrils in this passage signify the holy preacher's foreknowledge and expectation. While he desires the coming of the Last Judgment, the unveiling of the heavenly homeland, and the rewards bestowed on the righteous, he as it were breathes in the future through the nostrils.

*Isa 2:22

*Isa 2:22

52. But the glory of his nostrils is terror, because the unrighteous fear the coming vision of the strict Judge, which the righteous passionately await. The righteous person, you see, is considering his own struggles, and he wants to be paid his reward; he knows his case is righteous, and he expects the Judge's presence and his coming in fiery flame to punish the impious and to bring the innocent their reward of contemplating his reality; yes, he desires this with extreme longing. The one on the other hand who remembers his own unrighteousness is in dire horror of the coming Judgment, and he is afraid of scrutinizing his own actions, because he knows very well that if he is examined he will be condemned. So the glory of his nostrils is terror, because where the righteous person is glorified, the sinner is sentenced.

Let us see how the horse breathes through the nostrils what he does not yet see, and let us see how great is the glory with which he is lifted up when he already expects what is to come. See how the famous preacher looks upon his present labors and says, *I am already being poured out, and the time of my passing is at hand. I have fought the good fight, I have finished the course, I have kept the faith. There remains for me a crown of righteousness, and the Lord, the just Judge, will bestow it on me on that day.** And he rightly adds, *Not only on me, but on those who lovingly await his coming.** It is as if he said, "But on all those who are aware of their own good works." It is only those of course who know the worth of their own righteousness in the Judge's cause who lovingly await his coming. Since accordingly the righteous person has glory precisely there where the unrighteous is terrified, let him rightly say, *The glory of his nostrils is terror.** But while this holy preacher is awaiting the glory that is to come, while he is yearning to come before the face of the Judge, and while he is still kept waiting for the reward of his labor, let us hear what he does while he is still posted in this life. The next verse:

XXV. 53. *He digs the earth with a hoof.** A horse's hoof usually means perseverance in labor. What then does the hoof signify if not the holy preacher's perfection in virtue? Obviously when the hoof digs the earth it evicts worldly thoughts from the hearts of the listeners by the example of the preacher's labor. The hoof digs the

*2 Tim 4:6, 8
*2 Tim 4:8

*Job 39:20

*Job 39:21

earth in that it empties the listeners' hearts of worldly concerns when the good teacher shows that the world is held in contempt by his labor. Let us see with what hoof of virtue Paul shows himself digging the earth of his hearers' hearts: *Keep in mind what you have learned, accepted, heard, and seen in me; act upon it, and the God of peace will be with you.** And again: *Be imitators of me, brothers, as I am of Christ.** Accordingly the one who corrects others by his own example and action certainly digs the earth with his hoof.

*Phil 4:8-9
*1 Cor 11:1

We still have something else to explain in greater detail, however, about this digging with the hoof. Although the saints are on the careful lookout with their mind's eye on the things that are above, and although they trample upon all that flows by below with the foot of rigid contempt, because of the corruption of earthly flesh to which they are still tied, they often suffer dusty thoughts to be in their hearts. And when they externally persuade other people to desire heaven, they are always internally haranguing themselves with incessant questioning, lest they be polluted by some base thought remaining inside themselves too long. So this horse digs the earth with his hoof when any preacher scatters the worldly thoughts in his own mind by vigorous inspection. The horse digs the earth with his hoof when the one over whom the Lord is already master considers the heap of rubbish collected by his old thoughts and keeps ridding himself of them with tears. That is why Isaac is rightly described as having dug wells in a foreign country.*

*Gen 26:18-22

We obviously learn from his example that we who are troubled by our exile should pierce through the deep soil of our thoughts and, wherever we find the water of true understanding, never grow weary of drawing it from the earth of our hearts with the hand of our inspection. The foreigners, however, secretly fill in those wells, because of course when the unclean spirits see us intently digging in our hearts, they fill in the excavation with the crowded thoughts of temptations. That is why we must always empty the mind and dig in it without ceasing, lest anything should be left unquestioned and the earth of our thoughts be heaped up over us even to the point of a sickly swelling of distorted actions. That is why Ezekiel was told, *Son of man, dig under the wall.** In other words, "Break the hardness of your heart with repeated blows of questions." That is why the Lord told Isaiah, *Go to the rock and hide there in a ditch dug in the earth from the presence of the fear of the Lord and from the glory of his majesty.**

*Ezek 8:8

*Isa 2:10

We indeed enter the rock when we bore through the thickness of our lethargy; we hide in a ditch dug in the earth from the presence of the fear of the Lord when we evict worldly thoughts, and we are concealed in the lowliness of our minds from the wrath of the strict Judge. The more earth that is dug and ejected, the more bedrock is uncovered that is still below it. So also the more intensely we evict worldly thoughts from our minds and hide within ourselves, the more humble we will be.

54. Look well and see that the day of God's Judgment is at hand, and it is as though his very fearsome face were already uncovered, so it is all the more necessary that each one of us should fear him more intensely the more closely his majestic glory already approaches. What then is to be done or where can we flee? On what side can anyone hide from him who is everywhere? But see how we are ordered to enter the rock and to hide in a ditch dug in the earth, so that breaking through the hardness of our hearts we may obviously escape his invisible wrath there where we are taken away from the love of visible things and left alone in our hearts. That is how when the earth of depraved thoughts is evicted, the mind is hidden inside itself more safely because more humbly. That is why the people of Israel were ordered through Moses by the Lord that when they went outside for the necessities of nature they should take along a pointed stick in a sheath and hide their excrement in a hole filled up with earth.* *Deut 23:12-13

We are weighed down, you see, with the burden of corruptible nature, and certain superfluous thoughts break out like the heavy load of the digestive system. But we should carry with us a pointed stick in a sheath, obviously so that we may be always ready to reproach ourselves, always having with us the sharp goad of compunction; this goad should continually dig in the earth of our minds with the pain of repentance and bury anything rotten that bursts out. The excretions of the stomach, you see, are covered in a hole in the ground through the use of the pointed stick, and we rid ourselves of the superfluous thoughts of our mind by a delicate self-accusation in the sight of God, one that is concealed by the goad of compunction. Accordingly the saints never stop reproving and judging their own useless thoughts, so the Lord says of his horse, *He digs the earth with a hoof.** In other words, whenever he sees a worldly thought taking up space in his mind, he strikes it with hard blows of the repentance he has brought with him. So whenever the saints judge themselves internally with that strict delicacy, they no longer fear anything external, and the less they fear present evils, the more completely they prepare themselves for future goods. So he goes on,

XXVIII. 55. *He boldly exults and goes out to meet the army.** He boldly exults, because in this way he is neither daunted by adversity nor lifted up by prosperity. No adversity daunts a person whom no prosperity corrupts. This horse then is both strong and controlled. He has the energy of courage so as not to be hindered by

*Job 39:21

*Job 39:21

adversity, and he has the weight of one who is settled in mind so as not to be moved by prosperity. Time indeed flies, but on that account it cannot pull away the righteous person who cannot be moved. Those whom it moves of course it also pulls away; it throws down the wrathful whom flattery lifts up. The person who is well-disposed and subject to God knows how to stand fast amid transient things and how to fix the footsteps of his mind amid the passing events of time; he knows both how to avoid excitement over small things and how not to fear what is coming. He often laughs at adversity, because he knows how to occupy himself fruitfully with the labors brought on by his dismay, and because he suffers them patiently for the sake of truth, he is glad in that the merit of his virtue is increased thereby. That is why we read that the apostles exulted when they happened to suffer for Christ's sake, as it is written: *They left the council chamber rejoicing that they had been held worthy to suffer insult for the name of Jesus.** That is why when Paul was hard pressed by harsh persecution in Macedonia, he showed himself happy in the fact that he admitted himself afflicted thereby and said, *When we came to Macedonia our body could not rest.** It was as if he said outright that his spirit could rest in the care of souls while his body endured the suffering of persecution.

*Acts 4:41

*2 Cor 7:5

Against this horse therefore the swords of painful opposition are unsheathed by the adversaries of Holy Church, and the weapons of the patronage of worldly powers are gotten ready. Heretics are accustomed, you see, to defend themselves with powerful worldly people as if with weapons. All people who are without faith are also accustomed to fight the preaching of faith by having the powers of the world stirred up. But God's horse boldly exults and fears no external torture, because it seeks internal delight; it does not fear the wrath of worldly powers, because it even tramples upon the very delight in this present world through ecstasy. That is why Solomon says, *Nothing that happens to the just man frightens him.** That is why it is written of him elsewhere, *The just man is like a fearless lion; nothing frightens him.** Therefore the lion is not afraid to meet other beasts, since he is well aware that he will prevail over them all. So the righteous person's boldness is rightly compared to that of a lion, because when he sees anybody rise against him, he has recourse to the self-confidence of his mind, and he knows he will overcome all his adversaries, because he only loves the one whom he never unwillingly loses. Whoever desires external things that are taken away against his will is foiled by his own will through external fear. Contempt for worldly desires is unbroken virtue, because the mind is positioned on high, and he is raised up by the judgment of his faith away from base things; he is all the less touched by any of his adversaries the more safely he is defensively established on high.

*Prov 12:21

*Prov 28:1

56. Not only is this horse absolutely fearless toward those who are coming against it, but it even goes out to meet them. So the Lord rightly adds, It *goes out to meet the army.** We are often left quiet and unhurt if we do not care about trials of justice with depraved opponents, but if the soul's desire for eternal life has been inflamed and if it already looks upon the true light within, if it enkindles the flame of holy fervor in itself, inasmuch as the place allows, and insofar as the cause requires it, we should expose ourselves for the defense of justice and and oppose perverse people who dare to commit perverse acts, even when they are not opposing us. When therefore the saint opposes depraved evildoers, even

*Job 39:21

when he is not involved, it is rightly said about God's horse, It *goes out to meet the army.*

57. We can see that horse aroused by the heels of its rider against the armed enemy as the great ardor that inflamed Paul when the flame of zeal consumed him at Ephesus to force his way into the crowd gathered at the theater. It is written, *They were filled with wrath, and they cried out saying, "Great is Diana of the Ephesians," and the city was filled with confusion. They rushed with one accord into the theater, taking with them Gaius and Aristarchus of Macedonia, Paul's companions.* And this follows immediately: *Paul wanted to join the throng, but his disciples would not let him. Some also of the chief men of Asia, friends of Paul, sent him word, pleading with him not to enter the theater.** These words certainly teach us how impetuously he would expose himself to the hostile troops unless his friends and disciples held him fast with the bonds of love.

*Acts 19:28-31

58. But if we should face enemies, if we should keep seeking battle, if we ought always to keep ourselves on the course of our fervor, how is it that the same famous preacher avowed about himself, *At Damascus the governor of King Aretas was guarding the city of Damascus to take me prisoner, but I escaped his hands by being let down in a basket through a window in the wall.** How is it that this horse sometimes chooses to face the armed troops and sometimes hides from the hostile army as though he were afraid? Is it not that we must both be taught by his technical skill sometimes to desire constant battle with adversaries and sometimes to prudently avoid it? It is absolutely necessary that in all that we do we should place on one side of the mind's scale the weight of labor and on the other its fruit; when we consider the

*2 Cor 11:32-33

weight of labor to be greater than the fruit, then each one of us can escape the labor without detriment, as long as he occupies himself with other matters in which the profit of fruit can outweigh its labor.

When however the weight of the fruit subsequently shows that it either balances or outweighs the labor, the labor cannot be avoided without grave loss. That is why when the holy preacher perceived the excessively obstinate minds of persecutors at Damascus, he refused conflict and adversity on their account, because he knew well that he was going to profit many, whereas he saw that he was able to profit few or none at Damascus. He sought therefore to escape the battle and reserved his fighting ability for more successful battles. It was not then strength that was lacking to the place, but a place that was lacking to strength, and therefore the strongest soldier sought a field of battle instead of a doubtful siege.

But where he surveyed the necks of many adversaries to be subjected to the rightful king, he was not afraid to undergo war even at the risk of death. Just as when he was going to Jerusalem himself and his disciples were for disallowing it because of the prophecy of his coming sufferings, he testified for himself and said, *I am not only ready to be bound but to die in Jerusalem for the name of the Lord Jesus, nor do I hold my life to be more precious than myself.** Consequently he was unperturbed at his foreseen sufferings, and so he here seeks hostile troops, but in the former instance he showed that his flight was planned and not the consequence of fear.

*Acts 21:13; 20:24

59. In this matter we must weigh the facts: anyone who declines certain labors through planned judgment is praiseworthy; one who is courageous embraces more demanding labors for God's sake. People often, you see, call a cautious plan what is in fact abject fear, and they affirm that they have prudently escaped an attack when they shamefully turned and fled on being struck. So it is necessary when the cause of God is invoked and the question of a plan is put on the table that the weight of fear in the heart should be most carefully determined, lest fear should creep in through weakness, pretending to be reason through the outward form of a plan, and lest sin should call itself prudence; in that case the soul could not return to repentance, when it calls virtue what it wrongly perpetrates. It remains, therefore, that whenever we are beset by doubts and some adversity hangs over us, we should first fight internally against fear and inordinate haste, so that we neither fearfully draw back nor hastily attack. We are of course excessively hasty if we always defy adversity, and we are excessively fearful if we always hide ourselves.

60. But we will understand spiritual warfare better if we take the form of maneuvers from the example of material warfare. No one of course is a wise leader when he orders a frontal attack against hostile troops, nor is anyone a courageous leader who is always cautious and leads the army away from facing the enemy. The leader must know how sometimes to have the army cautiously avoid the enemy's frontal attack and sometimes to crowd them by outflanking. Perfect preachers surely exhibit this skill with solicitude when by sometimes diverting the full savagery of persecution they know how wisely but not slackly to give way; sometimes, however, they show contempt for an attack of persecution, and they can bravely but not hastily turn it aside. The saint, you know, when he finds it convenient, exposes his breast to blows, and even in death he blunts the flying arrows, so it is rightly said, *He goes out to meet the army,** about whom it is again well said,

*Job 39:21

XXIX. 61. *He scorns fear, nor does he fall back from the sword.** Let us see how he despises fear who

*Job 39:22

counts the very adversaries' swords that he tramples on. He says, *Who will separate us from the love of God? Will tribulation, or prison, or hunger, or persecution?** In fear some future pain is dreaded, but in the sword some present pain experienced from a blow is felt. Accordingly, since the saint does not fear future adversity, he despises dread, and since he is not even overcome by the striking of a blow, neither does he give way before the sword. For this horse therefore there are as many enemy swords as kinds of persecution, all of which he opposes and overcomes, because the love of life prepares him for death, but since we have heard how very stoutly he exposes his breast to arrows, let us now listen to what is done by the adversaries. The next verse:

*Rom 8:35

XXX. 62. *He will hear the quivers rattle above him.** In Holy Scripture the word *quiver* sometimes means the righteous and hidden counsel of God, but sometimes the secret contrivances of depraved people. The word *quiver* expresses the hidden righteous counsel of God as when the same blessed Job in an earlier part of the book testifies, saying, *Then he opened his quiver and shot at me.** In other words, "He uncovered his hidden counsel, and he wounded me openly with attacks." Just as the quiver contains arrows, so God's hidden counsel contains sentences, and it is as if an arrow were plucked out of a quiver when God pulls an open condemnation out of his hidden counsel.

*Job 39:23

*Job 30:11

The word *quiver* also designates the contrivances of depraved people, as when the prophet says, *They have filled their quivers with arrows to shoot at the righteous hearts in the darkness.** The wicked, you see, devise snares for the righteous, and they hide them in their secret contrivances just as if they were loading quivers with arrows, and in the dark places of this life, as if in physical darkness they shot at the righteous of

*Ps 10:3

heart, because their malicious arrows can both be felt as wounds and not be perceived in flight. Accordingly, since God's horse is not terrified by any adversity, the more it is opposed, the more eagerly it is led by its powerful intention against the armed enemy. Its persecutors in the very act of striking find themselves beaten; nevertheless, in their trouble they turn to counsel, prepare their traps, and as if from a remote place of hiding strike and wound. So it is rightly said in this passage, *He will hear the quivers rattle above him.** They wanted to strike him with a device hidden far away, since their open gathering and approach was in vain. This quiver actually did rattle above God's horse at that time when forty enemies made a plot to kill him and asked for Paul to be led from prison, so that they might kill him with the blows they had planned as if with a hidden ambush of arrows, since they could never overcome him with a planned public persecution. The quiver then rattled when the intention of a hidden contrivance reached Paul.

*Job 39:23

63. However, if we carefully observe, we will see something still deeper in the rattling quiver. Adversaries, you see, often take counsel against good people, and they initiate depraved investigations in order to think out the traps they want to spring on them. But those who should betray these very traps to the good people themselves decide and secretly transmit them in such a way as to make people think that punishments have been prepared, so that since the knowledge was secretly passed on, it is feared more, and wounds more suspected than inflicted trouble souls that hear them the more. The arrows in the quiver are hidden and rattle unseen, so that even so they foretell death. The quiver then rattles against the horse when the depraved devices deceitfully hidden against the holy preacher are more deceitfully revealed. Having been threatened by the rattling of the quiver that was meant to terrify, God's preacher is not terrified by the public insults cast like arrows against him close at hand. But when he is not terrified by these threats, the cruel persecutors reveal themselves to hurt him. So after saying, *He will hear the quivers rattle above him,** the Lord quickly adds,

*Job 39:23

XXXI. 64. *He will cast the spear.** Against God's preacher the spear is cast after the rattling of the quiver, when after public terrorization from close at hand he is already struck and suffers pain. But when the holy preachers in defense of the faith undergo punishment, they seize for that same faith those whom they can, and despite blows of the whip they do not give up, and when they patiently suffer wounds they prudently return the fire of arrows with preaching against the hearts of unbelievers. So it sometimes happens that the fierce persecutors complain, not so much because they do not weaken the preacher's heart, but because his words cause their side to lose more adherents. Since therefore they do not overcome him with blows, lest perchance they should lose more people who listen to him, they quickly take up the spear of reply against his spoken words.

*Job 39:23

65. So after he said, *He will cast the spear*, the Lord added, *and take up the shield.** After the fierce persecutor wounded the preacher's body with blows, he fortified the listeners' hearts with the words of his disputation as though with a shield. The saint therefore brandishes a spear if he has to strike, but is opposed by a shield to keep him from being heard. God's defenders, you see, have their own arrows for use in battle, and they penetrate the listeners' hearts all the more quickly when they are shot from the spiritual bow, that is, from the intimate tension of the heart. Paul had armed himself with these arrows for the war of faith when he said, *I labor even to the point of chains like an evildoer, but the word of God*

*Job 39:23

is not chained.* It is as if he said, "Yes, I am hit by the spear of punishment, but I still do not stop shooting the arrows of words. I suffer cruel wounds, but I pierce the hearts of the unfaithful people by speaking the truth." Let him say it then: *He will hear the quivers rattle above him. He will cast the spear and take up the shield.** Against God's horse indeed the counsels of depraved people resound, and the quivers rattle; the spear is cast, and pain is exacted, but since the resistance of disputation is also offered, the shield is raised. But is the horse's enthusiasm restrained by all this? The more the saint is opposed by persecution, the more sharply he is impelled to preach the truth, and while he patiently puts up with persecution, he hurries ardently to invite people to listen. So the Lord continues to speak well about his horse:

*2 Tim 2:9

*Job 39:23

XXXII. 66. *With fierceness and rage he covers the ground; he pays no attention to the sounding of the trumpet.** It was first said to the sinning human being, *You are dust, and to dust you shall return.** The trumpets are sounded when the powers of this world terrorize the saints and forbid them to speak. Accordingly, because the preacher burns with the zeal of the Holy Spirit, and even in a position of being punished he does not stop calling sinners to himself, he beyond doubt covers the ground fiercely, but since he is by no means afraid of the threats of persecutors, he pays no attention to the sounding of the trumpet. And since the trumpet proclaims the declaration of war, what else but the voice of worldly powers is the voice? Having shown contempt for resisters, it readies itself for the battle of death.

*Job 39:24
*Gen 3:19

67. This trumpet had been sounded by the chief priests when they flogged the apostles and forbade them to speak about God, as it is written: *They beat the apostles and charged them not to speak in the name of Jesus.** But let us see how the trumpet's sounding did

*Acts 5:40

not frighten God's horse. Peter said, *We must obey God rather than men.** He also told other persecutors, *We cannot refrain from speaking of what we have seen and heard.** The horse then did not fear the sounding trumpet, because the famous preacher despised the worldly powers and feared none of the threats that he heard.

*Acts 5:29

*Acts 4:20

68. Let us see how another of God's horses covered the ground, how no trumpet was able to terrify him: *More of them came from Antioch and Iconium in Judea, and having won over the crowd, they stoned Paul, and dragging him outside the city, they left him for dead. But when his disciples stood around him, he got up and re-entered the city; the next day he set off for Derbe with Barnabas. And when they had announced the good news in that city and taught many people, they returned to Lystra, Iconium, and Antioch to confirm the faith of the disciples.** Let us consider then what threats could restrain this horse when not even death itself was able to turn him aside from what he intended to do. See how he was attacked with stones, but he was not prevented from speaking the truth. He could be killed, but he could not be overcome. As though already dead he was thrown outside the city, but the next day we find him unhurt and preaching inside the city.

*Acts 14:18-21

O how strong was the weakness that was inside this person! O how victorious was his pain! O how overbearing was his patience! He is summoned by rejection to act; by blows he is caused to stand erect and preach salvation; by pain he is revived to drive away the weariness of labor. What adversity would overcome this person whom even pain revives? But he is God's horse, and he despises both arrow and quiver; he has only contempt for malicious counsel, and he is stronger than the brandished spear. He hardens his chest against the wounds of open persecution, and he breaks the opposing shield, because he subdues the disputation of those resisting his message by reasoning with them. He covers the ground, because he converts sinners in his own body by exhortation; he pays no attention to the noise of the horn when he hears it, because he tramples upon any terrible prohibition. What is said is of minor importance when he bravely perseveres in his labors and, what is still greater, exults in adversity. So he goes on to say,

XXXIII. 69. *Wherever he hears the noise he says, "Aha!"** By these words we are shown that in this passage the Lord says nothing about the horse devoid of reason. Nor can a brute animal say "Aha!" But when it is asserted that it says what it absolutely cannot say, the Lord indicates the one whom the horse signifies. The word *aha* certainly means exultation. Accordingly the horse hears a noise and says "Aha!" because when a courageous preacher understands that the battle of his passion is at hand, he exults at the exercise of virtue, nor is he afraid of the danger of conflict, because he rejoices at the triumph of victory. It is the horse's lot to say, "Aha," but the holy preacher's to rejoice at the moment of passion. But if the brave preacher desires the glory of his passion, and if he joyfully seeks to undergo the crisis of death for the Lord, how is it that Truth tells Peter, his bravest preacher, who stoutheartedly takes unto himself the virtue inherent in his name, *When you are old you will stretch out your hands, and someone else will tie you and take you where you do not wish*?* How can he rejoice at his passion, when someone else ties him and he is led where he does not wish to go? But if we consider how a soul trembles with the fear of death when his passion is approaching and still rejoices at the thought of the coming reward of the kingdom, we will understand how he unwillingly wills to undergo the danger of the glorious battle, because he both considers

*Job 39:25

*John 21:18

in death what he fearfully tolerates, and in the fruit of death he foresees what he desires and seeks.

70. See how Paul loves what he flees and flees what he loves! Does he not say, *I want to die and be with Christ,** and, *For me to live is Christ and to die is gain?** Yet he also says, *We who are in this tent groan in turmoil, because we do not want to lose what we have, but to receive more clothes, that what is mortal might be swallowed up by life.** See how he desires death and yet is afraid to lose the flesh! Why is this? Because even if lasting victory inspires joy, the very pain troubles him nonetheless in the present time, and although love of the reward to follow is victorious, it is not without groaning that the force of pain touches the soul.

*Phil 1:23
*Phil 1:21

*2 Cor 5:4

Just as when a brave soldier, seeing the time of battle close at hand, girds himself in armor, he both trembles and hastens, both shakes and rages; he seems as it were to be frightened and to grow pale and yet to be spurred on by violent anger; so also the saint, seeing the time of his passion draw near, is both shaken up by the weakness of his nature and strengthened by the solidity of his hope; he both trembles at the thought of his approaching death and exults at the thought of the truer life reached through dying. He certainly cannot cross over to the kingdom unless death intervenes, and that is why he both confidently doubts and doubtfully trusts; he both joyfully fears and fearfully rejoices, because he knows he will not reach the quiet prize unless he laboriously transcends the gap that lies between.

It is the same way with us when we want to expel sickness from our bodies: we sadly consume bitter drafts to clean ourselves out, while we rejoice at our following health. Because of course the body cannot be healed otherwise, we freely partake of the drink that disgusts us. When the soul realizes that life lies in bitterness, while it is upset over the feeling of dislike, it also is glad. Let the Lord then say, *Wherever he hears the noise he says, "Aha!"** because the brave preacher knows the announcement of battle; so although as a human being he shakes before the force of the blow, the certitude of faith lets him exult at the prize and reward. But he would never remain unhurt in this contest of his passion unless he reached that same passion while meditating with instant thought. The evil, you see, that is avoided by counsel, the soul undergoes by reason and by fighting against itself, because the less anyone is beaten by adversity, the more prepared for it he finds himself by foreknowledge. The heavy burden of fear is often lightened in practice, and death itself, while it troubles us unexpectedly, is even foreseen deliberately and often makes us feel glad. So the Lord goes on about the horse:

*Job 39:25

71. *He smells war from a distance.** It is as if he said outright, "Therefore he wins another battle, because he prepares his mind for battle before the battle is joined." To smell war from a distance means to foresee by thought some adversity that is still far away, lest perchance some evil should befall a person unexpectedly. Paul warned his disciples to smell this war at a distance when he said, *Put yourselves on trial and prove yourselves, whether you have faith or not.** It is as if he ordered them outright and said, "Bring forth the battles of persecution to your minds and weigh the deep and hidden thoughts of your hearts; find out what kind of people you will be and how you will be able to live through punishments."

*Job 39:25

*2 Cor 13:5

The saints smelled out this war from far away when they were either well situated in the peace of the universal church or at war with the heretics, or when they foresaw imminent tortures from persecution by those without faith. While they are living rightly they often receive evil in return for good, and they bear the insults of detraction with serenity, so that when an occasion of persecution arises, the enemy finds them so much more prepared and strong that not even the darts of false brethren within the church defeat them. The one, you see, who falls from the state of patience before the onslaught of wounds opened by tongue is witness against himself that he does not stand fast against the swords of obvious persecution. Since therefore the man of God practices in the present time against future adversity, and having practiced in small things exerts himself against greater opposition, it is rightly said of the horse that he smells battle from afar.

XXXIV. 72. *[He hears] the urging of the captains and the roars of the army.** The captains of the opposing army are the instigators of error, and it is of them that the psalmist says, *He poured contempt upon their leaders and led them aside, off the track.** Truth himself says of them, *If a blind person leads the blind, both together will fall into the pit.** The army of depraved persons, that is, the crowd, follows these captains, because they are the foolish followers of their evil precepts. It is noteworthy also that the captains are said to urge but the army to roar. Obviously this is because those who govern the unfaithful and the heretics urge on them the evil doctrines they order to be followed as if they were reasonable. The crowd that is subject to them, however, obeys their voices without judgment and cries out in confused frenzy, so they are said to roar as if with the minds of beasts. The howling of wolves is conveniently compared. The pack of reprobate sinners pants only with greed against the life and behavior of the faithful, so it is as if their cries were howls.

God's horse therefore scents the urging of the captains and the howls of the army from afar when any

*Job 39:25

*Ps 106:40

*Matt 15:14

holy preacher considers long before it is present either what the fabricators of error are able to devise against the chosen ones, or how the crowd subject to them can monstrously go mad. Paul sensed this urging by the captains when he said, *The hearts of the faithful are led astray by their sweet words and blessings.** He sensed the howls of the army when he said, *After my departure ravening wolves will come among you.** Peter sensed the urging of the captains when he cautioned the disciples about certain ones: *They will avariciously exploit you with lying words.** He sensed the howling of the army when he first said, *Many people will imitate their lustful practices by which the way of truth is blasphemed.**

*Rom 16:18

*Acts 20:19

*2 Pet 2:3

*2 Pet 2:2

73. Accordingly, now that we have recounted how every holy preacher and faithful captain in the war of persecution can show his quality, let us also describe every soldier of Christ using the image of this horse, so that the one who has not yet reached the stage where he considers himself a preacher, if he has already begun to live according to this word of the Lord, can recognize himself as expressed by it, inasmuch as he can gather from this how well he is known by God, namely that if he has reached greater heights, God certainly does not forget him but lets his speech be significant, even in small matters. Let us then repeat all that has been said about the horse and suggest in what ways God's soldier makes progress from the first moment of his conversion, how rapidly he grows from his smallest attainments even to the greatest, and by what stages he keeps going from the lowest attainments to the highest. So let him speak:

XXXV. 74. *Will you teach the horse strength or cover its neck with a neigh?** Every soul that the Lord mercifully keeps watching should show before anything else the fortitude of faith about which Peter said, *Be serious and watchful. Your adversary, like a roaring*

*Job 39:19

lion, goes around looking for someone to devour. Let your faith be strong and resist him.* To this fortitude the neigh is joined when that happens that is written: *He might believe with the heart and be justified and confess with the tongue and be saved.** The next verse:

*1 Pet 5:8-9

*Rom 10:10
*Job 39:20

XXXVI. 75. *Will you rouse him like the locusts?** Everyone who follows God's way is roused like a locust in the very beginning, because even if in certain actions our bent knees stick to the earth like those of a locust, yet in other actions our wings spread out and we are lifted up above the earth. In the beginning of our conversion, you see, good behavior is mixed with bad, when we intend to initiate new behavior while old habitual behavior is still active. The more we continue to fight against our bad actions every day, the less we are tripped up by their being part of our behavior in the meantime. Nor does the guilt of those actions condemn us any more when our minds carefully resist their depraved continuance. Worldly actions disturb us less when we begin a new life, because they are not allowed to remain with us any longer. Accordingly the Lord lovingly overlooks certain weaknesses of ours in the beginning of our conversion so that he may at length lead us on to heaven by perfecting us, so he lifts us up like locusts in the beginning; we are lifted up for the flight of virtue, so that we do not despair for the failure of worldly action. The next verse:

*Job 39:20

XXXVII. 76. *The glory of his nostrils is terror.** Since whatever is unseen is known by its odor, not without reason are the thoughts of our hope expressed by the use of the word *nostrils*, by which the coming Judgment, unseen by our eyes as yet, we nevertheless already see by means of hope. Everyone in fact who begins to live uprightly and hears how the righteous people are called to the kingdom through the Last Judgment rejoices thereat, but when he remembers that some evil thoughts are still left in him, he is afraid of the coming of that same Judgment concerning which he began to exult. He actually notices that his life is a mixture of good and evil, his thoughts are a jumble in a way of hope and fear. When he hears something about the joy of the kingdom his delight elevates his mind, but when on the other hand he thinks about the tortures of Gehenna, terror quickly seizes his mind. The glory of his nostrils is then rightly called terror, because his position is between hope and fear, and when he considers the future Judgment in his mind, he fears the same thing that is the cause of his glory.

His very glory is then terror for him, because in starting to be good, he is gladdened by the hope of Judgment, but because all evil is not yet at an end, he is not perfectly safe. But while this conflict is going on he has careful recourse to his mind, and, resisting the storms of such great fear, he disposes himself for the tranquility of peace alone; he makes every effort to be found free by the strict Judge. In fact he evaluates his fear of the Lord's presence as slavish, and lest he should fear the Father's presence, he behaves in such a way that he may recognize him as a son. In this way he learns to love the Judge with all expectation and, so to speak, to resist fear by fearing. He considers the rising of fear in the heart as a reaction of the flesh, and on that account he gives priority to the taming of the flesh with forceful subjugation. So after saying, *The glory of his nostrils is terror,** the Lord rightly continues, **Job 39:20

XXXVIII. 77. *He digs the earth with a hoof.** **Job 39:21
Digging the earth with a hoof obviously means taming the flesh by strict abstinence. The more the flesh is restrained, the more secure in heavenly hope the soul finds itself and rejoices therein. So when the earth has been dug, it is fittingly added, *He boldly exults*. Because he

bravely restrains what opposed him, he boldly exults in his fulfilled desires in eternal peace. The more strictly the body is restrained from forbidden actions, you see, the better disposed the mind is for heavenly desires. So Solomon was right to say, *Prepare your external work and accurately plow your field, that you may later build your house.** He in fact builds the mind a good house who first clears away the thorn bushes from the field of the body, lest the brambles of desires should grow in the field of the flesh and the whole interior building of virtues should collapse when the famine of goodness spreads. Everyone who finds himself in this state of war and in this battle, the more strictly he restrains his own body as if it were itself an ally of the enemy, the more quickly he sees through the enemy's tricks. So after the breakdown of the body and after the joy of the heart, he correctly adds,

*Prov 24:27

XXXIX. 78. *He goes out to meet the enemy.** The unclean spirits are the armed enemy, and they are armed with innumerable ambushes against us. And when they are unable to persuade us to do evil, they block our field of vision with evil images under the guise of virtues; they hide themselves under a certain kind of armor, lest they should be recognized naked in their malice against us. We go out to meet the enemy in arms when we foresee their ambushes in advance. Accordingly, having dug in the earth, we go out to meet the enemy in arms, and this means that having tamed the pride of our flesh, we scout out the tricks of the unclean spirits in a wonderful way. Having dug in the earth, we go out to meet the armed enemy, and this means that, having overcome the wickedness of the flesh, we engage the spiritual vices in battle. The person who still fights against himself feebly, you see, wages war in vain against the enemy troops outside. Those who are themselves subjugated to

*Job 39:21

the flesh: how can they strike back against the spiritual vices? How can anyone desire to win the struggle in the external battle if he still gives in when there is a private internal war going on against his own wanton pleasures?

79. Or at least we go out to meet the enemy army when we oppose them through intense exhortations as they set their ambush in someone else's heart. We come out to meet the enemy, as it were, moving from the place where we were to another place, when we in an orderly way put aside our own concern to forbid the unclean spirits to enter our neighbor's mind. So it often happens that the crafty enemy, the more they see the brave soldier of Christ prevail against them in someone else's heart, when he has already beaten them in his own interior struggle, the more alarmingly they tempt him within himself. While they are calling him back to protect his own heart, they are more at liberty to invade other hearts that he was protecting with his exhortation. And when they are unable to overcome him, they try at least to occupy him, inasmuch as the soldier of God is battling himself, while not he but the one he would defend is crushed. But the mind that is immovably fixed in God disdains the thorns of temptation; nor does it fear the darts of any kind of terror. It depends on the help of heavenly grace, and it heals the wounds of its own weakness in such a way that it does not abandon the souls of others. So he adds about this horse,

XL. 80. *He scorns fear, nor does he fall back from the sword.** He scorns fear, because he is not terrified by any temptation to the point of being silenced. Nor does he fall back from the sword, because even if a violent temptation should strike him, it does not cause him to give up the protection of his neighbor. That is why even Paul provides us with an example of his own unconquered way of life and tells us about the sword

*Job 39:22

wounds he received, showing us that he did not fall back from these swords. He had already won all the fights of the works of the flesh and been stabbed by the enemy sword of temptation of the flesh when he said, *I see another law in my body, resisting the law of my mind, and making me a captive of the law of sin residing in my body.** But from that same sword that he had beaten in himself he did not fall back in others when in fact he told his neighbors, *Do not let sin rule in your mortal bodies or obey its desires.** And again: *Mortify your members that are on earth. Avoid fornication, impurity, wantonness, and evil desires.**

*Rom 7:23

*Rom 6:12

*Col 3:5

A serious sword of temptation struck him, about which he himself said, *I was in more labors, more often imprisoned, beatings uncounted, dying often: from the Jews I received forty lashes fifty times less one; three times I was beaten with rods; once I was stoned; three times I was shipwrecked, being in the deep sea night and day.** All this and more he was able to suffer, and it tires us just to count it. But how great was his love of neighbor when he did not give in to this sword, so that after all these trials he added, *Besides all these external cares, there is my daily, pressing anxiety, the care of all the churches.** He is God's horse struck by the sword, but that blow did not turn him aside from his course, since he was a brave soldier in the spiritual battle and was himself wounded by the enemy, and he still urged others along to safety. But the more the ancient enemy saw himself despised so forcefully, the more painful were the darts he aimed at that hardened breast of the heavenly soldier. So he goes on,

*2 Cor 11:23-25

*2 Cor 11:28

XLI. 81. *He will hear the quivers rattle above him. He will cast the spear and take up the shield.** Because he sees that the efforts of the holy mind prevail against him and are profitable for others, the ancient enemy

*Job 39:23

rages still more to harm it, and he multiplies his temptations against it. So it often happens that those who have authority to govern others suffer more serious battles of temptation, inasmuch as while the captain in the war himself turns to flight, the crowded band of the resisting army is dispersed without difficulty, just as in a battle of physical bodies. And so the shrewd enemy inflicts different kinds of blows and wounds upon the heavenly army, now wounding them from ambush with arrows from the quiver, now casting spears against them from frontal attack, obviously because he hides the vices and other evils under the appearance of virtues while he opposes them with others that are easy to see.

When he sees that God's army is weakening, then he does not have to use disguises and trickery. But when he notices strong people resisting him, then beyond any doubt he prepares traps for their strength. When, you see, he sees any weak person enticed by the flesh, he openly presses upon that person's notice a bodily form that can be desired. But if he sees by chance that a person is proof against avarice, he inconveniently suggests the poverty of his household to his thoughts, so that while the mind is as it were dutifully occupied in the care of providing, it is being secretly led astray in the futile search for material things and wickedly seized. So an arrow wounds God's horse from ambush when the wily enemy hides vice under the cover of virtue. The spear, however, wounds at close quarters when outright wickedness tempts even the experienced warrior.

82. On the other hand, the enemy often casts both these weapons at the same time at the heavenly soldier, so that he might dispatch him with either one blow or the other. The deceptive adversary then tries to strike both ways, by open hostility and by hidden ambush, so that when the hidden arrow is suspected the spear in frontal attack is feared less, or while the spears in front are being avoided, the arrow's flight from ambush is not seen at all. He often proposes a temptation of lust that suddenly ceases by trickery, whereupon he quickly suggests pride over preserved chastity. There are also those who when they see many people fall from the citadel of chastity into the pit of pride neglect the custody of their own lives and drown in the impurity of fornication. And there are those who on the other hand flee from the impurity of fornication only to fall from the peak of chastity into the pit of pride.

The open sin of vice is therefore like a warrior openly brandishing a spear, and the sin of virtue is like an arrow from the quiver that wounds from hiding. God's horse, however, both defeats the spear in frontal attack when he tramples upon lust and detects the arrow loosed against his flank when he is pure and chaste and keeps himself from pride. So Solomon rightly speaks about both methods of fighting: *The Lord will be at your side, and he will keep your feet from stumbling.** His foot, you see, is moving forward, but he does not see what is in front of him if his eye is on his flank. On the other hand, if he is guarding his footsteps and has his eye on what is in front, he stops looking around. When we do anything with our attention held in front of us, it is as though we foresee where to place our feet, but when a sin secretly arises out of some power, it is as though our flank were uncovered for the flight of an arrow while we were looking toward the front.

But it often happens that when we are worried about the rising of a sin, we leave aside the practicing of a virtue, and it is as though, looking around at our flank, we do not see how to put our foot forward. So it is well said, *The Lord will be at your side, and he will keep your feet from stumbling.** God's soldier is protected by

*Prov 3:26

*Prov 3:26

the shield of divine grace, and he looks around and is aware of whatever may be aimed at his flank. He does not cease his step-by-step progress toward the front. And the deceitful, envious foe sees that he can by no means prevail through arrow or spear, so he moves against the shield, so that if he does not wound the resistant soldier in the chest, he may at least cut off the path of the forward-moving soldier by certain blows; by his very feints he makes it hard for him to proceed, and if he cannot defeat him, he at least resists him. But let us hear what God's horse does in the face of so many events of war:

XLII. 83. *With fierceness and rage he covers the ground; he pays no attention to the sounding of the trumpet.** The trumpet sounds against the horse when a sin crops up in front of a chosen person's mind in something that he does, constituting a strong and terrible temptation. But he covers the ground with fierceness and rage, because he shakes himself up with excessive zeal, and if he finds anything earthly in himself he rids himself of it by his daily progress. He pays no attention to the sounding of the trumpet, because by forceful inspection he carefully restrains every vice that arises from the praise of valor. Actually he would consider it the sounding of a trumpet if by chance he should fear the performing of a good action on account of something shameful that should arise. Accordingly he is not afraid to act bravely against noisy temptations, so he takes his stand in enthusiasm and does not worry about the sounding of the trumpet. On the other hand, when he sees he is making progress in virtue, lest he should be lifted up by that prosperity in virtues, he is often glad to be beset by temptations. So he properly adds,

*Job 39:24

XLIII. 84. *Wherever he hears the noise he says, "Aha!"** Evil success in fact has tripped up many people,

*Job 39:25

and peace that lasts too long has rendered many others insensitive. The enemy then has unexpectedly struck them down hard, because he found them neglectful as a consequence of being habitually undisturbed. So when the saints find that they make a great deal of progress and are prosperous in virtues, they are exultant at times at being beset by temptations by a certain disposition of God's providence; the more they humbly realize how weak they are from having been hit by the blow of temptation, the more stoutly they guard the honor of virtue that they have received. The horse accordingly hears the noise and says, "Aha," obviously because God's fighter sees himself fall into the power of temptation and considers it an advantage bestowed by God's providence, placing stronger trust in him precisely because of the adversity. Such battles of adversity do not prevail over him for the reason that they never try him unforeseen; he takes note long before from everything that happens and knows the vice that a new battle introduces. So he goes on,

XLIV. 85. *He smells war from a distance.** To smell war from a distance means to realize what battles with vices follow from the causes that preceded. As we have already often said, an unseen object is known from its odor, so the smelling of a battle from a distance means it is done as though by the whiff of nostrils, so by the foresight of thoughts, we ascertain hidden wickedness. The Lord rightly says about such smelling in praise of his church: *Your nose is like a tower in Lebanon.** It is through the nose, you see, that we discern odors and stenches. And what else does the nose signify but the far-seeing discernment of the saints? A lookout tower is built high, so that the coming of an enemy may be seen at a distance. Rightly therefore is the church's nose said to be like a tower of Lebanon, because when the

*Job 39:25

*Song 7:4

far-seeing discernment of the saints takes its position on high to carefully look all around, it detects a sin before it is committed, and when it watchfully discovers it, it forcefully avoids it. That is why Habakkuk says, *I will stand guard at my watch tower.** That is why Jeremiah warns the soul of every one of the elect, saying, *Set up a lookout post for yourself and watch in bitterness.** To set up a watch tower means to know beforehand by deep meditation that battles with vices are coming; the mind of the chosen one watches in bitterness, even if it enjoys a stable peace of the virtues, when it sees the evil ambushes set up, and it does not consent to wait quietly.

*Hab 2:1

*Jer 31:21

86. The soul is careful in the first place to do no evil and in the second place not to do good carelessly; after it has put away depraved actions, it strives to subject even righteous acts to itself, lest they should get beyond the mastery of the mind and turn into a sin of pride. As we have already said above, it often happens that evil arises out of good through the vice of carelessness, so we must meditate with watchful application on how arrogance arises out of teaching, cruelty out of justice, slack behavior out of dutiful love, anger out of zeal, sloth out of meekness. So when he performs these good actions, he sees what the enemy does against him here by making those vices arise. When he devotes himself to study for the acquisition of learning, he carefully prepares his mind for the battle of arrogance. When he rightly desires to avenge the misbehavior of certain ones, he most wisely avoids the consequence of cruel revenge that exceeds the right measure of justice. When he tries to tame himself by the pursuit of meekness, he is careful to guard himself from the loss of discipline. When he is incited by the urge of righteous zeal, he is careful above all to see that the flame of wrath does not burn hot above what is necessary. When he exercises restraint and uses great calmness and a quiet demeanor, he observes himself to make sure that he does not grow cold and insensitive. So because in the thoughts of the spiritual army every vice is carefully watched before it can secretly rise, it is rightly said about God's horse: *He smells war from a distance.** He carefully estimates how a multitude of wicked thoughts may rush in, so that he may not allow evil to enter his mind, not even a little. So he continues,

*Job 39:25

XLV. 87. *The urging of the captains and the roars of the army.** The vices that tempt us fight against us in the invisible battle with pride reigning over them, so that some of them are in charge like captains whom the others, like soldiers, follow. Not all sins occupy the heart by the same entrance, you see. But whereas the greater and fewer ones go first into the neglected mind, the smaller and innumerable ones are poured forth into it in large numbers. Pride is the queen of vices, and once she has taken over the vanquished heart completely, she soon hands it over to the seven principal vices, who are as it were her captains, to be destroyed. The army then obviously follows these captains, because from them without any doubt the oppressive multitudes of vices are born. We will clarify this fact better if we introduce by enumerating as far as we can the captains of this army one by one. The root of all evil is certainly pride, about which Scripture testifies, *Pride is the beginning of every sin.*[2]* Her first offspring of course are the seven principal vices, and they are brought forth from this poisonous root, being called vainglory, envy, anger, sorrow, avarice, gluttony, and lust.[3] Because he was sorry

*Job 39:25

*Sir 10:15

---

[2] This reflects the verse numbering of the Vulgate. Modern editions, however, have Sir 10:13.

[3] Today they are called the seven capital sins.

that we were captives of pride by these seven vices, our Redeemer came full of the sevenfold grace of the Holy Spirit to fight the spiritual battle of liberation.

88. But each of these vices leads its own army against us: from vainglory are born disobedience, boasting, hypocrisy, contention, obstinacy, discord, and presumption. From envy are born hatred, back-biting, detraction, elation over a neighbor's adversity, and sorrow over his prosperity. From anger are born a quarrelsome mind, insulting speech, outcry, indignation, and blasphemy. From sorrow are born malice, rancor, meanness, despair, laxness concerning the commandments, and wandering of the mind towards what is forbidden. From avarice are born treachery, dishonesty, deception, perjury, disorder, violence, and hardness of heart against mercy. From gluttony are propagated silly laughter, offensive humor, impurity, excessive talking, insensitivity toward intelligence. From lust are generated blindness of mind, inconsiderateness, inconsistency, rashness, self-love, hatred of God, desire for the present world, and horror or despair of the future world. Since therefore the seven principal vices bring forth such an immense multitude of vices out of themselves when they reach the heart, it is as though they draw troops and an army to follow them. Of these seven sins, five are spiritual and two carnal.

89. But they are all joined together by such a close relationship that only one is generated from one. Pride's first offspring is vainglory, which when it has overpowered and disabled the mind soon gives birth to envy. This is because the mind, once it has desired the power of an empty name, rots away lest someone else should be able to acquire that name. Envy in turn gives birth to anger, because the more seriously the soul is wounded by the internal sore of malice, the more likely it is to lose meekness and tranquility; it is as though a member of the body were touched with pain, so that the hand of opposing action feels pressed down by heaviness. From wrath in turn is born sorrow, because the mind is troubled, inordinately shaken, and confused for having given in to it, and when it has lost sweet tranquility, nothing but grief following on its troubled state nourishes it. Sorrow in turn becomes avarice, because after the confused heart loses internal joy, which did it good, it seeks its consolation outside itself, and the less recourse it has to internal joy, the greater is its desire to obtain external goods. After that happens, two carnal vices, namely gluttony and lust, are left over. But everybody knows that lust is born from gluttony, because in the very distribution of the members of the body the stomach and the genitals are closely connected; so when one of them is inordinately fed, the other beyond any doubt is aroused to undignified behavior.

90. The captains are rightly said to urge on and the army to roar, because the first vices insinuate themselves into the deceived mind according to a more or less rational order, but the ones that follow are innumerable, and they draw the mind on to all madness and confuse it with bestial noises. Vainglory ordinarily urges the subdued heart in a kind of rational way and says, "You should desire more goods, so that the more your wealth exceeds that of others, the more you can be profitable to others." Envy also ordinarily urges on the subdued heart as if rationally and says, "How are you worth less than those others? Why then are you not at least equal or superior to them? How much more are you worth than they? They should not then be your equals or superiors." Anger also ordinarily urges the subdued heart on as if rationally and says, "You cannot bear calmly the things that are happening to you. It is wrong for you, in fact, to put up with them patiently. Even if they can be resisted without much irritation, they will later overwhelm you immeasurably."

Sorrow likewise ordinarily urges the subdued heart on as if rationally and says, "What do you have to be happy about? Look at all the bad behavior you put up with from your neighbors! Measure the grief you feel, seeing that they turn against you with the gall of bitterness." Avarice as well urges the subdued heart on as if reasonably and says, "It is certainly not wrong for you to desire to have something, since you do not desire wealth, but are afraid of being in want, and you can put to better use what someone else wrongfully keeps." Gluttony too ordinarily urges the subdued heart on as if reasonably and says, "God has made all foods clean, and the one who refuses refreshing food does nothing else but spurn the proffered gift." Lust again ordinarily urges the subdued heart on as if reasonably and says, "Why don't you let yourself go for once and have your pleasure? You don't know what will follow you. You should not lose what time you have for desires, nor do you know what will quickly happen. If God did not want a man to get involved in the pleasure of sexual union, he would not have created the human race male and female in the beginning." Such are the captains' exhortations delivered in the secret heart when they are carelessly admitted and they familiarly urge us to do evil, and their whole roaring army obviously follows, because the unfortunate soul was once made a captive to the principal vices, and after many multiplied iniquities it turns to madness, so that it is already laid waste by inhuman and bestial behavior.

91. God's soldier, however, skillfully tries to foresee the battles with the vices, and he smells the war at a distance, taking careful thought to see what leading evils the vices would try to persuade the mind to initiate;

consequently he hears the urging of the captains with the wisdom of the nose. Because his foresight is long, he looks upon the confusion of the wickedness that is following, knowing as if by smelling the roars of the army.

Consequently, since we know that either God's preacher or any soldier in the spiritual battle is described by the words about the horse, let us now see the same warrior signified in the image of the bird, so that once we have learned about his courage through the horse, we may also learn about his contemplation through the bird. We have heard how much the saint endures through patience in the battles against the vices by means of the horse's greatness that was described; now let us notice through the image of the birds how far he flies through contemplation. The next verse:

XLVI. 92. *Does the hawk grow feathers through your wisdom, stretching out its wings toward the south?** Almost nobody is unaware that the hawk abandons its old wings every year, when its young is born, and it never stops growing feathers. But it is not that time of plumage that is mentioned here, when it grows in the nest, because then of course the nestling obviously cannot yet stretch out its wings toward the south. No, it is the annual time of plumage that renews the tired old wings, and actually domestic hawks require a warm and protected place for them to grow feathers conveniently. Wild hawks on the other hand stretch out their wings when the south wind blows, so that their members can be warmed by the hot wind and their old wings may relax. However, when there is no wind, they stretch out and bat their wings toward the rays of the sun, and in this way they create a hot wind for themselves, so that with open pores the old hawks leap up and the young ones grow.

What is the meaning, then, of the hawk growing feathers in the south wind, if not that every one of the

*Job 39:26

saints is touched by the wind of the Holy Spirit and grows warm? He or she stops acting according to the custom of the old life and takes on the form of the new humanity. That is what Paul admonishes us to do when he says, *You have taken off the old man together with his actions and put on the new.** And again: *Although our outer man gets worn out, still our inner man is renewed every day.** To fling out old wings means to lose a long-standing pursuit of sly actions, and the growing of new wings means to hold fast to a meek and simple way of living. The wings of the old way of life are heavy, but the feathers of a new change of life lift us up, and the more recent the change, the lighter the flight it makes possible.

*Col 3:9-10

*2 Cor 4:16

93. And he was right to say, *stretching out its wings toward the south.** When we stretch out our wings toward the south, in fact, we open up our thoughts by confession through the coming of the Holy Spirit, so that we are no longer free to defend ourselves and hide our thoughts, but instead we make them public by self-accusation. Accordingly the hawk grows feathers precisely at that time when it stretches out its wings toward the south, and every one of the virtues grows wings when we lay out our thoughts for the Holy Spirit by confession. He who will not uncover his old thoughts by admitting them hardly produces the works of the new life, and he who cannot mourn over what is serious cannot offer support. The power of compunction, you see, opens the pores of the heart and scatters the feathers of virtues, and when the mind earnestly accuses itself of sluggish dotage, it becomes young with brisk newness.

*Job 39:26

So let blessed Job be asked, *Does the hawk grow feathers through your wisdom, stretching out its wings toward the south?** Did you bestow intelligence on any one of the chosen ones, so that he might stretch out the

*Job 39:26

wings of thought at the breath of the Holy Spirit insofar as he cast off the weight of the old way of life and grew the feathers of virtue for use in his new flight? In this way he could obviously grasp that of himself he has no internal perception or alertness, nor could he by any of his own means bestow such on others. The new birth of the Gentiles can also be signified by this hawk, as if blessed Job could openly be told, "Look now on the future Gentiles and their plumage of virtues, and cast off the old wings of pride." It goes on:

XLVII. 94. *Will the eagle be lifted up at your nod and build his nest in inaccessible places?** In Holy Scripture the word *eagle* sometimes signifies the unclean spirits who seize souls, sometimes the powers of the present world, and sometimes either the most refined intelligences of the saints or even the incarnate Lord swiftly flying across the lowest places and quickly returning to the highest.

*Job 39:27

The word *eagle* describes the spirits waiting in ambush, as Jeremiah bears witness when he says, *Our persecutors were swifter than the eagles in the sky.** Our persecutors are really swifter than the eagles in the sky, because evil men accomplish so much against us that they seem to govern even the powers of the air by their malicious strategies.

*Lam 4:19

The word *eagle* describes the earthly powers, so that the prophet Ezekiel tells us, *A great eagle with an enormous wingspan and long legs and many colorful feathers came to Lebanon and took the crown of a cedar tree; he plucked off the greenest of its branches.** Who else but Nebuchadnezzar, the king of Babylon, is signified by this eagle? Its great wings symbolize his immense army, and its long legs the length of his reign; its full and colorful plumage represents his riches, and their immense variety his immense and united worldly

*Ezek 17:3-4

glory. This eagle came to Lebanon and took the crown of a cedar tree, plucking off its greenest branch; this means that Nebuchadnezzar took away Judea's loftiness, the nobility of that kingdom, as if it were the crown of a cedar tree, and in that he took away the very young royal progeny from the nobility of the kingdom, leading it captive, it was as if he plucked off its greenest branch.

The word *eagle* describes either the refined intelligences of the saints or the flight of the Lord's ascension. So that same prophet described the four evangelists, saying he saw them in the forms of four animals; he was a witness to the apparitions among them of the faces of a man, a lion, an ox, and an eagle.* He doubtless meant the fourth animal, the eagle, who abandoned the earth by flight, to signify John. He penetrated the internal mysteries through his refined intelligence, and he saw the Word. John himself also saw a vision in the Book of Revelation that did not differ from that witnessed by the Prophet Ezekiel. He writes, *The first animal was like a lion, the second like an ox, the third had a face like that of a man, and the fourth animal was like an eagle in flight.** And although each one of the animals can be correctly compared to each one of the evangelists, all four can also signify the Head whose members they are: one the way of human birth, another the slaughtering of a pure sacrifice through the death of an ox, another the power of legitimate authority through the roaring of a lion, another the vision of the human birth of the Word, as when the eagle sees the rising of the sun. He accordingly is a human being, because he really accepted our nature; he is a sacrificed calf who for us patiently died; he is a lion who through the power of his divine nature broke the chain of death that he accepted; finally he is the eagle, because he returned to heaven whence he had come. He is called a human being by his birth, a calf

*Ezek 1:10

*Rev 4:7

by his death, a lion by his resurrection, and an eagle by his ascent to heaven.

But the word *eagle* in this passage[4] signifies the refined intelligence of the saints and their lofty contemplation. The eagle's range of vision in fact surpasses that of all the birds, so that the rays of the sun should not close the eyes fixed upon it because of any glare of its own light reverberating. At the command of God then the eagle is raised on high; while obeying the divine voice, the life of the faithful is suspended in heaven. The eagle is said to build its nest in inaccessible places, because it disdains worldly desires and is already nourished by hope in the sky; it builds its nest in inaccessible places, because the faithful do not build the dwelling of their minds on a way of life that is low and base. That is why Balaam prophesied concerning the Kenite and said, *Durable indeed is your dwelling, as long as you build your nest in the rock.** The name Kenite is interpreted "owner," and who are owners in the present world, if not those who are naturally skilled in worldly wisdom? And they really build themselves a durable dwelling place if through humility they become like little children themselves and they are nourished by the loftiness of Christ. If they know themselves to be weak and are recognized in the high humility of the Redeemer, they place their mind's confidence where it can be fostered. They should not desire what is base, but transcend all that passes by letting their heart fly.

*Num 24:21

95. Let us see the eagle building its nest of hope in inaccessible places. He says, *As for us, our commonwealth is in heaven,** and, *He raised us up together with Him, and He made us sit with Him in heaven.**

*Phil 3:20
*Eph 2:6

---

[4] I.e. Job 39:27, cited at the beginning of XLVII.94.

His nest is in inaccessible places, certainly because he determines his counsel in heaven; he does not want his mind to fall into baseness, nor does he want to live in the lowest places through sordid human community. Perhaps Paul was being held in prison at that time when he testified that he was seated with Christ in heaven. But he was there where he had already fixed his ardent mind, not where the slothful flesh kept him out of necessity.

96. This, you see, is ordinarily a specific pattern for the chosen ones to follow: that they know how to make use of the course of the present life in such a way that they realize by the certitude of faith that they have already reached heaven, inasmuch as they see that all passing things are beneath them, and they trample underfoot by means of love for eternity all that is pre-eminent in this life. That is why the Lord says through the prophet to the soul that follows him, *I will lift you up above the great ones of the earth.** These things are, as it were, the lowlands of the earth: loss, insult, poverty, and wretchedness. Even the lovers of the world themselves, while they walk over the broad highway on the level ground, avoid the lowlands while trampling them down unceasingly. The highlands of the earth, on the other hand, are profit in wealth, flattery from subject peoples, abundant riches, honor, and high dignity; all who still walk according to base desires think those honors constitute greatness, and they esteem them highly. But once the heart is set on heaven, those things that seemed high are quickly perceived as wretched. Just as when a person climbs a mountain he little by little despises the land that lies below the higher his footsteps tend, so also the person who attempts to fix his attention on the things that are above, while the effort alone makes him see that the honors of the present world are nothing, is lifted up above the high places of the earth; in addition, what he formerly thought was beyond

*Isa 58:14

him when he was still held by base desires, after making progress in the things above he knows are below him. That is what the Lord promises that he will do in the passage quoted: *I will lift you up above the great ones of the earth.** That is what the Lord also testifies that he is able to do in the presence of Job alone: *Will the eagle be lifted up at your nod and build his nest in inaccessible places?** It is as if he said, "As he does at mine, and what I command externally, that I inspire internally by the grace that I bestow secretly." The next verse:

*Isa 58:14

*Job 39:27

XLVIII. 97. *He stays among the rocks.** In Holy Scripture when the word *rock* in the singular is mentioned, who else but Christ is meant? Paul is our witness when he says, *The rock was Christ.** But when the rocks are mentioned in the plural, it is obviously his members, namely the saints, whose solidity participates in his strength. The apostle Peter in fact does call them stones, saying *You are like living stones in a building made into a spiritual house.** This very eagle then lifts up the eyes of his heart toward the rays of the true sun, and he is said to stay among the rocks, because his mind takes its place among the sayings of the ancients and of the strong patriarchs. He recalls to his memory, then, the life of those who he knows have preceded him on the road to God, and he zealously builds himself a nest of holy meditation in their lofty fortitude. And when he silently thinks over their deeds and words, when he considers how wretched the honors of the present life are in comparison with eternal excellence, it is as though he were residing among the rocks while observing the base things of earth beneath him.

*Job 39:28

*1 Cor 10:4

*1 Pet 2:5

98. The lofty rocks of virtue can also be understood as the heavenly powers. The wind of our changeable nature no longer pushes them in this direction or in that like trees, because like rocks located in hard-to-reach places, they are strangers to any movement of changeability. Rather, they last in that eternity in which they are fixed, and they have the firmness of immovable loftiness. The saint then disdains the earth, and like an eagle he stays up in the lofty air; he is held up there through the spirit of contemplation, and he awaits the unending glory of the angels. While he is a guest in this world, he desires the lasting things that he looks upon, and he already has a place in the heights. So we correctly heard, *He stays among the rocks.** By the attention of the heart he resides among the heavenly powers that are already so firmly fixed through their eternal strength that they cannot be turned away by any variation of changeability to any side of guilt. So he fittingly continues,

*Job 39:28

XLIX. 99. *Among the sundered boulders he dwells, and on inaccessible cliffs.** Who are the sundered boulders if not the strongest of the angelic choirs, who, if not complete, are nevertheless fixed in their original state, who remained so when the Devil fell along with his group of angels? Yes, they are sundered, because a part fell and a part remained. They indeed stand whole through the quality of their merit, but through their numeric quantity they are sundered. The Mediator came to restore this sundering, so that once the human race was redeemed, he might make good the loss of the angels and might perhaps fill up the measure in the heavenly homeland in a more ample way. It was because of this sundering that it was said of the Father, *His intention was precisely this: that in the fullness of time he planned to restore all things in Christ, both the things in heaven and those on earth in him.** The things on earth are restored indeed in Christ, since sinners are converted to justice; in him the things in heaven are restored, since there the humbled human race returns whence the apostate angels proudly fell.

*Job 39:28

*Eph 1:9-10

But when he says, *on inaccessible cliffs*, he obviously means that the sundered boulders are those inaccessible cliffs. The glory of the angels, you see, is indeed inaccessible to the heart of sinful humans, because to fall for beautiful bodies means that the human being closes his eyes to spiritual reality. But anyone who has been so carried away by contemplation that by divine grace he is raised up already inserts his attention in the choir of the angels; he has his place in the heights, and he stops all base actions. It is not enough for him to look upon the splendor of angelic glory, unless he can see him as well who is above the angels. The vision of him, you see, is the real satisfaction of our mind. So having said that this eagle stays among the rocks, and that he dwells among the sundered boulders and the inaccessible cliffs, the Lord immediately goes on to say,

*Job 39:29

L. 100. *There the food of contemplation is found.** That is, from the choirs of angels the eye of the mind moves on to contemplate the glory of heavenly majesty, because with that glory yet unseen it is still hungry, and finally seeing it, that eye is satisfied. In fact it is written, *Because his soul has labored much, it will see and be satisfied.** And again: *Blessed are they who are hungry and thirsty for justice, because they will be satisfied.** What that food of our mind is we are clearly shown by the words, *Blessed are the pure of heart, for they shall see God.** But because the corruptible flesh interposes its weight, we cannot see God as he is, so it is rightly added:

*Isa 53:11
*Matt 5:6

*Matt 5:8

*Job 39:29

LI. 101. *His eyes look ahead from a distance.** As long as anyone is still continuing to achieve something in this life, he does not yet see God as he is, but only through riddles or through a mirror. So when we see close at hand, we perceive truly, but when we bend our gaze further away, we see darkly, with an uncertain vision. Since then the saints are lifted up in high contemplation and they still cannot see God as he is, it is rightly said about this eagle, *His eyes look ahead from a distance.* It is as if he said, "He intentionally bends his glance with vigor, but he sees nothing nearby, and he can by no means penetrate into the magnitude of his glory. The darkness of our corruptible nature beclouds the incorruptible light, even if it can be seen to some extent; nevertheless that light cannot be seen as it is, so he indicates how far away it is. But if the mind did not see it in some way, it would not see how far away it is, and if it saw it perfectly, it would certainly not see it as if through darkness. Consequently it is neither seen absolutely, nor on the other hand is it absolutely unseen, so it is rightly said that God is seen from afar.

102. We may at this point introduce the words of Isaiah and show how both first and last were expressed by the same Spirit. When he would indicate the virtues of the active life he said, *He who walks in justice and speaks the truth, who casts out avarice and calumny, he who excludes his hands from every bribe. He who closes his ears lest he should hear of the shedding of blood, and who closes his eyes lest he should see the doing of evil.** Then he immediately turns from the stages of the active life to those that belong to the climbing to the contemplative summit and adds, *such a person will dwell on high; his elevated stature is a rocky stronghold. He will be given bread, and his water will be faith. His eyes will see the king in his glory, and he will see the land afar off.**

*Isa 33:15

*Isa 33:16-17

Dwelling on high of course means to set one's heart on heaven; when our loftiness is a stone monument, it means that we accept the precepts of the great patriarchs and respect their examples, separating ourselves from every base thought; our loftiness is a stone monument when our mind is joined with the choirs and camps of angels, and we take our stand in the citadel of the heart to fight against the evil spirits who crowd around us setting their traps. Then we are also given bread, because our righteous attention is fixed on heaven, and we are fed with the contemplation of eternity. Our water is faith, because God's teaching promises here by hope what it displays there as gift. But the wisdom of this world is without faith, because it is not going to remain after death.

Our water is faith, because it inserts the words of life before death, and it displays them after death. Our eyes consequently see the King in his beauty, because our Redeemer in Judgment will be seen as man by reprobate sinners, but only the chosen ones will rise to see the loftiness of his divinity. It is, you see, like a certain ugliness to see the King only in the form of a slave in which he was scorned by the wicked. But the chosen ones see the King in his beauty, because they are snatched up outside of themselves, and they fix the eyes of their hearts on the very splendor of divinity. Since as long as they are in this life they cannot see that homeland of the living as it is, he goes on to say, *They will see a land afar off.** *Isa 33:17

But the Lord says here to Job, *Will the eagle be lifted up at your nod and build his nest in inaccessible places?** Isaiah says, *Such a person will dwell on high.** But Job is told here, *He stays among the rocks, among the sundered boulders he dwells, and on inaccessible cliffs.** Isaiah says: *His elevated stature is a rocky stronghold.* Again Job is told here, *There the food of contemplation is found.** And again Isaiah says, *he will be given bread, and his water will be faith. His eyes will see the king in his glory.** Finally, what is added here in Job—*His eyes behold it afar off**—Isaiah has also said: *he will see the land afar off.** *Job 39:27 *Isa 33:16 *Job 39:28 *Job 39:29 *Isa 33:16 *Job 39:29 *Isa 33:17

103. Let us consider how lofty an eagle Paul was, who flew all the way to the third heaven* yet had his place in this life and still foresaw God from afar and *2 Cor 12:2

said, *We see now as in a mirror obscurely, but then face to face,** and again, *I do not suppose that I have already attained the prize.** But although the eternal things that he saw were much less than they really are, and although he knew that he could not realize them perfectly, he tried unsuccessfully to get through to weak ears by preaching what he could barely make out as a reflection in a mirror. Actually, he spoke of himself as of another person when he said, *He heard secret words that people are not free to utter.** Internal words, therefore, however small or extreme they may seem to be, are lofty to devout preachers, but to weak listeners unattainable. So when holy preachers realize that their listeners are unable to understand the word of God, they confine themselves to the word of the incarnate Lord alone. So it is just as well that when the lofty eagle is here said to see the difficult places afar off, it is immediately added,

*1 Cor 13:12
*Phil 3:13

*2 Cor 12:4

LII. 104. *Its fledglings lick up blood.** It is as if he clearly said, "The eagle itself feeds on the contemplation of divinity, but its listeners can never grasp the hidden truths of divinity, so they are satisfied with knowing about the blood of the crucified Lord." Licking up the blood of course means venerating the weakness of the Lord's passion. That is why the same Paul who we just said flew away to the secret place of the third heaven also told his disciples, *I determined to know nothing among you but Jesus Christ and him crucified.** It is as if this eagle said openly, "Yes, I do foresee from afar that my food is the power of his divinity, but I pass on to you who are still children only the blood of his incarnation to lick up. He who by his preaching taught his weak listeners, you see, only about the blood of the cross, the loftiness of the divine nature having been kept silent, what else did he do but offer his fledglings blood? However, because the soul of every holy preacher, once

*Job 39:30

*1 Cor 2:2

released from corruptible flesh, is quickly led to the One who willingly fell in death for our sakes and rose from the dead, the Lord fittingly adds concerning this eagle,

LIII. 105. *Wherever there is a corpse, he is immediately present.** A corpse of course means that someone has fallen, and it is not without reason that the body of the Lord is called a corpse because of the fall of death. But what is said here about the eagle—*Wherever there is a corpse, he is immediately present*—Truth also promises concerning souls leaving bodies: *Wherever the body is, there the eagles will gather.** It is as if he said, "Because I, your incarnate Redeemer, preside in the heavenly seat, when I release the souls of the chosen ones, I too will bring them up to heaven."

106. However, what is said about the eagle—*Wherever there is a corpse, he is immediately present*—may be understood in a different sense. Every person who falls into the death of sin can suitably be called a corpse. He who does not have the vivifying spirit of justice lies inert as though lacking a soul. Because any holy preacher considers where the sinners are, he flies there anxiously, in order that he may shine the light of vivifying justice on those lying in the death of sin, so it is rightly said of this eagle, *Wherever there is a corpse, he is immediately present.* In other words he aims for that place where he expects to preach profitably, so that he may profit those lying in death from his own present spiritual life and by correcting them eat them. By changing their wickedness into uprightness, he would change them into his own members as if by eating. Behold him whom we have already used often as an example: Paul, when he visited first Judea, then Corinth, then Ephesus, then Rome, then Spain to announce the grace of eternal life to those lying in the death of sin—what else did he show himself to be but an eagle? Like an eagle he

*Job 39:30

*Matt 24:28

flies everywhere quickly, and everywhere he seeks out prostrate corpses, so that while doing God's will by profiting sinners he might as it were find his own food in their corpses. Yes, the food of the righteous is the conversion of depraved sinners, about which it is said, *Do not labor for perishable food, but for the food that remains for eternal life.** So when blessed Job heard of so many virtues of the saints, he is understood to have become speechless and to have been silenced by fear and admiration. So it goes on:

*John 6:27

LIV. 107. *The Lord added and spoke to Job: Does he who contends with God so easily cease speaking? Surely the one who argues with God should answer him.** The holy man did not suppose his merits were increased by so great an action of the whip, but rather that his vices were cut off. And since he did not know of any in himself, he thought himself unjustly stricken, and all that is left for the one stricken is to murmur against the stroke. The Lord however considered that the words he spoke proceeded not from the boastfulness of pride, but from the quality of his life, so he lovingly reproached him, saying, *Does he who contends with God so easily cease speaking? Surely the one who argues with God should answer him?* It is as though he said openly, "You who spoke so freely of your own actions, why were you silent about the life of the saints that you have heard? It was my part to argue and to doubt whether my strokes were just or not. Granted, you have spoken truly of your own good deeds, but you did not know what the purpose was of the strokes you have received, and although you do not have anything to be corrected now, you do have still further to grow. Now you know how high the citadel of virtue is to which I would raise many people: behold, I have recounted it. You considered your own state but did not know the loftiness of others. You have

*Job 39:31-32

heard, then, of the virtues of others, so answer, if you can, concerning your own."

But we know how he closed the eye of his heart through the darkness of pride, he who although he did what was right, neglected the consideration of the better merits of other people. On the other hand, he sheds light on his own works with the bright ray of humility who wisely weighs the good deeds of other people, because while he sees his own deeds and those done by others externally, he tramples upon the boasting of pride that attempts to break out internally on account of his singularity. It is on this account that God's voice was conveyed to Elijah, who supposed that he was alone: *I have kept for myself seven thousand men who have not bent the knee before Baal.** In this way could he not only realize that he was not the only one left, but he could avoid the pride of self-esteem that could have risen in his heart as a consequence of singularity. Blessed Job therefore is found to have done nothing depraved, but he learns how other people have also performed well, so that while he considers himself to have others equal to himself, he might humbly subject himself to him who alone is the highest.

*1 Kgs 19:18

BOOK 32

I. 1. The more the dignity of the holy man's virtues increases in the sight of God, the less dignified he subtly finds them to be, because the closer to the light they come, whatever lay hidden in them appears uglier to him externally, to the extent that what is internal seems too beautiful. Every person, you see, is enlightened by the touch of the true light and is shown to himself or herself, and when they realize what righteousness really is, they learn to see sin as it is. So it happens that our mind, however cold and numb it may be in human interaction, however much certain ones fall short without knowing it, however much our mind evaluates certain sins as nothing, nevertheless when it comes to the earnest wish for the heights of prayer, it girds itself for compunction; then the very eye of its compunction arouses it to a thorough look at itself, and it is tearfully rendered more vigilant.

When it abandons and neglects itself, you see, the mind grows numb with guilty lukewarmness, and it supposes that idle words or useless thoughts make it less guilty. But if it becomes warm by means of the fire of compunction, it awakens at the sudden touch of the breath of contemplation, and at those words and thoughts it previously thought to be of small importance it quickly takes fright, as being serious and death-dealing. It shrinks back from things that may be slightly hurtful as if they were most terrible, because it obviously allows nothing idle to enter it anymore, having become serious through the conception of the spirit. No sooner has it entered into itself than it senses as horrifying the things that resound externally, and the higher it has been raised by its progress, the more it avoids what is base, in which it wallowed when it failed. Nothing now nourishes the soul except what it had seen internally. It now tolerates with difficulty whatever finds entrance from outside to the extent that it is not what it has seen inside itself.

On the other hand, it finds the standard of judging the external things it tolerates from the sights it has been able to see fleetingly. When it contemplates lofty matters, you see, it is swept away to the higher realms, and going out of itself it already freely sees itself and understands in detail whatever of itself is left below itself. From this circumstance it happens in a wonderful way that, as was said above, where it becomes more dignified it seems to itself less dignified, and it feels itself further from righteousness when it is approaching righteousness. That is why Solomon says, *I tried everything in wisdom, and I said, "I will make myself wise," but wisdom remained far from me.** The wisdom that is sought is said to remain far away, because it seems higher to the one approaching it.

Those however who by no means seek it guess that they are as close to it as they are far from knowing the standard of its righteousness, because those who are sitting in darkness cannot admire the glorious light that they have never seen, and when they do not aim towards the form of its beauty, they themselves willingly become uglier every day. Whoever is touched by the rays of that light has his own misshapenness made obvious to him, and the more truly he finds how twisted he is by vice, the more keenly he considers the highest and knows how far he is away from the standard. So blessed Job transcends the virtues of the human race and wins the debate with his friends, but when God speaks he is taught higher

*Eccl 7:24

truths, knows himself, and becomes silent. He won the contest with those who spoke wrongly, but at the words of interior speech he righteously knew himself guilty. Of course he did not know why he was stricken, but on the other hand, because he was not respected by the whip, he silently accused himself. When we do not know God's judgment, you see, we must not discuss it with words but rather fear it with respectful silence; since the Creator does not make causes known by means of blows, he shows their justice by showing that he who is supreme Justice is the cause. Accordingly the holy man was reprehended first for speaking and then for keeping silence, so he makes known what in fact he thinks of himself. He says,

II. 2. *I have spoken thoughtlessly; what answer can I give?** It is as if he said, "I would defend my speech, if I had delivered it with the weight of reason." But after he is convicted of having used his tongue thoughtlessly, what is there left for him to do but to restrain his tongue by keeping silent? He goes on: *I cover my mouth with my hand.** In the usage of Holy Scripture the word *hand* customarily means "work," and the word *mouth* means "speech." So covering the mouth with the hand means covering up the sins of thoughtless speech with the virtues of good works. But what person can we find who, however perfect he or she may be, never sins by careless speech? James is our witness, who says, *Do not let many of you be teachers, my brothers. Actually we all do wrong in many ways.** And again: *Nobody can tame the tongue.** The Truth himself condemns sins of the tongue when he says, *Every idle word spoken by men must be accounted for on judgment day.**

*Job 39:34

*Job 39:34

*Jas 3:1-2
*Jas 3:8

*Matt 12:36

The saints, however, under the eyes of God try to cover up sins of the tongue with the merits of a good life, and they try to press down immoderate speech with the weight of good works. So in Holy Church we cover our mouths with our hands when her chosen ones every day cover up the vices of idle speech with the power of good works. It is written, *Blessed are they whose sins are forgiven, whose misdeeds are hidden.** But when it is elsewhere written, *Everything is naked and open to his eyes,** how could anything be covered, when to God's eyes everything is naked, and nothing could be hidden? But since anything we cover we put below, and when we cover it we lift up that with which we cover it, so that what is put under it is covered, we are said to cover the sins that we as it were put below when we give them up, and we put something else on top of them when we later choose the doing of good works and prefer them to sinning. He therefore who abandons former evil and does good later, through the good that he adds covers the wickedness that is past, over which he lays the merits of good works. Blessed Job then, who is the type of Holy Church, attaches himself to us by his words and represents us; so let him say as if in our place, *I cover my mouth with my hand.* In other words, let him say, "That which I said to the strict Judge, and, as I see, which displeases him, I hide from his eyes and cover with the covering of good works." The next verse:

*Ps 31:1

*Heb 4:13

III. 3. *I have said one thing that I wish I had not said; I have said another, but I will add no more.** If we examine in detail the words blessed Job has uttered, we find that he has spoken nothing wicked. If however we twist his words, which he spoke openly and truly, into some vice of pride, they will not yet be only two: no, they will be many. But since for us men to speak means to use words to reveal a hidden meaning, but for us to speak in the ears of God means also to reveal the thought of our mind by means of the expression of some action, blessed Job weighs himself in the scale of the

*Job 39:35

finest examination and confesses that he has fallen short in his second speech. It is one thing, you see, to say that it is wrong to do things deserving punishment, but it is quite another to say also that one is even murmuring against the punishment. Accordingly he who was pre-eminent among people in all his works before the Lord's reproach was growing higher still in the reproach, but he now realized that he was not so perfect in his former actions or so patient afterwards during his trials. So he accuses himself and says, *I have said one thing that I wish I had not said; I have said another, but I will add no more.* It is as if he said, "I thought I was upright among the people, but now that you have spoken, I find that I was depraved before my trials and rigid after them. *I will add no more,* since I even now understand from your speech that the better I understand, the more humbly I should search myself."

4. Since blessed Job typifies the church, these words of his can be suitable for all the chosen ones, so that when they know God they may realize that they have fallen short in one way or another, because they understand that they have sinned in word or deed or in neglecting love for God or neighbor. And they promise that they will add no more words, because through the grace of conversion they are doing penance, and they are careful to purify themselves daily even from the sins they have already committed. Because blessed Job accused himself in repentance for two misdeeds, he clearly showed that every sinner who repents should express sorrow for two things: that he did not do the good he should have done, and that he did evil that he should not have done.* That is why Moses spoke about rash oaths that a person might make either to do good or to do evil, if he remembers it after it was forgotten: *He should offer either a female lamb or a female goat from*

*Rom 7:19

*Lev 5:6-7

the flock and have the priest pray for him and for his sin. If, however, he cannot offer anything from the flock, he should offer either two turtle doves or two pigeons, one for sin, and the other as a holocaust.*

To make an oath means that we bind ourselves by a vow to divine service. And when we promise to perform good works, we pledge ourselves to do them well. But when we make a vow of abstinence or promise the chastisement of our flesh, we confess that we have done evil in the present time. No person in the present life is so perfect as not to sin; however dedicated to God one may be, and however loving one's devotion, one may do wrong in a small way. That is why we are ordered to offer sacrifice for sin. It may be either a ewe from the flock or a female goat. And what else does the ewe signify but the innocence of an active life? What does the female goat, which lives in pastures among the crags and inaccessible rocks, signify but the contemplative life?

So when people realize that they have not fulfilled what they promised and intended, they should zealously gird themselves up for offering sacrifice to God, either with the innocence of good works or with the lofty pasture of contemplation. And so they are correctly not ordered to offer both a ewe lamb and a goat from the flock, because the active life belongs to the many, but the contemplative life only to few. If we offer ourselves in this way, as we have seen that many people do and have done, it is as though we gave a ewe lamb from the flock. But when the wealth of the person offering is not equal to the offering of a ewe lamb or a goat, it is provided for the purification of the penitent sinner that two young pigeons or two doves may be offered.

We know of course that pigeons or doves utter moans instead of songs. What then do the two young pigeons or two doves signify but the two forms of our penitential cries when we do not get up and offer good works? First we weep bitterly for not doing what is right, and then for doing evil. So we are ordered to offer one turtledove for sin and the other for a holocaust. A holocaust means that the entire sacrifice is burnt up. Accordingly we offer one turtledove for sin when we utter a groan for guilt; with the other we offer a holocaust, because we have neglected the doing of good. We set our own depths on fire, and we burn with the fire of sorrow. Since therefore the penitent owes two groans, blessed Job, who is growing by means of the divine reproach and growing also in his own self-reproach, admits in repentance that he had said one thing and another. It is as if he said clearly, "Through negligence, then, I have been sluggish toward the good and have boldly rushed forward to do evil."

But the Lord answered Job from the whirlwind and said: Gird up your loins like a man; I will ask you, and do you answer me.* What it means for God to answer from the whirlwind, telling blessed Job to gird up his loins, what it means for God to ask, and what it means for a person to answer have already been shown in the course of the Lord's first speech. Since however I would spare the reader's weariness, I will above all avoid repeating what has already been said. Let us go on:

*Job 40:1

IV. 5. *Would you make my judgment invalid, or will you condemn me so that you could be justified?** Anybody who tries to defend himself against his trial attempts to rob judgment from the author of the trial. When he denies that he is being struck for his own guilt, what else is he doing but accusing the striker of injustice? Blessed Job's heavenly trials then were not intended to strike him in order to do away with his sins, but instead to increase his merits, inasmuch as in the time of rest Job was clearly shown in such a great state of holiness; consequently his

*Job 40:3

state of being crushed made clear the virtue of patience that also lay hidden in him. Accordingly, when he did not find any guilt in himself to account for the trials, and he did not discover that the trials were there for the sake of increasing his merits, he thought he was being unjustly struck, since he did not find in himself anything that needed to be corrected.

But lest his very innocence should be puffed up in an outgrowth of pride, it is corrected by the divine voice, so that his mind, freed from wickedness but repressed by strokes of correction, might be recalled to hidden judgment, and the heavenly decision, although unknown, might at least not be reckoned unjust. He should then believe everything that is out in the open to be righteous, since it obviously has God as its author. There is great satisfaction in a trial when the righteous will of the Creator is there. Since that will is accustomed to do nothing unjust, it is recognized as righteous even if hidden. When we are struck down for the sin of injustice, if in that very attack we are united with the divine will, we are quickly freed from our own injustice because of that union.

Whoever already undergoes a trial but still does not know the reason for the trial, if he embraces that very judgment against himself, believing it to be just, by that very fact his own injustice is corrected, and he gives thanks for the fact that he was struck down righteously. In the act of retribution he joins himself to God and rises against himself, and great is that justice already, because he unites himself to the Judge's will in his punishment, which he denied in his guilt. The holy man then had not been out of harmony with God by guilt, and as it were he was in difficult accord with him in his punishment. Nor did he believe that the trials that ordinarily are there to punish vice in him alone increased merit. So now he is rightly corrected, so that he might subject himself unknowingly to the hidden judgments, and he is asked, *Would you make my judgment invalid, or will you condemn me so that you could be justified?** It is as if he were freely told, "You are thinking about your own good actions, but you are unaware of my hidden judgments. If then you question my trials from your own merits, what else are you doing but rushing to indict me for injustice by justifying yourself?" The next verse:

*Job 40:3

V. 6. *Do you have an arm like God's, or can you thunder with a voice like his?** Because blessed Job's merits transcended those of the human race, the loving Creator and Teacher challenges him here to a consideration of the likeness of his great power, so that once he became aware of his own immense unlikeness he would be reduced to humility.

*Job 40:4

7. But when God's voice and arm are mentioned, we must beware above all lest the mind should suppose there is anything corporeal in God. We should fall into the heresy of the anthropomorphists if we should conclude that he who is uncircumscribed and who both fills and surrounds all things could be enclosed in a bodily envelope. But almighty God draws us on to the consideration of himself and yet humbles us to the point of our own dimensions; so that he might suggest the heights, he condescends to the lowest, inasmuch as the soul of the little ones is nourished by realities it knows in order to rise to the inquiry of those it does not know; he who exists far above that soul moves it when it hears words denoting realities close to it, so that using them as something like steps it may approach him. So it happens that through his Holy Scriptures God may draw certain similarities to himself sometimes from human bodies, sometimes from minds, sometimes from birds, sometimes even from things that are not objects of sensation and in fact not like him at all.

He often draws likenesses to himself from human bodies, as when the prophet told the Israelites, *Whoever touches you touches the pupil of his eye.** Another prophet tells hopeful people about him, *His shoulders will cover you.** It remains true nonetheless that in God's nature there are neither shoulders nor eyes; rather we ourselves see with our eyes and bear burdens with our shoulders. Because God sees all things, he is held to have an eye; since he puts up with us, and by the very fact that he puts up with us he preserves us, he is said to cover us with his shoulders; so the prophet says, *His shoulders will cover you.* It is as if sinful humankind (and humankind pleading forgiveness after sin) were told, "The Lord protects you with that same love with which he puts up with you. His shoulders will cover you, because while he carries you he protects you."

*Zech 2:8

*Ps 90:4

Sometimes God also draws a similarity to himself from human minds, as when the prophet tells Israel, *I have remembered you, because I pity your youth.** The Lord also compares Israel to a bride and says, *Even if she should forget, yet will I not forget you.** Everybody knows of course that God's memory is neither interrupted by forgetfulness nor restored by remembering. Rather, he abandons things by passing them by, and he is said to forget by comparison with the habit of a human mind; when after a long period of time he visits whom he wills, by comparison with our changeability he is said to remember. By what means then does forgetfulness weaken the power of his divinity? That praiseworthy memory does not essentially harmonize with forgetfulness. Nothing is remembered, whether past or present. How could God remember the past when the very things that pass are themselves always standing present at his nod? How could he remember what is not present when all that exists is by that very fact present

*Jer 2:2

*Isa 49:15

to him, since it is inside him? If it were not present to him, it would certainly not exist. By seeing what does not exist, he creates it, and by seeing what does exist, he contains it. Accordingly, whatever the Creator does not see essentially lacks existence.

Sometimes he draws a likeness to himself from birds, as when Moses said, *It spreads out its wings and catches them.** And the prophet: *In the shelter of your wings protect me.** Because God protects and feeds us little ones, and not with a heavy and burdensome hand, he cares for us with protection that is both light and soft when he displays his mercy toward us; as if with a bird's concern he spreads out his wings over us.

*Deut 32:11
*Ps 16:8

Sometimes because of our frailty he compares himself with infinite condescension to things that are not objects of sensation, as when the prophet says, *I will bear down upon you, as a cart bears down when it is filled with hay.** The life of the flesh is like grass, you see, as it is written: *All flesh is grass.** So since the Lord suffers the life of the flesh, he avows that he bears it like a cart bearing bales of hay. For him to bear the burden of hay means that he complains of bearing the burdens and wickedness of sinners. Well then, the Lord brings similarities to himself out of things that are far different from him. So we must carefully notice that at times some of these similarities to God are spoken by reason of his works, but at other times they indicate the real quality of his majesty. So when God's eye, shoulder, foot, or wing is mentioned, they indicate the effects of his works. However, when God's hand, arm, right hand, or voice is mentioned, such words indicate the Son, who is consubstantial with him.

*Amos 2:13
*Isa 40:6

The Son indeed is God's hand and God's right side, and the Father speaks of his ascension through Moses: *I will raise my hand to heaven, and I will swear by my* right hand.* The Son is the arm about which the prophet said, *To whom has the arm of the Lord been revealed?** He is the voice to whom the Father gave birth and said, *You are my Son. Today I have begotten you.** Of him it has been written, *In the beginning was the Word. The Word was with God, and the Word was God.** David proclaimed that the Father made everything through the Word: *He spoke, and it was done.** So for God to have an arm is the same thing as for the Father to beget a Son who works, and his thundering voice means that he displays his consubstantial Son to the world in a terrifying way. So when the Lord asked blessed Job, *Do you have an arm like God's, or can you thunder with a voice like his?** it is by a wonderful dispensation of love that he exalts him in the act of reproof, because the one whom he excels by comparison to himself he displays to all the world as a superior person before everyone else. So he goes on in the same vein:

VI. 8. *Surround yourself with beauty and rise up in loftiness; be glorious and put on splendid garments.** Unspoken are the words "like me." He surely surrounds himself with beauty of whom it is said, *The Lord is King, and he puts on beauty.** He rises up in loftiness before us when he shows himself to our minds as unreachable in his nature. Of course he is glorious, he who while he enjoys himself is in no need of additional praise. He puts on splendid garments when he assumes the chorus of holy angels whom he created for the sake of his own beauty, and he displays his glorious church like a kind of garment of glory without any spot or wrinkle.* That is why the prophet tells him, *You have put on confession and beauty, and you are clothed with light as with a garment.**

Yes, here below he puts on confession, and there later he puts on beauty; he makes sinners confess and do penance here, and later he displays them shining with the beauty of justice. He is dressed with light as with a garment, because in that eternal glory he is clothed with all the saints who were told, *You are the light of the world.** These words are said through the gospel, because at the transfiguration of the Lord on the mountain his clothing became as white as snow.* And in the transfiguration what else is foretold but the glory of the final resurrection? On the mountain his clothing became white as snow, because on the summit of heavenly glory all the saints, shining with the light of justice, will cling to him. But in suggesting how he joins the righteous to himself by the use of the words indicating the most beautiful garments, he also shows how the unrighteous are separated from him. The next verse:

*Matt 5:14

*Mark 9:2

VII. 9. *Scatter the proud in your anger.** You should hear whispered, "As I do? I both tolerate them in times of peace when they unite against me, and I sometimes come in strict vindication to scatter them in my wrath." But we should carefully notice in this matter that a serious error against faith is committed if anyone should by chance suppose that in that divine nature wrath or pacification should occur. The Creator of all things is immortal precisely in the respect that unlike creatures, he is unchangeable. That is why James says of him, *With him there is no change, no shadow of alteration.** And it is written elsewhere, *You, O Lord, judge in serenity.** And the prophet says, *The land has become a desert before the wrath of a dove, before the fury of the Lord.** Because he had first said *the wrath of a dove*, he added *the fury of the Lord.*

*Job 40:6

*Jas 1:17
*Wis 12:18

*Jer 25:38

The dove of course is a very simple creature, and since in God no uneven temper or wrath creeps in, the prophet called the Lord's fury "the wrath of a dove." So that he might show the power of the divine chastisement as serene, he used both words, *wrath* and *dove,* as if speaking clearly and saying, "He unshakably exerts judgment who punishes while remaining mild." Consequently, even at the Last Judgment he remains himself and unchangeable; he does not diverge, nor does he alter or fluctuate. Nevertheless he by no means shows himself to the chosen ones and to the reprobate sinners in the same form of unchangeability, but rather he will appear to the righteous as tranquil and to the unrighteous as angry. They bear within themselves a conscience as witness, so that their minds see the selfsame reality, but they are not equally dealt with, because their former acts of justice render God kindly disposed toward the former, and their guilt renders him terrible toward the latter.

And who will explain their dread when it falls to them in their misery both to see their own interior guilt and to see the just Judge standing before them? Actually it happens every day in the living of the present life that the hearts of mortals are taught about the quality of the coming Judge. When two people go to be judged, one is well aware of his or her innocence and the other of guilt; both of them observe the Judge, who is silent before passing sentence; the guilty debtor, however, suspects that the very silence of the Judge means serious wrath against himself. The Judge's stern attitude does not warn him of wrath; instead the memory of his own depraved behavior warns him, because even if an external sentence does not yet cry out that he is guilty, internally his conscience accuses him gravely.

On the other hand, the friend of justice looks upon the countenance of the discerning Judge, but he rejoices inwardly in the testimony of good by his memory, and since he has nothing to fear before him he sees that all is pleasant concerning himself. In this passage the Lord's fury is mentioned, but not a stern attitude of the divine nature; for the sinners, however, who are well aware of it themselves, there is the legal scrutiny of a righteous sentence. Although the sinners see him as a calm judge, because they are in no doubt that they are going to be struck by him, they see his actions as those of a judge who has a stern attitude. The next verse:

VIII. 10. *Look at every arrogant individual and humiliate him.** It is as if he said, "as I do." To account for the punishment of the arrogant, the guilt of the proud is rightly stated, because arrogance is generated from pride, not pride from arrogance. The Lord looks upon every single sinner, you see, in one of two ways: either he is converted from sin, or he is punished for sin. In respect to conversion, it is said, *Jesus looked at Peter, and Peter remembered and wept bitterly.** With respect to punishment it is elsewhere said, *The Lord's countenance is upon those who do evil, that he may rid the earth of their memory.** In both of these ways the arrogant person is laid low by humility: either by repentance he acknowledges his guilt, or by perishing he receives his punishment. The next verse:

*Job 40:6

*Luke 22:61-62

*Ps 33:17

IX. 11. *Look upon all the proud ones and put them to shame; trample upon the impious people in their own district.** Understand "as I do." The proud are put to shame in the presence of the Lord, either here below by those faithful to religion who condemn sin, or hereafter by feeling their own just punishment. As for the region of the impious, it is pride itself. It is written, *Pride is the beginning of all sin.** Where impiety originates, there it continues, although there is not much distance between pride and impiety. Excessive pride in fact leads to impious thoughts about the Creator. The impious person is then trampled in his own district, because the very pride that lifts him up oppresses him, and when he is carried away by his own proud thoughts, he hides the light of

*Job 40:7

*Sir 10:15 Vulg

justice from himself, which he ought rather to have discovered. While he advances externally against God by means of empty honors, he is often emptying himself internally with real misery. That is why the prophet says, *You hurled them down when they were lifting themselves up.** He did not say, of course, that you threw them down after they were lifted up, but instead while they were climbing, because this indeed is what it means for the impious to be cast down internally, namely to be lifted up externally by vainglory. It is ordained by God's judgment that in this case fault is not one thing and penalty another, but their fault is transformed into a penalty, so that when they are elated by the haughtiness of pride, their ostentatious external advancement is the same thing as an internal fall. The next verse:

*Ps 72:18

X. 12. *Hide them in the dust, and at the same time sink their faces in the pit.** It is as if he said, "as I do." Yes, the Lord hides both the impious and the proud in the dust with righteous judgment, because their hearts disdained the Creator's love. He allows them to be oppressed by the very worldly affairs that they chose. He dismisses their lives at the Last Judgment. They are in fact hidden from him, and he does not recognize them. Instead he says, *I do not know where you come from.** The lives of depraved people are hidden in the dust, weighed down by base and abject desires. Whoever still desires the things of the world, as it were, does not appear in front of the true light, because in fact such a person is hidden in the dust of worldly thoughts. The oppressed mind tolerates the dust of depraved thoughts that the wind of the most wicked temptations carries. That is why the prophet proclaims about every single soul that is weighed down with earthly thoughts, using the image of Ephraim: *Ephraim has become an unturned ash cake.**

*Job 40:8

*Luke 13:27

*Hos 7:8

Our attention is certainly well formed according to nature when it rises to God, but accustomed pleasure finds its wicked place in our way of life, and when it is present it pushes us toward the world. The ash cake is cleaner on its underside, but of course dirtier on top where it comes in contact with ashes. Whoever then neglects the attention by which he should seek God as it were turns away his cleaner underside, like the ash cake, and when he freely tolerates the cares of the world, he carries the piled ashes on top. However, he would turn the ash cake over if he brushed off the ashes of desires of the flesh, and he would display his best attention on top, that which he had contemptibly repressed inside for so long. But he refuses to be turned when, with his mind occupied with the love of worldly cares, he neglects to brush off the piled-up ashes and does not desire his best attention to rise, turning away his cleaner face to the ground.

13. He is right to add, *and at the same time sink their faces in the pit.** It is as if he said, "as I do." By a righteous judgment the Lord sinks the faces of proud people in the pit, because he casts down to the bottom the attention of the hearts of those who lift themselves up over other people. The one whose face is turned to the pit certainly looks upon the lowest things. And well is it said of the proud that their faces are sunk in the pit, because it is the lowest things that they seek, while they desire the highest honors in their pride. And the more they extol themselves and lift themselves up, the more they tend and rush towards the bottom. In fact while they seek worldly honors, their progress is toward the lowest things, even as in their pride they go after the highest. It is wonderful yet opposite when humble people seek heaven while they cast themselves down low, and the proud desire what is low while they extol themselves up to the highest by despising others. The

*Job 40:8

former join themselves to heaven while despising earth; the latter while extolling themselves are cut off from what is above. The latter by elevating themselves lower themselves, and the former in lowering themselves lift themselves up.

The psalmist rightly spoke about proud people: *He humbles the sinners all the way down to earth.** They embrace what is below, you see, and as long as they extol and elevate themselves, having lost heaven, what else do they seek but earth? For them this very tendency already means that they have fallen to the lowest place; leaving behind what is above, they have sought the lowest. Their face is proclaimed to be submerged in the pit, and rightly, because they follow after the lowest things, and they are tending towards the pit of hell. So it is righteous judgment that brings it about that those whom here below a voluntary aversion has blinded, there in the beyond the pit of punishment that they deserve hides them from the vision of the true light.

*Ps 146:6

Consequently, since the holy man was questioned with so great an intensity of the power of God that he was asked, *Do you have an arm like God's, or can you thunder with a voice like his?** and *Scatter the proud in your anger,* and *Look at every arrogant individual and humiliate him,** and since he was told other things that God indeed can do but that a person is hardly able even to hear, all those things that the Lord radically proposed he shows with a suitable end, and a conclusion that follows:

*Job 40:4

*Job 40:6

XI. 14. *Then I will admit that your own right hand can save you.** It is as if he openly declared, "If you can yourself do these frightful deeds that I have just mentioned, then I will impute all the good that you have done to you instead of to myself. If however you cannot kill other sinners with your mere glance, it remains true

*Job 40:9

that you cannot free yourself from the guilt of your own wickedness by your own power." This is how the divine voice told blessed Job that his own right hand could not save him. And yet there are some people who are far from the manliness of this man, and who have despised God's help, who are still confident in their own power to save themselves. For the sake of these people, what else should we pray except that if they have already received the gifts of good works, they should also receive this gift: that they may learn who gave them the others. So with the foregoing words the Lord gave notice of the magnitude of his power; now with the following words he displays the wickedness of the ancient enemy, so that the good servant, having first heard about the Lord's power, might know how much he should love him and, realizing the Devil's craftiness later, might learn how much he should fear him. So the prophet was right to say, *The lion roars: who will not be afraid? The Lord God has spoken: who will not prophesy?** *Amos 3:8

So after the power of his Creator was made known to Job, by no means should the adversary's power be hidden from him, so that he would all the more humbly subject himself to his Defender the more clearly he had realized his enemy's wickedness, and he would seek out his Protector the more ardently when he knew how terrible was the foe he escaped. It is abundantly clear that the one who has little understanding of the danger he escapes loves his Deliverer less, and the one who considers the adversary's power feeble supposes his Defender's relief of little worth. So the prophet who rightly attributed his escape to the Lord said, *I love you, Lord, my Strength.** He freely says, "I love you more *Ps 17:2 because I know my own weakness, and I know that you are my strength." That is why he says elsewhere, *Magnify your mercies, you who save those who hope*

*Ps 16:7

*in you.** Then indeed the mercies of the Lord become wonderful among us who are delivered when we realize through those mercies how grave were the dangers that we escaped.

15. The foregoing speech of the Lord made it clear to blessed Job how wonderful were the works of the later saints, in order that having heard about them, he might learn how low he should evaluate the best of his own powers. So now he is shown the enemy with whom he is at war, and the power and tricks of that enemy are clearly pointed out to him. And since he has been led to the conversation with his Creator, he is openly informed about the adversary's assertions. With the words that follow the Lord intimates to his faithful servant all the devices of the wily enemy, all his oppressive theft, all his ambushes and swooping, all his threats and terrorizing, all his persuasion and urging, all that he breaks in desperation, all his deceitful promises. Finally he lists the order of his battles and hesitations. He says,

*Job 40:10

XII. 16. *Here is Behemoth whom I made along with you.** To the name of Behemoth (unless it suggests the ancient enemy), transliterated from the Hebrew language, what animal corresponds in Latin? It clearly indicates the person of the one whose malice is added later on. But it has been written that God made all things together, so why does he say here that he made this animal along with the human race, when it remains true that he made everything at the same time? Again we must ask ourselves how God made all things at the same time when Moses describes creation as the work of six days, clearly distinguishing the different creations. We will understand it more quickly, however, if we carefully ascertain the causes of the origins of creation with refined detail. The matter of individual things was created at once, but the formed individual species were not created all at once, and what existed at once through the same matter did not appear together through the species that were formed.

When heaven and earth are described as made together we have spiritual creation and creation of bodies. Everything in heaven originated at the same time, and everything on earth is described as created and produced together. The sun, the moon, and the stars are reported as created on the fourth day in heaven. But what specifically appeared on the fourth day already existed on the first day, created in the matter of heaven. On the first day the earth is said to have been created, and on the third day the trees and all the green things were described as created, but what specifically appeared on the third day was of course created on the first day in the very matter from which the earth was born.

So it follows that Moses both distinguished creation by means of separate days in recounting all of it and afterwards maintained that everything was created together: *This is how heaven and earth issued forth in their creation, when the Lord made heaven and earth; no green plant was yet in the field, nor had any grass sprung up in the country.** Moses had recounted the creation of heaven and earth, of the green plants and the grass, on different days, but now he makes it clear that it was done on one day, so that he could show that all creation existed at once substantially, although the individual species did not appear simultaneously.

*Gen 2:4-5

That is why it is also written in Genesis, *God created man; he made him in the image of God; he made them male and female.** Eve was not yet described as created, and yet the human being is reported as male and female. But because the woman was beyond doubt to be produced from the side of Adam, she is already substantially counted with him from whom she was to be individually.

*Gen 1:27

We may consider the smallest quantity in itself, so that we may weigh the largest produced from it. The plants once created do not yet hold the fruit, nor does the fruit show its seed. The fruit and the seed, however, are within the plant before they are shown, because of course they are present in the substance of the root together, although they do not appear together as time goes on.

17. But since we have said that they were created together substantially, and we have found that some proceeded from others, by what manner or means is blessed Job informed that Behemoth was created? The angelic and human natures are not the same, nor did the human being proceed from the angel nor the angel from the human. Blessed Job is told that Behemoth was created for this reason: that every creature issues forth from the Creator. The Creator is never affected in his action by any extension of time, so there is no doubt about the simultaneous creation. Why then is Behemoth singled out, and why is it said that he was created in common with the other creatures in the general creation? Well, if we weigh the causes of created things with a detailed discussion, we will see that angel and human were created together, not in a common time frame but in the common knowledge by reason, together by the accepted character of wisdom, not by a formally conjoined nature. It was written about the human being, *Let us make man according to our image and likeness.** And Satan is told by Ezekiel, *You were the very image of character, full of wisdom and perfect in beauty in the delightful paradise of God.** The human being and the angel alone were created together and existed in all creation, because they proceeded distinct from all nature devoid of reason.

Since therefore in all creation no rational animal existed outside of angels and humans, not one creature

*Gen 1:26

*Ezek 28:12-13

capable of the use of reason existed, so nothing rational was created alongside the human being. Accordingly let the human being be told, and let the angel be told, that whoever has lost the power of loftiness has by no means lost the power of acute refinement found in rational nature. Let them be told, *Here is Behemoth, whom I made along with you.** Accordingly, when the human considers that the one who was made along with him as a rational creature has perished because of pride, in that neighbor's fall he should greatly fear his own perdition. In these words we must carefully notice that the Lord's voice openly censures the horrible teaching of the Manicheans that speaks of two principles and tries to assert that no shadowy nation was created. But how can it be said that no depraved nation was created, when the Lord declares that he made this Behemoth the author of all depravity through a nature rightly created? But let us hear what this Behemoth does, he along with whom Job was made, as we have heard, and lost. The next verse:

*Job 40:10

XIII. 18. *He eats hay like an ox.** If we turn over the words of the prophets carefully, we will find that they have been uttered by the same spirit as Job's. Isaiah, you see, looking upon sinners' lives being devoured by an ancient insatiable enemy, said, *The lion will eat straw like an ox.** What else is meant by the words *straw* and *hay* but the lives of people who live according to the flesh? Of these the prophet says, *All flesh is grass.** Accordingly Behemoth here and the lion there are the same animal. Hay here and straw there are the same food. But the mind wants to know why this beast that Isaiah calls lion and the Lord calls Behemoth, who in both passages eats hay or straw, is not called a horse instead of an ox. And we will know this more easily if in both animals we weigh the difference in their nourishment. Horses, you see, eat hay that is to a certain extent contaminated,

*Job 40:10

*Isa 11:7

*Isa 40:6

but they drink only water that is pure. Oxen, however, can drink water that is contaminated, but they eat only food that is clean. How is it then that Behemoth is compared to oxen, who graze only on clean pasture, unless it be as another prophet proclaimed about the ancient enemy, *His food is special*?* He finds no joy, you see, in seizing those who are involved in bad actions and willingly throwing them down into the pit with himself. He desires to eat hay like an ox, because he wants to tear with his tooth of evil suggestion the clean life of spiritual people.

*Hab 1:16

19. But I think we must ask how it is that Behemoth here, who eats hay like an ox, is said to consume the lives of spiritual people when, as was said above, the lives of those who live according to the flesh are signified by the word *grass*. His food will then not also be special if he tears and eats the food of those who live in the flesh. But this question will be quickly answered, since some people both are grass in God's eyes and rate the name of saints in human eyes. Before human eyes a life appears in one way, and before God's judgment a person's consciousness shows something else. Some then are special before human judgment, but in the sight of the Lord's far-seeing examination they are grass. Was not Saul grass in God's eyes, him about whom Samuel told the people, *You surely see whom the Lord has chosen*?* A little earlier it was even said, *Chosen and upright.** It was he whom the people sinfully deserved, and in God's sight he was actually reprobate, yet in the order of causes he was chosen and upright.

*1 Sam 10:24
*1 Sam 9:2

Because many people are grass, and they guess that they are chosen by human estimation, Solomon was right to say, *I saw the impious buried, who while they were still alive were in the holy place and were praised in the city as if they had done righteous deeds.** Because

*Eccl 8:10

many people are grass who are nevertheless protected by a rampart of support through sanctions, a certain wise person commands, *Go over, guest, and set the table.** The guest is told to go over and set the table, because anyone who is stationed at God's altar seeks his own glory through good works, and praise at the altar is extended by the display of his own purity, and yet in the sight of the Lord he is not counted among the citizens. His reputation advances among other people, and yet God excludes him as a stranger. Consequently he goes over to honor the table, because he refused to stay at the holy place, he who in all that he earnestly does runs mentally after human praise.

*Sir 29:33 Vulg

Since therefore some people earnestly lead a spotless life but do not wish thereby to gain favor within, Behemoth's food is rightly called "chosen," and yet he is said here to eat grass like an ox. It is as if the clean grass on the ground and in the lowest places lay in front of this Behemoth's mouth while a person pretended his life to be innocent by keeping the commandments, and yet through the acts that he presented as good, he did not lift up his heart to desire the higher things. What good therefore do they do who guard purity of life in themselves, those who through a base intention leave themselves on the ground to be found by the Behemoth's mouth? Since therefore almighty God implies what our enemy is doing, he now takes note of how he prevails, so that we might know the evil depths of his craftiness more easily and thus overcome it more quickly. The next verse:

XIV. 20. *His power is in his loins, and his strength is in his navel and his belly.** It states here that the male's seed for intercourse is the loins, but the female's source is in the belly. That is why Truth told his disciples, *Let your loins be girt.** That is why Peter, to restrain the

*Job 40:11

*Luke 12:35

heart from lust, gave this warning: *Gird up the loins of your minds.** That is why Paul, to express how Levi's priesthood was tithed by Melchizedek's sacrifice in the time of Abraham, when Levi still lay hidden in Abraham's body, said, *He was still in his father's loins.** But since the seed for a woman's lust is found in the belly, the prophet who decries Judea's wantonness under the image of a prostitute testifies, *On the day of your birth your umbilical cord was not cut.** The cutting of the umbilical cord on the day of birth means the denial of the flesh's lust on the day of conversion. It is difficult to stop something that has been wrongly started and to improve something that has been already badly formed, so Judea is reproached for her birth. Although she was born in God, she kept her umbilical cord uncut, because she did not deny the satisfaction of lust. Because therefore by the Devil's might both sexes are grievously overcome by the weakness of lust, against males his strength is in the loins, and against females in the belly.

*1 Pet 1:13

*Heb 7:10

*Ezek 16:4

21. But why when Behemoth started to eat this straw did his first deceptive argument add the fall of lust, unless it is crystal clear to everybody that after he once seized the human spirit, he quickly went on to the corruption of the flesh? What we know about the first human beings is that after they had committed the first sin of pride, they covered up their unseemly members, clearly indicating that after they tried between themselves to seize the highest interior reality, they quickly carried on their shamelessness into the external forum of the flesh. So here is Behemoth insatiably raging and trying to devour a whole person at once; first he takes hold of the mind by pride, and then he ruins the flesh with the pleasure of lust. By no means is his strength said to be in the loins and bellies of those who were thrown down, and rightly so, but *His power is in his* *loins, and his strength is in his navel and his belly.** It is as if it were openly said, "His strength is in his loins, and his power is in his navel and his belly, because they who were deceived by the coaxing of his shameful suggestions and gave themselves up to the movements of lust properly became his body." The next verse:

*Job 40:11

XV. 22. *He makes his tail as rigid as a cedar trunk.** There is much support in these words for the expression or teaching of ethics. But let us first discuss the violent actions of Behemoth, so that we may later uncover hidden things with more detail. Holy Scripture sometimes uses the word *cedar* to express the high excellence of heavenly glory, but sometimes it signifies the rigid pride of depraved people. The word *cedar* expresses the loftiness of heavenly glory, as when the prophet testifies, *The just man will flourish like the palm tree; like the cedar of Lebanon will he grow.** On the other hand, in the words of the same prophet *cedar* is used to signify the proud power of depraved people: *The voice of the Lord knocks down the cedars.**

*Job 40:12

*Ps 91:13

*Ps 28:5

What then is the tail of Behemoth here if not the posterior of that ancient enemy, when he enters his own special vessel, that man of perdition who is appropriately called Antichrist? Because he is sometimes allowed to lift himself up to worldly honors, sometimes to boast of signs and wonders of false holiness with the pride of power, the Lord's voice rightly compares his tail to a cedar. Just as the cedar, you see, surpasses other trees in height by constant growth, so at that time the Antichrist will temporarily obtain the glory of the world, and he will surpass human measure by the peak of his honors and the power of his signs. That spirit will in fact be in him who was created in the highest and did not lose the power of his nature, even when he was thrown down. His power is of course never revealed in the present time, because he is bound by the dispensation of divine authority. That is why John says, *I saw an angel come down from heaven. In his hand was the key to the abyss and a large chain. He took the dragon, that ancient serpent, called the Devil and Satan. He bound him for a thousand years and cast him into the deep. He closed it and locked him in.** We are told that he was bound and put in the abyss, because thrust back in the hearts of depraved people, he is confined by the power of the divine dispensation lest he should be free to hurt people in any way, so that although he can rage secretly in those he inhabits, he cannot break out with the violent seizures of pride. But it also suggests how he is to be set free at the end of the world there where it is said, *When the thousand years are over, Satan will be freed from his prison, and he will go out to deceive the nations.** By the number of a thousand the whole time of Holy Church, however long it is, is expressed for its perfection. And when it is over the ancient enemy is said to be set free, for a short time indeed, but with much power against us.

*Rev 20:1-3

*Rev 20:7

23. His rage enlarges his cruelty indeed, but heavenly mercy narrows it down to a brief space of time. That is why Truth himself says, *There will then be great tribulation, such as has not been from the beginning of the world until then, nor will there be again.** Therefore he goes on to say, *Unless those days had been shortened, no one would be safe.** Since accordingly the Lord sees that we are both proud and weak, he mercifully says that the days he first called especially evil are shortened, especially for the sake of terrifying the proud on account of the days of adversity and encouraging the weak on account of their brevity.

*Matt 24:21

*Matt 24:22

24. But we must seriously consider the fact that Behemoth here lifts up his stiff tail like a cedar, so that he rises at that time with a more terrifying appearance than he now discloses. What kinds of pain do we know that we do not boast that the martyrs suffered? Some were struck down unexpectedly by a thrust of the sword buried in the throat. Others were nailed to the gibbet of the cross, where death was both appealed to and rejected, repulsed and summoned. A saw with rough edges ground others down. The ironclad hoof attacked and scattered others. Ferocious beasts threatened to mutilate others. The multiplied force of whips tore the flesh from the inward parts of others. Others were buried alive, and earth covered them. Others were thrown down from great heights to their deaths. Others were thrown into the water, which drowned and sank them. Devouring flames consumed others until they were burned to ashes. When accordingly Behemoth here stiffens and stretches his tail in a still more evil way at the end of the world, how is it that he grows more dreadful in these contortions, unless it be what Truth himself says in the gospels: *False Christs and false prophets will arise, and they will work great signs and wonders, so that even the elect, if it were possible, might be led into error.**   *Matt 24:24

At the present time our faithful ones work marvels when they suffer perversity. At that time, however, even when the henchmen of this Behemoth start doing perverse things, the faithful will be working wonders. Let us therefore weigh what that temptation of the human mind will be when the upright martyr subjects his body to torture and the torturer works miracles right before his eyes. Is his virtue unshaken then from the very root of thoughts, when the one who crucifies him shines out with brilliant signs? Let it then be rightly said, *He makes his tail as rigid as a cedar trunk.** He will then   *Job 40:12 be high, you see, with prodigal veneration, and hard with the cruelty of torture.

25. Not only will his power be lifted up on high at that time, but he will be bright with the display of signs. That is why David says, *His ambush is hidden, and he is like a lion in his lair.** His obvious power would have sufficed for him to be a lion, even if he were not in ambush. On the other hand, it would have been enough for hidden craftiness for him to creep up out of ambush, even if he were not a lion. But the ancient enemy here is unrestrained in all his powers, so he is allowed to rage with both weapons, spreading out to fight the chosen ones both by force and by trickery: force through strength, and trickery through signs. Consequently he is rightly called a lion in ambush. His ambush is the sight of miracles; his leonine nature is worldly power. So that he can attract those whose wickedness is obvious, he shows off his worldly power, but so that he can also deceive the righteous, he pretends holiness by means of signs. He persuades the former by the pride in sheer size; he deceives the latter by ostentation of holiness.

*Ps 9:30

John speaks of Behemoth's tail here under the image of a dragon: *The dragon's tail moved and pulled down a third of the stars of heaven and let them fall to the ground.** Heaven is the church in the night of this present life; she contains the numberless virtues of the saints while she shines like the radiant stars on high, but the dragon's tail threw down the stars to the earth, because that posterior of Satan was lifted up by the boldness of an assumed man, and by obtaining certain ones whom he found like those chosen by God, he displayed them as reprobate sinners. So for the stars to fall from heaven to the ground means that some people, having given up the hope of heaven, took him as leader and panted after the campaign for worldly honors.

*Rev 12:4

26. That is why Daniel spoke against this dragon's tail with the image of Antiochus and said, *He overthrew* *the host and the stars and trampled on them, and he grew great even to the prince of the host; he took away the daily sacrifice, and he overthrew the place of sacrifice. Power was given him against the daily sacrifice because of sin, and truth will be cast down to the earth, and he will act and prosper.** He overthrew the host and the stars when he broke down some people who were shining with the light of justice and strong with the power of good works. He grew great even to the prince of the host, because he was extolled against the author of virtue himself. He took away the daily sacrifice, because he cut short the zeal for the life of the church in those whom he seized. Power was given him over the daily sacrifice on account of sin, because unless the merits of those who were perishing drove out those who were thought to be righteous, the adversary could never obtain them. Truth was cast down to the ground, because at that time faith in the reality of heaven will give way to the desire for a temporal life. He will bring it about and prosper, because at that time he will stride forward with unimaginable cruelty, without any resistance, not only in the minds of reprobate sinners but even against the bodies of the chosen ones.

*Dan 8:10-12

That is why Daniel again speaks out: *A king with brazen countenance who understands propositions will arise, and his power will prevail, but not by his own forcefulness.** The power of that man will not reside in his own forcefulness, but he will be extolled by Satan's might up to the glory of perdition. So he again says, *He will kill the mighty among the people of the saints according to his own will, and guile will prosper in his hand.** Of course he kills the mighty when he overcomes the bodies of those who are undefeated mentally. Or at least he kills the mighty and the people of the saints according to his own will, when he drags

*Dan 8:23-24

*Dan 8:24-25

those who were supposed to be mighty and holy by the nod of his own will. Deception prospers in his hand, because fraud is helped along by the work of his hand. Whatever he deceitfully says he confirms by working wonders, because whatever his lying tongue fabricates he displays as true by the action of his hand.

27. So he again speaks up: *He will even rise against the prince of the host, but he will be crushed by no human hand.** That is why Paul says, *So that he is enthroned in God's temple as if to show himself to be God.** And again: *The Lord Jesus will slay him with the breath of his mouth and destroy him by the brightness of his coming.** That is the same thing as what Daniel said: *He grew great even to the prince of the host.* Yes, Paul said, *So that he is enthroned in God's temple as if to show himself to be God.* Even what Daniel added—*he will be crushed by no human hand*—Paul also expressed: *The Lord Jesus will kill him by the breath of his mouth, and he will destroy him by the enlightenment of his coming.* Obviously the fact that he will be crushed by no human hand means that not in the war of the angels, not in the battle with the saints, but through the Judge's coming alone, by the breath of his mouth, Satan will be struck down by eternal death. This is Behemoth, whose pride Paul also mentions: *He is the adversary who lifts himself up against all that is called God and worshiped.**

*Dan 8:25

*2 Thess 2:4

*2 Thess 2:8

*2 Thess 2:4

Daniel speaks of him as the fourth beast, provided with ten horns, and immediately adds, *I was looking at the horns, and suddenly I saw another smaller horn sprout among them, and three of the first horns were thrown down before it, and as I looked eyes like human eyes appeared on it, and a mouth speaking boastful words.** What he describes is the eleventh horn of this beast, because the power of his kingdom is confirmed by

*Dan 7:8

wickedness. Every sin has the number eleven, because while it does what is twisted it exceeds the Decalogue's commandments. In goat hair sin is mourned, and so in the tent there are eleven veils of sackcloth.* That is why it is written in the eleventh psalm, *Save me O Lord, for there is now no saint.** That is why Peter, in his worry that the number of apostles remained eleven, when lots were cast wanted Matthias to be the twelfth. Unless he perceived something wrong to be signified in the number eleven, you see, he would not be in such a hurry to complete the number of apostles with the twelfth.

*Exod 26:7

*Ps 11:2

Since therefore a transgression is expressed by the number eleven, the very author of transgression is indicated by the eleventh horn of this beast. But it is a noticeably small horn that sprouts, so a real man is born; he inhumanly grows, so he grows until he links up with the energy of angelic power. But he tears out three horns that were there before his appearance, so he subjugated three nearby kingdoms to his dominion. He has eyes like human eyes and a mouth that speaks boastful words, because a human form is discerned in him, but his words lift him up above humankind. Paul spoke of this paradox: He *lifts himself up against all that is called God and worshiped.** Daniel for his part says, *a mouth speaking boastful words.**

*2 Thess 2:4
*Dan 7:8

So the one who Daniel says speaks boastful words and who Paul maintains lifts himself up against the worship of God is the same as the one whom blessed Job compared to the cedar of the word of God. Just like the cedar, he endeavors to reach the sky while he prospers in all arrogant deceit, forceful power, and mountainous pride. He is rightly said to stiffen his tail, because all his power is accumulated and concentrated in that one condemned man, so that through him he may bring about as many wonderful deeds of power as are his own concentrated resources with which he urges him on. But since we have heard what kind of head it is that rules over its evil members, let us now learn what the members are that stick to that head. The next verse:

XVI. 28. *The sinews of his testicles are intricate.** Behemoth here has as many testicles as he possesses preachers of his iniquity. Are not they his testicles who by pouring out the poisonous seed of error corrupt people's hearts with evil persuasion? And it is rightly said that the sinews of his testicles are intricate, obviously because the statements of his preachers are entangled with deceitful teachings, so that they might seem to be correct when they persuade the doing of perverse acts. Thus the interweaving of assertions, like intertwining sinews, even if they could be seen, could not be loosened. His testicles have intricate sinews, because the point of his preaching hides behind his deceitful arguments. But it often happens that while hearts are being infected with words, the preachers pretend innocence by their acts. They would never attract good people by persuasion, you see, if they displayed their perversity in their actions. But since this beast has testicles, and they are intertwined with intricate sinews, they pretend righteousness behind which they hide, while they preach perversity and corruption; they imitate their head, who like a lion in ambush both rages through the power of worldly authority and coaxes through an appearance of holiness.

But would that at that time only this beast could do such things and that it did not at the present time also have those testicles of lust with which to corrupt the inner parts of the faithful people! Nor is it only by the words of his mouth that evil is perpetrated, but he proposes worse evils because of the example given by the things that many people do. So many people have not seen the Antichrist, and yet they are his testicles,

*Job 40:12

because they corrupt the hearts of innocent people by the example of their actions! Whoever extols himself by pride, whoever is tortured by the desires of avarice, whoever is unhinged by the pleasure of lust, whoever is incited by the flames of unrighteous and excessive anger: what else are these but the testicles of Antichrist? As long as they freely involve themselves as his tools, they bring forth the offspring of error in other people by their example. The one does evil, and the other joins the one doing evil; not only does the latter avoid opposing the former, but he actively praises him. What else then is the one who, having lost the authority of the faith promised to God, bears witness to error but a testicle of the Antichrist? If anyone accuses such people, they quickly hide under some defensive veil, obviously because their sinews are intricate and badly involved, and they can never be freed from corruption. The next verse:

XVII. 29. *Their bones are like tubes of brass.** *Job 40:13
Bones in the body contain the members; the members are what are contained. This beast has both flesh and bones. There are some who are wicked, but they are kept in error by others, and the others are worse, those who keep others in error. What else then do we take the bones of Antichrist to be but certain people in his body who are stronger? In their hearts, of course, iniquity has intensely hardened, and so his whole bodily structure is stabilized through them. There are many people in this world who seem rich and are supported by possessions and power, and their might seems to be well founded, but they give these things away to their supporters and drag them into their own error. They entice some people with gifts to make them depraved; others they restrain with presents to keep them depraved. What else are these people accordingly but Antichrist's bones, who multiply by keeping evil people evil and in this way

carry the flesh in Antichrist's body? Sometimes they display sweetness of speech to deceive their audience, just like flowers that cover thorns, and what appears has fragrance, but it covers a sharp point. They mix sweetness with bitterness and softness with harm; they like to look admirable with power; with their skill at deception they humbly prostrate themselves as it were through relaxed conversation; they insinuate themselves through speech, while they deny pretensions by their outward behavior.

30. So the bones of Behemoth here are rightly compared to brass pipes; naturally like a metal deprived of sensation they have good-sounding speech, but they have no sensation that comes from a good life. They assert with apparently humble speech what their proud way of life disdains. That is why Paul says, *Even if I speak with the tongues of angels and men, if I have no love, I have become like sounding brass and tinkling cymbals.** Such a person indeed speaks what is good, but he does not seek through love the same good that he speaks, and so the sound he makes is more like brass or cymbal, because he does not feel in himself the words he speaks. There are those however in the body of this beast who are not decorated with honors or supported by riches or sporting the appearance of virtue or even experienced in the art of deception, yet they are anxious to seem what they are not. On this account they become even worse scoundrels against the lives of good people, and of them the Lord goes on to say,

*1 Cor 13:1

*Job 40:13

XVIII. 31. *His cartilage is like iron plates.** Cartilage has the appearance of bone but not the solidity. How is it then that his cartilage is compared to iron plates unless because those members of his that are weaker are worse evildoers? Other metals in fact are broken up against iron, and Behemoth's cartilage is said to be like iron, because those of his members who are not satisfactory for the display of power are stirred up more fiercely to kill the faithful people. Because, you see, they do not consider themselves capable of doing signs and wonders for Behemoth, they prove themselves faithful to him through acts of cruelty, and just because they do not have the power to corrupt innocent hearts by means of persuasion, they boast all the more of their power to kill the bodies of other good people. So it is well said, *His cartilage is like iron plates*, because what everyone considers weaker in Behemoth's body is what comes across as more evil. He is compared not merely to iron, but to iron plates, and rightly, because those whose cruelty is noised about all over the place apparently spread out like iron plates.

32. We may as well stretch the meaning of these same words of the Creator that we have already considered and discussed with a more searching hand of inquiry, and bring in a more abundant harvest of understanding for the purpose of moral improvement. We have heard how the ancient enemy took up the form of a man in order to act against the human race; it remains for us now to inquire about what he sets afoot in the human race by himself without the aid of a man. So here is what the Lord says:

XIX. 33. *He makes his tail as rigid as a cedar trunk.** *Job 40:12
The first suggestion of the serpent is of course slight and gentle, easy to rub out with the foot of virtue, but if it is negligently allowed to strengthen, or if it is freely allowed entrance to the heart, it accumulates so much force that it captures and forces down the mind and increases its weight to an intolerable degree. Accordingly the tail is said to become as rigid as a cedar, because once a temptation is received in the heart, wherever it then enters it becomes dominant as if by law. The head of this

Behemoth is grass, and its tail is a cedar, because the first suggestion is slight and easily knocked down, but in time it grows violent, and while the end of the temptation is approaching it grows effective.

Every suggestion can be overcome in the beginning, but what follows later can hardly be overcome. First like an ingratiating counselor it speaks to the soul, but once it has sunk the tooth of pleasure in it, it fastens itself almost irreversibly with a violent habit. So the tail is well said to become rigid. The tooth wounds and the tail binds, because the first suggestion strikes, but lest the stricken mind should be able to escape, the end of the temptation grows stronger and ties up the soul. Sin, you see, has three means of entrance: the serpent's suggestion, the pleasure of the flesh, and the consent of the spirit cause it to be committed; so Behemoth here opens its mouth and suggests unlawful acts, then drawing out pleasure, it fixes its tooth, and finally it demands consent by possession and stiffens its tail.

That is why some people by long custom reproach themselves for sins they have committed, and they flee from them because of judgment, but they cannot fight against them or avoid them in their actions, because as long as they do not cut off the head of Behemoth here, even unwillingly they are often tied up by his tail. And his tail grows hard as a cedar against them, because it grows from a slight pleasure at the beginning even to the violent holding on. Let him say it then: *He makes his tail as rigid as a cedar trunk.* So every person ought to flee the beginning of temptation inasmuch as we all know very well that we cannot quickly free ourselves from its end.

34. We should know as well that the serpent often introduces still greater guilt to those whom he has already grasped when he knows that they are approaching the end of the present life, and because he considers that he is going to use up the time for temptation, he accumulates a still heavier burden of wickedness for them. So Behemoth stiffens his tail like a cedar, because he makes those feebler at the end whom he seized at the beginning for depravity, so that the sooner his temptations are due to stop, the more stoutly they can be completed. Since, you see, he knows how to make their punishment correspond to his penalties, he tries harder before their death to magnify every sin. However, Behemoth here often already possesses the evil subdued heart, but divine grace repels the one whom the captive will brought in to itself, and the hand of mercy casts him out. And when Behemoth is expelled from the heart, he tries to embed fiercer spikes of iniquity, so that the mind embattled by him might feel those waves of temptation that it did not know when possessed by him.

This situation is well expressed in the gospel when it tells about an unclean spirit ordered to leave a man. When the boy possessed by a demon was brought to Jesus, it is written, *He threatened the unclean spirit and said, "Deaf and dumb spirit, I command you to go out of him and never enter him again." The spirit cried out and violently convulsed him before it went out.** *Mark 9:24-25 Notice that the spirit did not convulse the boy while it held him, but only in going out, obviously because it tears apart the thoughts of the mind worse when, forced by divine power, it already approaches its departure. And the person whom the mute spirit had possessed he abandoned with cries, because when a spirit possesses a person it often inflicts minor temptations, but when it is expelled from that person's heart it upsets him by means of more severe attacks. So it is well said, *He makes his tail as rigid as a cedar trunk*, because in possessing the heart Behemoth keeps growing in malice in his posterior part, and in abandoning the heart it strikes it with more violent torture. The Creator's admirable concern, however, reveals still more cunning details about Behemoth:

XX. 35. *The sinews of his testicles are intricate.** The sinews of his testicles are the death-dealing details of schemes. It is a fact that through them the strength of his craftiness gains power and corrupts the unstable hearts of mortal creatures. His testicles are depraved suggestions with which his passions burn for the corruption of the mind, and he generates the offspring of wicked deeds in the soul that he has raped. But the sinews of these testicles are intricate, because the details of these suggestions are tied up with intricate discoveries, so he may force some people to sin in such a way that if they want somehow to avoid sin, they cannot do it without falling into another trap of sin. So by avoiding one sin they commit another, and they can by no means extricate themselves from this guilt without involving themselves in consenting to another sin.

*Job 40:12

We can demonstrate this better if we offer an example of this hand-tying from everyday human life. In the church there exist three states: the married state, the state of chastity, and the state of leadership. That is why Ezekiel saw three liberated men: Noah, Daniel, and Job.* And when the Lord listed some in the field, others on the couch, and still others at the mill,* he obviously showed that there are three states in the church. We will succeed in making it clear if we distinguish each one from the others.

*Ezek 14:14, 20
*Luke 17:34, 36

36. This is how a worldly person cultivates friendships: he gets a second person leading a life like his own to bind himself by oath to keep his secrets in complete silence. But the one he swore the oath to is known to be one who committed adultery, and he even went so far as to try to kill the husband of the adulterous woman. The one who swore the oath then thinks it over, and he is assailed by contrary thoughts on that account. He is afraid to keep the situation quiet, lest his silence should make him an accomplice of the man's adultery and homicide, and he is afraid to publicize it, lest he incur the guilt of perjury. He is bound then by the intricate sinews of testicles, and whichever side he inclines toward, he is afraid of being subject to the contagion of transgression.

37. Another person abandons all that is worldly, and he seeks to break his own will in all things; he wishes then to submit himself to someone else's guidance, but he does not discern the one who should be in charge of him in God's sight with a careful enough scrutiny. By chance the one he chooses injudiciously begins to take charge, forbids him to do the works of God, and commands him to do worldly things. So the subject weighs the guilt of disobedience against the contagion of a worldly life; he is afraid to obey and afraid not to obey, lest by obeying he should abandon God by not following his precepts, or by not obeying he should disdain God in his chosen superior. Should he by complying with what is unlawful want something for God's sake that he would practice against God, or on the other hand by not complying make himself subject to the judgment of the one whom he had sought out as his judge?

Obviously this person through the defect of his own indiscretion is tied up with the intricate sinews of testicles, since whether he complies or surely does not comply, he is bound with the guilt of transgression. He was eager to break his own will, and his care results in the solidifying of his own will, even by disdaining his superior. He decided seriously to forsake the world, and he is forced to return to worldly cares even by someone else's will. They are indeed intricate sinews when the enemy's arguments tie us up in such a way that when we seek to untie the knot of guilt we are still more tightly bound.

38. Somebody else neglects to weigh the burden of ecclesiastical honors, and he rises to a place in the government as a favor. But since all that distinguishes us here below is more endowed with grief than adorned with honor, his heart is depressed by troubles, and he remembers guilt. We grieve at having been given work along with guilt, and we realize how inconvenient the place is that we have reached when we are dejected by its difficulty. Such a person realizes that he is under obligation along with the favors dealt, and he desires to abandon the sublime position he has attained, but he is afraid it would be a worse crime to abandon the care of the flock that he has received. He wants to guard that flock, but he is afraid lest it should be a worse fault to possess the guidance of pastoral relationship that has been bought. So he sees himself surrounded by a cycle of honors as if by sin.

As far as he can see, neither path is without the guilt of crime, whether he should abandon the flock he has received, or on the other hand a sacred action he has bought should be kept as a worldly possession. He is afraid on every side, and he suspects every path, lest by staying in a purchased official position he should mourn his unworthiness for it, which he cannot correct even by abandoning it, or instead deserting it while he tries to weep over another, or on the other hand involving someone else in the very betrayal of the flock. Since therefore Behemoth here ties knots in this way that cannot be loosened, so that the mind is often led into doubt when it tries to extricate itself from guilt and is in that way still more tightly tied up in guilt, it is rightly said, *The sinews of his testicles are intricate.** The arts of Behemoth's contrivances, you see, are as it were loosened and let go, only so that they may be more intricately tied and hold fast.

*Job 40:12

39. There is however something that can be done towards destroying his cunning, so that when the mind is caught between smaller and greater sins, if absolutely no door is open for an escape without sin, the lesser sin can always be chosen. For example, when someone is surrounded by walls to keep him from flight, he may speedily run to where a lower wall is found. Paul too, when he found some incontinent people in church, allowed for the lesser faults, so that he might keep away the greater, and he said, *Because of fornication, let each one have his own wife.** And since married people can only join together without guilt when they are joined not for the satisfaction of lust but for the raising of children, so that Paul might show that he had not allowed even this without guilt, albeit a smaller one, he quickly added, *This however I say by way of concession, not of command.** What is allowed but not commanded, you see, is not without vice. He of course saw a sin that he foresaw could be allowed. But when we are hung up by doubts we conveniently give in to lesser faults, lest we should commit more serious sins without forgiveness. In this way we often free ourselves from the intricate sinews of Behemoth while we pass on to greater virtues through the commission of minor faults.

*1 Cor 7:2

*1 Cor 7:6

XXI. 40. The next verse: *His bones are like tubes of brass.** What do our Behemoth's bones signify if not his counsels? Just as the body's position and strength consist in bones, so also in lying counsels all his malice rears up. Nor does he harass anyone with power, but by the cunning of death-dealing persuasion he kills. Again, just as the marrow irrigates the bones and refreshes them, so also Behemoth's refined presence slips into his counsel through the power of his spiritual nature and empowers it. His testicles, however, differ from his bones, that is, his suggestions from his counsels, in that

*Job 40:13

through the former he openly inserts what is hurtful, whereas through the latter, as if by good counsel, he draws us to sin; through the former he fights and wins, but through the latter he offers counsel and trips us. That is why his bones, or his counsels, are compared to tubes of brass. Pipes of brass are of course often adapted to the sound of singing, and when they move they sound to the ears like the fine singing of a sweet song; in this way they draw the interior mind out to experience pleasure, since what the ears hear is sweet, and they disarm the manliness of the heart with the breath of delight. Since the sense of hearing is attracted by pleasure, the mind's state of fortitude is weakened.

Very clever is his counsel; while he counsels comfortable forethought, he turns the heart away from its strong intention, and while sweet sounds are heard, they make us bend down to what is harmful. They are like bronze tubes that we freely hear, but they push the soul down from its internal attention to pleasure in external life. It is Behemoth indeed who especially busies himself with the development of deception, so that while he displays his perverse counsel as something useful, he is able to make his words sound appealing, inasmuch as having shown their usefulness, he can caress the mind, and having hidden their wickedness, he can corrupt it.

41. We will make all this clearer if we briefly expose a few of the arguments of his counsels. Suppose a certain person, being content with his own possessions, has decided not to get involved with any of this world's business undertakings, afraid of losing the advantages of his quiet life and scornful of the project of piling up wealth along with sin. To him the cunning enemy comes so that he may upset his intention of pious devotion, and he administers useful advice. He says, "Your present goods are sufficient for you, but what will you do when they are gone? If you do not provide more for when these are gone, what then? You have enough at present to provide for your children, but what will later be needed is still to be provided. What you have can be quickly gone if your watchful care stops preparing what is missing. Can worldly action not be set afoot and sin be avoided in that action insofar as you provide external income and do not alter internal uprightness?" Such are the arguments that he ingratiatingly instills, and he hides the ambush of sin in the worldly business that he foresees. His bones are therefore like tubes of bronze, because his dangerous counsels are softened for his listener by the silky voice of the counselor.

42. Another person has decided not only to resist the seeking of worldly advantage, but even to renounce all his possessions, so that he may place himself all the more freely at his heavenly master's service, as he has rendered himself unencumbered by abandoning and trampling upon his possessions, which could have prevented him. The enemy sneaks up to the heart of this person and makes this surreptitious suggestion: "Where did you get such reckless boldness, that you should dare think you can get by when you abandon everything? The Creator made you one way, but you dispose of yourself in another! If he had wanted you to follow his steps with the constraint of poverty, he would have made you stronger and more robust. Are there not many people who by no means abandon their worldly patrimony, and yet with it perform works of mercy and in that way purchase eternal goods and a place in heaven?" Such are his ingratiating suggestions, and he deceptively places before the lingering eyes death-dealing pleasures in those very possessions that he particularly warns the person to retain, inasmuch as, having seduced his heart, he draws it externally to soft pleasures and turns him away internally from the promise of perfection. Accordingly his bones are like tubes of brass, because while his treacherous counsels are rendering a charming sound externally, they introduce a dangerous cost internally.

43. Another person, having renounced all his external possessions so that he might gain the rank of higher discipleship, also gets ready to break his own will, so that by subjecting himself to the more upright will of another person he might renounce himself—not only his evil desires, but even his good wishes—for the consummation of perfection and might observe all things that were prescribed for him to do by the will of that other person. The enemy speaks the more gently to him the more ardently he tries to throw him down from that lofty place. He quickly softens his poisonous suggestion and says, "O how many wonders could you be able to work by yourself, if you never subjected yourself to someone else's judgment! Why do you diminish your own project beneath zeal for a better one? Why do you spoil the goodness of your intention when you try to extend it beyond what is necessary? What perverse deeds did you perpetrate when you acted according to your own will? When accordingly you are perfectly capable of living well yourself, why do you want to have someone else's judgment over you?" These things he gently suggests; then he gets ready specific ways of practicing pride in the person's own will. He praises the heart for its internal rectitude; then he slyly investigates how he can undermine it with depravity. His bones therefore are like tubes of bronze, because his secret counsels, while they gently delight the soul, turn it away from righteous intentions in a dangerous fashion.

44. Another person has completely broken his own will and already burned away many of the vices of the old man, both by changing his way of life and by tearful repentance. The more completely dead to himself he is and the less bound by his own iniquity, the more zealously he is incensed against the sins of others. The sly enemy, however, since he also knows that others can profit from the zeal for justice, says, as if he sought a favorable issue with words of advice, "Why do you exaggerate the duty to cure others? Would that you were strong enough to consider your own! Or do you not carefully evaluate the others to whom you turn your zeal when you are less careful to find your own faults to cure? And where is the profit in tending the wounds of others while neglect of your own causes them to fester?" He pretends to give counsel with these words while he deprives charity of zeal, and he ruins whatever good could have resulted from charity with the sword of lethargy that he has slyly introduced.

If, you see, we are commanded to love our neighbors as we love ourselves, it is fitting that we should burn with zeal for them against their vices as against our own. Since accordingly while smoothly counseling us he renders our mind a stranger to its own intention, it is rightly said, *His bones are like tubes of brass.** When his lying counsel sounds gentle to the ears of the soul, you see, it is as though he were singing with bronze pipes, so that when he soothes he also deceives. Behemoth here fights his battle much more softly when he busies himself in ambush under the pretext of weakness. But then he exerts his temptations harder when he hides the traps of iniquity from the eyes of the one being tempted behind a show of virtue. So he rightly goes on,

XXII. 45. *His cartilage is like iron plates.** What do we take cartilage to mean then, if not his pretense? Cartilage, you see, presents an appearance of bone, but it does not have the solidity of bone. Certain vices display an appearance of uprightness, but they emerge from the

*Job 40:13

*Job 40:13

weakness of depravity. Our enemy, you see, often covers up his malice so skillfully that he makes sins look like virtues to our deceived eyes. People expect a reward where they deserve to find eternal torments. People often act relentlessly in the retribution of vice, and this is called justice, whereas the unrestrained wrath of the righteous person is held to be meritorious zeal. On the other hand, sinners who should be cautiously weaned from their distorted behavior are instead broken by violent stress. Easygoing forgiveness is often passed off as meekness or respect, and offenders who are temporarily spared more than they should be are cruelly reserved for eternal punishment. Lavish giving is sometimes called compassion, and whereas wrongly retaining what has been received is a fault, it is worse for it to be thrown away, and this fault is not feared.

Sometimes stubbornness is held to be sparingness, and whereas it is a grievous fault not to give, it is supposed to be a virtue to keep what has been received. The obstinacy of bad people is often called persistence, and when the mind is not suffered to turn aside from its depravity, it more or less boasts in defense of its rightness. Inconstancy often pretends to be manageability, and because no one is completely trustworthy, everyone considers himself a friend to all. When fear is out of place it is thought to be humility, and when anyone is forced into a position of temporary fear, he keeps silence from the defense of truth; he supposes that in the divine order of things he shows his humility to those who are better than he. Sometimes proud words are supposed to mean the freedom of truth, and when truth is contradicted by pride, effrontery of speech is thought to be a defense of truth. Indolence often gets attention as if it were the restraint of a quiet person, and when it is a serious fault not eagerly to do what is right, it is supposed to be meritorious and virtuous merely to abstain from a bad action.

Spiritual restlessness is often called alert solicitude, and when not everyone puts up with silence, by doing what he likes a person supposes that he is exercising the virtue that he should exercise. Careless hurry in doing what ought to be done is often believed to be eager fervor that should be praised, and even when a desired good is ruined by untimely action, it is thought better to act as quickly as possible. Slowness in hastening a good action is often supposed to mean counsel, and when it is expected that due consideration will bring progress, a plotted delay overthrows it. Consequently, when a fault is looked upon as a virtue, it is necessary to think that the slower a mind is to abandon its vices, the less likely it is to be ashamed of the things it perpetrates; the slower a mind is to abandon its vices, the more likely it is to be deceived by the appearance of virtue, and the more likely to expect a reward in return for it. A fault is easily corrected in fact when we sense it to be a fault and are ashamed of it. Since therefore when a false step is thought to be a virtue it is very difficult to correct, it is rightly said, *His cartilage is like iron plates.** So because Behemoth here fraudulently displays his slyness behind a show of good, he holds the mind longer in sin.

*Job 40:13

46. That is why those who desire the way of holiness sometimes fall into error and are too slow to correct themselves. They instead evaluate what they are doing as correct, and as if they were cultivating virtue they devoutly persevere in a bad habit. They evaluate what they are doing as correct, and on that account they follow their own judgment more zealously. So Jeremiah said, *Her Nazirites were purer than snow, whiter than milk, more ruddy than old ivory, and more beautiful than sapphire; now their faces have become blacker than*

*Lam 4:7-8 *charcoal, and they are not recognized on the street.** After that, though, he quickly added: *Their skin is shriveled on their bones; it has dried up and become like wood.** What else is signified by the name of Nazirites but the lives of abstainers and continent people that are called whiter than snow or milk? Snow is water that has frozen and falls from the sky, but milk comes from the flesh, which is nourished by things below. What then do we understand by snow but the brightness of eternal life? What by milk are we shown but the administration of the worldly government?

*Lam 4:8

And since the continent people in the church often perform such wonderful deeds that many people who have chosen the heavenly life and many who have well administered the earthly life seem to be surpassed by them, they are spoken of as whiter than snow and brighter than milk. In fact their spiritual enthusiasm sometimes seems to surpass the life of the earlier and stronger patriarchs, so that it is rightly added, *Her Nazirites were more ruddy than old ivory.* Since the word *ruddy* is used, the flame of holy desire is signified. As for ivory, we know very well that the tusks of the largest animals are signified there. So they are more ruddy than old ivory, because these people are often before human eyes more fervent in zeal than some of the ancient patriarchs. And to express the whole message at once, it adds, They were *more beautiful than sapphire.* Sapphire in fact is the color of sky. And because they seem to surpass by their heavenly way of life many who precede and are on the road to heaven, they are reported to have been more beautiful than sapphire.

But when the mind well supplied with virtues often prospers even more than is convenient, it is induced to a certain self-confidence; then it is deceived by its own presumption, and it is darkened by a sin suddenly creeping in. So the prophet rightly adds, *now their faces have become blacker than charcoal.* They turn black from brightness, because they have lost God's justice by their own presumption, and they have even fallen into sins that they did not understand. And since after the fire of love they have reached cold lethargy, they are shown as compared to burnt-out charcoal. Sometimes, you see, people abandon the fear of God because of self-confidence, so that they even become colder than cold minds. Seeing them in this state, the prophet adds, *they are not recognized on the street. Street* is a Greek word* with the connotation "broad." *platea

What is narrower in fact to the human mind than the breaking of one's own will? And concerning that breaking, Truth himself has said, *Enter through the narrow gate.** What is broader than the project of resisting none of one's own will, and in whatever direction we are impelled by the will, there to go freely without hesitation? The one accordingly who through self-confidence lays aside the better judgment of holiness and goes his own way walks as it were the broad street. But they are not recognized on the street, because they had shown a different view of their lives when they broke their own wills and kept to the rough narrow path. And he is right again to add, *Their skin is shriveled on their bones.* What does the bone mean if not hardness and strength, and what is the skin if not softness and weakness? So their skin is said to be shriveled on the bones, because the hardness of virtue is sensed by those meeting them as the depraved weakness of vice. What they do, you see, is weak, but they are deceived by the confidence of pride, and they join it to strong feelings of mistrust, and where they sense great things in themselves, there they disdain the evil that needs to be corrected. So he rightly adds, *it has dried up and become like wood.*

*Matt 7:13

Their guilt in fact has been rendered so much less obvious that for them it seems even praiseworthy. And the prophet rightly affirms its dryness, since it has no greenness in his perception of it. So what Jeremiah sees as weak skin, blessed Job calls brittle cartilage, and what in Jeremiah is called bone for its hardness is in Job called iron plates. So here is Behemoth, who through his members at the end of time busies himself against the chosen ones with so much artifice and wickedness, and who even shows himself in so much hiding and ambush to deceive minds: let us hear about his nature and about his condition. He could not exercise himself in such wonderful evil works if his existence did not issue forth from a condition of greatness. That is why the Lord quickly with wonderful kindness, as if he would restore the causes of such great cleverness and such great courage, added the following words:

*Job 40:14

XXIII. 47. *He is the first of the ways of God.** It is as if he said outright, "On that account his strength is great enough to accomplish so many things, because in the nature of the world the Creator made him first by creating him substantially." What then do we take "the ways of God" to mean if not his actions? About them

*Isa 55:8

the prophet says, *nor are my ways your ways.** And Behemoth is called the first of God's ways, because when the Creator of all things acted, he created him first whom he made higher than the other angels. The prophet saw how high his primacy was when he said, *There were no cedars higher than he in the paradise of God, nor could the fir trees reach his height; the plane trees could not equal his green branches; no tree in the paradise of God was like him or approached his beauty whom God made*

*Ezek 31:8-9

handsome in his many thick branches.* Whom should we take to be meant by the cedars, firs, and plane trees if not that army of heavenly virtues with lofty height planted in the forest of eternal joy? But however high their condition, they did not surpass or equal him. His beauty was made foremost in the mass and multitude of his green branches, because he had precedence over the other legions, and his appearance rendered him more beautiful than the gathered multitude of angels embellished. This tree in the Paradise of God had as many green branches massed together as there were legions of heavenly spirits posted below him that he watched.

On that account he sinned without forgiveness and was condemned, because he had been created incomparably great. That is why the same prophet again tells him, *You were the seal of likeness to God, full of wisdom and perfect in beauty, in the delightful paradise of God.** He was about to say a great deal about his magnificence, but he embraced the whole with the first word. What good did he lack, you see, if he was the seal of likeness to God? Such a likeness on the face of a signet ring expresses by images whatever essence that face holds. And although the human being is created in the likeness of God, God gave the angel something more, so to speak, so the prophet did not say that the angel was created in the likeness of God, but he said that the angel was the seal of likeness to God, so that his being finer than nature is believed to express in him a more complete likeness to God.

*Ezek 28:12-13
(*Tu signaculum similitudinis Dei*)

48. That is why the same prophet adds the power of Behemoth's primacy, which he had already suggested: *Your covering was every precious stone: carnelian, topaz, and jasper, chrysolite and onyx, beryl, sapphire, carbuncle, and emerald.** He mentions nine kinds of stones, obviously because there are nine orders of angels. Holy Scripture tells us in fact about angels, archangels, thrones, dominations, virtues, principalities, powers, cherubim, and seraphim,* openly reporting and

*Ezek 28:13

*Col 1:16

mentioning how many distinctions there are among the citizens of heaven. Behemoth here is described as covered by those stones, because he possessed them like a garment ornamenting himself, whose brightness he transcended, since compared to them he was brighter. For a further description the prophet adds, *Worked gold was your setting, and your engravings were prepared on the day of your creation.** Worked gold was his setting, because he shone with the brightness of wisdom that he received at his good creation, but engravings are made for stones, so that set in gold they might shine together as united ornamentation. They would never clash with one another, because the gold would be poured out to fill the settings and unite the whole. So the settings for this stone were prepared on the day of its creation, obviously because it was created capable of love.

*Ezek 28:13

If he had wished to be filled with charity, with the angels standing as it were in positions of royal harness, he could have united with the stones. If he had shown himself permeable by the gold of charity in the society of the holy angels as an ornament in the way we have said, he would have remained fixed in royal order. This stone therefore had settings, but they were not filled with the gold of charity, because of the vice of pride. On that account, you see, stones are set in gold that they might not fall; so on that account he did fall, because although the Artist's hand had created settings, he disdained to be bound by the chains of love. But now the other stones whose settings had been created along with his are tied together by charity and are mutually permeable, and their reward is this: that while he fell, they deserved never again to fall or to be released from the royal harness.

The same prophet again saw the loftiness of this prince, and he added, *You were a cherub extending your protection on the holy mountain of God, and you walked unhurt among the fiery stones.** The cherub of course is interpreted "fullness of knowledge," and this person is called *cherub* precisely because he has undoubtedly transcended everyone in knowledge. He who walked unhurt among the fiery stones, because he had been ignited with the fire of charity among angelic hearts, was glorious in the light of his creation. He was rightly called *extending protection*, since all that we extend and protect we overshadow. And because by comparison with his own glory he is supposed to have overshadowed the glory of others, he is reported to have been extending protection. Behemoth covered and overshadowed the others, you see, because he transcended their majesty by his own greater excellence. His beauty there lay in his many green branches, in his being the seal of likeness, in his being a cherub, and in his being protective, and he here is called the first of God's ways by the Lord's voice.

*Ezek 28:14

49. On that account Ezekiel suggests here what such wonders mean and what Behemoth lost, so that God might show the terrified human being what he would suffer from the guilt of self-exaltation if being human he should grow proud, and if by striking, God should refuse to spare the one whom he had raised to such glory and brightness in his creation. The human being then should consider what the proud person on earth would deserve if even the angel who was the foremost of the angels in heaven was thrown down. That is why the prophet was right to say, *My sword has drunk its fill in the sky.** It is as if he said outright, "Estimate with care how wrathfully I should strike the proud ones of the earth, if I did not even spare my blows against those I created in heaven close to me for the sin of pride!"

*Isa 34:5

So since we have heard about so many powers of the ancient enemy and realized how great was the majesty in which he was created, who would not fall down in boundless terror? Who would not sink to the ground as if from a blow of despair? But since the enemy's displayed power effectively represses our pride, the Lord also comforts our weakness by uncovering the plan of his grace. So, having once called Behemoth the first of his ways, he quickly adds,

*Job 40:14

XXIV. 50. *His Maker has applied his sword.*** The sword of our Behemoth is nothing else but his hurtful malice. But by him who made his nature good is his own sword applied, because Behemoth's malice is restrained by the divine plan, lest it should be allowed to strike human minds as much as it wants to. So our enemy has great power, but he strikes less because the loving care of the Creator restrains his sword. So that he may hide within the folds of his consciousness, he may not extend his malice to encompass the deaths of human beings beyond what is allowed from on high by a righteous dispensation. So the fact that he does prevail often and mightily is due to the principle of his strong creation; however, he is sometimes beaten, and that is certainly because the Creator turns his own sword backwards. This very Behemoth is the first of God's ways, and he was allowed freedom to tempt the holy man. That is why he moved people, robbed flocks, made fire come down from heaven, troubled the air to raise winds, struck the house so that it collapsed, killed the banqueting youngsters, troubled Job's wife's mind and tricked her into an evil suggestion, and inflicted her husband with wounds in his flesh.

But the Creator turned back his sword against him and said, *Save his life.** And the gospel testifies and describes his weakness when the sword is turned back, because he could not remain in the possessed person, nor did he presume to enter the brute animals again

*Job 2:6

without permission, but he said, *If you cast us out, send us into the herd of swine.** We are shown how the sword of malice is turned back, since if the highest Power did not grant leave, Behemoth could not move against the pigs. How then could he by his own volition dare hurt human beings made in the image of God, about whom it is definitely said that he could not even presume to touch the pigs without orders?

*Matt 8:31

51. It is also noteworthy that when Behemoth is called the first of God's ways, the wild teaching of Arius is completely reasonably denied. Arius confesses the Son of God to be a creature, you see, but here is Behemoth displayed as the first of God's creatures. Arius is only left with the choice of preaching that the Son is no creature, or the folly of saying that he was created after Behemoth. However, since all that is applied is reduced to itself, Behemoth is rightly said to have applied his sword. His malice, you see, boils down to himself by his choice, since it is forbidden to be exercised against the lives of the chosen ones. He is however allowed to strike many because they deserve it, inasmuch as when they abandon God they make themselves the slaves of the condemned enemy. By the chosen ones, however, he is the more valiantly defeated the more humbly they submit themselves to the very Creator of all.

Accordingly, since Behemoth is the first of God's ways, and since by God's permission he shows himself to be unbearable, we clearly learn the greatness of the enemy we have to fight. So each one of us is left with one alternative: to subject ourselves as completely to our Creator as each one seriously weighs the violent resources of the enemy against us. What else but dust are we anyway? And what is he but one of the heavenly spirits and something greater, the highest? What then would we dare by our own strength, when we fight against the chief of the angels, being no more than dust? But the Creator of the heavenly spirits has assumed a body of earth, and in this way humble dust already rightly overcomes the proud angel.

We receive strength by clinging to true fortitude, that strength that the spirit lost, being put to flight by following himself. And it was fitting that he should be conquered by dust who abandoned the Creator and thought himself to be strong, and that being overcome he should discover that his pride lost the battle. He is extremely fierce in his hot breath, so that when the lowest things torture him, the human being ascends on high, and that flesh is taken up and remains in the heavenly places from which such a great spirit as he lies cast down without end. But the order of merit has changed places with that of mind. So, so indeed has pride deserved to be cast down, and so has humility deserved to be exalted, inasmuch as a heavenly spirit by self-exaltation endures hell, and humble earth reigns up in heaven without end.

BOOK 33

I. 1. Every proud person is as much a family slave of the ancient enemy who is portrayed by the Lord's voice with the name of Behemoth as he is puffed up by his prosperity in this life. For the proud, you see, elation grows along with honor, and with elation of course grows anxiety; their soul keeps getting pulled here and there, because desire grows along with possessions. Innumerable thoughts keep proliferating just like the grass of the field; they feed on these thoughts as if they were their desired fodder, nourishing also the hunger of Behemoth himself. So the Lord now says fittingly,

2. *The mountains bear plants for him.** In Holy Scripture when the word *mountain* in the singular number is used, sometimes the incarnate Lord is meant, sometimes Holy Church, sometimes God's covenant, sometimes the apostate angel, sometimes one of the heretics. However, when the plural *mountains* is used, sometimes it is the loftiness of the apostles and prophets or sometimes the pride of worldly powers that is meant. A mountain signifies the Lord when it is written: *It will happen in the last days that the mountain of the house of the Lord will be lifted up above the tops of the mountains.** The incarnate Lord is certainly a mountain above the tops of the mountains, and it transcends even the loftiness of the prophets. Again Holy Church is signified by a mountain when it is said, *Those who trust in the Lord are like Mount Zion.** *Zion* means lookout, and so the church is prefigured as a lookout who contemplates God. Again, the covenant of God is expressed by the mountain, as Habakkuk has said: *God will come from*

*Job 40:15

*Isa 2:2

*Ps 124:1

Lebanon, and the Holy One will come from the shadowy dense mountain.* He who promised his coming through the pages of the Old Testament came as it were to that place where as if by a promise he bound himself. And that very Old Testament, be it noted, is rightly called a shadowy dense mountain, because it is darkened by the dense obscurity of allegories.

A mountain again signifies the apostate angel, as the preachers are told about the ancient enemy under the image of the king of Babylon: *Raise a signal upon the dark mountain.** Yes, the holy preachers raise a signal upon the dark mountain when they exalt the power of the cross against Satan's pride, when he often hides under a cloud of pretense. Again the mountain expresses any heretic, as the psalmist says with the voice of the church, *I place my trust in the Lord. How can you say to my soul, "Fly like a bird to its mountain?"** When the faithful soul is told by a heretical preacher to abandon unity by confiding in an inflated teaching, he is persuaded to abandon the Lord and as it were to fly away to a mountain. Again the mountains signify the loftiness of the apostles and prophets, as it is written: *Your justice is like God's mountains.** And Paul's voice seconds it: *Let us become God's justice in him.** Or again as the psalmist, using the voice of the hopeful church, says, *I have lifted up my eyes to the mountains; from where will my help come?**

Again the mountains express the pride of worldly powers, about which the psalmist says, *The mountains will run like wax away from the face of the Lord.** Many, you see, who were at first inflated with high-flown rigidity, were afflicted with great fear when God appeared in the flesh, and they became like liquid through repentance. Or as the same prophet again says, *Mountains were raised, and fields descended.** The persecutors of

*Hab 3:3

*Isa 13:2

*Ps 10:2

*Ps 35:7
*2 Cor 5:21

*Ps 120:1

*Ps 96:5

*Ps 103:8

the Lord often come against him with pride, but they return from him humbled. So the mountains are raised through inflated pride, but the fields descend, obviously made flat through the knowledge of guilt.

3. Nevertheless some people remain suspended in the heights of their pride and disdain to bow humbly for the divine services, because they do not cease thinking of and perpetrating evil according to the wishes of the ancient enemy; so it is rightly said of Behemoth in this passage, *The mountains bear plants for him.* The worldly proud indeed bear plants for our Behemoth, because they feed him with the evil that they do. They bear plants for our Behemoth, because they offer him their own flowing slippery pleasures. *People will be lovers of themselves,* says the apostle.* He completes their description with the following words: *Lovers of their own pleasures and not of God.** What else is grass on the mountains, then, but fluid pleasures that are born in the hearts of the proud? Unless they had contempt for God in their pride, they would never perpetrate such slippery actions in their playfulness. Such indeed is the grass our Behemoth feeds on; he is hungry for the penalty of eternal death that is theirs, and he is satisfied with their depraved way of life.

*2 Tim 3:2

*2 Tim 3:4

The proud ones of this world, you see, even if they are at times impeded by the orderly course of the heavenly plan and cease from the perpetration of depraved actions, they still multiply depraved thoughts. Now they show themselves to have more power over other possessions and honors; now they use that same power to injure somebody else; now they let their own shifty actions guide them, and they lose consistency through smooth actions and pleasures. These people who, having received possessions from God, nevertheless think always of bad actions and not upright actions: what else do they do but fight against the Lord with his own gifts? So here is Behemoth: he always recognizes his own desires in the hearts of the proud; it is as if on the mountains he found grass, with which he keeps the belly of his malice filled. So the Lord rightly adds,

II. 4. *All the beasts of the field play there.** What else is meant by the beasts but the unclean spirits, and what by the field but the present world? That is why it is said about the prince of the evil spirits against Ephraim, *A beast of the field will cut them open.** Or as Isaiah says, *No evil beast will pass through her gates.** But we are taking the word *field* to mean the world, as the Lord also says: *The field is the world.** The beasts of the field then play in the grass on the mountain, because the demons are cast down in this world by their betters, and they are delighted with the evil deeds of the proud. The beasts play in the grass when the reprobate spirits lure human hearts to think bad thoughts. Is it not play for unclean spirits to deceive human hearts that were made in the image of God? Now they make false promises, now they mock them with false terrors, now they pretend to them that transitory joys will remain, now they make eternal penalties seem light as though they were transitory. He had without any doubt feared the illusion of these beasts who said, *My God, I trust in you, let me not be ashamed; let not my enemies mock me.**

Then, since the hearts of the proud stretch out toward every vice, so that they might be prepared by evil thoughts for any intruding evil spirit, it is correctly said of the mountain grass, *All the beasts of the field play there*. Because proud people let no evil pass by in their thoughts, there is no beast of the field that does not eat its fill of this mountain grass. Even if they sometimes run away from lust of the flesh, they commit the crime of internal lust by boasting of their own chastity. Even

*Job 40:15

*Hos 13:8
*Isa 35:9

*Matt 13:38

*Ps 24:2-3

if they grasp nothing external avariciously, they are absolutely not free of the enticement of avarice, because even if they solicit no goods, they try to steal praise for their forbearance by favoring people. The mountains therefore bear grass for our Behemoth, and all the beasts of the field play there, because in the hearts of the proud any evil spirit eats as much of it as every vice is born from pride. So now that we have heard what our Behemoth eats, we must now hear where he rests in the meantime through his depraved desire. The next verse:

III. 5. *He sleeps in the shade, hidden among the reeds in the marshes.** Shade in Holy Scripture sometimes means the Lord's incarnation, sometimes a cooling off of the mind after the agitation of thoughts of the flesh, so that the use of the word *shade* tends to mean this very cooling of the heart through heavenly protection. On the other hand, *shade* sometimes means the distancing of charity and the lethargy of a cold mind. That the Lord's incarnation, saving historical truth, is signified by the use of the word *overshadowing*, the angel's words testify when he told Mary, *The power of the Most High will overshadow you.** Since the word *shadow* expresses nothing but the combination of body and light, the power of the Most High overshadowed her in that her bodily womb received the incorporeal light. It was obviously from that overshadowing that her mind received all its coolness. Again, the word *shadow* expresses the cooling of the heart from heavenly protection, as the psalmist also says: *In the shelter of your wings protect me.** The waiting bride also expresses herself thus in the Song of Songs and foretells the coming of the Bridegroom: *I sat down beneath the shadow of the One I desired.** It is as if she said, "I rested from the heat of the desires of the flesh underneath the protection of his coming."

*Job 40:16

*Luke 1:35

*Ps 16:8

*Song 2:3

On the other hand, *shadow* expresses the distancing of charity and the lethargy of a cold mind, as it is written of the sinful human being that he followed a shadow.* He ran away from the heat of charity; yes, the human being abandoned the sun of truth and hid himself under the shadow of internal frigidity. So the voice of the self-same Truth speaks: *Wickedness will spread far and wide, and the love of many will grow cold.** That is why the first man was found hidden among the trees of Paradise after his sin during the hour after midday.* Since he had lost the midday heat of charity, he already languished under the shadow of sin as if underneath the cold air.

*Sir 34:2

*Matt 24:12

*Gen 3:8

6. Our Behemoth then finds a certain relaxation in sinners whom he made cold by removing them from the heat of the true sun, so he is said to rest underneath their shade. Sometimes, however, the shadow expresses with the addition of death the death of either the flesh or of any reprobate sinner who imitates the darkness of the ancient enemy by zeal for his depraved works. So the psalmist speaks with the voice of martyrs: *You have thrown us down in the place of torment and covered us with the shadow of death.** The shadow of death oppresses those chosen by God when the death of the flesh, which is the image of eternal death, detaches them from this life, because just as the former separates the soul from God, so the latter separates the body from the soul. Or at least the shadow of death oppresses them, because it is written about the ancient enemy, *His name is death.** All the reprobate sinners then are the shadow of death, because they imitate the depravity of his pride. They project his image like a shadow, because they drag the likeness of his malice along with them. They shut out God's chosen ones when they temporarily grow strong in violent persecution.

*Ps 43:20

*Rev 6:8

In this passage, however, the shadow of depravity is taken to mean that numbness in which Behemoth sleeps, because while he anxiously stays awake against hearts that are on fire with charity, he safely lies down in cold hearts. He cannot sleep in the hearts of saints, you see, because even if he briefly stations himself there at times, the very heat of heavenly desires makes him weary, and as often as he is goaded to leave, so much the more do the saints sigh with deep love for eternity. As many words disturb him as holy thoughts cry out from their hearts to heaven. So it happens that he is frightened by the weapons of good works, and he runs away in alarm from the sharp arrowheads of sighs to return to the cold hearts of reprobate sinners to seek a shade of malice that he can claim undisturbed. And he is shown to have found it when it is quickly added, *hidden among the reeds.*

7. In Holy Scripture the word *reed* or *cane* can mean either an abiding word, or a teacher's experience, or quickness of mind, or the brightness of earthly glory. The reed signifies the eternity of the Word, as when the Father's voice speaks through the psalmist: *My tongue is the reed of a swiftly writing scribe.** Since the words we speak are passing, but those we write remain, the Father's tongue is called a scribe's reed, because his Word is co-eternal, generated by him, and non-passing. Again the reed expresses written teaching, since the prophet promises Holy Church, *In the lairs where dragons formerly lived will arise fresh reeds and rushes.** In that sentence is actually contained what I wrote long ago in this very book, namely that the reed expresses the teaching of scribes and the rush means the freshness of what is heard. Again the cane, or surely the reed, signifies the swiftness of the mind, as when the Lord told the crowds of Jews in praise of John, *What did you go out to the desert to see? A reed shaken by the wind?** Obviously you should think, "No." John was certainly no

*Ps 44:2

*Isa 35:7

*Matt 11:7

reed shaken by the wind. No breath of tongues moved his mind controlled by the Holy Spirit in any of its parts.

Again the reed or rush expresses the brightness of earthly glory, as when Wisdom says of the righteous people, *The just will shine and be like sparks flashing among the reeds** A bed of reeds in fact is what the worldly life is called, and, yes, worldly people are like reeds: they progress through temporary external glory to the heights, as it were, but interiorly they are empty and lack the solidity of truth. That is why the kingdom of Judea is compared to a reed, as the prophet tells of the Lord when he appears in the reality of flesh, *A bent reed he will not break, and smoking flax he will not quench.** What else would he proclaim with the word *reed* but the earthly kingdom of the Jewish people, which was indeed thriving externally but hollow internally. And since the same people already lacked a royal family, and a foreign king ruled the kingdom, he was right to call that kingdom a bent reed, but what does the flax signify if not the priesthood, whose members certainly wore linen vestments? And the priesthood certainly lost the warmth of charity at the Lord's coming and consequently did not burn, since the fire of faith was gone, but only smoked. However, the incarnate Lord did not break the bent reed, nor did he extinguish the smoking flax; no, he did not knock over by his judicial power the Jewish kingdom that was already tottering or stamp out the priesthood that had no fire of faith, but he put up with them in his longanimity and patience.

*Wis 3:7

*Isa 42:3

8. So in this passage what else does the word *reed* signify but the minds of worldly people that are dedicated to passing glory? They are as empty inside themselves as they display themselves externally lofty and elegant; since they superficially chase after external glory, they have no internal solidity or weight. They are just like reeds, silly inside and empty, but externally they are handsome of form and good-looking; the more eagerly they seek external honors, the more constantly their hearts are driven by anxious thoughts. So Behemoth here is correctly declared to sleep hidden among the reeds, since he quietly holds on to the hearts of those whose appetites he instigates to desire passing glory and high positions; he quietly sleeps there in such a way as to prevent those he possesses from being quiet. They keep trying to surpass others with their highly honored positions, you see, and, like reeds, they prevail over the righteous people formally, as if over the bark of trees, through their purely external elegance. In this way they remain empty internally, and they offer Behemoth an interior place where he can rest.

That is why Truth says in the Gospel that a spirit is cast out and finds no rest in dry and waterless places; then when it enters the house it had left, it finds it empty and swept clean. So it enters with many others.* Since, you see, ground that is rained on is slippery, the hearts of righteous people are dry and waterless places that are dried out by rigorous training and free of the water of the concupiscence of the flesh. So here as well it is necessary to point out wherever Behemoth is found sleeping, so it is quickly added, *in the marshes.**

*Matt 12:43-45

*Job 40:16

9. The minds of worldly people, you see, are marshes, because the moisture from the concupiscence of the flesh that fills them makes them wet. In them our Behemoth has left the footprints of his iniquity as deep as his passing through those same minds has gone, as it were into muddy ground. Acts of pleasure are of course muddy places. The foot does not slip over dry ground, but when it is put down in wet places it hardly holds its ground. Those then who make their journey of the present life over places that are wet cannot stand straight as regards justice. Behemoth then sleeps in these wet places, because he finds rest in the slippery works of reprobate sinners.

Some people however imagine that the genitals are watery places. Well, if that is the case, what else do the watery places signify in fact but lust? So also the reed signifies the boasting of pride, and the watery places mean lust of the flesh. These then are the two vices that inhumanly dominate the human being: one obviously spiritual, the other carnal. Pride of course raises the spirit, and lust corrupts the flesh. The ancient enemy then, either through pride above all or through lust, presses the human race hard, and he sleeps hidden among the reeds in the marshes, and he holds the condemned human being underneath the sway of his dominion; yes, he holds humankind either through pride of the spirit or through corruption of the flesh. Some people however he possesses by both means, because once the spirit of pride lifts them up, not even the fear of corruption turns them aside from their swelling loftiness.

But do the teachers of virtue not keep watch against them daily and unceasingly inside Holy Church? Do they ever stop speaking out against base pleasures or encouraging the thought of the joys of the heavenly homeland? But the more desperately depraved minds cling to the lowest pleasures, the more obstinately they refuse to hear about the highest. Nor is it enough for them that they perish themselves, but they do what is worse: when they notice anybody arguing for correction, they resist the loud reproaches of the righteous people, lest at least some of the depraved receive correction. So he rightly continues:

*Job 40:17

IV. 10. *Shadows protect his shadow.** The shadows of the devil are of course all the wicked people. They are his devoted servants, who imitate his iniquity. They trail his body, showing the form of his image. Reprobate sinners are his plural shadows, so on the other hand every single sinner is his single shadow. Since evil people contradict the teaching of righteous people, and since the former do not let any wicked person be corrected by the latter, the shadows of our Behemoth protect his shadow, because inasmuch as any sinners do not know themselves well, they are quick to defend another sinner. His shadows protect his shadow, so the actions of the most wicked are protected by those who are more wicked: perverse patronage! They do this assuredly lest the guilt with which they are themselves bound should be corrected in others and that correction should eventually involve them.

So they cover up for themselves while they protect others, since when they consider that others being freely corrected will be confounded, they foresee that their own life will be impeded. So it happens that the full extent of crime is increased when it is defended, and the wickedness of each single person becomes easier to perpetrate the more difficult it is to punish it. The crimes of sinners, then, see greater increase the longer they go unpunished because of being defended by those in power. But such things seem normal, whether they happen outside the church or even inside Holy Church, the more openly God's enemies show themselves, and the more patronage is proffered to vices. Against him indeed they fight a defensive war, and they multiply in their defense all the things that displease him.

The Lord complains against these actions through the prophet under the image of Babylon and says, *Thorns and thistles will sprout in their houses and nettles in their strongholds.** What do we take the thorns to mean if not itching thoughts, and what else are the thistles but pricking vices? In the Babylonian houses, therefore, thorns

*Isa 34:13

and thistles sprout, because in the confused reprobate mind thoughts and desires spring up and are aggravated, and sinful acts sting, but those who do them also have their defenders, who are worse still. That is why he also added the sequel: *nettles in their strongholds*. Nettles have so many thorns growing thickly on them that they can hardly be touched. Thorns and thistles then sprout up inside, but outside, the nettles protect the stronghold all around, obviously because the wicked youngsters do whatever evil they want, but the evil elders protect them. That is why it is rightly said here in Job, *Shadows protect his shadow.** Since the worse evildoer is the protector, it is as though a shadow darkened a shadow, lest it be illuminated by the light of truth. The next verse:

*Job 40:17

V. 11. *The willows of the brook will surround him.** Although willow trees have no fruit, yet they do have such fresh greenery that even when cut down to the roots they can hardly be dried out and laid down. So in Holy Scripture the word *willow* is sometimes used to denote the freshness of good people and sometimes the sterility of reprobate sinners. If they did not express the lives of the chosen ones, you see, through their constant freshness, the prophet would never have said about the children of Holy Church, *They will sprout among the green plants like willow trees alongside the flowing waters.** Yes, the children of Holy Church sprout like willows among the green plants, and while they stand among the withering lives of carnal-minded people their vast numbers and abiding freshness of mind last long. And they are rightly held to sprout next to flowing waters, because every one of them receives the ability to bear abundant fruit from the teaching of Holy Scripture, which moves quickly through time.

*Job 40:17

*Isa 44:4

On the other hand, unless the lives of sinners were signified by the unfruitfulness of the willow, the psalmist would never have spoken against Babylon in the voice of the preachers and said, *On the willows there we hung up our instruments.** The willow trees inside Babylon are described, because they are all unfruitful and strangers to the love of the heavenly homeland, whose roots are found in the confusion of this world together with all the inner life of the heart. That is why the holy preachers do not play their musical instruments among the willows, but instead hang them up, because when they see the people with unfruitful and reprobate minds, they do not hold forth with their eloquent preaching, but rather mourn and are silent.

*Ps 136:2

But what else does the brook signify but the course of this mortal life? The prophet also says of it, *He drinks from the stream on the wayside, so he will lift up his head.** Obviously this means that our Redeemer made contact with the penalty of mortal life in a certain crossing over, and that is why he did not remain attached any longer to that death to which he freely submitted. So on the third day he rose and lifted up that head that he had laid down by dying. So what is it that is said here of our Behemoth, *The willows of the brook will surround him,** if not that the lovers of mortal life, as becomes those who are strangers to the fruits of good actions, hold on to him* more tightly the more the delight of passing pleasures fills them? As long, you see, as the love of life in the flesh inebriates their thoughts, it is as though the brook still washes their roots. It is clear that like willows they bear no fruit, so their leaves are green and fresh; because they are not weighty in speaking, they sometimes spout words of integrity, but they show no weight from good works. So it is rightly said, *The willows of the brook will surround him*, because any unfruitful people who are slaves to the love of worldly life are close followers of the ancient enemy by their

*Ps 109:7

*Job 40:17

*Behemoth

perverse behavior. But now that we have heard what is paid him by his clients, let us now listen as well to what he does with them. The next verse:

VI. 12. *He will swallow the stream and will not wonder; he has confidence that the Jordan will flow into his mouth.** What else is signified in this passage by the word *stream* but the flow of the human race that surges as it were from its birth, as if its origin were a fountain, but that in its passage flows on to the lowest level by dying? And who are they that are signified by the name *Jordan* if not those who have already received the sacrament of baptism? Because, you see, our Redeemer deigned to be baptized in that river, it follows that many others would be baptized in his name. Yes, it so happens that this very sacrament of baptism began with him. Our Behemoth was born at the beginning of the world, with only a few chosen ones escaping him, and he swallowed the human race that was flowing down to the depths as if it were some kind of a river, even until the time of redemption. Therefore it is rightly said here, *He will swallow the stream and will not wonder.**

But since after the coming of the Redeemer he also seized some of the faithful who neglected to live uprightly, it is rightly added, *He has confidence that the Jordan will flow into his mouth.** It is as if he said outright, "Before the redemption of the world he did not wonder that he swallowed the world, but he did something worse when even after the coming of the Redeemer he trusted his ability to swallow some of those who were sealed with the sacrament of baptism." He does in fact devour some of those who are placed under the name of Christianity, because he trips them up with an erroneous faith. Others he never turns aside from the correct faith, but he bends them for the sake of some depraved purpose. Others he does not bend so much as he wants

*Job 40:18

*Job 40:18

*Job 40:18

to the performance of impurity, but he twists their eager intention inside their consciousness, so that when their minds deviate from charity, not all their external works are right. They hold the faith but do not stick to the life of faith, because either they openly do what is wrong, or their actions are depraved because they do them with a misguided heart, even if they seem to be holy.

Because some people are faithful by confession but not by their way of life, here are the words spoken by Truth himself: *Not everyone who says to me, "Lord, Lord," will enter the kingdom of heaven.** He also says, *Why do you call me, "Lord, Lord," but do not do what I say?** That is why Paul says, *They confess that they know God, but they deny him by their actions.** That is why John says, *He who says he knows God but does not keep his commandments is a liar.** That is why the Lord complains about his very first people and says, *This people honors me with their lips, but their hearts are far from me.** So the psalmist also said, *They loved him with their mouths, but their tongues lied to him.**

*Matt 7:21
*Luke 6:46
*Titus 1:16
*1 John 2:4
*Isa 29:13
*Ps 77:36

It is hardly to be wondered at if our Behemoth, before the cleansing water, before the heavenly mysteries, before the bodily presence of the Redeemer, swallowed the river of the human race with the gaping mouth of deep persuasion, but this is a real marvel, this is really terrible: that he seized many with open mouth, prevailed over them, and dragged them to the depths of hell even after the Redeemer was known, even after the heavenly mysteries, and even after the cleansing water. Let it be said then, let it be said with the terrible voice of Truth, *He will swallow the stream and will not wonder; he has confidence that the Jordan will flow into his mouth.**

*Job 40:18

The Devil did not think it any great accomplishment, you see, that he took in the ones without faith, but with all his exertion he occupies himself with the death of those against whom he pines away on account of their regeneration. So let no one be so confident in his own ability as to have sufficient faith without works, since we know what is written: *Faith without works is useless.** Let no one suppose that he has completely escaped Behemoth's bite by only confessing his faith, because he has already swallowed the river, to be sure, but he is still thirsty for the Jordan, and as often as he has the Jordan in his mouth, so often does every Christian backslide into wickedness. We flee from his mouth indeed while faith holds us up, but we must take care with all zeal lest we hesitate on this slippery road. If we neglect caution in our walking, it is in vain that we keep on the right road by believing, because the road of faith indeed leads to the heavenly homeland, but it never leads anyone there who stumbles.

*Jas 2:20

13. We have in this matter something that we should evaluate in more detail. Those people, you see, about whom we have spoken and said to be represented by the Jordan, can be signified by the river. Those who have already known the faith in truth but neglect to live by faith can rightly be called a river, obviously because they flow down. The Hebrew word *Jordan* in fact speaks of their descent. There are those, you see, who desire the ways of truth and deny themselves; they descend from pride in their old lives, and when they desire eternity they make themselves complete strangers to this world. Not only do they not desire what is not theirs, but they even abandon what is theirs; not only do they not seek worldly honors, but even when such honors are offered them, they disdain them.

That is why the voice of Truth says, *If anyone wants to come after me, let him deny himself.** Those who deny themselves trample upon the wind of pride and present themselves to God's eyes as strangers to pride. That is

*Luke 9:23

why the psalmist says, *I will remember you from the land of the Jordan and of Hermon.** Jordan, as I have said, means descent, whereas Hermon means a curse or alienation. So the one who is reminded of the Jordan and of Hermon is reminded of God, because such a person denies himself and becomes a stranger to self; consequently such a one is called back to the memory of the Creator.

*Ps 41:7

But the ancient enemy does not hold this matter to be of great importance, since he holds those people who seek the earth by right of his tyranny. We know of course that the prophet bears us witness: *His food is special.** Nor does he regard it any wonder if he swallows them whom pride lifts up, avarice wastes away, pleasure enlarges, malice squeezes, anger inflames, discord separates, envy wounds, and lust debases and kills. So he will swallow the river and not wonder, since he does not consider it strange if he devours those who are running downwards through the very ardor of their lives, but his special interest is to seize those who, having disdained worldly ambition, are already contemplating union with heaven. So, when he has swallowed the river, it is added that he *has confidence that the Jordan will flow into his mouth.** He earnestly desires to seize from ambush those who, as he knows very well, are denying themselves honors in the present life for love of the heavenly homeland.

*Hab 1:16

*Job 40:18

There are some indeed who abandon the world and leave behind the empty joys of passing honors; they earnestly desire the lowest place of humility, and they go beyond the customary routines of human interaction by living good lives; they so advance toward the pinnacle of their interest that they are already performing powerful signs; nevertheless they do not protect their flanks by circumspection, so they are struck by the spear of vainglory, and terrible is their fall from heaven. That is why the eternal Judge, who scrutinizes the secrets of the heart, points them out and foretells their fall and ruin. He says, *Many will tell me on that day, "Lord, Lord, did we not prophesy in your name? Did we not cast out demons in your name? Did we not work many miracles in your name?" And then I will assure them, "I never knew you. Get away from me, you evildoers. I do not know who you are."** That is also why he says through the prophet, *The Lord has called judgment for the fire, and it has devoured a great abyss, and it has eaten away part of the house.**

*Matt 7:22-23

*Amos 7:4

Of course judgment is called for the fire, since the sentence of justice has already been passed, and the penalty of eternal fire has been given. The fire has devoured the great abyss, because it burns the evil and incomprehensible human minds that are even now hidden from humans themselves underneath signs and wonders. Part of the house is consumed, because hell devours even those who now boast of being counted among the chosen ones, as though their actions were holy. They are here called the Jordan who will there be called part of the house. The ancient enemy accordingly has confidence that the Jordan that is part of the house will flow into his mouth. It does in fact sometimes happen that even those who are now considered chosen are tripped up by his clever traps, and he kills them. But is there anyone whose hard heart these words of the Lord would not trouble? Whose constant presence of mind would not shake to the very interior roots of his thoughts when the terrible power of our enemy against us is clearly presented? Will there be no help or encouragement? There surely will be, since he continues,

VII. 14. *In his eyes it is as though a fishhook captured him.** We must take careful notice that God mercifully chooses the words of his Holy Scripture for our sakes, sometimes frightening us with severe threats,

*Job 40:19

sometimes restoring us with gentle words of comfort; he mixes terror with comfort and comfort with terror, so that while on our behalf he tempers either approach with a wonderful craft of teaching, we should be neither desperately afraid nor carelessly secure. After he has made clear the clever traps and unbridled fury of Behemoth by means of many long sentences, he forthwith commends the coming of his only begotten Son, our Redeemer. He also suggests by what sequence our Behemoth is to be done away with, so that since he has already struck our hearts with fear by recounting his power, he might also relieve our sadness more quickly by showing us his destruction. So after he said, *He will swallow the stream and will not wonder; he has confidence that the Jordan will flow into his mouth*,* he forthwith announces the very coming of the incarnate Lord and says, *In his eyes it is as though a fishhook captured him.**

*Job 40:18

*Job 40:19

Everybody knows that a fishhook shows bait but hides the sharp point. The bait provokes so that the sharp point may pierce. Accordingly our Lord, in coming for the redemption of the human race, made himself a kind of fishhook to kill the Devil. He assumed a body as a kind of bait that our Behemoth might desire to bring about the death of our flesh. Whereas he desired the Lord's death unjustly, the Devil lost us whom he held as it were justly. The Devil was captured by the fishhook of the Lord's incarnation, because when he desired him for the bait of his body, he was pierced by the sharp point of his divinity. In the Lord unquestionably was that humanity that the Devil drew to himself as a devourer, in him the divinity that would pierce him, in him the vulnerable weakness that would provoke him, in him the hidden power that would pierce the throat of the ravening beast. By the fishhook then he was captured, because where he devoured there he was killed.

Our Behemoth of course had known that the Son of God was incarnate, but he knew nothing of the plan of our redemption. He knew that the Son of God became incarnate for our redemption, but he surely did not know that he who was our Redeemer was going to pierce him through by dying. So it is well said, *In his eyes it is as though a fishhook captured him.** We are said to have something before our eyes when we see it placed before us. The ancient enemy of the human race accordingly saw its Redeemer placed before him whom he knowingly confessed and in confessing feared, and said, *What have you to do with us, Son of God? Have you come to torment us before the appointed time?** In his eyes then it is as though a fishhook captured him, because he both knew it and bit; he knew beforehand the one he should fear, and yet he did not fear him afterwards, since he was in fact his own food, and he hungered for the death of flesh.

*Job 40:19

*Matt 8:29

Accordingly we have now heard about our Head and what he did of himself; now let us hear what he does through his members. The next verse:

*Job 40:19

VIII. 15. *With a stake he will pierce his nose.** Just what do we take the stake—that is, a wooden peg whose end is carved to a sharp point in order to fix it into something—to mean if not the sharpened counsels of the saints? They pierce the nose of our Behemoth when they attentively watch out for his most cunning traps, and by outsmarting him they pin him down. Through the nose of course we detect odors, and once we happen to smell its fragrance, even if its source is very far away, we recognize it. By his nose, consequently, Behemoth's shrewd traps are signified, by which he perceptively attempts to recognize the hidden goodness of our hearts and with the most wicked persuasion to cause it to disintegrate. So the Lord pierces his nose with the stake, because he disarms his cunning traps and pierces them with the ready sensitivity of the saints. He frequently flies about over the roads good people take, setting traps so skillfully that through what he knows to be their good works he might find an opening for malice. When he sees that one person is given something, he incites another person to flaming discord; he sees the misery of the former, and he persuades the latter to get angry, so that when some good is done he suggests that it is not shared, and in this way he severs the concord experienced by souls and the goodness of communal favor. Since he cannot break the minds of righteous people by persuading them to do evil, he fusses about trying to sow evil seeds among them by their own good actions. But the saints overcome these traps of his as soon as they discover his wiles.

We can the more fruitfully explain all this if we call to witness one of the many defenders of truth, Paul, under whose ministry one of the Corinthians had committed the crime of incest.* The famous teacher delivered him over to Satan for the destruction of the flesh and for the satisfaction of repentance, and he reserved his spirit for salvation on the day of the Lord. By the sublime ability of a teacher that soul was turned over to him for the consummation of the penalty by whose influence he fell into sin, so that he who had been the instigator in the vice of wickedness should himself become the whip of discipline. However, once this good deed of repentance had been carried out, since he knew that the Corinthians were already moved with pity for him, he said, *Whatever you have forgiven anyone, I too have forgiven; if I have forgiven anything it is for your sakes in the presence of Christ.**

Then, thinking of the grace of communion, he said, *Whatever you have forgiven anyone, I too have forgiven.* It is as if he said, "I do not dissent from what

*1 Cor 5:5

*2 Cor 2:10

is good for you. Whatever you have done yourselves is my choice." So he quickly added, *If I have forgiven anything it is for your sakes*. It is as if he said, "I have added my agreement to what you have done, whatever act of mercy I have performed for your sakes. Your convenience therefore is my good, and my convenience is your good." Paul, who wrote about this union of hearts, immediately added an explanation to tell the Corinthians what it meant: *the person of Christ*.

It is as if we were to presume to say, "Why do you join the disciples so cautiously? Why do you either conform yourself to their actions or them to yours with such careful preparation?" He immediately adds, *So that we may not be outwitted by Satan*.* Then he adds his cunning traps and suggests how delicate was the perception with which he took hold of them, saying, *We are not ignorant of his devices*.* It is as if he might say in other words, "We are the Lord's appointed stakes, and we go around inspecting carefully and piercing the nose of our Behemoth, lest he should divert to some malicious purpose what our mind has begun to do well."

16. The sharp stake can signify the words of revealed wisdom through the flesh, so that since the nose draws in odors, Behemoth's nose symbolizes the scouting activity of the ancient enemy. When he was in doubt as to God's incarnation, he wanted to find out about it by pleading for miracles in his temptation, and he said, *If you are God's son, command these stones to be turned into bread.** Since accordingly he desired to know the smell of his divinity by means of obvious signs, it is as though he inhaled breath through his nostrils. But when Satan received the immediate response—*Not on bread alone does man live*,* and *You shall not tempt the Lord your God**—Truth struck with the sharp points of his sentences at the ancient enemy's hunting activity, and it

*2 Cor 2:11

*2 Cor 2:11

*Matt 4:3

*Deut 8:3; Matt 4:4
*Matt 4:7

was as though he pierced his nose with a stake. But our Behemoth stretches out his dishonest arguments, and still another one of his names is mentioned. He goes on:

IX. 17. *Can you capture Leviathan with a fishhook?** *Job 40:20
Leviathan is certainly said to mean "an addition to them." To whom, pray, if not to humanity? It was he in fact who once introduced the sin of prevarication and continues to spread it every day with his most base suggestions even to the point of eternal death. For them indeed he multiplies guilt with the interest of sin, and he doubtlessly accumulates penalties unceasingly. Leviathan can also be called *derision*. He first introduced himself by cunning persuasion as the one who would add divinity to human nature, but he robbed humans of immortality. He could therefore be called an addition to mankind by derision, since he promised to add to us what we did not have, and what we did have he deceptively removed.

But Leviathan was captured with a fishhook, because when through his henchmen he bit into the food of the Redeemer's body, the sharp point of divinity went through him. It was as though a fishhook took hold of the jaws that swallowed. In the Redeemer, in fact, the food of flesh was plain to be seen, and that is what the devourer wanted; the divinity was hidden during the passion, and that is what would kill Leviathan. In this deep ocean, in this immensity of humanity, he was avidly desiring the death of all humans and devouring the life of almost all beings; yes, this sea monster was swimming about here and there with open mouth, but the fishhook was suspended by a wonderful plan in the darkness of this deep ocean for the death of this sea monster.

The line of this fishhook indeed is that one spoken of in the Gospel, namely the line of descent of the ancient patriarchs. The Gospel states, *Abraham was the father of Isaac; Isaac was the father of Jacob.** So when *Matt 1:2

Abraham's other descendants are listed all the way up to the Virgin Mary and Joseph's name is added, it is as though a line were spun out, at the end of which the incarnate Lord, or this fishhook, is tied, which in this ocean of the human race this sea monster desired with open mouth, but that is why he would no longer be able to hurt by his bite through the ferocity of his partisans. So lest this sea monster should devour anyone he wanted to from ambush any more, or bring about human deaths, our fishhook holds back his ravening jaws and bites the one biting him. So God, indicating the incarnation of his only begotten Son to his faithful servant, says, *Can you capture Leviathan with a fishhook?** You should hear him answer, "I can. In fact I am sending my only begotten Son to become incarnate and kill that robber. When he sees the mortal flesh but not the power of immortality, it will be as though some fishhook killed the devourer precisely there where the piercing dart of power hides." The next verse:

*Job 40:20

X. 18. *Will you impede his tongue with a line?** You should hear, "As I do?" Holy Scripture, you see, sometimes uses a line to distinguish units of measurement, sometimes sin, and sometimes faith. To signify the shares of inherited land it is written, *The lines have fallen for me in pleasant places; yes, my inheritance is pleasant for me.** The lines indeed fall in pleasant places when, through a lowly way of life, shares in a better homeland receive us. On the other hand, sin is sometimes signified by a line, as when the prophet says, *Woe to you who drag wickedness along with lines of vanity.** Yes, wickedness is drawn along with lines of vanity when it continues to be carried through increasing sin. That is why the psalmist says, *The lines of sin have tied me up.** Just like a line that gets longer and is wound around, sin is not unreasonably compared to a

*Job 40:20

*Ps 15:6

*Isa 5:18

*Ps 118:61

line, since it is often found in a twisted heart, defended, and multiplied.

Again, faith is like a line, as Solomon testifies: *A threefold line is hard to break.** Obviously faith is woven from knowledge of the Trinity spoken by a preacher, and it remains strong among the chosen ones, but in the hearts of reprobate sinners alone it is dispersed. Consequently there is no reason that the word *line* in this passage could not be understood as either "sin" or "faith." Our incarnate Lord, you see, stopped Leviathan's tongue with a line, because appearing in the likeness of sinful flesh, the Lord condemned all the errors that Leviathan preached. That is why Paul testifies with the words, *For sin he condemned sin.** With a line the Lord impeded Leviathan's tongue when, through the likeness of sinful flesh, he destroyed all the arguments of his deception in the hearts of his chosen ones. See then how at the appearance of the Lord in flesh Leviathan's tongue was impeded, because when the Lord's truth was known, those false teachings were silenced.

*Eccl 4:12

*Rom 8:3

19. Where now is the error of the Academicians, who pretend to assert with certitude that nothing is sure, who with a brazen show demand faith from their listeners in their own assertions when they claim that nothing is true? Where is the superstition of the Astrologers, who, while they are looking up at the course of the constellations, make the lives of men and women depend on the motions of the stars, whose teaching the birth of twins often clearly shatters, when in one solitary moment of an hour these twins come forth and yet the kind of life they lead from that moment is not the same? Where are so many proclamations of falsehood that I shrink from recounting, lest I turn aside too long from my orderly exposition? But all these erroneous teachings have already been silenced, because the Lord's incarnation has tied up Leviathan's tongue. The prophet says the same thing very well: *The Lord will make desolate the tongue of the sea of Egypt.** The knowledge of worldly teaching is indeed the tongue of the sea that is rightly called the sea of Egypt, because it is darkened by the shadows of sin. The Lord has accordingly desolated the tongue of the sea of Egypt, because he has destroyed the false wisdom of this world by revealing himself in the flesh. And so Leviathan's tongue has been tied up with a line, because the old sinful proclamation has been restrained through the likeness of sinful flesh.

*Isa 11:15

20. If however faith is sealed with a line, the very same understanding nods to us again, because when faith in the Trinity is known in the world through the holy preachers, the world's teaching stops rising up against the minds of the chosen ones. That is why the prophet rightly tells the Lord, *You cause fountains and rivers to burst out; you have dried up the rivers of Ethan.** Ethan means the strong one, and who is the strong one but the one Truth mentions in the Gospel? *No one can enter the strong one's house or take away his goods without first binding the strong one.** The Lord accordingly causes the fountains and rivers to burst out when he opens up the flow of truth in his apostles' hearts, about which another prophet also speaks: *You will joyfully draw water from the Savior's fountain.** Being thirsty, we go to receive their teaching, and we take it away in the little bottles of our hearts full of truth. But Ethan's rivers dried up when these fountains started bubbling up, because by shining the ray of his truth the Lord dried up the teaching of the strong evil spirit. So Leviathan's tongue is tied up with a line, because faith in the Trinity spreads and the proclamation of error is silenced. But because he can no longer flaunt himself openly, he goes around here and there biting from am-

*Ps 73:15

*Mark 3:27

*Isa 12:3

bush. But with wonderful mercy the Lord watches out for him for our sakes and fights against him and his attempted deceptions. The next verse:

XI. 21. *Will you put a ring in his nose?** Just as the nose signifies ambush, so the ring signifies the almighty power of God. When that almighty power does not allow us to be caught by temptation, by a wonderful plan it surrounds and holds the ancient enemy's ambushes. A ring is accordingly put in his nose when, after the power of divine protection has surrounded his cunning, he is held back to keep him from prevailing against the weakness of human nature with all the fatal arguments he secretly instigates. The word *ring* can also mean the assistance of hidden judgment that is put in the nose of our Behemoth when his cunning cruelty is restrained. That is why the prophet, to keep Babylon from hurting the Israelites, tells its king, *I will put a ring in your nose.** It is as if he said outright, "In your thoughts you breathe ambush, but you bear the ring of my almighty power in your nose, and it will not let you fulfill your desires, so that the more ardently you pant for the death of good people, the emptier you return without taking their lives."

But the ring in this passage is called a sickle by Holy Scripture in John's Apocalypse. He says, *I looked and there was a white cloud, and on the cloud was sitting one like a son of man; he had on his head a golden crown, and in his hand there was a sharp sickle.** The power of God's judgment, you see, reaches everywhere, and that is why it is called a ring; since all that falls within its scope is connected, it is signified by the word *sickle*. Whatever is cut by the sickle, you see, in whatever direction it falls, is within a circle. And because the power of God's Judgment is by no means avoided, we are certainly within its scope wherever we might try to

*Job 40:21

*Isa 37:29

*Rev 14:14

flee, so that when the Judge is represented as coming, he is rightly said to hold a sickle, because he turns with power in every direction and surrounds everything with a cutting motion.

The prophet saw himself in the path of the sickle of Judgment when he said, *If I go up to heaven you are there, and if I go down to hell you are present. If I spread my wings to the light and dwell on the other side of the sea, even there your hand would lead me, and your right hand would hold me fast.** He saw himself inside a kind of sickle, and he realized that there was no way of escape open to him on any side, so he said, *Neither on the east nor on the west, nor even on the deserted mountains** (you should hear whispered, "Is there a way of escape"), but he quickly adds an all-embracing comprehension of divine power: *Because God is the Judge.** It is as if he said, "There is no way of escape on any side, because he who is everywhere is the Judge. Just as divine Judgment is signified by the sickle, because it forms a wall on every side, so also it is signified by the circle, because it hems us in on every side." So the Lord puts a ring in Leviathan's nose, because Leviathan is constricted by the power of God's Judgment within certain bounds, so that he cannot prevail as much as he wants with his ambushes. So let him say, *Will you put a ring in his nose?* You should hear, "As I do? In fact I confine his cunning ambushes with my almighty Judgment, so that he does not tempt as much as he wants, nor does he seize as much as he tempts." The next verse:

XII. 22. *Will you pierce his jaw with a hook?** The hook is not discordant with the concept of a circle, since it also constrains the flesh it reaches by enclosing it. But since a hook is extended horizontally, it signifies the more expansive protection of God's judgment in our regard. Accordingly the Lord pierces our Levia-

*Ps 138:8-10

*Ps 74:7

*Ps 74:8

*Job 40:21

than's jaw with a hook in that the ineffable power of his mercy takes hold of the ancient enemy's malice in such a way that he sometimes even loses those he has already trapped; it is as though after having committed sins they fell out of his mouth to return to an innocent life. And who would escape his jaw when once seized by it unless that jaw were pierced? Did he not hold Peter in his mouth when he denied Christ? Did he not hold David in his mouth when he sank in such a chasm of lust? But when both of these persons returned to life through repentance, our Leviathan in some way lost them through a hole in his jaw. Accordingly they who perpetrated such great evil later repented and returned, having been dragged away from Leviathan's mouth through a hole in his jaw. In fact, what human being would escape our Leviathan's mouth, so that he would commit no misdeed?

But this is how we know the great debt we owe to the Redeemer of the human race, who not only prevented us from entering Leviathan's mouth but even allowed us to return from his mouth. He did not take away the sinner's hope, but he pierced Leviathan's jaw so that he might show the sinner how to escape, so that he might at least flee after being bitten, after he had carelessly at first resisted fear of being bitten. Everywhere therefore we encounter the divine remedy, because he also gave us the command not to sin, and even gave us the remedy for sin, lest we lose hope. So we must above all be careful lest anyone find pleasure in sin and be seized by our Leviathan's mouth; nevertheless we should still not despair if we should be seized, because when we have perfect sorrow for sin, we will still find a hole in his jaw by which we can escape. If we are being chewed by his teeth but still look for a way of escape, we will find the hole in his jaw. Even the captive has a way of escape, the one who did not want to look out and keep from being seized. Consequently the one who has not yet been captured should run away from his jaw, but the one who has already been captured should look for a hole in his jaw. Our Creator then is loving and righteous.

23. But no one should say, "Since he is loving I sin venially." And no sinner should say, "Since he is just I have no hope of forgiveness for my sin." God frees us from the sin that we weep over, but everyone should fear the perpetration of anything if we do not know that it can be worthily wept over. Accordingly, before being guilty we should fear justice; after being guilty, we may be sure of mercy. Nor should we fear justice in such a way that we cannot be strengthened by any encouraging hope. Nor should we be so confident of mercy that we neglect to apply to our wounds the ointment of a worthy repentance. But we should always remember that the one we presume forgives us out of love also judges us strictly as well.

Accordingly the sinner should rejoice in the hope of his mercy, but the penitent should correct himself with the fear of his strict justice. Let the hope of our presumption then include the painful bite of fear, so that the righteousness of the Judge might terrify us to the point of correcting our sins, us whom the grace of forbearance invites to confidence in forgiveness. That is why a certain wise person said, *Do not say, "The Lord's acts of mercy are many; he will not remember my sins."** Then he forthwith added both his mercy and his justice: *Both mercy and anger belong to him.**

*Sir 5:6

*Sir 5:7

God's clemency pierces our Behemoth's jaw, and he meets the human race everywhere with mercy and power, since he has neither silenced any admonition of those who are free to be careful, nor denied the remedy of flight to those who have been captured. For this purpose in fact Holy Scripture has revealed the sins of such men, that is, of Peter and David: namely that the fall of the great might bring caution to the small. And for this purpose also the repentance and forgiveness of both are recorded: that the recovery of the lost might mean the hope of those who are perishing. No one could be proud of his own status when learning of David's fall, nor could anyone despair when learning that David was reinstated after his fall. See how wonderfully Holy Scripture humbles the proud with the same words by which it raises the lowly. It recounts one event by which the proud are recalled to humble fear at the same time as the humble are inspired with the confidence of hope. O new kind of medicine, incapable of evaluation; by means of the same formula it empties and dries the vessel that is full and relieves the dry vessel by filling it! It terrifies us with the fall of the mighty but strengthens us with their recovery!

24. Such in fact, yes, such is the mercy of God's plan, by which he both casts down the proud and supports us lest we collapse in despair. That is why he also advises us through Moses, *You must not take an upper or a lower millstone as a pledge.** We sometimes of course use the verb *take* in the sense of "taking away." That is why birds of prey[1] are sometimes called "takers." That is why the apostle Paul says, *You accept it if anyone represses you or preys upon you.** It is as if he said, "If anyone robs you." The pledge of a debtor of course is the confession of sin. A pledge is taken from a debtor when the confession of sin is already held from the sinner. The higher and

*Deut 24:6

*2 Cor 11:20

---

[1] There is a subtle play on words in the Latin, hard to render in English. The Latin verb in the quotation from Deuteronomy is *accipies*, translated into English as *take*. The word *accipitres*, nominative plural of *accipiter,* is usually translated *vulture* in English.

the lower millstone are hope and fear. Hope is offered up on high, but fear is pressed down below. But the upper and lower millstones have to be connected, since one is surely useless without the other. In the sinner's breast, then, hope and fear should be constantly joined, since he hopes in vain for mercy if he does not also fear justice; in vain does he fear justice if he does not also trust in mercy. We are therefore forbidden to take away the upper or the lower millstone in payment of a pledge, because the one who preaches to a sinner ought to arrange his preaching so perfectly that in reducing fear he does not abandon hope, or in abandoning hope leave him with fear alone. The upper or lower millstone is taken away if the preacher's tongue separates fear from hope or hope from fear in the sinner's breast.

25. Since the case required that we use David as an example, and we mentioned such a serious sin, the reader's soul might perhaps wonder why almighty God did not keep those whom he chose forever and whom he even raised up to the summit of spiritual gifts—why he did not keep them unhurt by sins of the flesh. So since we believe we can quickly satisfy such a query, we will briefly answer. There are those, you see, who have received gifts of spiritual power and through the grace bestowed on them have performed good works; thereby they fall into the sin of pride, yet they do not know how they have fallen. Accordingly the ancient enemy, who is already dominant inside, is allowed to rage externally as well, so that the one who has thoughts of pride falls into lust of the flesh.

We know on the other hand that it is sometimes a less serious sin to fail with respect to corruptible flesh than to sin by an unspoken thought arising from deliberate pride, but when pride is held to be a less shameful fault, it is less likely to be avoided. However, people are more ashamed of lust, because almost everyone knows it for a disgraceful act. That is why it often happens that some people rush on into lust after becoming proud; then they become ashamed of the evil of hidden sin from the obvious fall. Consequently they amend the greater sin after they have fallen into the smaller one, at which they are more grievously ashamed. They recognize their guilt in the smaller sin after they had believed themselves free of the greater. Sometimes our Behemoth, you see, by the Lord's loving plan, keeps drawing those who have grown lax onward from one sin to another, and while he strikes again and again, he loses the one he had seized there where he seemed to have won him over, and he is defeated himself.

We can consider therefrom with what great favor of mercy God keeps us safe within the fortified bosom of grace. See how the one who extols his own virtue returns through vice to humility. The one who extols the virtues he has received is wounded not by a sword, but so to speak by a remedy. What else is a virtue in fact but a remedy? What else is a vice but a wound? Since therefore we make a remedy a wound, God makes a wound a remedy, so that we who receive a blow from virtue are healed by vice. It is we who first distort the gifts of spiritual powers for the purpose of vice, so God assumes the allurements of vice for the practical skill of virtue, and he strikes at the state of safety so that he may use it, so that when we run away from humility, we may at length fall down and adhere to him.

But we must realize in this whole context that many people are more tightly bound by the things that bring them to ruin. So Behemoth here strikes at them with one vice so that they fall, and with another he ties them down to keep them from rising. Let a person then consider who the adversary is with whom he is at war, and if he happens to notice that he has already failed in some matter, let him at least then be afraid of being lured from one sin to another, so that he might earnestly avoid the wounds that are often deadly, because it is exceedingly rare that our enemy actually helps the chosen ones to be saved by means of wounds.

26. The jaws of our Behemoth can be understood as pierced in yet another way, namely that he is said to hold in his mouth not those who have already been completely entangled in sin, but those whom he is still tempting to sin by persuasion, inasmuch as his bite means to tempt anyone to sin by means of pleasure. He had received Paul, in fact, as someone to bite but not to swallow, when he harassed him with stings in the flesh after Paul had received so many heavenly revelations. So then, when he received permission to tempt him, he held him in his jaw, but his jaw was pierced. Paul in fact could have perished through pride, but he was tempted in order to keep him from perishing. That temptation accordingly was no whirlpool of vices but a safekeeping of merits, since our Leviathan contrived to wear him out with afflictions, but he did not devour him by forcing him to sin.

On the other hand, he would not lose those people who are proud of their holiness if he did not tempt them. They would certainly not be holy if they grew proud of the honor of their holiness, and they would be as much subject to his jurisdiction as they elevated themselves by their own virtues. But there is a wonderful procedure in God's plan, of such a kind that when people are tempted they are humbled, and when they are humbled they stop belonging to the tempter. So Behemoth's jaw is rightly said to be pierced, since when he grinds down God's chosen ones he loses them by the very act. When he tempts them and so loses them, he sees to it that they do not perish. The ancient enemy consequently helps along God's hidden plan since he willingly tempts the souls of the saints to ruin them, but he unwillingly helps them along to the kingdom by tempting them. His jaw then is pierced, because by tempting those he bites, he grinds them down and loses them by swallowing them. This act is accomplished not by human means, but by God's providence, that the very craftiness of the ancient adversary supports the advantage of the righteous people, inasmuch as when he tempts the chosen ones, in the very act of temptation he keeps them safe instead. So blessed Job is rightly asked, *Will you pierce his jaw with a hook?** You should hear, "As I do? I foresee and dispose all things, and I guard my chosen ones and keep them sound and durable, even when I allow their integrity to be somehow weakened here through the jaws of Leviathan." The next verse:

*Job 40:21

XIII. 27. *Will he multiply his prayers to you, or will he speak soft words to you?** You should hear, "as he does to me?" If, you see, those words were addressed to the person of the Son, Leviathan did speak soft words to that incarnate one in saying, *I know who you are, the Son of God.** Leviathan then multiplied prayers to the Son of God when through the legion of his subjects he said, *If you cast us out, send us into the herd of swine.** However, it could be understood more fittingly if he multiplied prayers to the Lord when on the day of the Last Judgment the wicked people who are Leviathan's body asked pity for themselves; at that time his members, actually reprobate sinners, will be late in crying out, saying, *Lord, Lord open the door for us!** They will be quickly answered: *I do not know where you come from.** Then also Leviathan will speak soft words to the Lord through his members when many sinners who belong to his body will say, *Lord, Lord, did we not prophesy in your name, did we not cast out demons in*

*Job 40:22

*Luke 4:34

*Matt 8:31

*Luke 13:25

*Luke 13:27

your name, did we not work many signs in your name?* They indeed will speak soft words in prayer when they repeat what they did in his name, what in fact they did with hard hearts when they stole praise for themselves. That is why they will quickly hear, *I do not know who you are.** The next verse:

XIV. 28. *Will he make a covenant with you?*—You should hear, "as with me?"—*And will you make him a slave forever?** You should hear, "as I do?" But we must carefully consider what this covenant is that our Leviathan makes with the Lord by which he will become his slave forever. When disagreeing parties make a covenant, you see, their intention is carried out so that each party should get what it wants and so that quarrels should be ended by the conclusion they have reached. Accordingly the ancient enemy, incited by the spark of his own malice, disagrees with the integrity of divine purity, but even while disagreeing he does not act contrary to the divine Judgment; although he always malevolently desires to tempt righteous people, the Lord only allows it to happen either by mercy or by justice. This freedom to tempt is called a covenant, in which the desire of the tempter is actualized, and yet in a wonderful way the will of the righteous Administrator is done by that means.

As we have said above, the Lord often delegates his chosen ones' instruction to the tempter, just as Paul, after the closing of Paradise, after receiving the secrets of the third heaven, lest he should be extolled by the very greatness of the revelations, had a messenger of Satan sent to him.* But as I have already said, God made use of this temptation, so that those who could have been lost through pride were kept from ruin by humility. It is by the secret action of God's plan that where the Devil's wickedness is allowed to rage, there God's kindness is lovingly brought to fruition. And it is

*Matt 17:22

*Matt 17:23

*Job 40:23

*2 Cor 12:3-7

well that by this covenant he is said to strike along with the Lord, and he is held to be God's slave, because there he obeys the will of heavenly grace where he expresses the anger of his own most evil will. He who while he is allowed to do his own will is bound by the will of heavenly counsel is then a slave by means of this covenant, so he may, so to speak, willingly tempt the chosen ones, and by tempting them unknowingly certify them.

29. But as long as he is enslaved for the good of the chosen ones in this life, he will be able to practice his wicked malice by tempting people; so in this passage he is not only said to be the Lord's slave by covenant, but he is said to be made his slave forever. So we are forced to investigate how he also performs his service after the present life is over; we must show how he serves the Lord in the unending future. He is certainly not allowed to tempt the righteous any more when they are in possession of the happiness of heaven and he surrenders himself to the eternal fire of hell before their eyes, because they are absolutely not to learn from temptations in that heavenly homeland where they are already being rewarded for the labor of temptation. But at that time our Leviathan with his body, that is, with all the reprobate sinners, is handed over to the avenging flames by which he is to be tortured without end.

While the righteous people are observing these tortures, they wax strong in God's praises, because they discern both the goodness with which they are rewarded and the punishment of the damned that they have escaped. The universe will then be so beautiful, when hell will rightly torture the impious people and eternal happiness will rightly reward the pious ones. Just as the color of black is applied first in a painting, so that the brighter colors of red and white may be painted over it and show up better, so also at that time God, who is a good manager, first displays the evil and then shows the happier joy of the blessed, after having demonstrated the punishment of reprobate sinners in front of the righteous people. And although that joy of theirs at seeing the Lord may not be such that it can grow, they realize all the more how much they owe their Creator, in that they see both the goodness they receive as their just reward and the evil that, having been helped by his mercy, they have overcome. Therefore, if the temptation of our Leviathan was advantageous for the righteous here below, and his condemnation is also profitable for them at the end, he is God's slave forever, and he unknowingly serves the praises of God, so that his penalty at the end is righteous, and his will here below is unrighteous. The next verse:

XV. 30. *Will you mock him as you would a bird?** How is it that our adversary was first named *Behemoth*, and then *Leviathan*, and is now compared to a bird to mock his ruin? In fact *Behemoth*, as I said before, is a wild beast displayed as a four-legged animal, since like an ox he is said to eat hay. *Leviathan* on the other hand, captured with a fishhook, is undoubtedly known as a sea serpent. Now, however, he is presented with the likeness of a bird, since it is said, *Will you mock him as you would a bird?** Let us then ascertain why he is called first a wild beast or a draft animal, then a dragon, and finally a bird. We will more quickly know the meaning of these names if we carefully search out the craftiness of his holding back.

*Job 40:24

*Job 40:24

From heaven he assuredly came to earth, and he now no longer lifts himself up to a longing for the hope of heaven. He is then both an irrational and a four-legged animal because of the foolishness of impure action, a dragon through hurtful malice, and a bird through his light fine structure. Because he is unaware of what he does against himself, he is a wild animal with brute senses; because of his desire to hurt us maliciously he is a dragon; because he lifts itself up proudly by the fine texture of his nature he is a bird. Again, because in his wicked actions God's power possesses him for our advantage, he is a beast of burden; because he secretly bites he is a serpent; because he sometimes disguises himself as an angel of light through untamed pride, he is a bird. Accordingly it is true that Satan provokes the human race with a kind of inexpressible skill of wickedness, but it is by those three vices especially that he tempts us most strongly, some obviously to lust, others to malice, and others to pride.

31. It is not without reason therefore that Satan is named by the very actions he attempts to set afoot as draft animal, bird, or dragon. To begin with, in those he provokes to the folly of lust he is a draft animal; in those he provokes to the malice of hurting other people he is a dragon; in those he incites to ambitious pride as if they understood things that are high, he is a bird; nevertheless, he is all three together—draft animal, dragon, and bird in those whom he soils with lust, malice, and pride. Through just as many forms whose images he induces in their hearts, he involves them in evil practices. He is named by the many different practices whose forms and images he assumes in the minds of those whom he deceives. So when he tempts the heart of one with lust of the flesh but does not win him over, he changes the temptation and incites his heart to malice; unable to take the form of a beast, he appears as a dragon. If he cannot ruin a person with the poison of malice, he parades all that person's good qualities before his eyes and lifts up his heart to pride. So the dragon could not trip him up, but then he creates an illusion of vainglory and flies like a bird before the eyes of his thoughts. And this bird in fact is lifted up against us with so brutal a size that he is impeded by no natural weakness. He does not have to worry about physical death, but he sees our Redeemer in mortal flesh, and he is inflated with a greater wind of pride. But precisely where he is lifted up on the wings of pride against his Creator he finds the pit of his own death. He falls headlong by the death of the Redeemer's flesh, which in his pride he eagerly sought; there he suffers the pit where as the food of his malice he desired the death of the righteous one. Let him therefore say, *Will you mock him as you would a bird?*

In fact the Lord made fun of the bird when he displayed his food in the passion of his only-begotten Son but hid the pit. He saw indeed what his mouth received, but he did not see what his throat held. Although he confessed him as the Son of God himself,* he thought he died as a pure man, for whose death he incited the souls of the persecuting Jews to cry out. But in the very hour of the Lord's being handed over Satan is already understood to have known tardily that he (Satan) would be punished by the very death of the Son of God. So he even terrified Pilate's wife with dreams,* so that her husband might stop the persecution of the Just One. But the matter was already determined by the unfolding of an internal plan, so it could not be opposed by any contrivance. It was expedient in fact that the death of the Just One who died unjustly should destroy the death of sinners who died justly. But our Leviathan was ignorant of this fact up until the time of the Lord's passion, and like a bird being mocked he fell into the pit of the Lord's divinity even as he was biting into the food of his humanity. The next verse:

XVI. 32. *Or will you bind him for your female slaves?** You should hear, "As I do?" Although the condition of slavery is despised, manhood is active, but when the female sex accompanies that condition,

*Matt 8:29

*Matt 27:19

*Job 40:24

it is lowly. The Lord of course rightly says that Leviathan is tied up, not for the masculine but for the female slaves, because he who comes to redeem us sends out his preachers against the pride of the world; he chose the foolish instead of the wise, the weak instead of the strong, and the poor instead of the rich. So the Lord tied up this strong Leviathan for his female slaves, because as Paul testifies, *God chose the weaklings of the world to shame the strong.** Solomon says for his part, *Wisdom has built herself a house; she has hewn for herself seven pillars. She has sacrificed her victims, mixed her wine, and set her table, she has sent out her handmaids to the tower and walls of the city,* to invite her guests.* Yes indeed, Wisdom built her house when the Only-begotten Son of God, by means of the soul,[2] created a human body for himself inside the virgin's womb.

*1 Cor 1:27

*Prov 9:1-3

In this way the Only-begotten Son's body is called a house of God, just as a temple is so called. This means that the one unique Son of God is both the One who inhabits and the one who is inhabited. And this truth is rightly taken in another sense, if the house of wisdom is called the church. The church indeed cut out seven pillars for herself in that she separated the minds of the preachers from the love of the present world and built them into her own structure, and because these pillars are connected by the power of perfection, they are signified by the number seven. She offered her sacrifices when she allowed her preachers to be slain in persecution. She mixed her wine when she preached the mysteries of the divinity and the humanity together to us. She set her table when she revealed and prepared for us the meal of Holy Scripture. She sent out her female

---

[2] This means of course that he united the body to himself through the soul. Only God can create. See Book 31.XXII.42.

slaves to the market and to the city walls to call us, because she endeavored to have preachers who were weak and poor to gather the faithful peoples to the heavenly building of the spiritual homeland.

That is why the Lord praises Nathanael in the Gospel* but does not count him among the chosen preachers: such people would come, you see, to preach the Lord, those who had nothing to show in praise of themselves, so that their actions might be recognized as being for the sake of truth alone, to the extent that it might be clearly seen that they were not suitable of themselves for those actions. Accordingly it was so that a wonderful power might shine out through the preachers' mouths that a more wonderful action preceded: namely that there was no merit in the preachers themselves. The Lord sent the female slaves, and he tied up the strong Leviathan, because he displayed the weak preachers to the world, and he restrained all the powerful ones who belonged to Leviathan's body with the chain of his dread.

*John 1:47

Leviathan himself is bound by the female slaves when by means of the weak preachers the light of the truth shines out, and the ancient enemy is not allowed to rage as much as he wants against the minds of the chosen ones. Rather he is coerced by signs and works of power, lest in the captivity of unbelief he should hold all those he desires to hold. He then does this by his own power who gives those who are not strong power against the ancient enemy. But now, since the Lord mentions those he sends against him, he adds what those who are sent in fact do. The next verse:

XVII. 33. *Friends will beat him, and dealers will divide him.** Our Leviathan is beaten as often as his members are separated from him by the sword of the Word of God. When wicked people, you see, hear the word of truth and are stricken by holy fear, they break

*Job 40:25

away from the imitation of the ancient enemy, and so his very body is divided when those depraved people who had joined it are removed from it. He calls them friends, however, whom he earlier called female slaves. In addition, he calls them merchants whom he first called friends. The holy preachers of course were first female slaves through fear, later friends through faith, and finally even merchants through action. The weak people are in fact told, *Fear not, little flock; it has pleased the Father to give you a kingdom.** Those who are growing stronger are likewise told, *I have called you friends, because I have made known to you all that I have heard from my Father.**

*Luke 12:32

*John 15:15

Those who at the end are going out for the work of merchants are commanded, *Go out to all the world and preach the gospel to all creation.** The preaching of the faith is in fact a kind of business deal wherein the word is given and faith is received by the listeners. Yes, it is a kind of business deal when preaching is given and faith is returned by the people. They impart faith, and forthwith they take on their holy life. If righteous preaching had not been a business deal, the psalmist would never have said, *Take up a psalm and sound the timbrel.** For a timbrel to sound, you know, an animal's skin must be dried. What then does the line *Take up a psalm and sound the timbrel* mean, if not "Take up a heartfelt song and give back a temporary mutilation of the body"?

*Mark 16:15

*Ps 80:2

If heavenly preaching were not a business deal, Solomon would never have spoken of Holy Church by means of the type of the valiant woman: *She makes fine clothes and sells them, and she hands over girdles to the Canaanite.** What else do muslin or fine clothes signify but the refined texture of holy preaching? In it the mind lightly rests, because the faithful soul is warmed by heavenly hope. That is why Peter witnessed the animals

*Prov 31:24

on the muslin sheet where the souls of sinners were mercifully gathered and held in the gentle rest of faith.* Yes, the church weaves muslin and sells it, because she bestowed the faith with speech that she had woven by believing, and she received from those without faith a life correctly lived. She handed over a girdle to the Canaanite, because she tightened up the loose works of the Gentiles with the energy of justice that she demonstrated, so that they might keep the precepts in their lives: *Let your loins be girt.**

*Acts 10:11-12

*Luke 12:35

So the Lord sends out his preachers; by searching he finds his female slaves, by transaction he makes them friends, by enriching he displays them as merchants. Formerly in their weakness they feared the threats of the world; now they arise to the level of sharing the knowledge of God's plan. Enriched with virtues, they are led on even to the business dealing of faith, so that by scolding and convincing the very members of our Leviathan, they can cut him off as sternly as, when they have become the bridegroom's friends, they unite themselves more truly to the love of truth and take away from Leviathan the souls of sinners; as quickly as, when they become more effective business agents, they display themselves as the best stocked repositories of virtues. So then God's preachers have taken in a most praiseworthy manner our Leviathan's possessions from him and distributed them; the voice of truth from the prophet promises, *If you separate the precious from what is base, you will be as my mouth.** He indeed separates the precious from the vile who disconnects human souls from the reprobate imitation of the ancient enemy. And God's mouth rightly says that such a person beyond doubt pronounces God's word. The next verse:

*Jer 15:19

XVIII. 34. *Will you fill a net with his skin or a boat with his head?** What is meant by a fishnet or a

*Job 40:26

fishing boat but the individual churches of the faithful that make up one catholic church? That is why it is written in the Gospel, *The kingdom of heaven is like a fishnet thrown into the sea that gathers in all kinds of fish.** Obviously the kingdom of heaven is another name for the church, whose behavior the Lord raises to the heights, and thereby she already reigns here in the Lord by her heavenly life. She is also rightly compared to a fishnet cast into the sea that takes in all kinds of fish. When she is sent into this Gentile world she rejects none but receives the bad with the good, the proud with the humble, the wrathful with the meek, and the foolish with the wise.

*Matt 13:47

On the other hand, we take our Leviathan's skin to mean the fools in his body, and his head to mean those who are prudent. Or perhaps the skin's being external means the slaves who are subject to this extreme end, whereas the head means those who are the leaders. And the Lord rightly follows the established order and declares that he is going to fill the fishnet and the fishing boat, that is, his church and the devout faithful, first with Leviathan's skin and then with his head, because as we have said above, he first chose the weak so he could shame the strong. He chose the fools of this world to put the wise to shame.* He first collected the illiterate and later the philosophers; he did not teach the fishermen through the lecturers, but with marvelous power he humbled the lecturers through the fishermen. Let him then say, *Will you fill a net with his skin or a boat with his head?** You should hear "As I do? Yes, I first gather the extreme and the weak inside the church of the faithful, as if they were the Devil's skin, and afterwards I subject his head to myself, that is the prudent adversaries."

*1 Cor 1:27

*Job 40:26

The next verse: *Will you place your hand over him?** That is, "As I do? It is in fact my wonderful power that

*Job 40:27

restrains him, and I do not allow him to rage beyond what is expedient, and I turn away his rage as much as I allow it for the advantage of my chosen ones." Well, certainly placing his hand over Leviathan means to beat him with his powerful energy. Accordingly blessed Job is interrogated thus: *Will you place your hand over him?** It is as if he were clearly asked, "Will you restrain him with your own power?" So he quickly and rightly adds,

*Job 40:27

*Job 40:27

XIX. 35. *Remember the struggle, and add no more.** Another plan of God's judgments on that account often attacks his servants who have great merits; it either threatens them, or flogs them, or presses heavy burdens upon them, or imposes difficult labors upon them, because his wonderful power foresees that if they continue quiet, free, and tranquil, they will not be able to bear the adversary's temptations but will fall prostrate with their minds wounded. So while they are preoccupied externally with strokes of the whip or with burdens to be tolerated, God hides them from undergoing the darts of temptation internally. It is a practice of medicine in fact often to cause internal heat to be focused on itching of the skin, so that an external wound might cure an internal hurt. So it sometimes happens by dint of a remedy of God's plan that an internal wound is healed by the operation of external pain, and by the cutting action of external strokes of a whip the internal rottenness brought about by vices is expelled from where it could have occupied the mind. Yet it often happens that people are themselves unaware of an obvious fault, and they are tortured by pain or by forced labor; then they burst out with complaints against the righteous and almighty Judge, apparently little perceiving that strong adversary against whom they are fighting. If they really paid careful attention to his insufferable powers, they would never murmur against their external sufferings.

36. But these latter only seem grievous to us because we refuse to consider the more grievous war against the hidden enemy. And against that war, as we have said, we are defended when we are buffeted. As long as we are afflicted, we are hidden. Before our flesh can be fortified by the immortality of the resurrection, if it suffers no affliction, it is restrained by temptations. Everybody knows it is much better to burn with fever than with the fire of vices. And yet when we are attacked by a fever, because we neglect to consider the heat of vices that could have taken possession of us, we murmur at being struck down by a fever.

Everybody knows it is much better to suffer harsh servitude from people than to be subject to caresses by demonic spirits. And yet when we are worn out by the yoke of the human condition through the high Judgment of God, we break out with complaints, and it is no wonder, since we pay too little attention to the fact that if no condition of servitude oppressed us, perhaps our free mind would be a worse slave to many wicked deeds. So then we believe that the things we put up with are grievous, because we do not see how harsh and intolerable are the battles of the crafty enemy against us. Our mind would consider any burden light if it could weigh the battles of the hidden adversary that could be fought against it. What if almighty God should lift the burdens we suffer now and at the same time withdraw his help from us and leave us subject to the temptations of this Leviathan himself? Where would we go while so fierce an enemy is raging if we were not defended by any protection of our Creator?

Since therefore blessed Job was unaware of any fault of his own while he was suffering these harsh trials, lest he should perchance fall into the vice of murmuring, he should remember what was to be feared, and he should then be told, *Remember the struggle, and add no more.** It is as if he were clearly told, "If you considered the hidden foe's war against you, you would not blame me for any of your sufferings. If you take heed of the sword your adversary wields against you, you will hardly take fright at your father's whip. You see the whip I beat you with, but you do not notice the strong enemy from whom I save you by beating you." *So remember the struggle, and add no more.** "In other words, the weaker you perceive yourself to be against the enemy's war, the more readily you should submit to the father's discipline. So when you suffer the blows of my attack, you should call your enemy to mind so you can bear it with equanimity; then you will not treat any of your sufferings as harsh, since by means of that external torture you will be free from internal suffering." Since, however, our Leviathan coaxed Job with false promises about God's mercy, the Lord first terrified him with the thought of his great power, and then inspired him with careful consideration by saying, *Remember the struggle, and add no more.* But in order that he might make clear Leviathan's unpardonable guilt, he forthwith added,

*Job 40:27

*Job 40:27

XX. 37. *Behold, his hope is going to deceive him.** This fact however is to be understood about him in such a way as to include his body, which means all the wicked people who do not fear the strictness of God's justice and console themselves in vain with his mercy.

*Job 40:28

However, he quickly returns to our consolation, and he foretells the future destruction of the Last Judgment, saying, *And he will plunge down while all the people are looking on.** He will indeed plunge down, because when the eternal and terrible Judge appears, and while the legions of angels are standing, and while the whole ministry of heavenly powers is watching, with all the

*Job 40:28

chosen ones being led forth to witness the spectacle, this cruel and powerful beast will be brought captive to the middle of the court along with his body, which amounts to all the reprobate sinners to be committed to the eternal fire of hell at the words, *Depart from me, you accursed, into the eternal fire prepared for the Devil and his angels.** O what a sight that will be when this most savage beast is displayed before the eyes of the chosen ones, who in this present wartime could have terrified them excessively if he could have been seen.

*Matt 25:41

But it happens by God's admirable hidden plan both that by his grace the warriors vanquish him now without seeing him, and later that, already led captive, he is seen by the happy winners. Then the righteous acknowledge in full the debt they owe to God's help when they see what a powerful beast it was over whom they are now victorious in their weakness; then they will see how savage the beast is and how much they owe to the grace of their Protector. Our soldiers will then return from this battle bearing the trophy of virtues; they will have received their bodies when they already find entrance to that eternal judgment chamber of the heavenly kingdom, and the first thing they will see is the mammoth power of this ancient serpent, lest they should estimate as contemptible the danger they had escaped. It is well said then, *And he will plunge down while all the people are looking on.** The death they will witness will at that time inspire joy—of him whose life now tolerated by the righteous makes war on them every day with torture. But we will hear these things as if we were forthwith to question the Lord, saying, "O Lord, when you knew very well how strong this Leviathan was, why did you raise him up to fight against us in our weakness?" If so he will forthwith answer, *It is not as if I were cruel in raising him up.** And it is as if we were immediately to

*Job 40:28

*Job 41:1

ask the reason or how it is that he is not cruel in raising up him about whom we know very well that God allows to plunge in everywhere and devour everything. And so he replies forthwith,

XXI. 38. *Who then can resist my presence? And who has given me anything that I should return it to him?** In these two verses the Lord reveals both the force of his power and the whole weight of reason. To satisfy his power he said, *Who then can resist my presence?* And for the sake of reason he said, *And who has given me anything that I should return it to him?* It is as if he said, "It is not out of cruelty that I raise Leviathan up, because I have the power to free my chosen ones from his forcefulness, and again I do not condemn reprobate sinners unjustly, but I act reasonably. In other words I can both marvelously free those I kindly choose and abandon those I not unjustly reject."

*Job 41:1-2

No one in fact has given God anything first, so that divine grace should support that person. If we should anticipate God by acting rightly, what of the prophet who said, *His mercy will anticipate me*?* If we have offered some good work in order to merit God's grace, how about the words of the apostle Paul: *You have been saved by grace through faith, and this is not your own doing, Instead it is God's gift, not a result of works*?* If our love anticipated God, what of the words of the apostle John: *It is not that we have loved God, but that he has loved us first*?* And what about the Lord's words reported by Hosea: *I will love them willingly*?*

*Ps 58:11

*Eph 2:8-9

*1 John 4:10
*Hos 14:5

If without his gift we follow God by our own strength, what about the public witness of Truth in the Gospel: *Without me you can do nothing*?* Did he not say, *No one can come to me, unless the Father who sent me draws him on*?* Did he not also say, *You did not choose me, but I chose you*?* If we so much as forestall the gifts of good

*John 15:5

*John 6:44
*John 15:16

works by our own strength and by thinking rightly, why is it that Paul again cleverly tells us that all the confidence of the human mind gives way of itself from the very root of the heart? He says, *Not that we are sufficient of ourselves to think anything of ourselves, but our sufficiency is from God.** No one then anticipates God by merits, so that he might hold him a debtor, but in a wonderful way he is an equal Creator towards all, and he first chooses some people, while he righteously abandons others to their own reprobate behavior.

*2 Cor 3:5

39. However, God neither shows his chosen ones kindness without justice (in that he pursues them with harsh afflictions), nor on the other hand shows justice without mercy to reprobate sinners (in that he puts up with equanimity with those whom he later condemns for all eternity). If then both the chosen ones receive advance grace and reprobate sinners receive whatever they deserve, and if both the chosen ones find mercy that they should praise and reprobate sinners have nothing to complain of about justice, it is rightly said, *Who has given me anything that I should return it to him?** It is as if he said outright, "There is no reason that I should be compelled to spare reprobate sinners, because I owe them nothing on account of their actions. On this account, in the heavenly homeland they receive no reward whatever, because when they could have merited it here below, by their own free will they scorned it. The chosen ones, however, had formed their own free will correctly, since their mind was inspired by grace to remain aloof from worldly desires.

*Job 41:1-2

40. The good that we do, of course, is both God's and ours: God's through his anticipatory grace and ours through the conformity of our free will. If it is not God's, why do we give him thanks in eternity? On the other hand, if it is not ours, why do we hope for rewards and recompense? Since then we do not unreasonably give thanks, we know we are anticipated by his gift, and on the other hand, since we do not unreasonably expect a reward, we know our free will conforms, and we choose the action we perform. The next verse:

*Job 41:2

XXII. 41. *Everything under heaven is mine.** It is clear to everybody that not only the things that are under heaven, but also the things in heaven, the things created in the sky, are called his and serve his will, by whom they remember that they were created. Why then does he speak only of the things below, saying, *Everything under heaven is mine*? But since he is speaking of the Leviathan, who no longer has a place in the heavenly seat in the sky, he states that everything under heaven is his, so that he may teach us that he also who fell from heaven is subject to his authority. It is as if he said, "This Leviathan here has lost my blessedness, but he has not escaped my dominion, because even these powers serve me who are my adversaries because of their depraved acts. The next verse:

*Job 41:3

XXIII. 42. *I will not even spare his powerful words composed for the sake of prayer.** Who will suppose, who hardly knows he has read these words, that the Devil himself might be begging forgiveness for his sins? But perhaps that man—whom this Leviathan here is going to make his own vessel at the end of the world, whom, as Paul testifies, *the Lord Jesus will kill with the breath of his mouth and destroy by the illumination of his own coming**

*1 Thess 2:8

—perhaps that man, terrified at the presence of such high majesty, unable to activate his own powers, is reduced to prayers. This event however might be better understood in relation to his body, that is, all his wicked members, who come too late to utter words of prayer, which they now hold in contempt as far as putting them in practice. That is why Truth says in the Gospel, *At last the foolish virgins came and said, "Lord, Lord, open the door for us."** And he will answer them: *I know you not.** But since the power to pray is said to compose words, he urges us rather to understand in relation to the present time what we have spoken about Antichrist's future body.

*Matt 25:11
*Matt 25:12

43. There are, you see, some people within Holy Church who mouth frequent prayers but do not live a life in accord with prayer. They seek the heavenly promises in their petitions, but they steer clear of them in their actions. They even shed tears in their prayers at times, but when after the time of prayer their minds are attacked by pride, they immediately swell up with the arrogance of self-glorification. When incited by avarice they quickly burn with the fire of a greedy thought. When tempted by lust they forthwith pant with illicit desire. When persuaded by anger the flames of madness quickly engulf their mind's meekness. As I have said, even when they are moved to tears in their prayer, with their prayers at an end they are struck by the suggestions of evil habits, and they never remember their tears for desire of the eternal kingdom.

Balaam clearly pointed this out when he saw the tents of the righteous Israelites and said, *Let my life end with the death of the righteous, and let my end be like theirs.** But when the time of compunction had passed, he offered counsel against the lives of those whom he had wanted to be like in his death, and when he found an opportunity for avarice, he quickly forgot whatever he had wished for in his innocence. That prayer then never has the weight of virtue that it would have by persevering in love. On the other hand, it is rightly maintained about Hannah's tears, *Her face then was no longer averted.** This was obviously because her mind never lost through the ineptitude of frivolous

*Num 23:10

*1 Sam 1:18

joy what the ordeal of groans, uttered during the time of prayers, had sought. The effort of prayer in the case of some people, however, is turned instead to the objective of business, and concerning these Truth says in the Gospel, *They devour the houses of widows under the pretext of praying long prayers. They will receive a more serious judgment.** *Mark 12:40

Since therefore the petitions of the wicked people who are members of this Leviathan's body are by no means pitied, and since their prayers are belied by their actions, it is rightly said here, *I will not even spare his powerful words composed for the sake of prayer.** *Job 41:3 Since the words refer to the power to compose prayers, the vanity of the prayer is clearly unmasked. The true prayer, you see, means bitter groans emitted in compunction, not words composed to sound right. But since the ancient enemy enlarges himself the more wickedly with multiplied arguments the more relentlessly he is cut off, and since the Lord considers his hidden traps the more exactly the more merciful he shows himself toward us, it is rightly added,

XXIV. 44. *Who will uncover the appearance of his clothing?** Our Leviathan in fact tempts the minds of *Job 41:4 religious people differently from those wholly given up to the world. To the depraved he openly offers the evil that they desire, but he lies hidden from good people and fools them with the appearance of holiness. To the former as if to members of his own family he clearly puts himself forward in his wickedness, but to the latter as if to some kind of strangers he makes himself look pale under an appearance of integrity, so that he might introduce the evil that he cannot show them publicly covered with a veil of good deeds. In the same way, his members, when they cannot hurt anyone with outright depravity, often put on a cloak of good action. They indeed show themselves at work in evildoing, but they lie with an appearance of holiness.

Wicked people of course, if they made a bad showing, could not be received by those who are good, but they put up a kind of good appearance, so that when good people receive in them an appearance that they like, they also receive the evil they avoid mixed with that show. That is why, when Paul espied certain ones serving the interest of their stomach under the veil of preaching, he said, *Even Satan disguises himself as an angel of light. So it is no wonder that his minions transform themselves into ministers of justice.** Joshua feared this transformation, and when he saw the angel he asked whose party he belonged to: *Are you with us or with our adversaries?** Obviously if his power was hostile, by the very fact that he held him suspect he would willingly shrink from the appearance.

*2 Cor 11:14-15

*Josh 5:13

Since therefore our Leviathan is setting afoot a wicked deed, he often puts on an appearance of holiness; because it is only by God's grace that his mantle and disguise could be detected, it is well said, *Who will uncover the appearance of his clothing?** You should hear the Lord's voice say, "Who but I? In fact it is I who inspire my servants' minds with the grace of most refined discernment, that with his malice uncovered they see the naked face of the enemy that he covers and hides in the disguise of holiness." And since he tries to corrupt the minds of the faithful sometimes by outward show and sometimes by suggestion—he acts at times by deed and at times by persuasion—he adds,

*Job 41:4

XXV. 45. *And who has entered into his presence?** You should hear, "Who but me? I tear to pieces the words of his suggestions through the discretion of my chosen ones, and I make it clear that the case is not as it has been declared to be." His words seem to promise

*Job 41:4

good, but the end thereof is ruin. To enter into his presence means therefore to see through his cunning words, so that we never consider their meaning, but their real intention. Adam wanted to enter his presence when he neglected to weigh carefully the intention of his persuasion; he thought in fact that he received divinity through him, and in this way he lost the grace of immortality. Accordingly where he carelessly stood without understanding his words, there he presented himself before him to be swallowed whole. The next verse:

XXVI. 46. *Who will open the doors of his countenance?** The doors of his countenance are wicked teachers, who are on that account called doors of his countenance, as everyone enters through them, so that our Leviathan may be seen in the supremacy of his power. Just as Holy Scripture is accustomed to call the saints the gates of Zion (Zion in fact is interpreted "watch tower"), we are not wrong in calling the holy preachers the gates of Zion, since it is through their lives and teaching that we enter the hidden places of heavenly contemplation. So also by the doors of this Leviathan those of the master of error are signified, those by which crooked preaching is received, and for the wretched listeners the road to ruin is opened. But these doors are in fact in human eyes, often open for bringing people in, but on the other hand closed for discovery, because they have a correct appearance, but in fact they recommend deviant behavior. They are therefore closed for discovery, because to keep from being recognized internally, they are fortified externally by an appearance. The Lord however opens these doors with a wonderful power, because he makes the hypocrites' minds comprehensible for his chosen ones. *Who will open the doors of his countenance?** You should hear, "Is it not I who make the masters of error appear openly to my chosen ones with transparent rec-

*Job 41:5

*Job 41:5

ognition, when they are hidden behind an appearance of holiness?" And because when Antichrist comes he will win over the very highest powers of this world, it is by their twin error that in his rage he tries to draw people's hearts to himself, even after the preachers have been sent. And the powers have been so far unsettled as to bend, so that the Lord rightly adds concerning this Leviathan,

XXVII. 47. *There is ground for alarm through the cycle of his teeth.** With a difference of words he wanted to insert these teeth of Leviathan in another way than when he used the word *doors* above. Crooked preachers, you see, are his doors, because they open the entrance to ruin. They are his teeth, because they seize those led into error and cut them off from the solidity of truth. In the same way we take the teeth of Holy Church to be those who by their preaching grind down the toughness of sinners. That is why Solomon tells her, *Your teeth are like flocks of shorn sheep coming up out of the water.** They are not ineptly compared to the shorn and bathed sheep, because they are living a harmless life, and in the bath of baptism they have put aside the old fleece of their former way of life. So also the teachers of error are signified by Leviathan's teeth, because they bite and tear the reprobate life to pieces, and they chop up as a sacrifice of falsity those whom they have led astray from the integrity of truth. Their preaching in fact could have been easily scorned by the listeners, but dread of the worldly powers joined itself to that preaching and exalted it before human judgment.

*Job 41:5

*Song 4:2

48. So we are rightly told, *There is ground for alarm through the cycle of his teeth.** In other words the crooked powers of this present world protect the evil preachers. Yes, many of these powers are eager to rage against and terrify those whom they desire to seduce by their speech, and the fear they inspire is expressed

*Job 41:5

through the circular action of their teeth, as if it were said openly, "These wicked teachers grind up people with their persuasion, precisely because there are those among them who afflict those who are weak minded with terror." What then will that time of persecution be like, when some with words and others with swords rage against us and try to turn aside the piety of the faithful? Who is there, even if he be weak, who would not despise the teeth of this Leviathan, if terror did not also fortify the worldly powers all around?

But against the faithful a double cunning is practiced, because they are first addressed with flattering words and then ordered by threats of brandished swords. The exercise of both of these approaches (that is, both speech and power) is compressed in John's Apocalypse in a brief sentence where it is said, *The power of the horses is in their mouths and in their tails.** The mouths of the teachers of course signify knowledge, but the tail is worldly power. The tail is naturally situated at the rear, and it signifies the temporal power of this world, which is of secondary importance. The apostle Paul wrote of it as follows: *I seek one thing: that forgetful of what is behind, I may stretch forward to what is ahead.** Behind is everything that passes, and ahead is everything that is coming and that remains. As for these horses, that is, these most wicked preachers, everywhere they run under impulse of the flesh, and their power is in their mouths and their tails; they indeed preach crooked doctrines in persuasive voices. They are backed up by worldly powers, and they use what is behind to exalt themselves. Because they can seem despicable, they exact reverence for themselves from their wicked hearers, through the very people by whose patronage they are supported.

And so not unreasonably Leviathan's fear is described here also through the circular appearance of

*Rev 9:19

*Phil 3:13

his teeth, because he acts with the help of much terror. So in their crooked preaching, even if there is no declaration of truth, temporal power is surely to be feared. That is why the psalmist also describes this Antichrist rightly when he says, *Distress and trouble are under his tongue; he sits in ambush with the powerful.**³ Because of his crooked teaching, force and distress are under his tongue; because of his apparent miracles he sits in ambush, but because of the honor of worldly power he hides out with the powerful. Accordingly, since he profits from both false miracles and worldly power, it is stated that he both sits in hiding and accompanies the rich, so it follows that:

*Ps 9:28 Vulg

XXVIII. 49. *His body is like a combustible shield.** In Holy Scripture the word *shield* is sometimes used for the winning side, sometimes for the opposite side. A defensive shield often means God's protection, but it sometimes also indicates human resistance. As an example of God's protection the psalmist says, *You have surrounded us with the shield of your good will.** He says the Lord surrounds us with a shield, because those he protects with his help, he also rewards and surrounds. Again the same psalmist uses the word *shield* for human resistance when he says, *There he broke the horn, the bow, the shield, the sword, and the battle.** The horn of course means the pride of the arrogant, the bow the ambush of those who strike from a distance, the shield the stubborn endurance of resistance, the sword an imminent strike, and the battle a mental action against the Lord. And all this destructive activity takes place in the church, when the minds of those who resist God are tamed by the yoke of humility that is placed upon

*Job 41:6

*Ps 5:13

*Ps 75:4

---

³ In the Vulgate Psalm 9 is not separate from Psalm 10.

them. That is why the same psalmist says, *He will destroy the bow and break the armor, and he will burn the shields with fire.** The Lord destroys the bow when he unmasks the hidden devices of those who sit in ambush. He breaks the armor when he threatens the human patronage that had reared itself up against him. He burns the shields with fire when he ignites the minds of sinners who defend themselves with stubborn endurance, and he lights the fire of repentance and confession in them with the heat of the Holy Spirit.

*Ps 45:10

But it is incumbent upon us to study intently what is said in this passage of Job about the comparison of the body of our Leviathan to combustible shields. A shield is certainly strong enough, but when it wears out it is as fragile as any combustible instrument. Even if shields are combustible, then, they are strong enough to withstand the blows of arrows, yet they are still combustible. They are not penetrated by the blows of arrows, but they collapse into fragments by their own fragility. This Leviathan's body (that is, all the wicked people who are obstinate and stubborn but whose lives are fragile) is compared to combustible shields. When they hear the words of preachers, you see, they do not allow any darts to reach them, because in all the sins they commit they raise the shield of proud defense. When any of them is convicted of the guilt of his iniquity, he does not immediately think up ways of amending his sin, but rather of what he can use in support of his defense. He is not then pierced by any arrow of truth, because he uses the words of holy censure as a shield of proud defense.

That is why Jeremiah rightly says about the Jews who protect themselves with proud defense against the Lord's commandments, *Give them back, O Lord, payment according to the works of their hands.** And he again adds the same thrust more expressly: *Give them the*

*Lam 3:64

shield for their heart that your hands have fashioned.* The work of the Lord is surely his humanity, able to suffer when it appeared among human beings; when the Jews whose wisdom was pride saw that humanity they disdained it, and they scorned the idea of believing him to be immortal whose ability to suffer seemed mortal. And when they saw his humility while they were persistently arrogant in their pride, with all due care they determined not to let the holy words of preaching penetrate their minds. So while the Lord was giving notice of their evil deeds, he gave them his work as a shield for their hearts. His judgment was exact, you see, in displaying to them their own obstinate pride against him in the very act in which he also labored in weakness for our sakes. They repudiated the very words of preaching, because they scorned the weakness of the Lord's passion. They had therefore a shield in their hearts that was the Lord's work, and they turned that shield against him, because in their wisdom, which was pride, he who was humble for their sakes appeared despicable to them.

*Lam 3:65

50. This shield, as I have already said above, was first held by that sinner who, when the Lord asked why he had touched the forbidden tree, referred the sin not to himself, but to the woman whom the Lord had given him, though he answered that he had received the fruit; he wanted to have the guilt rebound indirectly to the Creator who had given him the woman who had suggested such things. The woman was also questioned, and she in turn held the shield when she replied that she was not guilty either, but she let the guilt bounce back to the serpent's persuasion, saying, *The serpent deceived me, and I ate it.** She in turn wanted to redirect the blame to the Creator obliquely, since he allowed the serpent to enter there, who was going to persuade her to do such things. The serpent of course was not questioned since

*Gen 3:13

there was no question of his repentance. The couple however whose repentance was sought presented the shield of most wicked defense against the words of that most righteous censure. That is why even now the practice of sinners remains defense against an accusation of sin, and where guilt should end, there it is piled up. So the Lord was right to say, *His body is like a combustible shield.** This is because all the wicked, lest they should receive words of censure, are ready to raise the shield of defense against the darts of adversaries. But Leviathan's body obviously covers us with still more emphasis when he goes on to say,

*Job 41:6

*Job 41:6

XXIX. 51. *It is connected by scales interlaced.** It is said that the dragon's body is covered with scales so that it cannot be quickly penetrated by projectiles. So the Devil's entire body, that is, the multitude of reprobate sinners, when it is censured for its iniquity attempts evasion by recourse to whatever excuses it can find, and it covers itself with some kind of scales for protection to keep from being pierced by an arrow of truth. Whoever when he is caught desires to excuse himself instead of weeping for his sin covers himself with a kind of scales, while the holy preachers are pelting him with the sword of truth. He has scales, and that is why the arrow of the word cannot find a way to penetrate his breast. That arrow is repelled by the hardness of flesh, so that the sword of the spirit cannot fix itself in him.

52. The wisdom of the flesh hardened Saul against God, when no arrow of the Gospel preaching reached his heart. But after he was pierced by the powerful rebuke from heaven and blinded by the notice from on high—in fact he lost the light so that he might regain it—he came to Ananias to be enlightened. And in that enlightenment he lost the hardness of his defenses, so that it was correctly written about him, *Something like* *scales fell away from his eyes.** The hardness of a garment of flesh had obviously held him fast, and that is why he did not see the rays of the true light. But after his proud resistance was overcome, the scales of defense fell away. They surely fell from his bodily eyes under Ananias's hands, but they had already fallen from the eyes of his heart at the Lord's previous rebuke. When he lay prostrate, you see, pierced by the spear of the heavenly assault, with a now humble and wounded heart, he asked a question: *Lord, what do you want me to do?** The scales having been rejected, the arrow of truth had obviously already reached the very inside of the heart; then, with the arrogance of pride defeated, he confessed him as the Lord whom he had fought, and not knowing what to do, he asked him.

  It is easy to see where the fierce persecutor is and where the ravening wolf.* Behold, he has already turned into a sheep who hesitates before the shepherd's path that he should take. And it is noticeable that when he asked, *Who are you, Lord*?* he got no answer from the Lord, such as, "I am the only-begotten Son of the Father," "I am the Beginning," or "I am the Word before the world was." Since Saul disdained to believe in the incarnate God and despised the weakness of his humanity, he heard the following words from heaven about what he had expressed contempt for: *I am Jesus of Nazareth whom you are persecuting.** It is as if he said, "You must hear me say from the heights what you in the lowest despise about me. You disdained on earth the idea that the Creator of heaven had come; now then, know on earth the man who came from heaven, so that the more you fear the appearance of weakness in me, the more you can certify what has come to be in heaven as a superior power. Prostrate yourself then; I am not at all laying out before you the fact that I am God before the

*Acts 9:18

*Acts 9:6

*Gen 49:27

*Acts 22:8

*Acts 22:8

world came to be; instead you hear from me what you disdain to believe." After he said *Jesus* in fact he also added *of Nazareth* to express his earthly habitation, as if he would say more clearly, "Accept the weakness of my humility and lose the scales of your pride."

53. We must realize, however, that these scales of defense, however much they cover almost the whole human race, press against the minds of hypocrites and crafty people in a more special sense. These latter, you see, shrink as much more frantically from confessing their faults as they are foolishly ashamed of looking like sinners to other people. When their show of holiness is rebuked and their hidden malice found out, their outward show interposes itself and engages the scales of defense, turning aside the sword of truth. That is why the prophet rightly speaks against Judea: *There the bogey lay down and found its rest, and there the groundhog had its hole.** The bogey of course means any of the hypocrites, and the groundhog malicious people who protect themselves with various kinds of defense. The bogey is said to have a human face but the body of a beast, just as all the hypocrites first present a holy appearance based on reason, but it is a beastly body that follows, because the works that they set afoot are really evil under the appearance of good.

*Isa 34:14-15

By the word *groundhog*, however, is signified the defense of malicious minds, obviously because when a groundhog's head appears his feet and body are seen as well, but as soon as he is seen he wraps himself in a ball, pulls his feet in, and hides his head; thus in the hands of the one holding him he is totally lost sight of, and all that was seen before is gone. Exactly in this way do malicious minds behave when they are caught at their excessive behavior. The groundhog's head is seen when the beginning of a sinner's misdeed is noticed.

The groundhog's feet are seen when it is known by what steps his wickedness was perpetrated. Nevertheless he has quickly brought forward his excuses, and the malicious mind retracts his feet inwardly, because he hides all the traces of his wickedness. He withdraws his head, because with a surprising defense mechanism he pretends that he never started any evil action. Just like the groundhog, he remains like a ball in someone's hands, because the one who caught him suddenly loses all he had already found out but holds the sinner wound up in his own conscience; he who had found out already and seen the whole action is deceived by the evasion of guilty defense and now knows nothing at all.

The groundhog then has a hole among reprobate sinners, because the malicious mind rolls itself up and hides inside itself in the darkness of its defense. But in the sense that sinners excuse themselves, and in the sense that they becloud with a shadowy defense the eye of the person who caught them, the eye still fixed upon them, the word of God also shows us how sinners are supported by those who are like them. The next verse:

XXX. 54. *Each one is joined to the other, and not even a breath gets between them.** Such are the scales of sinners, and lest any breath of life from the mouths of preachers should penetrate, they are both hardened and connected. Similar guilt unites them, and crooked defense causes them to crowd together with shared defiance, so that they can find common protection by defending one another in turn in their misdeeds. Each one fears for himself when he sees another warned or corrected. That is why they unanimously rise up against the words of reformers, since they protect themselves in each other. So it is well said, *Each one is joined to the other, and not even a breath gets between them.** They protect one another in turn in their wickedness

*Job 41:7

*Job 41:7

with proud defense, and they by no means allow any breath of holy exhortation to get between them. And he still more openly confirms their fatal agreement, saying,

XXXI. 55. *One will stick with the other, and holding on to one another they will never be separated.** If separated they could have been corrected, but instead they persist united in the obstinacy of their iniquity; the more separated they are daily from knowledge of justice, the less able they are to be separated from one another by any reproof. Just as bad as it is for good people to be disunited, it is as dangerous for the bad not to be disunited. Unity hardens people in perversity as long as they remain on good terms, and the more incorrigible they are, the more like-minded. A wise person talks about this unity of reprobate sinners: *The synagogue of sinners is a ball of flax.** The prophet Nahum also says, *Like brambles intertwined is a crowd of revelers drinking together.** A banquet of reprobate sinners is in fact delight in temporal pleasure. They drink together in such a banquet because they agree to get drunk on the enticements of their pleasures.

*Job 41:8

*Sir 21:10

*Nah 1:10

Accordingly a similar guilt unites the members of our Leviathan, that is, all the evil persons whom the word of God compares to scales joined together for mutual defense; so it is rightly said, *One will stick with the other, and holding on to one another they will never be separated.** Holding on, they cannot be separated; because they remember that they are like one another in all things, so they are forced to come to one another's defense. Now having described his body, our exposition returns to the description of Leviathan as head, and we proceed to speak of what the ancient enemy himself does in the time of the final persecution:

*Job 41:8

XXXII. 56. *His sneezing fits have the brightness of fire.** We will explain this more easily if we first ascertain how this sneezing occurs. When we sneeze,

*Job 41:9

a gust of air is released from the chest, and if it does not find an open path of escape, it reaches the top of the head, so the congested air gets out through the nose and the whole head is agitated. Leviathan's body then, whether we take it as evil spirits or as reprobate sinners who stick to him by the similarity of wickedness, has a surge of air rise from its chest; this happens when pride rises from the present world's powers. It does not find a path of release, as it were, because it extols itself against the righteous people, and God arranges that it cannot prevail as much as it wishes. The air then rises as far as the top of the head, which it agitates, because Satan's pride accumulates and agitates perception with more force at the end of the world. The head then is agitated when the very mover of evil spirits rises through the one called Antichrist, and he moves more violently in the persecution of the faithful. The accumulated pressure of air then escapes through his nose, because all his wicked pride shows itself in the obvious gusts of his malice.

A sneeze accordingly agitates the head with exceeding force, and the sneeze of this Leviathan is called that final agitation by which he enters a condemned person, and through that person he rules the reprobate sinners. At that time he moves with such great power that he even troubles, if that should be possible,* the chosen members of the Lord. In fact he performs such great signs and prodigies that the power of his miracles seems to shine out with an appearance of the light of fire. Since therefore his agitated head dares to shed the light of miracles, his sneeze is rightly called the brightness of fire. Because he moves to persecute the righteous, he shines in the eyes of reprobate sinners with the power of signs. And since the worldly wise embrace his tyranny, and because he sets afoot all the evil that he does by their advice, the passage continues,

*Matt 24:24

XXXIII. 57. *His eyes are like the eyelids of dawn.** His eyes are of course fixed in his head and serve the purpose of vision, so they are not unreasonably called his counselors. In fact they foresee how his actions should be performed with crooked devices, and they light the way for his malicious workers as if for his feet. They are rightly compared to the eyelids of dawn. We take the eyelids of dawn naturally to mean the final hours of the night, during which night opens its eyes as it were and already shows the start of approaching light. The prudent worldly people, accordingly, who are adherents of the malice of Antichrist by their crooked counsel, are as it were eyelids of the dawn, and they declare the faith in Christ that they find to be a kind of error of night while promising that the veneration of Antichrist is the real morning. They promise of course that they are going to dispel the darkness and declare the light of truth by means of illuminating signs, because they can convince nobody of what they wish unless they declare that they are offering something better.

*Job 41:9

That is why that very serpent in Paradise spoke to the first human beings, pretending to offer them something better, as if he were opening the eyelids of the dawn, and he reproved the ignorance of their unspoiled minds, promising the knowledge of divinity. It was as though he were banishing the darkness of ignorance and declaring the divine morning of eternal knowledge as he said, *Your eyes will be opened. You will be like gods knowing both good and evil.** In the same way that other condemned man will come in his time, he whose eyes are compared to the eyelids of dawn; his wizards will repudiate the simplicity of true faith as if it were the darkness of the night that had passed, and they will point to Antichrist's lying signs as if they were the rays of the rising sun. But our Leviathan not only

*Gen 3:5

has eyes to foresee evil with malicious intentions, but he also opens his mouth to pervert the minds of human beings, because through crooked preachers he incites the hearts of their listeners to love the deceit of error. So the Lord rightly adds,

XXXIV. 58. *Torches come out of his mouth.** Those who foresee are called eyes, and those who preach are called mouths. But from this mouth torches come, and they set the mouths of the hearers on fire with love of faithlessness. So where they shine as if by wisdom, there without any doubt they burn by means of depravity. But we are shown how this wisdom can be their light when he forthwith goes on to say,

*Job 41:10

XXXV. 59. *Like pine torches they are set on fire.** See how exactly their hypocrisy is described already, they whose preaching is compared to pine torches! When a pine torch is first lit, you see, it has a sweet odor but a faint light. It is the same way with these preachers of Antichrist; they take unto themselves an appearance of sanctity, but the works they perform are the works of evil. They give off an odor that seems innocent, but their light is darkness. Their odor comes from their pretense of justice, but they burn in darkness by perpetrating what is evil.

*Job 41:10

John describes their malice fully in the Apocalypse where he says, *I saw another beast rising from the earth, and it had two horns like the horns of a lamb, while it spoke like the dragon.** He has already recounted the description of the first beast, that is, Antichrist, in an earlier verse. After that he says that this second beast rose, because after him the multitude of his preachers boasts of earthly power. Rising from the earth is in fact equivalent to pride in earthly power. This beast has two horns like those of a lamb, because the hypocrisy of holiness is a lie claiming to have what the Lord alone

*Rev 13:11

had in reality, that is, wisdom and life. However, under the appearance of the lamb the serpent's poison is injected into the reprobate sinners who are listening, so it is rightly added at that point, *It spoke like the dragon.** This beast then, which is a multitude of preachers, if it spoke boldly like the dragon would not look like the lamb, but it put on an appearance like the lamb so that it might set afoot the dragon's work. Both of these facts are expressed here by the pine torches that light up the darkness as an effect of malice, and by the sweet smell that arises from a similarity of life.

*Rev 13:11

60. But we are certainly not to suppose that it is only then that the preachers of Antichrist are to appear, or that they are now absent from human deception. Even now, before his actual appearance, some people preach him with their voices, and many more with their actions. Are they not preachers of his hypocrisy, who after they receive sacred orders from God hold on to the fugitive world with all their desires, and who pretend that their actions are virtuous when they are in fact all vices? But the more the minds of the chosen ones hold on to the interior light, the more exactly they should learn to distinguish vice from virtue.

Is it any wonder that we do in a spiritual fashion what we see money changers do daily in a material way? First they ascertain the coin's quality,* then its outward appearance, and finally its weight, lest what they take for gold is really brass, or what is true gold be dishonored by an outward counterfeit appearance, or what both is true gold and has a straightforward appearance does not carry a full weight. So it is with us when we notice a stranger working wonders: we should use the balance in our mind as if we were skilled money changers. We should first use our discretion to examine the gold, lest vice should hide under the appearance of virtue, and the

*silver, gold, or brass

action of a depraved intention should be softened by a look of rectitude. If then the quality of the intention be approved, the outline of the impressed image should be questioned, and whether the said quality originates from accredited minters, from the ancient fathers, in other words, and whether it is vitiated by any error as regards the similarity with their lives. So when the quality of the coin has been probed through the intention, and the correct appearance ascertained through a good sample, it remains to find out if it has the full weight. If then the good effect that shines in the signs and miracles does not have full perfection, it must be carefully weighed with caution and full consideration. If not, then an imperfect reality might be taken for a perfect one, and it might turn into a loss for the one who accepts it.

Accordingly, if the preachers of Antichrist do not know how the strength of a pure intention qualifies the things that they perpetrate, and hence whether they hold true minted quality, how do they know whether their actions show no search for the kingdom of heaven but rather a desire for the best of worldly honors? Or do they not see that they are at odds with some monetary value when contrary to all righteous reverence they persecute the righteous people? How in fact do they display in themselves a weight of integrity when not only are they strangers to the assiduous search for perfect humility, but they never even touched the entranceway of that humility? That is the very reason that the chosen ones can know how to disdain the signs that they work, those whose actions are obviously at odds with all that the holy fathers did and are remembered for. However, the chosen ones themselves, even while they see all these signs, while they disdain and are in horror at the life and miracles of Antichrist, nevertheless suffer a cloud of doubts in their hearts, because even while his malice elevates himself through these prodigies, their own clearer vision is darkened. So he again rightly adds,

*Job 41:11

XXXVI. 61. *Smoke came out of his nostrils.** The stare of his eyes is cut off by the smoke. Accordingly we are told that the smoke came out of his nostrils, because momentarily a cloud of darkness appeared in the hearts of the chosen ones on account of his treacherous miracles. Smoke came out of Leviathan's nostrils, because an alarming darkness confused the eyes of good people as a result of its lying prodigies. It is then indeed that in the hearts of the chosen ones, after those terrible signs have been witnessed, a dark thought gathers like a cloud. That is why, as I have already said, the mouth of Truth speaks in the Gospel: *False Christs and false prophets will arise, and they will work great signs and wonders, so that even the elect, if it were possible, might be led into error.**

*Matt 24:24

We must then earnestly seek out in this matter both how the chosen ones might be led into error and why the words *if possible* are said (as if it were subject to doubt) when the Lord is expected, who knows beforehand everything that is to happen. But since it is true both that the hearts of the chosen ones are struck by an alarming thought, and that they are unmoved by any inconstancy, the Lord includes all this in one brief sentence: *so that even the elect, if it were possible, might be led into error.* It is as though one were already in error if one's thoughts were shaken, but he immediately adds *if possible*, because it is undoubtedly impossible that the chosen ones should fall completely into error. But even the very fervor of souls is expressed in this dark smoke when he immediately adds,

*Job 41:11

XXXVII. 62. *Like a heated and boiling pot.** Every soul at that time is like a heated and boiling pot, because it suffers attacks from its own thoughts as if they were the foam of burning liquid. It is both burning zeal that moves them and the very oppression of the time that holds them enclosed within as if they were lidded pots. That is why when John wrote about the signs wrought by this beast, he also added, *So that he even caused fire to come down from heaven.** Actually fire coming down from heaven means that the flames of holy zeal come from the heavenly souls of the chosen ones. Our Leviathan is elsewhere called not only a serpent but even a ruler, since he governs the unclean spirits and people who are reprobate sinners, as Isaiah says: *A basilisk will come forth from the root of the snake.** It is incumbent upon us then to inquire with all diligence how the basilisk kills, so that from the actions of the basilisk its malice may become better known to us. The basilisk in fact does not kill with a sting, but it consumes with its breath. A gust of air often has such an effect that whatever the basilisk touches even at a distance with only the breath of its nostrils decays.

*Rev 13:13

*Isa 14:29

63. At this we are compelled to conclude that since smoke is said to come out of Leviathan's nose even before his first appearance, every day human hearts are affected by this death-dealing smoke from his nostrils. As we said above, this smoke weakens the fixed stare of our eyes, so it is rightly said that that smoke comes out of Leviathan's nostrils, through whose evil inspiration depraved thoughts arise in human hearts; they blunt the attention of our minds, lest we should see the internal light. Leviathan brings about darkness by the exhaled breath of his nostrils, and the amassed heat of multiplied thoughts arising from the love of material life gathers in the hearts of reprobate sinners through his inspirations and ambushes. He generates as it were dense masses of smoke while he piles up the most useless anxieties for the present life in the minds of worldly people.

This smoke from Leviathan's nose sometimes even reaches the eyes of the chosen ones. The prophet in fact suffered internally from this smoke when he said, *My eye was troubled at the wrath.** He was oppressed by the outpouring of the smoke, and he said, *My heart is troubled in my breast, and even the light of my eyes is gone from me.** Yes, this smoke assails the attention of the heart, because it troubles the tranquility of internal peace with a cloud of darkness. But God cannot be known except in tranquility of heart. That is why the same prophet also says, *Be free and know that I am God.** But the mind cannot be free when it is oppressed by the pouring out of this smoke, because the coils of worldly thoughts powered by the love of the present life keep twisting around inside it. So the light of eternal freedom is lost in this smoke, because the eye of the heart is confused by anxious cares and darkened by them.

*Ps 6:7

*Ps 37:11

*Ps 45:11

64. But this smoke troubles the souls of the chosen ones in one way, and in another way it blinds the eyes of reprobate sinners. From the eyes of good people, it is dispersed by the breath of spiritual desires, lest the wretched thoughts prevail with the density of the smoke. However, the more freely this smoke accumulates in the minds of depraved people through abominable thoughts, the more lightsome thoughts founded in truth are taken from them. The more the clouds of smoke increase, the more immoral desires are fostered in the hearts of the reprobate sinners.

65. We well know the windings of this smoke, because even when they wind, rise, and are dispersed, other windings rise from below, and even if some depraved desires pass, others rise along with carnal thoughts. The wretched mind in fact often sees what has already passed, but it does not see what is still there. It is glad that it is no longer subject to certain vices, but it neglects to be on its guard and to groan at the others that move up to occupy their place, to which perhaps it will succumb more wickedly. So it happens that while some vices pass, others keep rising, so this serpent retains its place in the hearts of reprobate sinners unceasingly. So the prophet Joel was right to say, *What the cutting locust left the swarming locust ate; what the swarming locust left the hopping locust ate; what the hopping locust left the destroying locust ate; wake up you drunkards and weep.**   *Joel 1:4-5

What else does the cutting locust mean that crawls along with its whole body but the vice of lust? It so ruins the heart that it holds that love of its former purity cannot rise. What is meant by the swarming locust that moves by flying leaps if not vainglory exalting itself by means of empty presumption? What does the hopping locust signify whose whole body is involved in feeding the stomach if not the vice of gluttony? What does the destroyer do but set on fire whatever it touches, and what else but wrath does it signify? So the swarming locust eats what the cutter left behind, because when the vice of lust leaves the mind, vainglory frequently takes its place. Because it is no longer laid low through love of the flesh, the mind boasts of chastity as if it were holy. What the swarming locust left behind the hopping locust ate, because if vainglory (which often arises as if motivated by holiness) is resisted, then the mind too readily gives in either to gluttony or to the satisfying of some desire or ambition. The mind that does not know God, you see, is led the more boldly to the satisfying of some desire of advancement the less it is controlled by any desire for human praise. What the hopping locust left behind, the destroying locust ate, because when gluttony is resisted by abstinence, the mind is dominated more fiercely by impatience and anger; like a blight on growing plants it eats up the harvest and ruins it. So the fire of impatience causes the fruit of virtue to decay. As long as vices give way to vices, one plague eats up the field of the mind while another leaves it.

66. So then Joel follows up with the phrase, *Wake up you drunkards and weep.** They are apparently called drunkards who, being confused by love of this world, do not sense the evils they are undergoing. What else in fact does it mean to say, *Wake up you drunkards and weep,* but shake off the dream of your insensitivity and avoid all these plagues of vices that fall upon you one by one in your ruined hearts? Stay awake and weep. The smoke then rises out of Leviathan's nose in as many circling coils as the base plagues consume the fruits of the heart with their secret whispering. The Lord solicitously expresses the force of this smoke when he quickly adds, *Like a heated and burning pot.** The pot is heated when the human mind is aroused by the persuasion of the hostile enemy, but the pot is burning when the mind is already hot even through consent and is set on fire with desires ignited by perverse persuasion. It raises just as many waves by being churned up as it dares to commit evil acts externally.

*Joel 1:5

*Job 41:11

The prophet had foreseen this heating of the pot of the carnal consciousness coming from Leviathan's smoke when he said, *I see a boiling pot turned away from the north wind.** It is from the north, you see, that the pot of the human heart is heated when the spiritual adversary sets it on fire by instigating it with illicit desires. It is he who said, *I will take my seat on the mount of the covenant, at the edge of the north.** And the mind that Leviathan once took over through the breeze of evil persuasion he heats up with a fire set beneath it, and not content with present evil, he keeps heating up the desires without stopping. So by desiring some contemptible things, the mind disdains others already obtained. Some-

*Jer 1:13

*Isa 14:13

times the mind is avid for its own advantage, sometimes it contradicts someone else's convenience even at its own disadvantage, sometimes it satisfies the illicit desires of the flesh, sometimes as though in a certain peak experience, caught in a thought of pride, having put aside the care of the flesh, it lifts himself up totally in a wind of pride. Consequently, since the heart is led by various desires and is incited by our Leviathan's instigation, his smoke is rightly said to be like a heated and boiling pot, and the consciousness is blown up by so much heat from his temptations that its prideful thoughts expand within. Truth more clearly explains what happens with other words as the Lord adds,

XXXVIII. 67. *His breath sets the coals on fire.** *Job 41:12
What else does he call coals but the minds of reprobate sinners that were set on fire by worldly concupiscence? They burn, of course, when they desire anything worldly. Desires naturally burn, and they will not let the soul remain quiet and whole. So Leviathan's breath sets the coals on fire as often as his secret suggestions draw human minds to illicit pleasures. Some of them he inflames with the torches of pride, others with envy, others with lust, and still others with avarice. He placed a torch of pride near Eve's mind when he tempted her to treat the words of the Lord's commandment lightly;* *Gen 3:6
he set Cain's soul on fire with envy when God's acceptance of his brother's sacrifice made him sad, and that is what caused him to go so far as the crime of fratricide.* He set Solomon's heart on fire with the torch of *Gen 4:5
lust when he subjected him to such an intense love of women that he was even led to the veneration of idols, and while he followed the pleasures of the flesh he forgot the reverence due to the Creator.* He also burned *1 Kgs 11:4
up Ahab's soul with fire when he forced him to covet someone else's vineyard with impatient desires, and in

this way he even constrained him to commit murder.* *1 Kgs 21:2
So strong is Leviathan's breath with which he breathes on coals that he inflames human minds to perform illicit acts with the application of secret suggestions. So he quickly goes on:

XXXIX. 68. *And flames escape from his mouth.** *Job 41:12
The flames in his mouth are of course the very instigation of secret words. He speaks words of evil persuasion to anyone's soul, but flames escape from his mouth, because the soul burns with desires when instigated by his suggestions. He makes suggestions daily, and he never stops making suggestions until the end of the present life. But at that time he grows still more terrible, when he comes through that condemned man and shows himself more openly in the glory of this world. Then a thicker smoke comes out of his nostrils, and a more widespread instigation strikes at human hearts that are terrified and in admiration over his signs. Then his breath heats up coals more violently, because the minds of reprobate sinners, which he finds already hot with the love of worldly glory, he incites with the wind of his suggestions, even to the wickedness of inflicting cruelty. Then flames escape from his mouth, because whatever he speaks himself or through his preachers is fire by which the barren wood is burnt up. So their minds are touched by the fire of worldly concupiscence, those who never desire to become as precious metals.

Those people therefore who do not want to be affected by the flames from his mouth according to the directive of the teacher of truth should be careful to be found not as wood, straw, or stubble, but as gold, silver, and precious stones.* The easier one shows oneself to be *1 Cor 3:12
convinced by him, you see, the more liable that one is to be burnt up by the fire of his persuasion. While we by no means concede that the mind residing in this corruptible

flesh is never touched by the heat of his persuasion, still it remains true that when the mind is burned by his evil wind, it must turn to the work of prayer without ceasing. The water of tears will extinguish the flame of his suggestions more quickly.

BOOK 34

I. 1. Since we carry a body from this world, let us consider the end of the universe from the point of view that we are part of it. We will more easily understand the nature of the end of the world if we carefully take notice of what we carry about the world. Our life energy thrives more actively through the years of adolescence, but in our old age we wither because of the multiplying bodily weaknesses that we carry, and the longer our lifetime is extended for us to be preserved, the more we daily fail instead of dying, and we live from moment to moment. In the same way the world's time grows longer with the passing years, and it is affected by the misfortunes that frequently happen; where it feels the advancing years, there it senses the cost of salvation. Troubles increase with the passage of time, and we more weakly tolerate a diminishment of life the longer our life lasts.

So the ancient enemy is let loose with all his power against Job, and that enemy, who himself had already died for having lost the blessed state of his heavenly creation, will then be completely extinguished when he is denied liberty to tempt and is bound for the eternal fire. So the one who is going to tempt approaches the final end of the world in a more ruthless frame of mind, because the closer he senses himself to be to the penalty, the greater is the ferocity to which he is aroused. He calculates of course that the time is near when he will lose the permission of most wicked freedom, and the shorter the time that restricts him, the greater is the extent of the cruelty that enlarges him, as that angelic voice told John: *Woe to you, earth and sea, because* the devil has gone down to you, and great is his anger, because he knows his time is short.* Therefore his great anger grows hot at that time, lest he who could not remain in the blessed state should rush into the pit of his condemnation accompanied by only a few. It is then that he craftily figures out whatever his wickedness can accomplish; it is then that he lifts up his proud neck higher, and through that condemned man he carries, he wickedly demonstrates all that can prevail in a temporal sense. So the voice of God rightly speaks up now:

*Rev 12:12

II. 2. *Strength will reside in his neck.** And what does the neck of our Leviathan signify if not the extension of pride? It is the neck that he lifts up against God, and he even rises with the pride of power and the pretense of holiness. The prophet Isaiah bears witness that the neck symbolizes pride when he accuses the daughters of Jerusalem, saying, *They walked with stiff necks.** So we are told that strength resides in our Leviathan's neck, because power is added to support his pride. Whatever is proudly extolled at that time, you see, and whatever is craftily devised, is carried out with the help of worldly power. That is what the prophet Daniel foresaw and spoke of: *Guile will prosper in his hand.** The guile in his hand is of course dishonest power, because he can forcefully carry out whatever he wants in his wickedness for a short time. We are told that his guile prospers, because his malicious guile is not impeded by any difficulty. Our Leviathan, you see, tends to have an ample supply of instruments of his own, which can execute wickedly what they wickedly desire and thus add to the pile of his wickedness.

*Job 41:13

*Isa 3:16

*Dan 8:25

3. When the chosen ones are by chance weakened, you see, and they give in to illicit desires, they are often kept in that state by the hand of the divine gift, and they experience no effects of their wretched will. When, however, a wholesome contrary attitude arises from their prayers, their moral inability is often cured, and in their interior disposition a wonderful process occurs by which a change of their evil will is brought about by conversion, while their weakness forbids perfection. That is why, under the image of any individual soul, the Lord speaks through the prophet about the weakness of Judea while she is following depraved paths: *Behold, I am going to surround your path with thorns, and I will surround you with a stone wall, and you will not be able to find your own paths. You will follow after your lovers and not reach them; you will search for them and not find them. Then you will say, "I will go and return to my first husband, because I was better off then than I am now."**   *Hos 2:6-7

The paths of the chosen ones are surrounded by thorns, and they feel the pain of their stabbing in the things that they desire in a worldly sense. It is like a stone wall that blocks their way when it is the difficulty of perfection that resists their desires. Their souls are in fact seeking their lovers, but they do not find them, when by following evil spirits they never reach the pleasures of this world that they so desire. It is rightly added that this difficulty soon bids them say, *I will go and return to my first husband, because I was better off then than I am now.* Her first husband is of course the Lord, who joins a chaste soul to himself by introducing the love of the Holy Spirit. It is he then whom every person's mind loves when it finds so much bitterness, resembling the pricking of thorns, in the very pleasures that it desires in the world. So when the soul starts feeling the sting of the world's adversities (the world that it loves), then it understands fully how much better off it was with its former husband.

4. Accordingly adversity often cures people who have gone astray through a depraved will. It is of course less to be feared that they should find prosperity after they have desired unrighteousness, since it is more difficult to amend evil that is based even on perfect prosperity. As for our Leviathan then, who along with his members is set apart for eternal tortures, the deceit in his hands is so guided and the stiffness of his neck so maintained that he fulfills his base desires against good people in this world with crooked skill; so true is this that the less present adversity stands against him, the less future prosperity awaits him. And since everyone who familiarizes himself or herself with Leviathan's friendship by means of perverse behavior first loses the true riches of the mind, the Lord rightly adds,

III. 5. *Poverty goes before his face.** The word *face* usually denotes knowledge. That is why it is written, *My face will go before you.** In other words, knowledge will be the guide. We should know, however, that in Holy Scripture poverty connotes one thing when used for the chosen ones and something else when used for reprobate sinners. The poverty of the chosen ones means that when the true riches of the heavenly homeland are given back to their souls, they who reside in the wretched exile of this present life should remember how poor they are. They in fact sigh without ceasing for those riches about which Paul says, *That you may know what is the hope of his call, what are the glorious riches of his inheritance in the saints.** And since they by no means see them as yet, they intensely groan in the meantime at the wretchedness of this poverty.

Jeremiah had surely comprehended this poverty when he said, *I am a man who sees my poverty in the rod of his indignation.** The rod of God's indignation is his intended stroke. The human being suffered God's indignation when he was evicted from Paradise and lost the true riches of interior joy. But since all the chosen

*Job 41:13

*Exod 33:14

*Eph 1:18

*Lam 3:1

ones unceasingly face the fact that they have fallen into the poverty of the present life from the state of easy native possession, it is rightly said, *I am a man who sees my poverty.* All those then who still desire what they can see do not understand the evil of the present state of pilgrimage, and they cannot see that they are suffering. The prophet David was contemplating this poverty when he said, *My strength in poverty is weakness.** We are thus told that strength in poverty is weakness, because the soul, having fallen in this state of pilgrimage and been beaten back by the distress of its state of corruption, is hindered from the contemplation of that which it has lost.

*Ps 30:11

6. Reprobate sinners, however, cannot contemplate poverty, because as long as they follow after the things they see, they neglect the thought of what is invisible that they have lost. Therefore their state is properly called a state of want, since they are filled with vices and empty as regards the riches of virtue. It often happens to them that they are lifted up through insane pride while they never consider their loss a headlong fall, nor do they realize that they are destitute as regards good works. That is why the preacher at Laodicea is told by the angel, *You say you are rich and prosperous and have need of nothing, and you do not know how wretched you are, nor how pitiable, poor, blind, and naked.** She asserts that she is rich who extols herself by a pretense of holiness, but she is accused of poverty, blindness, and nakedness. She is surely poor because she lacks the riches of virtues, blind because she does not even see the poverty she suffers, naked because she lost her first garment, and still worse because she does not even know she lost it.

*Rev 3:17

Since accordingly, as we have said, the poverty of reprobate sinners is the self-denial of merits, it is rightly said of Leviathan, *Poverty goes before his face.**

*Job 41:13

Absolutely no one is admitted to his or her knowledge unless first undressed as regards the riches of virtues. First he cuts off good thoughts, and then as it were he turns on for them the open knowledge of his wickedness. Yes, poverty is said to go before his face, because vigorous ability is first lost so that his familiar knowledge may afterwards be experienced. Or surely he creeps up on many people so deceitfully that they can never become aware of him, so that he can dispose of their virtues as long as he does not let them see his malice and craftiness; so we are told that poverty goes before his face, as if he said openly that when he tempts from ambush he despoils them before he can be seen.

That is why the prophet says about Ephraim, *Strangers have consumed his vigor, and he did not know it.** Strangers surely tend to be understood as the apostate angels who eat up our strength when by distorting the power of our mind they devour it. That is what Ephraim unknowingly suffered, because being tempted by the evil spirits, he both lost the power of the soul and did not know what he had lost. So poverty goes before Leviathan's face, because he despoils the minds of the negligent people whom he tempts before those who are tempted know about the ambush. So what was said before—*Strength will reside in his neck*—shows his violent force, whereas what follows—*Poverty goes before his face*—signifies refined deceit.

*Hos 7:9

7. Although we know what is meant by the fact that poverty goes before his face, there is another point that we must consider more sternly. Before our Leviathan appears in the guise of that condemned man whom he assumes, by a terrible process of a secret plan the church is deprived of the signs of power. Prophecy is concealed, the grace of healing is taken away, the virtue of prolonged abstinence decreases, the word of preaching is silenced, and lavish miracles are taken away. The heavenly plan by no means takes away all these things utterly; it is just that she does not as at earlier times display them openly and frequently. This reality comes about by means of a wonderful plan by which piety and justice are wrought together in accord with divine government.

While Holy Church appears more commonplace in this way, deprived of the power of signs, it happens both that the rewards of good people grow greater, because they venerate the church in the hope of heaven and not because of the signs that she presents, and the minds of bad people are quickly shown to be against the church; they neglect the following of the invisible reality that she promises, because they are not impressed by visible signs. Accordingly, since the humble faithful are deprived as it were of the multitude of manifest signs, the hidden plan holds a terrible trial, more generous in mercy for those who are good but heavier in righteous anger for those who are bad. So before our Leviathan becomes manifest and conspicuous, in large part the signs of power in Holy Church cease, and we are told, *Poverty goes before his face.**   *Job 41:13

First, you see, abundant miracles are taken away from the faithful, and then that ancient enemy shows himself against them through public prodigies, so that where he exalts himself through signs, he is beaten more stoutly and praiseworthily by the faithful without signs. However, even for the faithful in that battle, signs will not be lacking, but the enemy's signs will be so many that ours will seem either few or none at all. In fact their virtue becomes stronger than all his signs when it tramples down with the heel of internal constancy all the terrible things he does. But the malignant enemy shows himself to be as fierce and brutal against them as he groans at their contempt of the growing fame of his miracles. Accordingly he gathers himself for their total ruin, and he collects all the reprobate sinners with united cruelty to kill the faithful; he imposes his ferocity as strongly as he desires to move perversely against them, so that no member of his body should resist his intention. So the Lord rightly adds,

IV. 8. *His carnal members stick to him.** Leviathan's carnal members are all the reprobate sinners who do not rise to the recognition of the spiritual homeland by desire. His carnal members are those who are joined to those who behave perversely and who precede them in acting wickedly. Paul speaks like that in a contrary sense of the body of the Lord: *You are the body of Christ member by member.** A member of a body is one thing, and a member of a member is another. A member of a body is of course a part of a whole, whereas a member of a member is a small part of a large part. A member of a member is as a finger to a hand or a hand to an arm; a complete member of a body has reference to the complete body. Accordingly, just as in the spiritual body of the Lord we speak of members of members, and we are speaking of those who are governed by others in God's church, so also in that reprobate congregation of Leviathan there are carnal members who by their evil behavior are joined together with others who are wicked. But because in the unjust enemy from first until last there is perfect agreement in perverse behavior, the word of God mentions that the carnal members adhere to one another. So they unanimously sense what is perverse, and there is no division or dispute among them on that account. At that time also no argument or disagreement will separate them, and consequently they will violently prevail against those who are good, because they agree on what is evil. Just as we have already said above that disunity among good people is dangerous, so it is still

*Job 41:14

*1 Cor 12:27

more dangerous when there is unity among those who are evil. In fact the unity of reprobate sinners places as many difficult obstacles on the road of good people as their gathering is oppressive for them.

9. Paul foresaw how dangerous the unity of reprobate sinners would be for him when he found himself placed among the Sadducees and Pharisees, so he said, *It is about the hope and resurrection of the dead that I am being judged.** Thereupon the crowd of those in attendance burst out in contrary expostulation, and the confused multitude divided into two parties, opening for Paul a way of escape, because he whom the united crowd of persecutors had confined was let loose once that crowd became divided. Accordingly the righteous people escape when the unrighteous are divided, because the wishes of the chosen ones are perfectly fulfilled when the army of reprobate sinners is disordered by discord. This fact is nicely signified by the dividing of the Red Sea. When the water was divided into two parts, you see, it was opened for the chosen people to cross to the promised land, because when the unity of evildoers is shattered, the minds of good people are led to the fulfillment of their desires. If the unity of bad people had not been injurious, God's providence would never have separated the languages of the haughty people in such wide diversity; if the unity of bad people had not been injurious, the prophet would not say about the enemies of Holy Church, *Destroy them, O Lord, and confound their tongues.**

*Acts 23:6

*Ps 54:10

Accordingly, since our Leviathan is at that time to be unrestrained as regards his power, he is to be allowed also to have unity among reprobate sinners in order to enhance his malice, so that he can exert his power against us forcefully to the extent that he fights us not only with the robust power of boldness, but also with the massive bulk with which he is endowed. But who can equal this power? What mental power would not shake with fear from the very root of thought at the weight of so proud and compact a covenant? So because he sees us shake with fear through our weakness, God's pity forthwith adds what he does on his own account. The next verse:

V. 10. *He will send against him flashes of lightning that will not be borne to any other place.** What else is signified by the term *flashes of lightning* but the fearful sentence of that final Judgment? They are called *flashes of lightning* because they of course strike those to whom they are sent and burn them forever. Paul had seen a flash come upon him when he said, *The Lord Jesus will kill him with the breath of his mouth and destroy him by the illumination of his coming.** These flashes of lightning, however, which will be let loose against him will not be sent to any other place, because the righteous people will be rejoicing, and those flashes will only strike the reprobate sinners. After the threshing of the present life, you see, when the wheat sighs underneath the chaff, the winnowing shovel will distinguish between the wheat and the chaff in that Final Judgment, so that neither will the chaff be found on the threshing floor of the wheat, nor will any grains of wheat fall into the fire of the chaff. Those lightning flashes, then, will never touch any other place, because their fire will burn not the wheat, but the chaff. No penalty however will reform Leviathan, so the Lord continues and adds,

VI. 11. *Leviathan's heart will harden like a stone.** Yes, the heart of the ancient enemy will harden like a stone, because no repentance or conversion will ever soften it. No, only the blows of eternal retribution are ready for him, so the Lord rightly adds the following: *He will be hardened as by hammer and anvil.** The one who wields the hammer also fastens the anvil that alone

*Job 41:14

*2 Thess 2:8

*Job 41:15

*Job 41:15

is fit for the blows. For this purpose alone is the anvil set in place: to receive blow after blow. Consequently Leviathan is fastened like the hammer's anvil, because he is tied up by the chains of hell so that he may be beaten by repeated blows of eternal recompense. He is in fact struck in some way whenever any of the righteous people are saved while he waits in ambush, although also decaying with groans. It is on the anvil actually that new utensils are formed; Leviathan, however, is not changed by so many blows into a new utensil.

So Leviathan is correctly compared to an anvil, because by his persecution we are reformed, but he is himself always subject to blows, although never changed into a useful utensil. We leave him then to his eternal blows, while we are always struck by his temptations at the hand of the eternal Craftsman and are changed into little utensils formed by him. We then receive repeated blows from him only so that we may come to the eternal household as useful utensils. But Leviathan, like an anvil, is made fast, because while he goes around the world tempting, his position is in hell, where he is already sentenced to blows without wandering. The next verse:

VII. 12. *When he has been given up, the angels will be afraid, and those who are terrified will be purified.** Holy Scripture sometimes combines past with future in this way; sometimes it uses future tense instead of past or past tense instead of future. It uses future instead of past when John writes about a woman who is going to give birth, and says that she gives birth to a son who will rule the nations with an iron rod.* In this way was announced the coming incarnation of the Lord, which had already taken place. On the other hand, the past is used instead of the present when the Lord speaks through the psalmist: *They have pierced my hands and feet, and they have counted all my bones.** In these

*Job 41:16

*Rev 12:5

*Ps 21:17-18

words the appearances of the Lord's passion are described as though having already taken place, but in fact they were announced as going to take place far in the future. So concerning what is written here—*When he has been given up, the angels will be afraid*—there is nothing wrong with understanding the words spoken in the future tense as describing past events. Nor do we lose the sense of correct understanding if we believe that when our Leviathan fell from the citadel of the blessed the chosen angels were fearful because of his loss, so that when his fall into pride excluded him from their number, their very fear strengthened them to stand fast. So it follows: *those who are terrified will be purified.**

*Job 41:16

13. They were purified because he left heaven with the reprobate legions, and they alone were left behind in the heavenly seats who lived in eternity in the blessed state. Leviathan's fall then both terrified and purified them. It terrified them lest they should proudly despise their Creator, but it purified them because at the exclusion of the reprobate only the chosen ones stayed. God, the architect of the universe, knows how to use even the evil action of the reprobate for the good conduct of those who remain loyal, and he turns the collapse of the fallen into the good progress of those who remain, so when the sin of the proud ones was punished, an increase of merit was both found and strengthened for the humble angels. After the former proud angels fell, those who stayed were given the gift of never being able to fall. The holy angels then looked upon the loss of those who shared their nature; now they stand fast, more cautious as well as stronger. So with the Lord Creator of the universe arranging matters in a wonderful way, those chosen spirits profit from the ruin and loss to their homeland, as the kingdom was built up more sturdily where it had been partly ruined.

14. Because Holy Scripture often calls the church's preachers angels, in that they announce the glory of the heavenly homeland, we may take the angels mentioned in this passage to mean the holy preachers. That is why when John wrote to the seven churches in the Apocalypse, he spoke of the angels of the churches,* *Rev 1:4, 20 in other words, those who preached to the people. That is why the prophet said, *The angels of peace will weep bitterly.** The prophet Malachi also said, *The lips of* *Isa 33:7 *the priest hold knowledge; men should seek the Law from his mouth. He is the angel of the Lord of Hosts.** *Mal 2:7 Paul says for his part, *Great is the mystery of holiness, revealed in the flesh, justified in the spirit, shown to angels, preached to the nations, believed in the whole world, and taken up in glory.** So he who said that after *1 Tim 3:16 the hidden plan appeared to angels, and who added that it was preached to the nations, obviously used the name of angels for the holy preachers and signified thereby that they were messengers of truth.

15. *When he has been given up, the angels will be afraid, and those who are terrified will be purified.* If these words are interpreted as referring to the future, when the strict Judge is to come, the final condemnation of our Leviathan is signified, that is, when he is to be taken away from this world through the wrath of Judgment—he who at the present time is tolerated by a remarkable stay of meekness. Indeed he is cast away from here by such a tremendous weight of terror that even the holy preachers have their courage shaken. *When he has been given up, the angels will be afraid*, it says, because when he is seized by the whirlwind of justice, those who might still be in the body will be struck by fearful terror, and even the messengers from the heavenly homeland will be shaken. However courageous and perfect they may be when they are still here clothed with flesh, they cannot be free of any feeling of fear when confronted by such a tornado of terror. But when our Leviathan is seized, and when all the elements are shaken at his destruction, hope in the closeness of the kingdom gladdens the holy preachers, those who, as I have said, are at that time still in their bodies, and whom the weakness of the flesh troubles at the sudden display of wrath. There will then be in them both happy fear and fearful safety, because they will be both certain of remuneration in the heavenly kingdom and terrified by fear of so fierce a tornado because of the weakness of the flesh.

16. Let us then consider how the conscience of the wicked will be struck at that time, when even the lives of the righteous people will be troubled. What will they do who have hated the Judge's coming when even those who love it become frightened of such a terrible Judgment? And since the holy preachers' insides are baked by this fear, which removes any rust that remains in them from vices, after he said, *When he has been given up, the angels will be afraid*, he forthwith added, *and those who are terrified will be purified*. But since we know the end of Leviathan, let us now hear what he does before his ruin. The next verse:

VIII. 17. *When the sword overtakes him, neither spear nor armor will be able to stand.** In Holy Scripture the sword sometimes means either holy preaching, or eternal damnation, or temporary tribulation, or the ancient enemy's anger or persuasion. The sword means holy preaching when Paul says, *The sword of the spirit is the word of God.** The word *sword* signifies eternal damnation where it is written about heretical preaching, *Even if their children are many, their end is the sword.** However numerous his posterity may be here below, they will be consumed by eternal damnation. The sword is taken to mean temporary tribulation where it

*Job 41:17

*Eph 6:17

*Job 27:14

is said about the coming troubles of Mary, *The sword shall pierce your very soul.** Finally the sword signifies the wrath or persuasion of the ancient enemy when the psalmist says, *You freed your servant David from the evil sword.**

*Luke 2:35

*Ps 143:10

Kind indeed is the sword of holy preaching by which we are struck so that we may die to sin. But evil is the sword of the devil's persuasion by which anyone is struck with evil, so that he may be cut off from the way of righteousness. The sword of the ancient enemy is that condemned man who is to be assumed by him for the purposes of his service in the future. He sharpens that sword with malice and deception, and he pierces the hearts of weak people with it. Leviathan's sword grasps that condemned man when he receives him. On the other hand, if the word *sword* signifies his wrath, we are rightly told not that he took the sword, but that the sword took him. In fact he turns to such insanity that when he wants to be master of all, he is mastered by his wrath. Accordingly, when we take up wrath for the purpose of justice, we take up the sword, and possessing it under the impartiality of Judgment, we are in control. The one however who is seized by the precipitation of fury is held, not to grasp the sword, but to be grasped by the sword. He does not hold wrath and possess it, but by fierce wrath he is held.

18. It is clear to everybody, however, that we stab the adversary with the spear, but we are protected from the adversary by means of armor. With the spear we inflict wounds, and with armor we are protected from wounds. What else then does the spear signify but the dart of preaching, and what does armor signify if not the courage of patience? Our Leviathan then, who unleashes anger and every kind of cruelty by means of the reprobate person whom he takes over, is said to be caught by the sword. Through the display of immense power at that time he shows us whatever evil he is able to do. Neither spear nor armor can stand against him then, because he comes as Antichrist, and such great power will he seem to possess that if heavenly help is not present, he will even blunt the sharp point of preaching and put to naught the patience of suffering. Unless heavenly grace sustains the life of righteous people, the spear will not stand, because the power of preachers is broken; nor will armor provide resistance, because the patience of constancy will collapse and be pierced. So he adds,

IX. 19. *He will treat steel like straw and bronze like rotten wood.** Above he called a spear what now he names steel. What there he called armor, here he signifies as bronze. Steel is sharpened, you see, in order to wound the adversary, whereas bronze is almost never weakened by rust. By steel we understand the spear of preaching, and by bronze the constancy of patience. Under the name of Asher, Moses says of Holy Church, *Her shoe leather shall be steel and bronze.** Shoe leather is in fact taken to mean the fortification of preaching in Holy Scripture, since it is written, *Let your feet be shod with the preparation of the gospel of peace.**

*Job 41:18

*Deut 33:25

*Eph 6:15

Since therefore steel signifies virtue and bronze perseverance, steel and bronze are called shoe leather, because preaching is protected by the sharpness of steel and by constancy. With steel, preaching penetrates evil opposition, but with bronze it patiently preserves the good it had laid down. Preaching then forthwith repeats the church's perseverance more openly and says, *Just as the days of his youth, so will the days of his old age be.** But when our Leviathan takes up the sword that Holy Scripture calls Antichrist to put into practice his wicked designs, he will consider steel to be straw and bronze like rotten wood. Unless divine grace protects us, he

*Deut 33:25

will burn up the power of preaching like straw with the fire of his iniquity, and he will reduce the constancy of patience to dust as if it were rotten wood. The sharp point of steel and the hardness of bronze will fail when both the meaning of preaching is blunted and the longanimity of patience is blown away by the violence of his power.

20. Unless divine help should strengthen the chosen ones, how will the weak be described when even the strong are reckoned as straw? What then will our Leviathan do with the straw when he will reckon even steel as straw? What will he do with rotten wood when he will reduce the hardness of bronze to be like rotten wood? O, how many will there be who esteem their own powers to be like steel or bronze, and who will find themselves in that time of fire and trouble to be like straw? How many will there be who are hardened with the hardness of bronze and steel by depending on divine assistance after having been afraid of their weakness resembling straw? Against their adversaries they will be as much stronger with God's help as they remember how weak they were of themselves. But the higher Behemoth lifts himself against God's chosen ones by miracles, so much the more forcefully do all the saints constrain themselves to utter words of preaching against him. But he* possesses the minds of reprobate sinners so completely that he is never so challenged by the outbursts of truth as to let them loose.

*Behemoth

X. 21. *The bowman will not put him to flight.** What do we take the arrow to mean, if not the words of preachers? When such arrows are loosed by the voices of preachers who live right, they reach the hearts of those who listen. Holy Church had been hit by such arrows when she said, *I am wounded by love.** The psalmist's voice speaks of these arrows: *Children will shoot arrows at them and wound them.** Obviously the

*Job 41:19

*Song 2:5; 5:8

*Ps 63:8

words of humble people pierced the souls of those who are proud. The coming champion is told of these arrows, *Your arrows are sharp, O most powerful king; the people's hearts fail before you.** The bowman accordingly is the person who with the bow of holy attention fixes the words of correct exhortation in the hearts of listeners.

*Ps 44:6

Since therefore our Leviathan has only contempt for the words of preachers, and when he has gnawed the minds of reprobate sinners by his evil persuasion he immovably eyes the spears and stays with the reprobates, it is rightly said, *The bowman will not put him to flight.* It is as if he straightforwardly said, "The arrow of the holy preacher will not dismiss him from the hearts of reprobate sinners, because anyone whom he has seized already despises the preachers' words and does not hear them." So in his righteous anger against sins already committed, concerning those whom he has left in the hand of the ancient enemy the Lord says through the prophet, *I will send adders among you, snakes that cannot be charmed.** It is as if he said, "With righteous judgment I will hand you over to such unclean spirits as you cannot cast out with the exhortations of preachers as if they were voices of charmers." Since, however, our Leviathan cannot be moved from the reprobates' hearts by the arrowheads of holy preachers, his very contempt for the saints comes into play when he goes on,

*Jer 8:17

XI. 22. *For him sling stones are turned into stubble.** What but Holy Church is the sling reckoned to be? When the sling is cast, stones are hurled from it, and the adversaries' chests are struck. In the same way, when Holy Church is led with the changing times to a return of turbulence, strong people issue forth from her, by whose means wicked hearts are assailed as it were by blows from rocks. That is why the Lord told the prophet

*Job 41:19

about wise teachers, *They will devour and tread them down with the slingers of stones.** The holy teachers then lead others into virtue and devour enemies when they change them into their own body by the force of their way of life. The slingers bring these enemies into subjection when they teach the strong people in Holy Church to strike the hard-hearted and proud enemies. That is how the most monstrous Goliath was killed by a sling stone,* because the Devil's pride was brought down by a special stone of Holy Church.

*Zech 9:15

*1 Sam 17:49

He is Leviathan who, having entered that condemned man, despises the strong people in the church as weaklings and temporarily constrains them, so that it is now said, *For him sling stones are turned into stubble.** It is as if he said outright, "He reduces the power of the saints to the feeble likeness of stubble, because their tongue had as it were pelted his chest with harsh blows." In fact he is then to apply all the brute strength of his wickedness and to prevail against the saints with as much bodily savagery as was his pain at their overcoming him spiritually. And since he knows he will not prevail against them spiritually, he is to use up all the resources of his savagery against their flesh. It is no wonder if he has only contempt for human strength when he even disdains the eternal torture of heavenly Judgment that will be his lot. So the Lord continues,

*Job 41:19

XII. 23. *He will consider the hammer as stubble.** It is as if he said, "He despises even the weight of his notice that comes down to strike him for his punishment." In Holy Scripture, you see, the word *hammer* sometimes signifies the devil, by whose means the sins of evildoers are punished at the present time; sometimes however it is taken to mean a blow from heaven by which the chosen ones are either struck from a higher source, so that their crooked paths may be straightened, or righteous

*Job 41:20

anger may punish reprobate sinners, so that they may already receive the eternal punishment they deserve that will be shown them hereafter. The prophet for example testifies that the use of the word *hammer* indicates the ancient enemy when he asks, *How does it happen that the hammer of the whole earth is both struck down and broken?** It is as if he said, "Look at the one through whom the Lord struck down his vessels, who were to be formed for use in his service! Who can guess by what cataclysm at the coming of the Last Judgment he threw him down for eternal condemnation?"

*Jer 50:23

Again the hammer means a blow from heaven, such as is indicated when Solomon was building the temple, when it is said, *When the house was being built it was done with perfectly quarried stones, so that no hammer, axe, or iron tool could be heard in the house as it was being built.** What else did that house signify but Holy Church that the Lord inhabits in heaven? At her building the souls of all the chosen ones were set like well-finished stones. When she is built in heaven, no hammer of discipline is heard in her anymore, because we the hewn and perfect stones are led there so that we may be set in places befitting our merits. Here below, in the outskirts of the city as it were, we are shaped, so that we may arrive there without reproof. It is here that the hammer, the axe, and all the other shaping tools are heard.

*1 Kgs 6:7

But in the house of God no sounds are heard, because in the eternal homeland all the sounds of blows are finally silenced. Never does the hammer strike there, because no affliction attracts notice. Never does the axe strike, because for those who are received within, no external sentence of severity is passed. Never are iron tools heard, because no kind of chain whatever is felt there anymore. Accordingly, since the hammer's descent from above signifies the weight of a heavenly blow, how is it that our Leviathan has only contempt for the hammer, unless he disdains to notice any fear of a heavenly blow? He considers the hammer to be no more than straw, because he prepares himself for the weight of righteous anger as if for the slightest of terrors. So the Lord still more eloquently adds,

XIII. 24. *He derides the swiftly flying spear.** The Lord lets fly his spear against Leviathan, because he threatens to carry out a strict sentence of death against him. His letting fly the spear means that he is ready to turn his strict glare against him for eternal death. But the apostate spirit despises the Author of life even with his own death in view, and he derides the swiftly flying spear, because he foresees anything grave, anything horrible as coming to him from strict Judgment, and he fears no suffering; rather he clearly sees his inability to escape eternal torments, so he assumes insensitivity in his evildoing. When the worldly wise consider Leviathan's often confining himself with so much defiance and so much alarm to all that he desires, they turn their hearts to the service of his tyranny, and with all the wisdom they possess by God's gift they turn away from God to serve his enemy. So he rightly continues,

*Job 41:20

XIV. 25. *The rays of the sun will be below him.** When the sun is mentioned figuratively in Holy Scripture, sometimes it is the Lord, sometimes persecution; sometimes it means to show something up in a clear light, but sometimes the understanding of wisdom is intended. The Lord himself is signified in the Book of Wisdom when it proclaims that all the impious people will say on the day of the Last Judgment when they know their condemnation, *We have gone astray from the road of truth, and the light of justice did not shine upon us; nor did the sun rise for us.** It is as if he said outright, "The ray of internal light did not shine for us."

*Job 41:21

*Wis 5:6

That is why John said, *The woman was clothed with the sun, and the moon was under her feet.** We take the sun to mean the illumination of truth, but since the moon wanes when a monthly period has passed, we take it to mean changing times. Holy Church then is protected by the brightness of the heavenly light, so she is as it were clothed with the sun, but since she shows contempt for all that is subject to time, she treads on the moon with her feet.

*Rev 12:1

On the other hand, the sun signifies persecution, since Truth says in the Gospel that the seed germinating without roots withered at the sun's rising, obviously because the word that landed in the hearts of time-bound people ripened in a moment of time, and when the heat of persecution arrived it withered.* Again the sun sometimes signifies a display in clear light, as when the prophet proclaimed that the Lord of all appears to people's eyes, saying, *He pitched his tent in the sun.** It is as if he said, "He revealed the mystery of assumed human nature in the light of a clear vision." The same prophet* heard the divine voice through Nathan: *You acted in secret, but I will perform this word in the sight of all Israel in full view of the sun.** What else does the *full view of the sun* signify but the knowledge of clear sight? The word *sun* is also used for the knowledge possessed by the wise, since we find written in Revelation, *The fourth angel poured out his bowl on the sun, and he was given power to afflict people with heat and fire.** Obviously the pouring out of the bowl on the sun means to call for the punishment of persecution on the people who are famous for their reputation of wisdom: *and he was given power to afflict people with heat and fire.* When the people who are wise, you see, are won over because of torture, they are touched with the error of evildoing, and their example is enough to persuade

*Matt 13:5-6

*Ps 18:6

*David

*2 Sam 12:12

*Rev 16:8

the weak, who then burn with worldly desires. The downfall of the strong of course makes the loss of the weak more frequent.

And the sun signifies the incisiveness of wisdom, as Solomon says by means of a comparison: *The wise will endure like the sun, but the fool will change like the moon.** So in this passage,* what else do the rays of the sun signify but the incisiveness of wisdom? Since accordingly there are many people in Holy Church who seemed to shine with the light of wisdom but then were convinced by persuasion, terrified by threats, or broken by torture, so that they were thrown down before the sedition of our Leviathan, it is rightly said, *The rays of the sun will be below him.** It is as if we were clearly told, "Those who seemed to shed rays of light within Holy Church through their incisive wisdom and to shine on high through the authority of their upright conduct prostrated themselves to the power of our Leviathan by wicked deeds; no longer did they preach upright conduct, so that they shone on high, but instead they perversely served and obeyed him." The sun's rays are then beneath him when even some of the learned people do not raise their pointed spears by acting freely, but prostrate themselves before the feet of our Leviathan both by their perverse actions and by their wheedling flattery; so intelligence that like the sun was above them by the gift of heaven was thrown down before the ancient enemy's feet for the sake of earthly desires.

*Sir 27:12
*of Job

*Job 41:21

So even now, when any of the learned teachers subject themselves by the downfall of flattery to earthly powers or evildoers for the sake of temporary advantage or honor in daily life, it is as though they prostrated themselves before the feet of the coming Antichrist together with the rays of the sun. Behemoth then even humbles the light of heaven below himself while he tramples upon the learned minds through their fatal assent. The rays of the sun throw themselves down at our Leviathan's feet as often as those who seem to shine with the light of teaching find errors in Holy Scripture with their misdirected perceptiveness, and with crooked understanding they cast themselves down before his deviations. Since they lift themselves up against the honest preaching of truth, they become Leviathan's slaves by their false perceptions. The rays of the sun are beneath Leviathan as long as any learned people, or those in whom the light of intelligence predominates, either lift themselves up in pride over those whom they despise or put aside their better thoughts to dirty themselves with grubby desires of the flesh, or if they forget heaven and get involved in worldly affairs, or if they do not remember that they are earth and boast idly of their knowledge of heaven. So it is rightly added,

XV. 26. *He throws down gold from him as if it were clay.** The word *gold* in Holy Scripture is sometimes taken to mean the glory of the divine nature, sometimes the brightness of the heavenly city, sometimes the virtue of love, sometimes the shining of worldly honor, sometimes the beauty of holiness. For example, the word *gold* signifies the interior glory of the divine nature, as when the form of the bridegroom is described in the Song of Songs: *His head is finest gold.** Since God is Christ's head,* and none of the metals is brighter than gold, the Bridegroom's head is called gold, because his humanity is governed for us by the glory of his divinity.

On the other hand, the word *gold* is taken to mean the brightness of the heavenly city, just as John testifies that he has seen it: *the city itself was pure gold as clear as glass.** The gold of which that city is made is obviously said to be like glass, so that the gold might shine and the glass be seen as transparent. Again, the word *gold*

*Job 41:21

*Song 5:11
*1 Cor 11:3

*Rev 21:18

signifies love, so the angel John saw speaking to him was girded with a golden cincture around his breast,* because the citizens of heaven no longer had chests subject to the fear of punishment, nor were they divided from one another by any divergence, but they were united by love alone. To have a golden cincture around one's breast means that all thoughts of changeable feelings are restrained by chains made up of love alone.

*Rev 1:13

Again the word *gold* signifies the brightness of worldly honor, as the prophet says, *Babylon is a golden cup.** And what does Babylon's name mean if not the glory of this world? She is said to be a golden cup because while she displays the beauty of the world she makes foolish minds drunk with desire for her, so that they might desire earthly beauty and have only contempt for invisible beauty. Eve was inebriated by this golden cup with her first willful act, about which sacred history has this to say: when she desired the forbidden tree, she saw that it was lovely to behold, that it was a delight to see, and she ate its fruit.* Babylon then is a golden cup, because she displays a vision of external beauty but no feeling for interior righteousness. On the other hand, the word *gold* signifies the radiance of holiness, because the prophet Jeremiah laments that the radiance of justice in the Jewish people was traded for the darkness of wickedness with the words, *How has the gold been disfigured? How has its high color been transformed?** It is just as we said above: Gold is darkened when the darkness of wickedness follows and the beauty of justice is abandoned. Bright color is changed when radiant innocence turns into the repulsiveness of sin.

*Jer 51:7

*Gen 3:6

*Lam 4:1

27. The word *clay,* however, signifies in Holy Scripture sometimes the ubiquity of things made of earth, sometimes the evil teaching that smacks of impurity, and sometimes the enticement of desires of the flesh.

It signifies the ubiquity of earthly things, as when the prophet Habakkuk says, *Woe to the person who multiplies goods that do not belong to him. How long will you keep piling up thick clay against yourself?** He weighs himself down with thick clay who piles up earthly goods by avarice and confines himself with the heavy weight of his own sin. On the other hand *clay* signifies the one who devises a teaching that inculcates impurity, as when the same prophet tells the Lord, *You sent your horses into the sea and troubled many waters.** It is as if he said, "You have opened up a road for your preachers through the doctrines of this world that smack of the dirty things that belong to earth." The word *clay* also expresses a desire for sordid pleasures such as those the psalmist deplores, saying, *Deliver me from the mud, so that I may not sink.** The clay that sticks of course means the filthy desires and concupiscence of the flesh that defile us.

*Hab 2:6

*Hab 3:15

*Ps 68:15

*of Job

28. In this passage,* then, gold signifies the brightness of holiness. There is in addition no reason that we should not take the clay to mean either avarice for worldly possessions, or contagious wicked teachings, or the filth that accrues to pleasures of the flesh. But there are many people who are now inside Holy Church and who seemed to shine with the brightness of justice, but whom our Leviathan later tripped up either by concupiscence for worldly possessions, or by the contagion of erroneous teachings, or by their own pleasures of the flesh, and who beyond any doubt threw down their gold like so much clay. Throwing down gold like clay certainly means trampling underfoot a person's pure way of life through illicit desires, so that they who formerly blushed at the sight of his glowing life of virtue might also follow his muddy footsteps. The ancient enemy will in fact later mock some people with an appearance of holiness, while he traps others with the repulsive vices of a life according to the flesh. Then indeed he will act openly in such matters, but at present he secretly takes over the hearts of many people, just as the apostle Paul said: *So that he may be revealed in his own time, since the mystery of iniquity is already at work.** As often then as he throws down gold like clay underfoot even now, just so often does he distract the thoughts of those who live in chastity through evil habits of the flesh. As often as he tramples upon gold like clay, so often does he scatter their pure thoughts through base desires. He will act all the more violently in this way later on, when he is subject to the loss of his liberty, and he will then perpetrate what he wants with less restraint.

*2 Thess 2:6-7

29. Perhaps someone will wonder why a merciful God would allow such things to happen, namely that our Leviathan should—either now by his cunning suggestions or later by that condemned person whom he will possess—either make subject to himself the rays of the sun, that is, various learned and wise people, or throw down beneath himself gold like clay, that is, people who are radiant with the brightness of holiness by soiling them with vices. But our quick answer is this: the gold that Leviathan could cast down underfoot like clay was never gold in God's sight. The people who could be seduced at a time when they would not return seem in the eyes of men and women to lose holiness as if it were a garment, but in God's eyes they never had it. People are often in fact secretly involved in many sins, but with one solitary virtue they appear to have greatness. But even this one virtue becomes vain and fails; as long as people notice it, it is undoubtedly praised, and such praise is eagerly welcomed. So it happens that even this virtue is no virtue in God's sight when it hides what is displeasing and profits from what is pleasing.

What then could be meritorious in the Lord's eyes, when evil is hidden and goodness is public? Pride, as we have said, is often hidden, while purity is noticed, and just because chastity remains long obvious, it is lost near the end of life, because pride has remained covered up and unrepented even to life's end. One person is free to give alms, so he distributes his own property; he is however a slave to many acts of injustice, or perhaps his tongue is active in detraction. It often happens too that the person who was merciful is goaded toward the end of his or her life to greed and cruelty. This certainly happens by just judgment, so that the one who pleased people publicly lost the wherewithal to please them, and he or she never took the trouble to correct what was displeasing to God. Some others try to practice patience, but they are not afraid to envy other people or to keep malice in their hearts, so they get impatient sometimes, because they harbored pain too long. All these people are partly gold and partly clay. And even the gold is cast down when hidden sins require it, and even the virtue that was publicly famous was dissipated. But we will appreciate the price of the work if we carefully weigh virtue of a higher order.

30. Almighty God, you see, often puts up with people's hidden sins for a long time and freely gives his chosen ones their public good conduct for their future advantage. There are people, you see, who abandon the world, but not at all completely, and they eagerly take hold of the narrow way that they are not going to persevere in, but they incite others by their own example to seek out the narrow way, those who are going to persevere in it. So it often happens that the former seem to live a good life in the sight of others, but their way of life is not for their own sake but for that of others who are chosen; yes, those who are not going to persevere incite others by their own example to seek out a good way of life, those who are going to persevere in it. We often see others enter upon the way and hasten on towards a specified place, while others who see them start to follow them, so both groups make for the same place together. However, it often happens that a critical moment arrives and a sudden collision takes place, so that those who were in the lead turn around, and those who followed reach the goal. It is exactly the same when those who are not going to persevere seize upon the road of holiness.

There is a reason that those who are not going to finish start upon the road of virtue, and it is this: that they may show the way by which those who are going to come later should walk. Their case serves the progress of the chosen ones, and the advantage is not meager, because when the latter notice the fall of the former, they become fearful for their own state, and the ruin that condemns the forerunners humbles the followers. In this way they learn to put their trust in the protection of heavenly help, since they can see many people along the way who have fallen on account of their own strength. So when reprobate sinners seem to act well, they point out a clear road, as it were, to the chosen ones who follow them, but when they go bad and fall into a wicked path, they point out to the following chosen ones where they should avoid the pit of pride. So let our Leviathan go and put the sun's rays beneath him, casting down the gold as if it were clay. Almighty God knows how to derive benefit from the evil of reprobate sinners to comfort his chosen ones, while those who are going to reach him make progress toward him by their own merits, and if they ever think proudly, they are often set right by the downfall of others. But if Leviathan acts in this way even with those whom he honored by showing them some virtue, what do you think he will do with those whose mind is in some way not lifted up away from worldly concupiscence? The word of God gives us an answer clearly expressed when he says,

XVI. 31. *He will make the deep sea boil like a pot.** What else but the life of worldly people is meant by the sea, and what by the deep but their deeply hidden thoughts? And our Leviathan causes this deep sea to boil like a pot, because it stands to reason that at the time of the final persecution his zeal will be aroused to urge the souls of reprobate sinners to light the flame of cruelty against the lives of the chosen ones. Then the very depths of the sea will boil like a pot, when Leviathan sets the hearts of the lovers of this world on fire with a blazing heat, and what they have kept closely hidden inside their malice during this time of peace they will let burst out in a furious rage of persecution; they will let loose through sudden freedom of open cruelty all the hatred of ancient spite that they have held back so long. Because they were persuaded by a fatal mistake they become such zealous slaves of Antichrist that they then consider themselves truer worshipers of Christ. So after he said, *He will make the deep sea boil like a pot*, he goes on to say fittingly,

*Job 41:22

XVII. 32. *He makes the sea boil like ointment.** When ointment is boiled, of course, it gives forth a sweet fragrance. Accordingly, since our Leviathan seduces the hearts of reprobate sinners in such a way that whatever they do out of the wickedness of unbelief they think they are doing for the sake of truth and correct faith, what they are doing for religious zeal smells sweet to them. That is why Truth says in the gospel, *Anyone who kills you will think he is worshiping God.** Accordingly they boil like a pot while they are carrying out their persecution with cruelty, but for them that very persecution is redolent with the fragrance of ointment,

*Job 41:22

*John 16:2

while their minds are deceived by vain suspicions, and they suppose that they are offering worship to God. In holy Scripture, you see, the odor of ointment ordinarily signifies the reputation for virtue. That is why, when the bride in the Song of Songs desires the presence of the Bridegroom, she says, *We run following the odor of your ointments.** And the apostle Paul, knowing that he has the odor of the praise of virtue, says, *We are the sweet odor of Christ toward God.** *Song 1:3

*2 Cor 2:15

So our Leviathan seizes for the use of his lost instrument such ministers as have the reputation of praise and the clothes of virtue to do the work of cruelty. He then says, *He will make the deep sea boil like a pot*, and quickly follows up: *He makes the sea boil like ointment.** What therefore makes the sea boil like a pot through the fire of cruelty is the same fire as drives those who hold the false title of virtue for their judgment; it is as if he displayed how the ointment boils so that they might become as fierce in cruelty as they suppose themselves deserving a reward as if for religious zeal. This is righteous divine judgment, that those who neglect to cultivate and keep the habit of religious loyalty are deceived by the odor of its trace. That is why for the sake of adding to their delusion as they are perpetrating their cruelty, even signs and wonders follow, as we learn from the next verse:

*Job 41:22

XVIII. 33. *The path shines in his wake.** We are told that Leviathan's path shines after him, because wherever he goes the glow of his miracles leaves excessive admiration, and whether his own or his ministers' machinations do it, he is crowned with signs that lie. So, as we have already made clear often enough, Truth says in the gospel, *False christs and false prophets will arise, and they will work great signs and wonders, so that even the elect, if it were possible, might be led into error.** *Job 41:23

*Matt 24:24

Leviathan's path then glows in his wake, because he makes the works of those whose hearts he enters shine with wonders; thus the deeper the darkness of error in which he keeps those minds, the brighter shines externally the light of those miracles that he works through them. The memories of some people, however, still hold the words of the prophets and the precepts of the Gospel, and they know very well that the signs he displays are false and that the punishment to which they deceptively lead is real. But since our Leviathan does not fool their hearts with a false show of holiness, he disguises himself for them with different makeup. Leviathan is aware that some people know about all his deception but also that they love the present life, so he immediately relieves their minds of the fear of the coming punishments and claims that the strict Judgment will at some time come to an end; in this way he cunningly deceives them and wins them over to the pleasures of the moment. So the Lord rightly adds forthwith,

XIX. 34. *He will reckon the abyss to be as it were aging.** The psalmist testifies that the eternal incomprehensible judgments are familiarly called by the name of abyss, saying, *Your judgments are many and deep.** The word *age,* however, is sometimes used to indicate that the end is near. As the apostle says, *What is of long standing and growing old is close to its end.** Our Leviathan then will reckon the abyss to be growing old, as it were, because in this way he fools the hearts of reprobate sinners, and he plants in them the notion that the coming Judgment will in some way come to an end. Accordingly he reckons that the abyss grows old, because he thinks that the heavenly notice for punishment is to come to an end someday. Therefore that ancient persuader relieves his members, that is, the minds of the evildoers, concerning future penalties that he counts

*Job 41:23

*Ps 35:7

*Heb 8:13

on as having a certain end, so that he can let their sins increase without an end of repentance, and so that their sins here below may still less have an end in that his members suppose that later punishments for sin will come to an end.

35. There are then those who neglect to put an end to their sins here below, because they suppose that the Judgments upon them later will someday have an end. I will give a brief answer to such as these: If the punishments of reprobate sinners were someday to end, then also the happiness of the blessed ones would have a future end. Of himself Truth has said, *These people will go to their eternal punishment, but the righteous will go to eternal life.** Consequently, if the threat were not true, then neither would the promise be true. They say, however, that he threatened sinners with an eternal penalty so that he might prevent them from further sins, since he should threaten his creatures with eternal punishment, not bring it down upon them. To these I give a quicker answer: If he uttered false threats to turn them away from unjust acts, then he also uttered false promises, so that he might incite them to acts of righteousness. Who would accept such nonsense on their part? They assert with their own promises that the punishment of reprobate sinners is going to end, and by their own assertion they also deprive the chosen ones of their reward and repayment. Who would accept such nonsense on their part? They try to argue that it is not true what the Truth himself threatened concerning eternal fire, and while they are occupying themselves with showing that God is merciful, they are not afraid to preach that he is a deceiver.

*Matt 25:46

36. They say, however: there should be no endless punishment for a crime that has an end. Almighty God is certainly righteous, and when no eternal sin has been committed, no eternal torture should be used to punish it. We shall reply quickly by saying that they would be speaking the truth if when the righteous and strict Judge comes, he should weigh not humans' hearts but their actions. Wicked people, you see, have sinned finitely, because their life has an end. They would have preferred to have unending life, so that they could have kept sinning without an end. They desire sin more than life, so they want to live here below permanently, so that they may never stop sinning as long as they are alive. So it is the strict Judge's righteous duty to see that they are never without punishment, those whose minds in this life never wanted to be without sin, and that no end is granted to the wicked person's retribution, because as long as that person was able, he refused to put an end to his crimes.

37. But they say: No righteous person is gratified by cruelty, and the sinful servant is commanded by his righteous master to be killed, precisely so that his sinfulness may stop. So then he is killed for a purpose, since his master gets no pleasure out of cruelty. But the wicked are handed over to the fire of hell, so for what purpose are they always going to burn? Since it is certain that the loving and almighty God is not gratified by the torture of the wicked, why are those miserable people tortured, if their guilt is not wiped out? So we answer them quickly, that precisely because almighty God is loving, he is not gratified by the suffering of miserable people, but because he is righteous, he is not satisfied by the eternal punishment of the wicked. But all the wicked are punished with an eternal penalty, and it is for their own wickedness. Furthermore, they are burned together for a purpose, and that purpose is that all the righteous should both see that the happiness they receive is in God, and that they should perceive in these miserable ones the penalty they have escaped; they should realize in this way to what extent they are eternal debtors to God's grace, and at the same time how great is the evil that is punished that with God's help they were able to avoid.

38. Again they say, How is it that they are saints if they are not praying for their enemies, whom they will see being burnt up at that time? Did not the Lord say, *Love your enemies and pray*?* We again answer quickly: They pray for their enemies during that time when they can influence their hearts for conversion and fruitful repentance and when those enemies can be saved by that conversion. What else should they pray for in regard to their enemies but the apostle's words: *That God might give them repentance, and that they might escape the Devil's traps by which they are confined and return to his will*?* But how are they to pray for them at that later time, when they can no longer be converted from the way of wickedness to the works of righteousness?

*Matt 5:44

*2 Tim 2:25-26

The reason that human beings condemned to the eternal fire cannot be prayed for later is the same as that for the devil and his angels who are being reserved for eternal punishment now. The same reason governs the fact that the saints should not pray for disloyal and impious human beings who are already dead, since they already know that they were set apart for the eternal penalty and that they were already in the presence of the righteous Judge; in this way the righteous avoid rendering fruitless the virtue of their prayer. But if at the present time the righteous people who are still alive do not at all pity the unrighteous who have died and been condemned, when they know that the behavior of their own flesh is subject to Judgment, how much more immovably will they look upon the tortures of the wicked at that later time when they themselves will be denuded of every trace of corruption and will already be closer to the state of righteousness to which they will keep clinging more tightly? So their minds then, by the very fact that they are clinging to the most righteous Judge, will also absorb from him the power of immovability, so that they will never again be free to feel anything discordant with the exactitude of his internal law.

But now, since an appropriate opportunity had presented itself for me to reply to the Origenists, I will return to the stated order of my exposition, from which I had departed. So after the merciful Lord showed us our Leviathan's cunning devices, openly foretelling all the external oppression that he was violently to force upon the chosen ones and all the charming persuasions he was to plant internally for the reprobate sinners, he quickly and briefly injects something about his savage power:

XX. 39. *There is no power on earth comparable to his.** We are told that his power on earth is greater than that of all others, because even though he fell below human beings by the moral quality of his action, he transcends the human race by the power of his angelic nature. Even though he lost the blessed state of interior happiness, he did not lose the greatness of his own nature, and by his power he still exceeds all human resources, even if he lies below the merits of the saints because of having been cast down. So the recompense the saints deserve grows when they fight against him, and they win the victory over him when he boasts of his superiority over human beings as if by right, through the power of his nature.

*Job 41:24

XXI. 40. *He has been so made that he fears nothing.** His nature has been so made that he should have feared his Creator chastely, that is, with sober fear, with secure fear, not with the fear that perfect love casts out, but with the fear that remains forever, the fear that is born of perfect love. The loving fear of a wife for her husband is different, and the fear of a sinful handmaid

*Job 41:24

for her master is different again. The adversary had been so created, you see, that as long as he lovingly feared his Creator with a happy fear, he would also fearfully love him. But by his perversity he became such that he would fear no one. In fact he hated being the subject of the one who created him. God, you see, is above all beings, so that nothing is above him. Leviathan, however, aspired to have the highest pinnacle for himself, and he yearned for the right to possess that twisted freedom so that he could both rule over all other beings and have none above him. He said, *I will ascend above the tops of the clouds; I will be like the most high.** He therefore lost that likeness by the very fact that he proudly desired to be like him in elevation.

*Isa 14:14

He who ought to have imitated God's perfect love in his subjection, emulated his elevation, and he lost through pride what he could have simply imitated. He would in fact have been high if he had been content with participation in the elevation that was true. But when his pride desired an elevation for himself alone, he lost his right to the participated elevation. He forsook the Source with whom he ought to have stayed when he desired to be his own source. He abandoned the one who could have been enough for him when he judged that he could be enough for himself. The more he lifted himself up against the glory of the Creator, the more he fell inside himself. The one whom free servitude exalts, captive liberty casts down. When someone is set free here below so that he or she needs fear nothing, by that very freedom that person's hands are painfully tied. The Judgment of heaven orders all things in a wonderful way, so that the freedom Satan desired bound him, and he who feared absolutely nothing lies under the threat of every punishment. Yet he could have ruled over all the elements if he had wanted to fear the one he should have feared. Possessing all things, he would have only feared the One, and now he does not fear even that One, and yet he suffers all punishments.

41. So it happens that in order that he might fear nothing—he fears nothing, obviously, because he does not even fear God, but neither does he fear the sufferings he is to undergo. Would it not have been easier for him to avoid suffering by fearing than to undergo it without fear? His desire for elevation turned into mental stiffness, so that through his inflexibility, he who longed for preeminence through honor no longer feels himself unfortunate. He did not win the right to power that he sought, but he did find a kind of remedy for his pride in the stupidity of insensibility. And because he could not surpass all opposition by attack, by contempt he prepared himself for everything. His pride is described still more exactly in what follows:

*Job 41:25

XXII. 42. *He sees all that is lofty.** In other words, he looks down from on high upon everyone, and they are as if placed below him, since his project is to move against the Creator, and he has only contempt for the idea of supposing anyone to be like him. This attitude also fits his members very well, because all the evildoers, elated by the inflation of their hearts, despise with the arrogance of pride all those whom they see. And even if they should ever respect them externally, they are so great in their own internal estimation that in their secret heart they treat as of secondary importance the lives and merits of everyone else, and they look down on them as inferior to themselves, because through their own proud thoughts they have placed their own hearts in a tower of considerable height. The prophet says of such as these, *Woe to you who are wise in your own eyes and prudent according to your own lights.** And Paul says for his part, *Do not be wise in your own conceits.**

*Isa 5:21
*Rom 12:16

That is why the divine rebuke came to King Saul: *Although you may be little in your own eyes, did I not make you the leader of the tribes of Israel?** He indeed is little in his own eyes who imagines himself unequal in merit when compared to others. In fact whoever lifts himself up in his proud thoughts over the merits of others considers himself great. Reprobate King Saul, however, did not remain steadfast in the good he did at the beginning, because haughtiness at the power he had received caused him to swell up with pride. David on the other hand always conducted himself with humility and deferred to Saul in comparison; when he later found an opportunity to strike at his furious adversary he spared him and prostrated himself in a humble profession: *Whom are you persecuting, O King of Israel, whom are you chasing? Is it not a dead dog and an outcast?** At all events he had already been anointed as king, and at Samuel's entreaty when he poured oil from his horn upon his head, he learned that God's grace had preserved him for the government of the kingdom, when Saul had already been repudiated. Yet he cast himself down with a humble mind before the persecution of his adversary, whom he knew that God's judgment had made subject to him. Consequently, he humbly deferred to the one whom he knew to be incomparably inferior to himself through the grace of divine election.

*1 Sam 15:17

*1 Sam 24:15

Accordingly, let them who still do not know what their place is in God's sight learn how to humble themselves before their neighbors, when the very ones who have been chosen humiliate themselves before those to whom—as they already know—internal judgment has preferred them.

43. This tends to be a special pattern for the chosen ones: that they always have an internal sense of what they are in themselves. That is why that very David says of himself, *If I had not humbly thought of myself but extolled my own self.** That is why Solomon calls little ones to wisdom, saying, *Whoever is a little one, let him come to her.** No one of course who has not yet despised himself learns God's humble wisdom. That is why the Lord says in the Gospel, *I praise you O Lord, Father of heaven and earth, because you have hidden these things from wise and prudent people and revealed them to babies.** That is why the psalmist again says, *The Lord guides little ones.** That is why the teacher of the Gentiles says, *We became like children among you.** That is why he admonished his followers, saying, *Think of others as better than yourself.**

*Ps 130:2
*Prov 9:4
*Matt 11:25
*Ps 114:6
*1 Thess 2:7
*Phil 2:3

Since every unjust person evaluates whomever he thinks of as less than himself, the righteous person should on the other hand try to consider any of his neighbors as better than himself. The result should not be that when someone humbles himself before another, the other is moved to pride. No, Paul rightly warns both parties, saying, *Think of others as better than yourself.* Thus in my secret thoughts I prefer the other to myself, and on his part, he prefers me to himself, so that on both sides the heart is rightly repressed, and neither one is unduly lifted up by being honored.

44. But reprobate sinners who are Leviathan's members have only contempt for the idea and the practice of this form of humility, and even if they sometimes show themselves as humble in appearance only, they neglect the internal effort of practicing humility. And it often happens to them that if they perform any good act of whatever type, be it the smallest, they forthwith turn away the attention of their mind from all their evil deeds, and their whole attention is focused on the last good thing they have done. With that, they already consider themselves saints, and they forget all the sins they have committed and remember only the one good deed they have performed, which by chance they have not even been able to do completely. The opposite often happens to the chosen ones, so that they may be redolent with the grace of many virtues, but one vice, be it one of the smallest, tires them out with its assaults, inasmuch as they consider their own weakness in one part of themselves, and concerning those virtues that prevail in them, they boast not at all; even though their weakness causes them trouble, they humbly preserve their strong points. Consequently the reprobate sinners carelessly focus their attention on the one good thing they have done, be it one of the smallest, while they do not even realize the extent of the grave sins in which they are sunk. On the other hand, the chosen ones are often troubled by one small fault they have committed in weakness, but it happens by a wonderful providence that they do not omit continuing to do the great good they have been drawn to do.

45. The unit of righteous internal measurement is so arranged that both the righteous people are assisted by evil and the reprobate sinners are made worse by good, since the former make use of slight evils in order to increase their good actions, and the latter make use of meager good to augment the evil they do. The former naturally make more satisfactory progress in doing good whenever they are tempted by evil, but the latter fall more deeply into evil the more they boast of good. In this way the reprobate makes a bad use of good, and the righteous makes a good use of bad. The case is similar to what often happens to the person who is infected by a fatal disease by eating too much of a healthy food; another person might by using a moderate amount of the poison of a snake in a carefully prepared remedy to defeat the suffering of snakebite. The former refused to eat healthy food as it should be eaten, and so he fatally died from the food by which other people live in a healthy way; the latter person was careful to use the poison of a snake with caution, and so he regained his health while others grew worse and died.

However, we call the venom of a snake not depravity pure and simple, but a hint of depravity, by which, though we often refuse and resist, we are still tempted; it is turned into medicine precisely when the mind is alerted by virtues to notice the temptations used against it and consequently humbled. Consequently, when the wicked are rejected by the decision of that internal evaluation, whatever works they do and whatever virtues shine, they are complete strangers to the sense of humility. They are of course members of our Leviathan, about whom the heavenly voice said, *He sees all that is lofty.** This concerns not only himself but also those whose hearts he claims, and they as it were disdain all others from the heights they inhabit.

*Job 41:25

46. We should notice, however, that our Leviathan, whose name signifies the body of a beast, is described as looking down from above, obviously because his proud heart stretches out to cover even his body, and it is especially designated by the eyes. They are in fact inflated by the haughtiness of pride as they look down from above, and being forced to look down, they lift themselves up higher. Unless pride showed itself through the eyes as if through something like windows, the psalmist would never have spoken to God in this way: *You will save a humble people but humble the eyes of the proud.** Unless pride were poured out through the eyes, Solomon would not have spoken of Judea's self-exaltation: *His generation includes those who have proud eyes, and whose eyebrows are lifted up on high.** Accordingly our Leviathan is signified by the body of an animal, its

*Ps 17:28

*Prov 30:13

pride extends to its bodily form, and its rule is exercised more obviously through the eyes, so the ancient enemy is apparently being described to us as looking down from on high to see us. But since we have spoken a great deal to explain the enemy of the human race, the mind's great desire now is that one thing especially be explained more fully at the end of the Lord's speech, so that his members might be pointed out to us with a brief summary.

XXIII. 47. *He is the king of all the sons of pride.** In order that our Leviathan might fall under all that has been said above, he has been driven by pride alone. Nor would all those branches of vice wither unless the root had first decayed. It is in fact written, *Pride is the beginning of all sin.** Through pride Leviathan fell, and through pride he laid low the man who followed him. With pride as a spear he attacked the safety of our immortality, the spear that killed his own blessed life. Accordingly the Lord ended his speech at this precise point, so that when he numbered pride among all Leviathan's other sins, he might call it worse than them all. The fact that it occupies the end of the list of his sins also shows that it is the root of them all. Just as the root of a tree is underground, but from it the branches extend themselves above the ground, so pride is hidden within, but from it sins keep sprouting openly. No sins would appear publicly, of course, if they had not secretly occupied the mind. That is what makes our Leviathan's perception boil like ointment, whence he also strikes human minds with a certain heat of madness, but it shows how what is done openly overturns the mind of the one who is struck. Pride first bursts out internally, and later it spouts its works externally.

48. But since an occasion has arisen to talk about pride, we ought to discuss it with more careful detail,

*Job 41:25

*Sir 10:15

and to show in what ways and how often it arises in human minds, creeping up on them secretly. Other vices in fact only oppose the virtues by which they are destroyed; for example, anger opposes patience, gluttony opposes abstinence, and lust opposes continence. However, pride, which I have called the root of all the vices, is never content with the destruction of one virtue, but rises up against all the members of the soul. Like a general deadly disease that infects the whole body, pride invades the soul, and whatever the soul does, even if it shows itself as a virtue, is turned not toward God, but to vainglory. Like a tyrant taking over a besieged city, pride rushes into the mind, and the richer a person is whom it seizes, the harsher is the dominion it exercises over him, because the greater a virtue's practice is without humility, the wider becomes the dominion of pride.

When the mind is taken captive, whoever suffers pride's tyranny in himself first loses accuracy of judgment, because the eye of his heart is closed. Everything that other people do right of course displeases him, and only what he does himself pleases him, even if done badly. The works of others always displease him, and he always admires his own work, because whatever he has done he thinks he has done in a special way, so he shows off through a desire for honor, and his own thoughts show favor to himself. Since he considers himself better than everybody else, he walks alone among all his widely flung thoughts, and he quietly shouts his own praises. His mind is sometimes even led to such arrogance that he proudly goes beyond all bounds to spout his excellence in words. But the more immoderately someone else is praised in his presence, the more quickly he himself is ruined. So it is written, *The heart is lifted up before falling.**

*Prov 16:18

That is why Daniel writes, *The king walked in Babylon's courts, and he spoke out, "Isn't this Babylon, the great city I built for my home with the strength of my arm and the glory of my beauty?** But he quickly adds how quickly the punishment followed this act of pride and says, *The words had hardly left the king's mouth when the heavenly voice struck: "King Nebuchadnezzar, you are now addressed: The kingdom will be taken from you, and you will be driven from among men; you will dwell among beasts in the wilderness. You will eat hay like the ox until seven times pass over you."** See how quickly mental pride blurts out brazen words, and the Judge's patience equally proceeds to the sentence; the latter falls just as strictly as the former lifted itself up in arrogance without restraint. And since he counted up the good things, of which he boasted, he heard counted up the bad things with which he was struck down.

*Dan 4:26-27

*Dan 4:28-29

49. We ought to realize, however, that the pride itself about which we are talking here possesses worldly reality as well as spiritual reality. One person grows proud over gold, another over speech, another over weak earthly things, another over high heavenly virtues; nevertheless, in God's eyes it is one and the same matter that is in question, in whatever ways it comes to human hearts, and whatever clothes it wears to appear before them. When a person first waxes proud over worldly honors and is then extolled for holiness, pride never abandons his heart, but it comes to him habitually, so that he does not know it when it changes clothes.

50. We should also realize that pride tempts leaders in one way and subjects in another; it suggests to the leader's thoughts that it is only by the excellence of his life that he has surpassed others, and if anything has been done well by him, pride brings up in his own mind unseasonably what has been done. Pride tells him that he has pleased God in a special way, so that it may advance its hints the more easily, and it calls to witness even the very reward of the power given him, saying that unless almighty God had singled him out as the best of all, he would not have put all those others under his rule. Pride quickly exalts his mind and shows him how base and useless his subjects are, so that there is no longer a single one whom he can consider worthy to speak with on an equal basis. Accordingly his even disposition quickly changes into wrath, since he despises them all, and he complains excessively about the perception and way of life of them all; his anger grows beyond all bounds to the same extent that he considers those who have been committed to his care to be unworthy of him.

51. On the other hand, when pride tempts the hearts of subjects, it tries above all to bring it about that they completely neglect to consider their own actions, so that in quieting their thoughts they make themselves judges of their superiors; they inconveniently notice what they should reprove in the superior's actions and never see what should be corrected in their own. The more they turn their eyes away from themselves, the more dreadful is their downfall, because those who stumble on the journey of this life come to ruin when their aim is to be elsewhere. They indeed claim to be sinners, but they do not go so far as to be handed over to the control of a noxious person. While they express contempt for his actions and despise his orders, they end up in the madness of supposing that God does not care about human affairs, because they complain about being subjected to the one whom they reprehend as if by right. That is how they wax proud against the Creator's judgment while they show arrogance against their superior, and while they pass judgment upon their guardian's conduct, they also revolt against the very wisdom of him who arranges all things. In fact they often insolently go against their superior's express commands, and they call this pride of theirs "free speech."

In this way pride even claims to be a kind of righteous freedom, just as fear often calls itself humility. Just as many people keep silent out of fear, and yet they suppose that their silence indicates humility, so some people speak impatiently out of pride, and yet they suppose that their speech indicates righteous freedom. But sometimes subjects do not express the insolence that they feel, and those who can hardly contain their garrulousness sometimes out of the pure bitterness of an internal grudge hold their silence. They hold back their words of effrontery with mental pain although they are accustomed to speak roughly, but their silence is worse, because they hear words of correction for some sin they are committing, and although they are furious they hold back their answering words. When they are agitated thus severely, they often blurt out words of complaint from these violent feelings.

And when their superior hinders them ingratiatingly, they become more furious because of the very meekness with which they are thus hindered. And the more considerately their mind is judged as weak, the more coarsely is it aroused. Such people indeed know nothing of humility, which is the mother of virtues, so they lose all result of their labors, even if they may seem to be doing what is good, because the sturdy height of the rising building is not steady, and it is not at all rendered solid like a rock through a vigorous foundation. Their building grows only to fall, because they do not carefully acquire a foundation of humility before the massive structure of the building. But we expose their internal project better if we focus on their external behavior in a few words.

52. For all those who are bursting with pride in their thoughts there is noisy speech, bitter silence, looseness in cheerfulness, fury in sadness, dishonor in action, honor in imagination, erect posture in approach, malice in response. Their minds are always strong enough to impose insults, but weak when it comes to sustaining them, slow to obey but quick to provoke others, indolent in doing what they should and can do well, but always ready to do what they neither should do nor can do well. Such a mind in a person who will not desire it will not bend for any exhortations, but it wants to be forced to do what it secretly desires; because it is afraid to look base on account of its desires, it chooses to be forced to do its own will.

53. Accordingly, since I have said that human souls are tempted in one way by temptations of the flesh and in another by temptations of the spirit, let the former hear, *All flesh is grass, and its boasting is like the flower of the field.** Let the latter hear what some people heard after miracles were worked: *I do not know where you come from. Get away from me, all you evildoers!** Let the former hear, *If riches increase, do not set your heart on them.** Let the latter hear that after the foolish virgins came back with lamps out of oil, they were shut out from the wedding feast inside.* Again, since we have already said that magistrates are tempted in one way and employees in another, let the former hear what a certain wise man said: *They have made you leader; do not exalt yourself; rather act toward them as one of them.** Let the latter hear, *Obey your leaders and be subject to them. They are always vigilant, as becomes those who are going to render an account for your lives.**

When the former boast of the power they have received, let them hear the eager voice of Abraham telling a certain rich man, *Remember, son, that you have received good things in your life.** Let the latter hear, when their complaints burst out against their leaders, what Aaron's and Moses' voices answered the mur-

*Isa 40:6

*Luke 13:27

*Ps 61:11

*Matt 25:12

*Sir 32:1

*Heb 13:17

*Luke 16:25

muring people with: *What are we? Your grumbling is not against us but against God.** Let the former hear, *The fathers of orphans and the judges of widows will be upset in his presence.** Let the latter hear what the contumacious subjects heard: *The one who resists those who are given power resists God's ordinance.** Let them all together hear, *God resists the proud but gives grace to the humble.** Let them all hear, *The one whose heart is lifted up is impure in God's sight.** Let them all hear, *Why are you proud when you are earth and ashes?** Against the plague of this sickness let us all hear what the master, Truth, teaches: *Learn from me, for I am meek and humble of heart.**

*Exod 16:8

*Ps 67:6

*Rom 13:2

*Jas 4:6
*Prov 16:5
*Sir 10:9

*Matt 11:29

54. For this purpose the Only-begotten Son of God took on himself the form of our weakness;* for this purpose did the Invisible one appear not only visible but even contemptible, for this purpose did he accept being made a laughing stock and target of insults, for this purpose did he become a mockery and a reproach, for this purpose was his torment in the passion, so that a humble God could teach human beings not to be proud. How great is this virtue of humility, when he who is inestimably great became truly small in his passion only for the sake of teaching it? Since the devil's pride made itself the origin of our perdition, God's humility found itself the instrument of our redemption. Our enemy indeed was created along with all other creatures, and he wanted to seem proud above all other creatures. Our Redeemer, however, remained great above all creation, but he deigned to become small among them all.

*Phil 2:6-7

55. But we uncover the cause of pride better and open the foundation of humility if with a brief commemoration we count up the words of the author of death and those of the Creator of life in turn. The former said, *I will ascend to heaven.** The latter said through

*Isa 14:13

the prophet, *My soul is filled with evil, and my life has drawn near to hell.** The former said, *I will raise my throne above the stars in the sky.** The latter told the human race after it was expelled from its home in Paradise, *Behold, I am coming, and I will live in your midst.** The former said, *I will take my seat on the mount of the covenant, at the edge of the north.** The latter said, *I am a worm and no man, the reproach of men and the outcast of the people.** The former said, *I will ascend above the tops of the clouds; I will be like the most high.**

*Ps 87:4
*Isa 14:13

*Zech 2:10

*Isa 14:13

*Ps 21:7
*Isa 14:14

About the latter it was said, *While he was in the form of God, he did not consider it robbery that he should be equal to God; yet he emptied himself and took the form of a slave.** Through his members he says, *Lord, who is like you?** The former, however, says through his own members, *I do not know the Lord, and I will not let the Israelites go.** The latter says on his own account, *If I said I do not know him, I would be a liar like you, but I do know him, and I keep his word.** The former said, *The rivers are mine because I made them.** The latter said, *I cannot do anything of myself,** and *The Father is in me, and he does the works.** The former showed him all the kingdoms of the earth and said, *I will give you all this power and their glory, for to me they have been delivered, and I give them to anyone I wish.** The latter said, *You will indeed drink my cup, but the seat at my right hand or at my left is not mine to give; rather it is for those for whom the Father prepares it.**

*Phil 2:6-7
*Ps 34:10

*Exod 5:2

*John 8:55
*Ezek 29:9
*John 5:30
*John 14:10

*Luke 4:6

*Matt 20:23

The former said, *You will be like gods, knowing both good and evil.** The latter says, *It is not for you to know the times or the seasons that the father has reserved in his own power.** The former wanted God's will to be disdained and his own to convince, so he asked, *Why did God order you not to eat from any of the trees in the garden?** And a little later he said, *God knows that*

*Gen 3:5

*Acts 1:7

*Gen 3:1

as soon as you eat it your eyes will be opened.* The latter says, *I do not seek my own will, but the will of the Father who sent me.** The former says through his members, *Let there be no meadow where we do not pass our time of pleasure; let us crown ourselves with roses before they wither; let us leave traces of our delight everywhere.** The latter foretells his members, *You will mourn and weep, but the world will rejoice.**

*Gen 3:5
*John 5:30
*Wis 2:8-9
*John 16:20

The former teaches the minds of his subjects nothing else but the desire for the highest place, transcending all equals by the pride of their minds, transcending the society of all people by their pride and arrogance, and even to lift themselves up against the Creator's power. It is just as the psalmist says: *They move on as their heart is disposed; their thoughts and words concern evildoing; from on high they plan oppression.** The latter experienced spittle, slaps, blows, the crown of thorns, the cross, the lance, and death; he only advised his members, saying, *If any man would serve me, let him follow me.**

*Ps 72:7-8
*John 12:26

56. Since accordingly our Redeemer rules the hearts of humble people, and this Leviathan on the other hand is called king of the proud, it is common knowledge that pride is the most obvious signal of reprobate sinners, and humility contrariwise that of the chosen ones. Consequently, when it is known what each one has, we find the king under whom each one fights. Everyone, you see, carries about with him a kind of title of his work, by which it is easily shown under what leader's power he serves. That is why the Gospel says, *By their fruits you will know them.** So, lest the members of this Leviathan should deceive us by working miracles, the Lord showed us a sign by which they could be revealed, saying, *He is the king of all the sons of pride.** Even if they sometimes put on a false appearance of humility, they can never

*Matt 7:16
*Job 41:25

hide themselves in all situations, because their pride cannot long remain hidden, and if it is covered up in one action, it shows itself in another. Those however who fight under king humility are always fearful, and they look around on all aspects of a situation to fight against the spears of pride; they keep their eyes fixed on their own bodies as it were against possible blows, while they first of all protect humility in themselves.

BOOK 35

I. 1. Since this is the last book of this work, and the most difficult passages have already been treated, so that those that are left are less obscure, we are now free to speak more leniently and more casually. We are as it were on a vast wide sea, and we already perceive the coast, so we take down the sails of our attention, and we let ourselves be led by a different force than we did at first, yet we still go on, thrust forward by the same breath of wind. It is as though the wind of our solicitude has fallen, but its movement is still there, and itself more gentle, it urges us on to our coastal harbor. Accordingly, after the Lord has described to his faithful servant how strong and cunning an enemy Leviathan is, and when he has made his power and deceit clear, blessed Job replies to both and says,

2. *I know that you can do everything, and no thought is hidden from you.** Against Leviathan's inhuman powers he begins, *I know that you can do everything.* But against his hidden devices he adds, *and no thought is hidden from you.* So he quickly reproaches Leviathan himself and says, *Who is this who hides his counsel without knowledge?** In fact Leviathan does hide counsel without knowledge, because although he is hidden from our weakness by much deception, he is uncovered for us by the holy inspiration of our Protector. Without knowledge he hides counsel, because although he hides from those who are tempted, he cannot hide from the One who protects those who are tempted. Accordingly, once we have heard of the power and deception of the devil and heard also of the power of our Creator, which

*Job 42:2

*Job 42:3

both firmly represses the devil and mercifully covers us, we beseech you, blessed Job, that you refuse to hide from us what you sense of yourself. The next verse:

II. 3. *And so I have spoken foolishly and said what is utterly beyond my knowledge.** All human wisdom, however far reaching its influence may be, compared to God's wisdom amounts to foolishness. All human attainments, however righteous and however beautiful they may be, when compared to God's righteousness and beauty are neither righteous nor beautiful and amount to absolutely nothing. So blessed Job might think he had spoken wisely if he had not heard words of superior wisdom. In such a comparison all our wise words are foolishness. In fact anyone who has spoken wisely to human beings and then heard God's judgment wisely knows his words to be unwise. That is how Abraham knew that he was only dust speaking to the Lord: *I who am dust and ashes speak to my Lord.** That is why Moses, instructed in all the wisdom of Egypt, heard the Lord speak and knew he was of stumbling and slow speech. Then he said, *Please, Lord, I am not eloquent, but since yesterday and the day before, when you spoke to your servant, I am of stumbling and slow speech.**

That is why Isaiah saw the Lord sitting on a high lofty throne; afterwards he saw the two seraphim covering their faces with two wings and their feet with two wings while they flew with two wings; then he heard one call to the other, *Holy, holy, holy is the Lord God of hosts.** Returning to himself, Isaiah said, *Woe is me for my silence. I am a person with unclean lips, and I live among people with unclean lips.** He forthwith added how he knew about his unclean state: *I have seen the King, the Lord of Hosts with my own eyes.** That is also why Jeremiah, on hearing God's voice, knew that he could not speak and said, *Ah, ah, ah, O Lord God, I*

*Job 42:3

*Gen 18:27

*Exod 4:10

*Isa 6:1-3

*Isa 6:5

*Isa 6:5

cannot speak; I am only a child.* That is why Ezekiel spoke of the four animals and said, *A voice came from above the firmament over their heads, and they stood still and folded their wings.** What does the flight of the animals mean if not the loftiness of the evangelists and teachers? What else are the animals' wings but the contemplation of the saints that lifts them up to heaven? But when a voice is heard above the firmament over their heads, they stand still and fold their wings. When they hear the internal voice of heavenly wisdom, they in some way fold the wings of their flight, obviously because they know that they are unable to contemplate the very height of truth. So when they knew the heavenly power, they folded their wings at the voice coming to them from on high—this act means to humble one's own powers and out of consideration for the Creator to do nothing else but look downcast.

*Jer 1:6

*Ezek 1:25

So is it also with the saints who hear God's judgments: the more progress they make in contemplation, the more contempt they have for themselves, knowing that they are nothing or almost nothing. So let blessed Job reply to God's speeches, and with progress in wisdom let him know himself for a fool and say, *I have spoken foolishly, saying things that were exceedingly beyond my understanding.** See his self-accusation in tune with his progress in knowledge! He believes that he has gone excessively beyond what he knows, because he realizes that the Lord's words showed his hidden wisdom more than he had supposed. He goes on:

*Job 42:3

III. 4. *Listen, and I will speak; I will question you, and you must answer me.** For us to hear means that we incline the ear turned in one direction to the sound coming from another direction. On the other hand, for God hearing means—since he is not strictly speaking outside of anything—to receive our desires that rise up

*Job 42:4

beneath him. Consequently God knows the unspoken thoughts of the heart, and for us to speak to him does not mean that we utter thoughts with voices from the throat, but rather that we cling to him with ready desires. So whereas someone who asks a question wants to know something he does not know, for a human being to question God means to realize in his presence that he does not know. For God to answer, then, means that he teaches with hidden inspiration those who humbly realize that they do not know. So blessed Job said, *Listen and I will speak.** It is as if he said, "Mercifully receive my desires, so that while your merciful love receives them it may help me, and many more desires may rise up to you."

*Job 42:4

As often as good petitions receive an effective response, they are multiplied. Accordingly it is written elsewhere, *I cried out because you answered me.** He did not say, "Because I cried out you answered me," but *I cried out because you answered me*. He who spoke had been heard, and when he was heard his pleading was successful, so he cried out, *I will question you, and you must answer me*. It is as if he said, "I realize from contemplating your knowledge that I did not know. Now answer my question. In other words, teach me in my foolishness for my own humble recognition." The following words make it clear that his question arose from a humble desire, and he asked God to answer him as though led by his intense longing. He announced that he was going to ask, but he did not follow up with a question. Of himself he felt only humility, and knowing he would receive mercy from the Lord, he forthwith added,

*Ps 16:6

IV. 5. *I have heard of you by the hearing of the ear, but now my eye sees you.** Apparently these words make it clear how much better it is to see than to hear and how different he is now than he was formerly; consequently he has made progress through his trials. So he has seen

*Job 42:5

the light of truth more clearly with his internal eye; therefore he distinguished the darkness of his human nature, and he saw better.

V. 6. *On that account I blame myself.** The less a person sees of course, the less displeasing he finds himself. The more light of grace he has received, the more blameworthy he finds himself. When all a person's surroundings internally support him, he attempts to correspond to the rule that is above him. And since some human weakness still impedes his progress, he discerns that the part still lacking is not small. Everything then becomes burdensome to him that does not correspond to the internal rule. So blessed Job looks into that rule after having made progress through his trials and blames himself with great conviction, saying, *On that account I blame myself.* But since there is no knowledge of personal guilt unless lamentation of repentance follows, he rightly adds after his self-accusation,

*Job 42:6

VI. 7. *And I do penance with dust and ashes.** To do penance with dust and ashes of course means that after having contemplated the highest being one knows oneself to be nothing more than dust and ashes. That is why the Lord in the Gospel told the reprobate city, *If the mighty works that were done in you had been done in Tyre and Sidon, they would have repented long ago in sackcloth and ashes.** Sackcloth of course signifies harshness and the compunction of sinners, whereas ashes signify the dust of death. On that account the use of both words together tends to signify repentance, so that with the compunction of sackcloth we realize that we have done wrong, and with the dust of ashes we carefully evaluate what has become of us through judgment. Let us then consider the stinging vices in the wearing of sackcloth, and let us consider in the ashes the righteous penalty of vices that follows the sentence of death.

*Job 42:6

*Matt 11:21

Accordingly, since out of sin the shame of the flesh has risen, let the human being see the roughness of sackcloth as the deeds he did with pride, and let him see in ashes where he has arrived by continuing to sin. Sackcloth can also signify the sorrowful compunction that succeeds remembrance and repentance. When blessed Job said, *On that account I blame myself*, you see, he experienced the rubbing of sackcloth in a way, and his mind was troubled by the severe pain of self-reproof. With ashes he does penance, because he has carefully noticed what his first sin has made him through just judgment, and he says, *I do penance with dust and ashes.** It is as if he said outright, "I do not wax proud on account of any gift from my Creator, because I have been taken from dust, and I know I will return to dust through the sentence of death that has been passed."

*Job 42:6

8. Accordingly we have heard all Job's speeches, and we also know the answers given by his friends, so we could turn our minds to the scrutiny of the internal Judge's sentence and tell him, "Lord, we have listened in your presence to the two conflicting parties: we have heard Job himself rehearse all the arguments of his case in this matter, and we have also taken cognizance of his friends who defended the honor of your justice against him. You know the position our minds take between the two sides. We cannot of course reproach them for their words, with which, as we understand, they took up your defense. But now the conflicting parties stand waiting for your decision. Disclose then, Lord, the fine precision of your discernment and its indiscernible principle, and show us who has spoken the truth in this dispute. The next verse:

VII. 9. *After the Lord had spoken these words to Job, he turned to Eliphaz the Temanite and said, "My wrath is kindled against you and your two friends, be-*

cause you have not spoken the truth before me, like my servant Job."* O Lord, the sentence of your judgment has shown us how far short the blindness of our righteousness falls from the light of your justice. Behold, by your judgment we now recognize blessed Job as the winner, whose speeches about you we had thought sinful. By your judgment they were condemned who thought themselves to surpass blessed Job's righteousness in speeches on your behalf. Accordingly, since we have realized from God's decision how we should evaluate the two parties in the dispute, let us now weigh the words used in his sentence more exactly. How then is blessed Job reproved earlier, if in comparison to his righteousness his friends are not at all remembered to have spoken the truth in the Lord's sight? Or is that judgment now confirmed that the Lord spoke about Job to the ancient enemy: *Have you noticed my servant Job? There is none on earth like him.**

*Job 42:7

*Job 1:8

But what does this mean if he is both praised in front of the enemy and personally reproved, both reproved in his own person and preferred to the speeches of the friends, unless it is this: the holy man surpasses everyone by virtue of his merits, but by the very fact that he is human he could not escape reproof in the eyes of God? The holy man indeed still lives this earthly life, so he has something that the rule of God's scrutiny can judge, even if he already has something praiseworthy in comparison to other human beings. Accordingly blessed Job thought it was for sin that he was struck and not for favor; he supposed that vices were being curtailed in him, not that merits were being increased. He was reproved because he guessed that his trials were intended for some other purpose, and yet he achieved precedence before his friends who withstood him in the internal Judge's decision. So we clearly gather the greatness of

Job's righteousness in building a case for his innocence of action against the speeches of the friends, and in God's judgment even against the defenders of God's judgment he is preferred.

But at the beginning of the book we heard Satan telling the Lord concerning Job, *Just reach out and touch all his possessions, and see if he does not curse you to your face!** Upon this petition blessed Job was allowed to be touched by loss, bereavement, wounds, and offensive words, because of course God, who had praised him, knew that the holy man would never stoop to the sin of cursing, as the devil had maintained he would. Just as we said before, whoever supposes that blessed Job sinned in his speeches after his trial openly judges the Lord to have lost his claim. And while the Lord was speaking to the devil, although he declared Job's present good qualities, he did not promise Job's perseverance; however, we must realize that he would never have maintained Job's justice and allowed him to be tempted if he had not foreseen that his righteousness would remain in temptation. Consequently, anyone who supposes that Job succumbed to temptation when God allowed the devil to tempt him blames God for ignorance in allowing it.

10. We should then truthfully approve of Job's words, lest we should wrongfully blame God's providence. And surely, as far as human judgment is concerned, his friends were supposed to have spoken much that was truer in their speeches. But Truth himself displayed another principle that was hidden when he said, *you have not spoken the truth about me, as my servant Job has.** "About me," he said, that is, "within," where many lives are displeasing that externally please human beings. Therefore that saying is too cautious in its praise of righteous couples: *They were both righteous before*

*Job 1:11

*Job 42:7

God.* To appear righteous in the eyes of human beings is not safe praise. Human approbation often goes to some great person as though it were of God, but almighty God does not acknowledge the one who as it were is approved of himself. That is why the psalmist carefully prays, saying, *Guard my life in your presence.** No doubt even the way that is turned away from truth frequently seems right to human eyes. Notice that he did not say, "You did not speak the truth about me as Job did," but he said, *as my servant Job has.* Obviously the introduction of the idea of service lets him mention Job under a certain particular viewpoint, so that all Job had said in defense of God showed his humble truthfulness, not any haughty pride. But God is righteous and merciful, and he both strictly blames the friends from righteousness, and in his mercy kindly converts them. The next verse:

VIII. 11. *Take for yourselves seven bulls and seven rams, go to my servant Job, and offer the holocaust for yourselves. My servant Job will pray for you; his prayer I will accept, so that your folly will not be held against you.** See how righteous and merciful God is. He neither overlooks faults without scolding nor forgives guilt without conversion. He is a physician for internal sickness who first notices the decaying wound and then prescribes a remedy for health to be restored. But as we have already often repeated, blessed Job's friends are types of heretics, and when they try to defend God they offend him instead. Their words are in fact rebellious against the truth, although they falsely assert themselves to be servants of the truth, but almighty God frequently implants them in the body of the church through knowledge of the truth, and even their conversion is often mercifully obtained; through the forgiveness that Job's friends receive, their conversion is signified.

*Luke 1:6

*Ps 5:9

*Job 42:8

12. We must above all notice that they do not of themselves offer the sacrifice for their conversion, but they are ordered to offer it through Job. It is no wonder that when the heretics renounce their errors, they are absolutely not able to placate God's anger against them by the offering of a sacrifice by themselves, but they must be converted to the catholic church signified by blessed Job, so that they may obtain salvation by means of the prayers of her whose faith they impugned through false assertions. The Lord said, *My servant Job will pray for you; his prayer I will accept, so that your folly will not be held against you.** It is as if he openly told the heretics, "I will not accept your sacrifices. I will not listen to the words of your petitions, unless Job intercedes for you. I do recognize the words of his confession of me as truth. Then you may lead forward your bulls and rams and offer them for the sacrifice of your conversion, but you must apply to the catholic church that I love for your salvation at my hands. I wish to forgive your sin against me through her and let her obtain your safety, because she has suffered your lassitude.

*Job 42:8

13. It is only through the church that the Lord willingly accepts sacrifice, and only the church faithfully intercedes for those who are going astray. That is why the Lord commanded concerning the offering of the lamb, *Let it be eaten in one house, and let no part of its flesh be offered outside the house.** The lamb is consumed in one house, because the true sacrifice of the Redeemer is offered up in the one catholic church. God's law prohibits any of his flesh to be taken outside, because it forbids what is holy to be given to dogs.* It is she alone in whom the good work is fruitfully accomplished, so that the day's wages are given only to those who have labored in the vineyard.* It is only she who keeps safe with the bond of charity those who have their place in

*Exod 12:46

*Matt 7:6

*Matt 20:8

her. So the flood waters surely raise the ark up high, but they kill whomever they find outside the ark.* *Gen 7:17-23

It is only in the church that we contemplate the heavenly mysteries. That is why the Lord told Moses, *Here is a place near me. You will stand on the rock.** And *Exod 33:21 afterwards: *I will take away my hand and you will see my back.** Because it is only from the catholic church *Exod 33:23 that the truth may be glimpsed, the Lord said there was a rock near him whence he could be seen. Moses was put on a rock so he could contemplate the Lord's beauty, because unless a person firmly grasps the solidity of faith he or she has no knowledge of God's presence. The Lord spoke of this solidity when he said, *Upon this rock I will build my church.** What else then does the Lord *Matt 16:18 mean when he tells Job's friends, *Go to Job*, but "Go up to the rock"? What does *his prayer I will accept, so that your folly will not be held against you** mean if not *Job 42:8 what is said in this passage:* *you will see my back?** *of Exodus In other words, you will understand the mystery of his *Exod 33:23 incarnation that will be revealed later.

14. However, because the heretics have only contempt for the idea of standing on the rock, they do not look at the back of the passing Lord; in fact their position is outside the church, and they do not know the mysteries of his incarnation. As we have said above, the bulls signify the neck of pride, and the rams signify the leadership that the heretics hold, having persuaded the people who are led like flocks. About the proud heretics who corrupt the minds of the weak with their evil persuasion it is said, *The council of the bulls is held among the cows of the people.** *Ps 67:31

Since they drag the peoples along with them like flocks of sheep, the bulls are sometimes called rams. It is the rams of course that lead the flock. That is why Jeremiah upbraids the people and says, *Your leaders are like*

*Lam 1:6   *rams.** Accordingly, when heretics return to holy church they forsake the posturing of pride and never again lead the crowds of people to their ruin as if they were flocks of sheep following them; therefore blessed Job's friends are ordered to offer bulls and rams. The offering of bulls and rams in sacrifice means to slaughter the pride of leadership with humble conversion, so that by taming the proud neck those friends may learn to follow by obedience, those whose whole effort was formerly devoted to the teaching of leadership. This pride of theirs is also rightly expiated by seven sacrifices, because heretics who return to the church through the offering of humility receive the gift of the spirit in the form of seven graces, and since they had been wasting away with long-lasting pride, they are made new with grace.

15. The number seven actually has a certain perfection according to the worldly wise, since it is composed of the first odd and the first even combinations; the first odd combination is of course three, and the first even four. The number seven is made up of those two numbers, which result in twelve when they are multiplied. Whether we multiply four by three or three by four, we reach the product twelve. Now it is by a gift from above that we receive the preaching of truth; consequently we despise and trample underfoot the knowledge determined by pride. Beyond any doubt our faith is secure in retaining this: that upon those whom the Spirit has filled with the seven gifts, he perfects and bestows not only the knowledge of the Trinity, but also the practice of four virtues, namely prudence, temperance, courage, and justice. The Spirit thus increases in a way the resources of those people whom he enters, since it is by the knowledge of the Trinity that they are enabled to practice those four virtues, and through the action of the four virtues they finally reach the revealed reality of the Trinity. The number seven then is received among us, though in a far different way, because it fully and not vainly results in twelve, since faith increases works, and works perfect faith. The holy apostles too were chosen as twelve who were to be filled by the spirit with sevenfold gifts of grace, and they were sent to the four directions of the world to make the Trinitarian God known. Yes, the twelve were chosen, so that even from their very number the reasonable cause would shine out, and the three high ones would be preached in the four low directions.

16. So whether it be for that reason or for any other reason, in Holy Scripture at any rate the sacred number seven sometimes signifies the safe repose of eternity, sometimes the universality of the present time, sometimes the universality of Holy Church. The perfection of eternity is certainly meant by the number seven when the seventh day is called holy and made so by the Lord's rest on that day. It is no longer said to have an evening, because the rest of eternal happiness is not cut short by an end. That is also why the seventh day is ordered to be celebrated as a holiday in the Jewish Law, so that it may symbolize eternal rest. That is why in the cycle of years the number seven, multiplied by seven with one year added, results in the number fifty, and the jubilee year is celebrated so that the fiftieth year may signify the most sacred repose of eternal happiness. That is why after the Lord had frequently risen and appeared, he is described as having celebrated a banquet with seven disciples for the last time, because those who were made perfect in him might also be satisfied in the eternal banquet through him.

17. Again, the number seven signifies the whole course of the present time. Thus the seven days show us the total course of the present life. The number seven is also a type of Holy Church, who lives out all this time preaching in the world in the same way as the ark of the Lord marched around the city of Jericho seven times with trumpets blowing, ending in its destruction. That is why the prophet says, *I praised you seven times a day.** He also signified that he spoke of the entire complete time of his prayer, saying, *His praise is always on my lips.** We are still more clearly shown that the number seven indicates the totality of the present life when the number eight follows seven. When another number also follows seven, its addition signifies that time is ended by eternity. That is in fact what Solomon forewarns us about when he says, *Give a portion to seven and even to eight.**

*Ps 118:164

*Ps 33:1

*Eccl 11:2

The number seven indeed tells us that what is done in seven days expresses the present time, but the number eight signifies eternal life, which the Lord opened for us with his own resurrection. He rose on the Lord's day,* the day that follows the seventh or the Sabbath, so the eighth day is found after creation. It is then rightly said, *Give a portion to seven and even to eight, because you do not know what evil is going to happen on earth.** It is as if we were clearly told, "Deal with worldly matters in such a way that you do not forget to desire eternity." It is necessary, you see, that you provide for the future by good works, since you do not know what troubles will follow the coming Judgment. Accordingly we go up to the temple by means of fifteen steps. From that ascending of the temple by seven and by eight we learn respectively how carefully we should deal with worldly business and seek the eternal mansion with diligence.

*Sunday

*Eccl 11:2

The value of one cent then rises to ten, and finally the prophet sings a hundred and fifty psalms. It is because of this number seven, which symbolizes worldly action, and that of eight, which symbolizes eternity, that the number of the faithful staying in the Upper Room was a hundred and twenty, and upon them the Holy Spirit came down. Seven added to eight makes fifteen, and if in counting the fifteen we continue increasing gradually, we eventually reach the number of a hundred and twenty. Obviously they learned from this outpouring of the Holy Spirit that they should transcend worldly values by endurance and seek for eternity by earnest desires.

18. Again, the number seven symbolizes the universality of Holy Church. John wrote of seven churches in the Apocalypse, and what else but the universal church did he want us to understand by them? In order that the same universal church might be signified as full of the spirit's sevenfold gifts, the prophet Elisha is described as having breathed into the dead body of a child seven times. The Lord came down upon the empty people in the form of seven and inspired them, and the spirit mercifully bestowed upon them the gifts of seven graces. Because then the universality of Holy Church is often signified by the number seven, blessed Job's friends were ordered by God to go to him to offer their holocausts. But they must absolutely be watchful and see that they keep the mysteries of this sevenfold number intact; those whose post is outside must first join the universal Holy Church and then finally ask forgiveness for the guilt of their first act of pride.

For their sin they must offer seven sacrifices, because they will not receive forgiveness for their guilt unless they rejoin that universal peace from which they cut themselves off; they must be helped by the Spirit who has the seven gifts. Let the Lord then say, *Take for yourselves seven bulls and seven rams; go to my servant Job, and offer the holocaust for yourselves. My servant Job will pray for you; his prayer I will accept, so that your folly will not be held against you.** It is as if he

*Job 42:8

openly told returning heretics, "Join yourselves to the universal church through humble repentance and obtain from me through prayer that forgiveness of which you are unworthy yourselves; through that act you learn how to be truly wise, and so before me you first destroy that folly of wisdom in yourselves." It goes on:

IX. 19. *You have not spoken the truth in my presence, as has my servant Job.** The Lord had already pronounced these words a little previously, and yet he adds the same words now, repeating himself. What does this mean if not that he confirms by repeating it the sentence he had already passed in judgment? Moreover, so that the righteousness of blessed Job and the friends' own unrighteousness might be more clearly displayed, the Lord's praise of Job and his censure of the friends are again produced by repetition, so that the words that were held internally might show up more clearly by external repetition. When the king of Egypt realized, you see, the fearful time of famine that was coming by means of the images of cows and ears of corn in his double vision, he heard the voice of the saintly interpreter say, *The fact that you dreamed the same thing twice is an indication that the thing is decided.** So from this fact we can gather that whatever is repeated in God's word is confirmed all the more stoutly. Since we have heard the Judge's decision, let us also listen to those who received his sentence to know what they did.

*Job 42:8

*Gen 41:32

X. 20. *So Eliphaz the Temanite, Bildad the Shuhite, and Zophar the Naamathite went and did according to the word of the Lord, and the Lord accepted Job's intercession.** We shall however not go into the interpretation of their names, since we remember having spoken of it at the beginning of this work. But we must carefully notice the order of forgiveness as it was previously spoken, so that the Lord is said to have received

*Job 42:9

in the sacrifices not the friends but Job's intercession. But since anyone who tries to intercede for others wins support for himself by this act of charity rather than otherwise, the text resumes:

XI. 21. *The Lord in turn was appeased by the repentance of Job when he prayed for his friends.** In fact Job was already shown to us above and heard praying for his friends when it was mentioned that what we had said was done: *They went and did according to the word of the Lord, and the Lord accepted Job's intercession.** But we are clearly shown that even when he did penance for himself he deserved a hearing, just as quickly as when he loyally interceded for the others, when it was immediately added, *The Lord in turn was appeased by the repentance of Job when he prayed for his friends.** He effectively made his prayers win a hearing for himself when he also offered them for others. The sacrifice of prayer is more easily accepted when it is offered before the merciful Judge out of love for one's neighbor. And everyone really gains more in this way if he also offers that sacrifice for his adversaries. That is in fact what Master Truth has said: *pray for those who persecute you and speak falsely against you.** He also said, *When you stand up to pray, forgive anything you may have against anyone, so that your Father in heaven may also forgive you your offenses.** In the same place we are shown how much Job obtained for himself when he interceded for others. The Lord continues:

*Job 42:10

*Job 42:9

*Job 42:10

*Matt 5:44

*Mark 11:25

XII. 22. *The Lord gave Job double quantity of all he had before.** Of all that he had lost he received back double, because the approval of consolation wins us release from temptation through the kindness of the Judge. Temptation tries us less than the reward consoles, so that we may realize from the deserved reward that what we had to undergo was pretty small, although we supposed

*Job 42:10

that we had suffered grave pain from the force of the blow. That is why afflicted Judea was told, *For a brief moment I left you alone, but with great acts of mercy I will gather you.** Sometimes, however, the weight of affliction decides the extent of consolation. So it is elsewhere written, *According to the multitude of sorrow in my heart, your consolation, O Lord, rejoiced my soul.** He indicates that he was comforted by the very measure of his former afflictions, and he cries out that he rejoiced according to the multitude of sorrow he had experienced. The reader's instruction is not meager if he contemplates the stages of recompense. Correction follows excess, repentance follows correction, forgiveness follows repentance, and reward follows forgiveness.

*Isa 54:7

*Ps 93:19

Job was struck down, you see, by the permission of God's plan, and he was even afflicted by the words spoken by his friends; then he was comforted by the gifts of God's kindness. So he should also be warmed by human love, so that joyful consolation should greet him all around after bitter suffering and adversity had wounded him all around. So the story continues:

XIII. 23. *Then all his brothers came to see him, and all his sisters, and all those who had known him before, and they ate bread with him in his house, and they nodded their heads at him.** What else does the eating of bread signify but charity, and what the nodding of the head but admiration? So it rightly follows, *And they comforted him for all the misfortune that the Lord had brought upon him.** To comfort those who have been stricken by sorrow means to rejoice with them because of their pardon after having been stricken. The more a person is perceived to rejoice at his neighbor's restored health, you see, the more he gives evidence of having grieved at its loss.

*Job 42:11

*Job 42:11

XIV. 24. *And each one gave him one ewe lamb and one gold earring.** Even if all these words have been

*Job 42:11

written strictly literally, nevertheless the gift offerings force us to the recourse of the mysteries of allegory. Nor should we take these words lightly: namely *ewe lamb*, one, *gold earring*, one. Even if offering one ewe lamb is not strange literally, it is very strange for only one gold earring to be offered. But what does a lamb have to do with an earring, or what an earring to do with a lamb? Consequently the purpose of these gifts forces us to consider even the first, which superficially at least is related to the literal truth, as requiring the search for the mysteries of allegory. Since accordingly Christ and the church, that is the Head and the Body, are one person, we have often said that blessed Job signifies the figure either of the Head or of the Body. Keeping the literal truth intact, therefore, we may consider as a type of Holy Church what was written: *The Lord gave Job double quantity of all he had before.** So Holy Church, even if she now loses many people because of the attacks of temptation, receives at the end of the present world a double share of her possessions when she has received the full count of Gentiles, and has even the Jews who are then found come running to her faith. So it is written, *Until the full number of Gentiles enters in; then all Israel will be saved.** So also in the Gospel Truth says, *Elijah is going to come and restore everything.** At the present time the church loses the Israelites whom she was unable to convert by preaching, but Elijah comes to preach at that later time, and he will gather whomever he finds until the church fully regains what she lost.

*Job 42:10

*Rom 11:25-26
*Matt 17:11

25. Or at least for the church to receive double her possessions at the end means that she rejoices at each one of us receiving both the joy of the soul and the incorruption of the body. And so the prophet says concerning the chosen ones, *They will possess double inheritances in their own land.** John the apostle also

*Isa 61:7

says about the saints who pled for the end of the world, *Each one was given a white robe, and they were told to rest a while longer, until the number of their fellow servants and brethren should be complete.** We have already said long ago that each of the saints receives a garment before the resurrection, because they only enjoy happiness of the soul, but at the end of the world they will have two garments, because along with the soul's happiness they will also possess the glory of the flesh.

*Rev 6:11

26. But the words that come next certainly do announce the conversion of the Jewish people only at the end of this world. It follows: *Then all his brothers came to see him, and all his sisters, and all those who had known him before, and they ate bread with him in his house.** Then indeed do Christ's brothers and sisters come to him when as many Jews as can be found are converted. It is from that people, you see, that he assumed the substance of his flesh. Then accordingly his brothers and sisters come to him when from that people who belong to him by race, either those who are going to be strong like brothers or weak like sisters, hasten to him by knowledge of the faith and zealous devotion. Then they hold a banquet of festive celebration with him, when they hardly condemn him as a mere man any longer, mindful of his native closeness, but they rejoice at being joined to his divinity. Then they eat bread in his house when, having put aside the observance of the letter of the law that has been surpassed, they feast in Holy Church on the essential fruit of the mystical word.

*Job 42:11

The words *all those who had known him before* are rightly added at this point, because they certainly had known him before whom they despised as a stranger in his passion. No one in fact who had learned the fullness of the law was ignorant of the fact that Christ was to be born. King Herod, you know, was terrified by the arrival of the magi, and he undertook a serious inquiry of the priests and leaders to find out where they anticipated the future birth of Christ. Their immediate response was, *Bethlehem in the land of Judea.** So they already knew him whom at the time of his passion they despised in their ignorance. Their previous knowledge and later ignorance is rightly and briefly signified in Isaac's blindness. In his blessing of Jacob, Isaac both foresaw what the future would bring and lacked the knowledge of the person who was attending him.* The people of Israel were in the same case; they received the mysteries of prophecy, but they kept their eyes closed in contemplation, because they did not see the presence of him concerning whom they foresaw so much that was coming. They were strictly unable to discern the one who was standing before them, the power of whose coming they had long before announced.

*Matt 2:5

*Gen 27:23

Now see how they come at the end of the world and recognize the one whom they had known beforehand. See how they eat bread in his house, how they are nourished by the food of the sacred word in Holy Church. See how they cut themselves off from all the insensitivity of their former lethargy. So the text continues, *they nodded their heads at him.** So what does the head signify if not the leading role of the mind? The psalmist says, *You have anointed my head with oil,** as if to say, "You have poured the oil of charity over my mind when it was parched from its thoughts." The head is nodded then when it is touched by the fear of truth, and when it is shaken by its own impassivity. So let the parents come to the feast, and having rid themselves of lethargy let them nod their heads; in other words let those who were related to our Redeemer according to the flesh at some time or other receive the food of the word with faith and lose the hardness of their former

*Job 42:11

*Ps 22:5

impassivity. So also Habakkuk says, *His feet stood still, and the earth trembled.** When the Lord stands still the earth beyond doubt moves, because when he impresses our hearts with the footsteps of his fear, every earthly thought in us trembles. So in this passage* the nodding of the head means the shaking of the mind's impassivity and a drawing near to the knowledge of faith by means of the footsteps of a readiness to believe.

*Hab 3:5-6

*of Job

27. But since Holy Church is now afflicted by the hatred of the Hebrews, and she will later be relieved by their conversion, it is rightly added, *And they comforted him for all the misfortune that the Lord had brought upon him.** Obviously they comfort Christ, and they comfort the church, those who come to their senses after their mistaken infidelity of old, and they abandon the perversity of their ways by which they had resisted those who taught what is right. Is it not an oppressive grief to preach fruitlessly to hard-hearted people, to accept the labor of pointing out the truth, and to derive no fruit of that labor in the conversion of those who listen?

*Job 42:11

On the other hand, however, there is great comfort for preachers in the later progress of those who listen. Change and progress obviously mean relief for the speaker. It is noteworthy that they refused to comfort the one beset by trials, but they come to comfort him after the trial, obviously because the Hebrews during the passion disdained the preaching of faith, and they confirmed his humanity from his death while expressing contempt for belief in his Godhead. So the Lord says through the psalmist, *I expected one who would suffer together with me, and I found none; I looked for someone to comfort me, and I found none.** Absolutely no comfort did he find in his passion, he who from contempt for death even suffered as enemies the people he came to die for. Accordingly after his trials his rela-

*Ps 68:21

tives came to comfort him, because even until now the Lord suffers in his members, but in the last days all the Israelites will hasten to believe when they recognize the preaching of Elijah, and they will come back to the protection of him from whom they had fled.

That remarkable banquet will be held with a great concourse of peoples. Then after his trials Job will appear healed, when the Lord after his passion and resurrection is known by converts and believers alike to live in immortality in heaven through the certitude of faith. Then Job's reward is finally seen, when God is believed in his majestic power as he is, and those who formerly resisted him are seen subjected to his faith. So at the end of the world the Hebrews will gather to believe, and they will devoutly offer sacrifices to the Redeemer of the human race in the power of his divinity as if to the healed Job. As the text rightly continues, *each one gave him a ewe lamb and a gold earring.** What else does the ewe lamb signify but innocence, and what the earring but obedience? The ewe lamb is the simple soul that listens and is adorned with an earring or the grace of humility.

*Job 42:11

28. But since an occasion has arisen for expanding on the virtue of obedience, we may perhaps discuss that virtue slightly more carefully and attentively and show something of its great value. It is the only virtue to start with that introduces and guards other virtues in the mind. The first man received the commandment that he was to keep, that by which, if he would obediently submit himself, he would reach eternal happiness without effort. That is why Samuel said, *Obedience is better than sacrifice, and giving heed is better than the offering of fat rams, because rebellion is equal to the sin of divination, and the refusal of acquiescence is as the crime of idolatry.** Obedience therefore is proposed in

*1 Sam 15:22-23

accord with the law of sacrifice, because with sacrifice someone else's flesh is slaughtered, but with obedience one's own will is offered.

The more people's pride and judgment are repressed in God's eyes, and they immolate themselves with the sword of the commandment, the sooner God is pleased with them. On the other hand, disobedience is called the sin of divination, so that the greatness of the virtue of obedience might be clearly shown. What is better, you see, is displayed by what is worse, and its praise is felt thereby. If rebellion is equal to the sin of divination, and refusal of acquiescence is equivalent to the crime of idolatry, obedience alone possesses the merit of faith, without which everyone is guilty of infidelity, even those who seem to have faith. So Solomon displays obedience when he says, *The obedient person speaks of victories.**

*Prov 21:28

Yes, the obedient person does speak of victories, because when we humbly subject ourselves to someone else's voice, we conquer our own hearts. And so Truth speaks in the Gospel: *The person who comes to me I will not cast out, because I have not come down from heaven to do my own will, but the will of him who sent me.** So what? Would he reject those who came to him if he were doing his own will? Who is there who does not know that the Son's will does not differ from the Father's will? But because the first human being wanted to do his own will, and for that reason he was exiled from the joy of Paradise, the second human being came to redeem mankind, and while he was ready to do the Father's will and not his own, he taught us to remain within that will. Accordingly, since he does the Father's will and not his own, he does not cast out those who come to him; no, he gives us his own example and subjects us to obedience, and so he closes the door to our going out. So he says somewhere else, *I cannot do anything of myself,*

*John 6:37-38

but as I hear, so I judge.* Consequently he orders us to follow obedience all the way to death. So if he judges as he hears, he then also obeys when he comes as Judge. Then lest obedience should seem to be a hard task to us all the way to the termination of the present life, our Redeemer shows us that he observes obedience himself even when he comes as Judge. What is extraordinary if the human being who sins subjects himself to obedience in the brief span of the present life, when the Mediator between God and humanity, he who rewards those who obey, does not abandon obedience?

*John 5:30

29. We must realize, however, that evil may never be done through obedience, although the doing of good should sometimes be put off on account of obedience. Nor was there any evil in the tree of Paradise that God forbade humans to touch. Rather it was better for the human being created good by God to grow through obedience, and it would have been fitting for that human being to be steered away from good, inasmuch as by avoiding good he would have shown himself a more humble subject of his Maker, and consequently more virtuous in his acts. But notice what is said in Genesis: *You may eat from all the trees of Paradise, but the tree of knowledge of good and evil you must not touch.** For God, who forbids those subject to him any good, whatever it may be, it is necessary that he should grant many things that are good, lest the obedient minds should somehow perish if they should abstain from all things that are good and be internally depressed. So the Lord granted all the trees of Paradise for food when he forbade only one, since he did not wish his creature to die but to make progress; it was just as easy to forbid one as to allow freedom for all.

*Gen 2:16-17

30. But sometimes prosperity in this world as well as adversity is in order for our sakes, so we must above all realize that there are times when if we are to have anything of our own, there is no such thing as obedience; on the other hand, there are times when there is a modicum of obedience if we are not to have something of our own. If success in this world is to be grasped, you see, and when the higher place is demanded, the one who obeys in order to gain them loses the value of obedience for himself, if his own desire pants to gain them. He is certainly not guided by obedience when he does the bidding of his own ambitious urge in order to gain prosperity in this life.

On the other hand, when contempt of this world is demanded, and when we are ordered to achieve ignominy and insult, unless the soul desires these things for itself, the merit of obedience diminishes if the person unwillingly sinks to the level of this world's contempt or refuses to do so. Obedience is in fact cultivated to its own harm when a person's own wishes never join the mind in any sense for the purpose of accepting the world's scorn. Obedience then should have its own part even in adversity, and in prosperity on the other hand it should absolutely not have its own part, inasmuch as even in adversity the more a person's desire conforms to the divine plan, the more he can boast; as for prosperity, the more detached one is from boastfulness, even in accord with God's will, the truer that person's obedience will be.

31. But we will make the value of this virtue clearer if we mention the actions of two men for the heavenly kingdom. When Moses was guarding sheep in the desert, the Lord called him by means of an angel speaking from the fire, so that he might bring about the freedom of the whole nation of the Israelites. But because he was of himself of a humble disposition, he was at first afraid of the honor offered him of such a large responsibility, and he had recourse to the excuse of weakness. He said, *Please, Lord, I am not eloquent, but since yesterday and the day before, when you spoke to your servant, I am of stumbling and slow speech.** And neglecting himself, he requested another, saying, *Send him whom you will send.** See how he speaks to the Creator of the tongue and complains that he has no tongue; he wanted to avoid accepting the power of so great a responsibility.

*Exod 4:10

*Exod 4:13

Paul too was advised by God that he should go up to Jerusalem, as he told the Galatians: *I went up to Jerusalem with Barnabas along with Titus. I went with a revelation.** He was on the journey when he met the prophet Agabus, who told him how much adversity awaited him in Jerusalem. It is written of course that this same Agabus took Paul's belt and bound his own feet with it, saying, *This is how they will bind the owner of this belt in Jerusalem.** Paul, however, forthwith answered, *I am ready not only to be bound but even to die in Jerusalem for Jesus' name, nor do I hold my life to be more precious than myself.** By the guidance of revelation accordingly he went to Jerusalem, experienced adversity, and even freely desired it. He heard fearful tidings, but he still more ardently desired them.

*Gal 2:1-2

*Acts 21:2

*Acts 21:13; 20:24

So Moses of himself had no desire for prosperity, but he prayed against accepting a place at the head of the people of Israel. Paul on the other hand was led to adversity by his own wish, because he gained knowledge of misfortunes that threatened him, but by devotion of the spirit he even fervently desired still more painful experiences. The former wished to avoid the honor of present power ordered by God. The latter, when in God's plan harsh and difficult experiences were in the offing, eagerly prepared himself for even greater hardship. The undaunted courage of both of these leaders has gone before us and taught us that if we would really win for ourselves the prize of obedience, we must either struggle for prosperity in this world only at God's command, or on the other hand struggle for adversity by our own choice.

32. We should take note however that in this passage* the ewe lamb is offered along with the gold earring, and the gold earring along with the ewe lamb, obviously because obedience is always an ornament for innocent minds, as the Lord testifies: *My sheep hear my voice; I know them, and they follow me.** For blessed Job therefore no one offers an earring without a ewe lamb or a ewe lamb without an earring, since in fact no one who is not innocent obeys his Redeemer, and he cannot be innocent who despises obedience. Accordingly obedience itself must be observed, not with slavish fear but with the affection of charity, not with fear of punishment but with the love of justice, so all those who come to the banquet are reported to have offered a golden earring. So, as you can see, charity shines in the obedience they display, because just as gold outshines all other metals, so charity outshines all other virtues.

*of Job

*John 10:27

33. The many heretical sects, however, can have neither innocence nor true obedience; consequently those who come to the knowledge of faith offer a lamb, but only one; they offer an earring, but only one. This means that they come in such wise that they remain innocently and obediently in the unity of Holy Church. The one certainly cannot be divided into numbers, because this thing that we call one is not a number. So they offer a ewe lamb, but only one; they offer an earring, but only one. This means that they come to Holy Church with innocence and obedience; they bring a mind that is undivided by schism or sect.

34. We may open the eyes of faith and contemplate that ultimate banquet of Holy Church concerning her reception of the people of Israel. To that banquet the great Elijah will certainly come and act as the host of those invited to the banquet, and then the friends and the relatives will come with gifts to the one whom they had derided a little before when he was subjected to trials. When Judgment Day is near, the very power of the coming Lord will be already in some way shining through upon them along with the precursor's voice or certain unexpected signs. And when they rush forward to forestall his wrath, they will hasten the time of their own conversion.

The converts then come with gifts, because they are venerating him whom they had derided in his passion slightly earlier; they offer the fruits of virtues in place of gifts; they beyond any doubt complete with their offering what we perceive as already accomplished in large part and what we believe remains to be perfected: *The daughters of Tyre will adore him with gifts.** Then indeed will the daughters of Tyre adore him with their plentiful gifts, when the minds of the people of Israel that are now subjected to the desires of this world will bring the gifts of their confession of faith to him, finally recognized, whom they had denied in their pride. And although at the very time when Antichrist is drawing near, the lives of the faithful will seem to be less virtuous, even when the hearts of the strong will be seized by fear in the conflict with that grave son of perdition,* at the preaching of Elijah not only will many of the faithful be strengthened to remain firm with Holy Church, but as we have said above, many of the unbelievers will be converted to the knowledge of faith, in such a way that whoever are left of the people of Israel who had previously been completely rejected will come running to the bosom of mother church with all manner of loving devotion. So the text now happily continues,

*Ps 44:13

*the Antichrist

XV. 35. *The Lord then blessed the latter days of Job more than the former ones.** We believe that these events literally happened, and we hope that they remain to come about mystically. The last days of Job are more blessed than the first ones, and as far as the receiving of the people of Israel is concerned and the pressing end of the present world, the Lord comforts the pain of Holy Church with the gathering together of many souls. The more obviously she notices that the time of the present life is pressing on towards its end, the more abundantly she is enriched. The preachers richly blessed by Holy Church in the last days were foreseen by the psalmist, and he said, *Their fruit will abound even in old age, and they will continue to preach.** In old age their fruit will abound, because while their lives go on, their strength always produces better fruit, and the profit of their merits continues to grow along with the passing of time. They will continue to preach, because while they are preaching about heaven, even as they bravely endure adversity, their bravery also abundantly increases the profit of souls. The next verse:

XVI. 36. *He had fourteen thousand head of sheep, six thousand camels, a thousand yoke of oxen, and a thousand she-asses, and he had seven sons and three daughters.** The opening verses of the story showed that Job had seven thousand sheep, three thousand camels, fifty yoke of oxen, and fifty she-asses before the trial he suffered. All these were lost through his misfortunes, but now they have been restored in double measure. His children, however, have been restored to the same number as those he had lost. Previously he had seven sons and three daughters, and now he has been described as receiving seven sons and three daughters, so that those who had died are shown to be alive. It was said, *The Lord gave Job double quantity of all he had before.**

*Job 42:12

*Ps 91:15-16

*Job 42:12-13

*Job 42:10

But the Lord again added to Job just as many children as he had lost; yes, the ten whom he had lost were again restored in the flesh to the same number of ten. The ten who were lost were saved in the hidden life of souls. If anyone desires to be fed with the food of mysteries, it is necessary that he should know that we see intellectual animals in the previously mentioned animals, without considering the point of the story. We can understand, you see, that in these animals there is signified the totality of the people of faith who are gathered together. That is why the psalmist speaks to the Father about the Son: *You have put all things under his feet: sheep and all cattle, as well as the beasts of the field.** That is why the same prophet, seeing the simple people abiding in Holy Church, said, *Your animals will dwell there.**

*Ps 8:8 LXX

*Ps 67:11

37. What then do we take the sheep to mean if not innocent people, what the camels if not those who transcend the evil behavior of other people by the curving mass of their gushing vices, what the yokes of oxen but the Israelites subject to the law, what the she-asses but the simple minds of the Gentiles? The psalmist testifies that the noun *sheep* means innocent people when he says, *We are his people, the sheep of his pasture.** Nor do those who neglect the welfare of innocent people eat their fill of the interior pasture.

*Ps 94:7

38. Holy Scripture sometimes uses the word *camel* to designate the Lord, and sometimes the pride of the Gentiles is like a growing mound curving at the top. Because however the camel sometimes willingly bends down to have burdens loaded upon it, it not unreasonably signifies the grace of our Redeemer, who by the fact that he deigns to take on the burden of our weak nature willingly descends from his powerful height. That is why he has the Evangelist say, *No one takes it from me, but I lay it down myself. I have power to lay down*

*John 10:18 *my life, and I have power to take it up again.** He also says elsewhere, *It is easier for a camel to go through a needle's eye than for a rich person to enter the kingdom of heaven.** What does the use of the words *rich person* signify but anyone who is proud, and what the word *camel* but Christ's own condescension? So the camel went through the needle's eye when our Redeemer himself passed through the narrow gate of his passion even to the point of accepting death. And his passion was like a needle in that its sting involved bodily pain. It is easier then for a camel to go through a needle's eye than for a rich man to enter the kingdom of heaven, because unless he first took upon himself the burden of our weakness through his passion, showing us in this way the opening of humility, our rigid pride would never bend down to the level of his humility.

*Matt 19:24

On the other hand, the camel signifies the winding character of Gentiles that is full of vices. Moses tells us that the day was already low when Rebecca, seated on a camel, saw Isaac go out in the field, and she immediately alighted from the camel and covered her face with a veil, ashamed of letting him see her. Whom else does Isaac signify in that when the day was almost over he went out to the field, but him who at the end of this world, as if arriving at the end of the day, went out as if into the field? Although he was invisible, he made himself visible in this world. When she was seated on the camel Rebecca saw him, because the church coming from the Gentiles awaited him, while she was still supported by vices and not yet spiritually but naturally motivated. But she straightway alighted from the camel, because she abandoned the vices with which she had previously covered herself with pride, and she took care to veil herself, because seeing the Lord, she was ashamed of the weakness of her behavior, and she who had previously freely ridden the camel got down and covered herself with shame afterwards. So then the church was converted from her former pride through the words of the apostles, and just like Rebecca getting down from the camel, she covered herself with a veil. To her it is said, *But then what good did those things do you, which embarrass you now?**   *Rom 6:21

39. As for the oxen, they sometimes signify the madness of lust, sometimes the painful courage of preachers, and sometimes the humble Israelites. Solomon shows us how the word *oxen* indicates the madness of lust by means of a comparison; after having first declared the wantonness of a woman of evil enticement he added, *They are quick to follow her like oxen led to the slaughter.** On the other hand, the words of the law testify that the word *ox* expresses the labor of preaching, where it is said, *Do not muzzle an ox when it is treading out the grain.** It is as if it were said openly, "Do not forbid a preacher of the word to receive his stipend." Again the word *ox* expresses the people of Israel, as the prophet exclaims when he is foretelling the Redeemer's coming: *The ox knows its owner, and the ass its Lord's crib.** He makes the ox signify the people of Israel who bear the yoke of the law, but the ass signifies the Gentile people, who are given up to pleasure and completely savage.

*Prov 7:22

*Deut 25:4

*Isa 1:3

40. The word *asses* or *she-asses* signifies at times the wantonness of lust, at times the meekness of simple people, or at times, as we have said, the folly of Gentiles. It is openly declared that the use of the term *asses* signifies the wantonness of lust when the prophet says, *Their flesh is asses' flesh.** On the other hand, the word *she-asses* signifies the life of simple people, and this is expressed when our Redeemer was on the way to Jerusalem and he is reported to have ridden an ass. Jerusalem, you know, means the vision of peace. What

*Ezek 23:20

then is signified when the Lord, seated on an ass, sets out for Jerusalem, except that he possesses and leads simple minds all the way to the vision of peace by means of his sacred seat? Again, that the word *asses* signifies the folly of the Gentiles, the prophet testifies: *Blessed are you who sow seed over all the waters, and tame ox and ass.** Sowing seed beside all the waters means preaching the fruitful words of life to all the peoples. Taming ox and ass means binding the ways of the Israelite and Gentile peoples by means of the chains of heavenly precepts.

*Isa 32:20

41. Therefore, having preserved the literal truth of the passage, we not unreasonably believe that the people of Holy Church are signified by all these animals under blessed Job's name, inasmuch as the dispensation of the Holy Spirit has arranged all that has been written in a wonderful way, so that they inform us as to the past and promise what is to come. Let us acknowledge then in the sheep the faithful and innocent people of the Jews who had long been fed and satisfied with the feed of the law. Let us recognize in the camels the simple people who came to faith from the Gentiles; formerly they were found with a kind of deformity of body under an impious rite, and they appeared to be extremely offensive, full of evil-smelling vices. Because Holy Scripture, as I have said before, is often careful to repeat itself, it stoutly confirms that these same Israelites can be understood as the oxen who are as it were tamed by the yoke of the law. The Gentile people on the other hand, as we have said, may be signified by the asses; these latter bent themselves down for the worship of stones, with their backs foolishly curved over and with unresisting minds, and they served idols like brute animals.

Accordingly when Holy Church was under intense pressure in the beginning and subject to numerous trials, she lost both the people of Israel and even many of the Gentile peoples, that is, those she could not win, but she receives them back double in the end, because the number of the faithful of both nations that are in her keeps growing greater and greater. So the yokes of oxen can be understood as the preachers. When the Lord sent them out to preach, as the Gospel bears witness, he is said to have sent them two by two,* either because there are two commandments of love, or because there can be no society of less than two; so the holy preachers should realize from the very manner of their being sent forth how much they should love the concord of society. As we have said, the asses may signify the minds of simple people, but Holy Church receives two asses and two oxen, because when the holy preachers had been hard pressed by fear they kept silence during that long trial, while the minds of simple people were terrified, and they were afraid of confessing the truth; the less able they were to act at that time, the more courageously they now confess the truth and lift up their voices.

*Luke 10:1

42. We have said a few words to show how the church is signified, recalling that we have spoken at greater length in the beginning of this work to show how these words signify the Head of the same Holy Church. Accordingly those who wish to have greater satisfaction on these points should read the second book of this work. If however we want to know at this point in greater detail why there were a thousand yoke of oxen, a thousand she-asses, but six thousand camels and fourteen thousand sheep, we may briefly say that the number one thousand is held to symbolize perfection by the worldly wise, because it yields a perfect cube of the number ten. Ten by ten yields a hundred, which is already a square number, but flat. So if we want the height of a solid square, we again multiply 100 by 10 to get 1000. Six on the other hand is a perfect number in that it is the first to be completed by its parts. Six is made up of one, two, and three, half of which is one and two, and three completes it, since six is the sum of one, two, and three. There is no other number before six that can be divided into its parts, and into which the parts are added.

We transcend all this, however, through the high science of Holy Scripture, and we find there how the numbers six, seven, ten, and one thousand are perfect. The number six is perfect in Holy Scripture, because when the world began, the Lord completed on the sixth day the work he began on the first day. The number seven in Holy Scripture is perfect, because every good work is accomplished through the Spirit with seven virtues, so that faith and works finish together. The number ten in Holy Scripture is perfect, because the law is completed by ten commandments, and all infractions are held within the number ten, and as Truth reports the workers in the vineyard are each paid a denarius.[1] Now to get a denarius three are added to seven. The human being is composed of body and soul and seven qualities.

The human person's life has three spiritual and four bodily qualities. In the love of God, you see, three spiritual qualities are invoked, since the law says: *You shall love the Lord your God with your whole mind and your whole soul and with all your strength.** The four bodily qualities are obviously contained in hot, cold, wet, and dry matter. The human being then is made up of seven qualities, and it has been said that he gets paid a denarius, and when he receives the grace of the

*Matt 22:37

---

[1] *Denarius* of course is Latin, and it refers to a Roman coin whose original value was 10 asses. Modern translations have *penny*, which is closer to the Hebrew or Aramaic.

heavenly homeland his seven qualities are added to three heavenly ones, so that the human being might receive the contemplation of the Trinity, and as the pay for his work he might live fulfilled by a denarius.

Or perhaps the seven virtues are what he works with in this life until he receives payment for them in the contemplation of the Trinity, so that the life of laborers is repaid with a denarius. But everyone who is perfect also receives a denarius in this life, when to those seven virtues faith, hope, and charity are added. The number one thousand is also taken by Holy Scripture to be a perfect number, because it is used to signify the whole world, so it is written, *The word he commanded for a thousand generations.** We should certainly not think that the world is confined to a hundred generations, so what else could a thousand generations mean but all the generations that there are?

*Ps 104:8

Finally blessed Job received fourteen thousand sheep. Since there is in Holy Church a perfection of virtues, it is extended to both sexes, so that the number seven is duplicated. But there are six thousand camels, because those who disappeared from her long ago because of their evil-smelling vices now accept a fullness of labor in her.

Job receives a thousand yoke of oxen and a thousand asses, because he raises both the Israelites and the Gentiles, the learned and the simple, after their falls into temptation to the summit of perfection. He receives seven sons and three daughters, because to those who are born with seven virtues in their minds he adds faith, hope, and charity for complete perfection, so that the fewer virtues that are lacking to the faithful he brings, the more truly he can rejoice in his offspring. But now we have with great brevity covered this much, so we can concentrate on the names to be ascertained for the daughters as well. The next verse.

XVII. 43. *He named the first Dies, the second Casia, and the third Cornustibii.** Because these names are words for virtues, the translator has rightly taken care not to give them the form found in the Arabic language, but to translate them straightforwardly into Latin. Who does not know in fact that *Dies* and *Casia* are Latin words? As for *Cornustibii*, although the word is not *Cornus* but *Cornu*, followed not by *Cantantium Fistula Tibium*,* but *Tibia*,† by not at all preserving the correct gender in the Latin language I imagine the translator preferred to express the matter simply, but to keep the style of the language from which he was translating. Or perhaps in compounding one word out of two, *cornu* and *tibia*, he was at liberty to give both words, translated into one part of speech in Latin, whatever gender he preferred.

*Job 42:14

*English: Pipe of Singers

†feminine gender, not neuter

So what does it mean when blessed Job's first daughter is named *Dies*, the second *Casia*, and the third *Cornustibii*, if not that it is the entire human race that is chosen by the kindness of the Creator and by the mercy of the Redeemer and is signified by these names? The human being, you see, like the day, shone forth from his creation, because his Creator sprayed him with the light of inborn innocence. But by his own choice he fell into the darkness of sin, because he abandoned the light of truth, and he hid himself in the night of error, because he is elsewhere said to have followed a shadow.* But the generosity of his goodness did not forsake our Creator, but he moved against the darkness of our wretched state; he exercised still greater power to recall from error and redeem the creature whom he first created for justice by his power. After his fall, you see, the human being lacked the initial steadfastness with which he was created, so the Creator supported him against the internal war of opposing corruption with many virtues that he gave him. These virtues indeed of

*Sir 34:2

those who were progressing came to the knowledge of other human beings as sweet fragrant odors. That is in fact how Paul expresses it: *We are the sweet odor of Christ toward God.**

*2 Cor 2:15

That is what Holy Church speaks of as a sweet fragrant odor in her chosen ones. She says in the Song of Songs, *While the King was on his couch, my nard gave forth its fragrance.** It is as if he said more clearly, "As long as the King hides himself from my gaze in the secret resting place of heaven, the lives of the chosen ones will be lived with the wonderful odors of virtues, and because they do not yet see him whom they desire, the fire of their desires burns more ardently." As long as the King remains on his couch, indeed, the bride's nard sends forth its fragrance, and while the Lord remains quiet in his blessed abode, the virtue of the saints in the church administers to us the grace of high sweetness. Accordingly, since the human race was first created in the shining light of innocence, and was later redeemed and spread the odor of sweetness by the doing of good works, Job's first daughter was rightly named *Dies* and the second not unreasonably named *Casia*. In fact the latter daughter was surely rightly named *Casia*, since she spreads out widely with the odor of a sublime way of life.[2] The human being, you see, was created righteous in his very beginning and was then in no need of as many virtues as he needs now, because if he had chosen to remain as he was created, he could have conquered the enemy stationed outside him without difficulty. But after the adversary once broke into the internal human

*Song 1:11

---

[2] The Latin *casia* is an aromatic tree or shrub, perhaps a species of the genus cinnamomum, widely used in perfumes and medicines (*Oxford Latin Dictionary* [Oxford: Clarendon Press, 1982], s.v. *casia*).

being through his own consent, it takes much more effort to cast out as victor him who at first as assailant could have been ejected without trouble.

44. Much indeed must now be displayed that was unnecessary in Paradise. There is now need for the virtue of patience, the laborious teaching of doctrine, chastening of the body, constant prayer, confession of sins, and the shedding of tears, all of which the human being did not need at creation. He received goodness and well-being, you see, at his first creation. The sick person is given a bitter draft to drink, so that he may recover from disease and reach a state of health. As for the healthy person, she is not ordered to take anything in order to be well, but is told what to avoid in order not to get sick. Now then, when we can by no means keep the health we have, we undertake major efforts, but we take care to regain it when it is lost. And since all these efforts on behalf of our restoration are supported by influential opinions in Holy Church, the second daughter's name, *Casia*, deserves to have fragrance, so that whereas the first daughter, *Dies*, stands out with the dignity of creation, the second, *Casia*, has the fragrance of courage from the grace of redemption. So it happens that the said coming Redeemer is greeted by the prophet: *Your robes are all fragrant with myrrh, aloes, and cassia; from the ivory steps*[3] *the daughters of kings rejoice to join your train.**

*Ps 44:9-10

But what do such words as *myrrh, aloes*, and *cassia* signify, if not the sweetness of virtues? And what do ivory steps signify but the climbing of those making progress with efforts of great courage? The Redeemer is accordingly coming, and he wears robes redolent of

---

[3] Unfortunately the Latin Vulgate knows nothing of an "ivory tower" but only "ivory steps."

myrrh, aloes, and cassia, because he mercifully deigns to wear his chosen ones and to waft abroad the fragrance of the myrrh of virtue. In them the same odor is taken up the ivory steps, because in them the reputation of virtue is not based on a pretended appearance, but is produced by a true and solid climbing of works. It is rightly added, *From the ivory steps the daughters of kings rejoice to join your train.* Holy souls, you see, had been brought forth from the ancient fathers for the knowledge of the truth, and they rejoice to follow the Redeemer's train, because from the fact that they did well they claim no praise for themselves.

The third stage of the human race consists in the new state of the resurrection of the flesh, when it is raised to that harmony of eternal praise, and so the third daughter is named *Cornustibii*. And what else but the song of joy is meant by *Cornustibii*? It is there that we really find the fulfillment of the prophet's words: *Sing the Lord a new song.** It is there really fulfilled when the singing of God's praise is no longer a work of faith, but it will be sung on account of the reality of contemplation. There our Creator receives from us true songs of his praise, who made the human race *Dies* by creating it, *Casia* by redeeming it, and *Cornustibii* by raising it to himself. We have been created as light; now we have been redeemed as cassia; in the future we will be *Cornustibii*, raised up for the exultation of eternal praise. But before the bride reaches the marriage chamber, she gets rid of all life's offensiveness, prepares herself for the love of the Bridegroom, and adorns herself with comely virtues. She makes efforts to please the judgment of the internal master, and when she has been raised up by internal desires she transcends the base behavior of human association. So we are rightly told about blessed Job's daughters,

*Ps 149:1

XVIII. 45. *No woman was found in all the world as beautiful as Job's daughters.** The souls of the chosen ones, you see, transcend by the splendor of their beauty all the people found on the earth in human associations. The more they afflict and despise themselves externally, the better disposed they are internally. That is why the church is told by the psalmist, *The King has desired your beauty** when she is adorned with the beauty of the chosen ones. And he adds a little later, *All the glory of this daughter of kings is within her.** If she sought external glory, she would not have that internal beauty desired by the King. Even if many people shone with the adornment of virtues, and even if they surpassed the merits of everyone else by their perfect lives, nevertheless, those who, being aware of their own weaknesses, are not able of themselves to go on in the pursuit of higher attainments are content to sit in the church's lap and be loved by her. As long as they manage to avoid evil they are satisfied, even if they do not contrive to attain the higher good as much as they desire. However, the Lord receives them kindly and admits them into his presence as a fitting reward. So it goes on:

XIX. 46. *Their father gave them a share in the inheritance along with their brothers.** Because then of the merit of the perfect, they are said to be beautiful, but as being a type of the imperfect, they also receive, as if they were weak, a share in the inheritance along with their brothers, It was not the custom of the ancients for the female heirs to receive an inheritance along with those of the masculine gender, because the severity of the law preferred strong individuals and disdained those who were weak; its intention was to favor strictness, not kindness. But when our loving Redeemer came, no one was aware of his or her weakness, nor would anyone lose hope of getting a share in the heavenly inheritance.

*Job 42:15

*Ps 44:12

*Ps 44:14

*Job 42:15

Our Father did allocate to women a right to share in the inheritance among men, and he admits the weak and humble among the strong and perfect to their share in the heavenly inheritance. The Truth himself says in the gospel, *In my Father's house there are many mansions.** With the Father there are many mansions, because in that state of happiness, no one is treated differently or receives a different place in accordance with different merits, nor does anyone feel deprived because of being different, since whatever anyone receives is enough for that person. Accordingly sisters come along with brothers to the inheritance, because the weak ones are admitted there along with the strong, inasmuch as anyone who is not raised up because of imperfection is not shut out from the division of the inheritance because of lowliness. Paul talks about those mansions that are distributed because of merit. He says, *There is the glory of the sun, the glory of the moon, and the glory of the stars. Star differs from star in glory.** The next verse:

*John 14:2

*1 Cor 15:41

XX. 47. *After these events Job lived a hundred and forty years, and he saw his children and his children's children up to the fourth generation. Then he died an old man and full of years.** Holy Scripture rarely uses the phrase *full of years* except for someone whose life is being praised by the same Holy Scripture. The one whose days are empty of course is the one who, however long he lived, consumed the days of his life with vanity. On the other hand, the one is said to be full of days whose days never passed without purpose but had the daily reward for good works from the righteous Judge, and after they had passed they were preserved.

*Job 42:16

48. But since there are those who would wish to see these words also interpreted as a type of the church, it is incumbent upon us to rejoice at their spiritual understanding to the point that their wishes must be obeyed. So if fourteen is multiplied by ten we get one hundred forty. The life of Holy Church is rightly computed as the product of ten and four, because she is the custodian of both testaments, and she lives according to the Decalogue of the Law as well as according to the four books of the Gospel. Her life accordingly goes on to the summit of perfection. Although the apostle Paul wrote fifteen letters,[4] Holy Church keeps only fourteen, so that she might point out from the very number of his letters that the famous teacher explored the secrets of both the Law and the Gospel.

Blessed Job is rightly said to have lived after his trials were over, because Holy Church was also first buffeted by the blows of discipline and later strengthened by a perfect life. She also saw her children and her children's children up to the fourth generation, because in this life whose years unfold according to four seasons, she daily gazes on new offspring born for her through the words of preachers even to the end of the world. Nor is it incompatible with truth that we should say that seasons should correspond with generations. What else, you see, is any succession but the offspring of a race? After the butler of the king of Egypt had a dream about three bunches of grapes that he picked, the aforesaid Joseph interpreted it in the sense that the three bunches were three days. If therefore three bunches could signify three days, why could not four generations also signify four seasons?

Holy Church accordingly sees her children when she sees the first young shoot. She sees her children's children when she realizes that other faithful are born to faith from those same faithful. When the church is old and dies full of days, it means that light follows as the reward of daily works after the weight of corruption is

---

[4] Gregory may be referring here to the letter to the Laodiceans mentioned in Col 4:16.

left behind, and it is exchanged for the incorruption of the spiritual homeland. She dies full of days for whom the falling years do not pass but are stabilized by retribution for acts that stand firm. She dies full of days who keeps working at what does not pass during this passing time. That is why the apostles are told, *Do not labor for perishable food, but for the food that remains for eternal life.** Holy Church then does not lose her days, even when she abandons the present life, because in her chosen ones she finds the light increasing as much as she now guides them cautiously and solicitously in every temptation. The church does not lose her days, because she does not neglect the vigilant weighing of herself daily in this life, nor is she stuck in any idleness as regards all the good that could be done.

*John 6:27

Solomon says of her therefore, *She considers the ways of her household, nor does she eat idle bread.** She does consider the ways of her household, because she investigates in detail all her conscientious thoughts. Nor does she eat idle bread, because what she perceives in Holy Scripture by intelligence she shows before the eyes of the eternal Judge by displaying her works. She is said to die, because when she is absorbed in contemplation of eternity, her awareness of changing things dies, so that in no way can anything live anymore that impedes the sharpness of that internal vision. She sees internal things much more truly to the same extent that she dies to all that is external.

*Prov 31:27

Let us then believe that in blessed Job as one member of the church that death and plenitude of days has been accomplished, and let us hope that it is to take place in the whole church together, inasmuch as the truth of the event has been so preserved as to realize a future prophecy. The good things we know about the lives of saints are nothing if they lack truth, and if they lack mystery, they do not amount to much. So the Holy Spirit describes the lives of good people for us, and lets them shine upon our spiritual intelligence; in this way the meaning of the story upholds the literal truth, and the soul remains fixed in its own understanding midway between past and future; thus our hope is fixed upon the future, and our faith upon the past.

49. And so the work is done, and I can see that it is incumbent upon me to return to myself. Even when we try to speak correctly, you see, our mind is often scattered outside itself. When we concentrate on the words by which our integrity of soul is to be expressed, that integrity is minimized, because the words draw our soul to externals. So after a public speech we must return to the meeting house of the heart, so that as if I were in a kind of consulting hall, I might call the thoughts of my mind together to the discernment of myself, so that I might see whether I had carelessly spoken evil or not spoken well of what is good. The good is spoken rightly then, when the one who speaks desires to please only the One from whom he received what he speaks. And even if I do not find that I have spoken any evil, nonetheless my defense is not that I would never speak it.

If on the other hand by God's gift I have said anything good, I obviously confess that it is my fault if I have said it less well. So returning to myself internally and putting aside the leaves of words and the branches of sentences, when I inspect the very root of my intention with minute watchfulness, I know that my wish has indeed been to please God above all with my work. But with the same intention by which I try to please God, I do not know how the intention of human praise has inserted itself stealthily. When I now discern it after all is done, I find that I have done otherwise than I know myself to have begun. It is often thus with our intention: we begin correctly under the eyes of God, but the intention of human praise follows, hidden close by, and seizes it on the way, as it were. In the same way food is consumed by necessity, certainly, but in the very act of eating gluttony stealthily creeps up, and delight mixes itself with the act of eating. That is why it often happens that when we begin to eat for the sake of health, we complete the feeding of the body for the sake of pleasure.

It is to be confessed therefore that when our good intention desires to please God, a less good intention sometimes joins it by stealth, and that intention wants to please men and women with God's gifts. If we strictly discuss these things with God's help, what place of salvation remains for us among these pitfalls, when even our evil deeds are strictly evil, and even the good that we think we have can never be purely good. But I think this to be a compensation for my work: that all that I secretly blame in myself I unhesitatingly and openly speak in the ears of the brothers. Because I did not hide my thoughts in my exposition, in my confession I do not hide my sufferings. In the exposition I have made plain the gifts; in confession I uncover the wounds.

Because in this so great human race there is no lack of little ones who should be instructed by my words, neither is there any lack of great ones who could have mercy on my known weakness; in both of these ways I confer assistance on some brothers as far as I can, and hope for it from others. I have spoken to the former to instruct them what to do; to the latter I confess openly what they should pardon. I do not keep from the former the medicine of words: I do not hide from the latter the torture of wounds. Therefore I beseech whoever reads these words to offer for me the comfort of their prayers to the strict Judge and wash with their tears anything sordid they find in me. When the power of prayer and of the exposition is compared, let my reader surpass me in recompense; if he accepts words from me, let him shed tears for me.

Afterword

It is now some twenty-one years since I started the American English translation of Saint Gregory the Great's *magnum opus*, the *Moralia in Job*. I didn't know what I was getting into. I knew it was long, of course, filling three huge tomes of Corpus Christianorum Series Latina, itself a great undertaking of Brepols publishers going back to the 1960s and perhaps earlier, filling in Migne's gaps with more scientific methods of determining ancient texts. It is a great tradition going back to the patristic and medieval copying of ancient texts.

I was just feeling my way at first, heavily dependent on Cassell's and on the New Latin Dictionary from Oxford, England. I used as well the nineteenth-century Oxford translation, which was ultra-literal, but very helpful. I naturally found Gregory's Introduction and Letter to Leander easy to follow, especially because of his human admissions and humble sharing. He doesn't speak very much about the Byzantine court, but only about the monks he brought with him and whose life he shares. His duties as *apocrisiarius* no doubt did not consume much time, and he was not yet pope. He enjoyed his life among the monks and found it restful, though he does complain about his many illnesses, especially his stomach trouble. He was very sensitive to his audience and altered his presentation from time to time, especially when they requested more moral or allegorical adaptations. He explains his method of composition at the end of the Introduction, going over the copyists' texts and making additions or subtractions as seemed appropriate. He disclaims any slavish use of Donatus (a famous grammarian possibly of Cicero's time). His style is somewhat scholarly, but mostly conversational. His thought is quite intricate, making him resort to long periods with complex phrasing. His Latin is not easy. He rewards study, however.

He interprets the entire Book of Job. I am not aware of any other father, Latin or Greek, who accomplished such an enterprise. I have not counted the words, but I am sure they run into thousands, perhaps millions. His vocabulary is immense, and he uses words in unusual senses. His sentence structure is often baffling, making abundant use of past and present participles. One sentence can often cover half a paragraph or more. One paragraph covering two pages is often frequent. He makes abundant use of images. The image of a ship coming into or leaving port is especially dear to him. His use of the phrase *servitor servitorum Dei* may be the first in the Western church, but I'm not sure of that.

I learned a lot in the process. Chiefly I learned that the Latin words I thought I knew, I did not know at all, or at least not cumulatively. As we all know, words have a history and different contexts. That is why we speak of classical, patristic, late, early medieval, scholastic, and even modern Latin. And each of the early writers has his own style. Gregory has his, Augustine has his, Jerome has his, Hilary has his, Cassian has his, etc. Gregory of course was heavily influenced by Augustine, especially in his anti-heretical writings. But Gregory's knowledge of the classics is probably greater, since he probably never left Rome, other than for his sojourn at the Greek capital. As he admits, his Bible is mainly Jerome's Vulgate, though he sometimes refers to the Greek Septuagint. His knowledge of Greek is probably not extensive. His stay at Constantinople may not have exceeded three years.

What some may find interesting is that he considers Elihu as the target of the Lord's strictures, "Who is this wrapping up statements in unskillful sentences?" (Book 28.III.11). No doubt some modern interpreters would agree with him—and find some present-day examples as well!

Well, I won't say it hasn't been a lot of fun. It has. Nor that I have enjoyed every minute of it. There have been some man-sized headaches sorting out those complex clauses and getting them to make sense in English. Sometimes the exact sense of the Latin word was difficult to pinpoint. But yes, I did find it a source of enjoyment. I also learned much that I could not have learned elsewhere, and for that I am grateful. And speaking of gratitude, I would like to express the great debt I owe Fr. John Eudes Bamberger, to whom I dedicated this work of translation. I owe him more than I can rightly express, both for his encouragement back in my formative years to keep up the study of Latin, and for his appreciation and encouragement at various stages of the present work. Alas, he passed away two years ago at the end of a long, difficult illness. I also want to thank Fr. Mark Scott and Marsha Dutton, my two long-suffering editors. And last, but not least, I want to thank Mark DelCogliano for his generosity in providing an informative introduction for each volume. A work like this is always the result of many hands, and to all I say thanks for being part of it.

> Br. Brian Kerns
> Abbey of the Genesee
> Piffard, New York

Comprehensive Scriptural Index
VOLUMES 1–6; JOB 1:1–42:16

Scriptural references are cited by Book and Maurist paragraph (i.e., Arabic numerals). For example, 23.28 refers to Book 23, paragraph 28. Commas separate references within a single book, and semicolons separate references from different books (e.g., Genesis 3:19 is cited in Books 2, 8, 11 (three times), 12, 13, 15, 18, 29, and 31. The letter L refers to Gregory's Letter to Leander, which serves as a preface to the entire work, P refers to the Preface to Volume 1, and 4P refers to the Preface of Book 4, which numbers its paragraphs separately from the rest of the book.[1]

Gen		3:5	5.54; 22.30;	3:24	12.13
1:3	8.21; 9.75		24.14; 29.18;	4:1-8	20.76
1:5	8.21		33.57; 34.55	4:3-8	20.75
1:11	19.29; 29.52	3:6-7	5.54	4:4-5	22.28
1:12	6.54	3:6	21.4; 33.67;	4:5	33.67
1:26	4.25; 9.75; 32.17		34.26	4:6-7	11.12
1:27	5.64; 32.16	3:8	28.6; 33.5	4:7	3.23; 4.36
1:31	9.46	3:9	2.6	4:10	13.26
2:2-3	1.18	3:12	4.39, 50; 22.30	4:17	8.92;
2:2	6.43	3:13	22.30; 33.50		16.15, 15 n. 1
2:4-5	32.16	3:14	21.5	4:25	8.92 n. 5
2:7	18.81; 23.28	3:15	1.54	5:3-18	16.15 n. 1
2:15	19.34	3:17	4.2	5:3	16.15
2:16-17	35.29	3:19	2.57; 8.57; 11.5,	5:18	16.15
2:23	14.72		15, 61; 12.6;	6:3	14.72
3:1-5	30.60		13.26; 15.37;	6:6-7	9.12; 20.63
3:1	4.6; 24.14; 34.55		18.44; 29.20; 31.66	7:17-23	35.13

[1] I am grateful to Emily Stuckey for creating the index for all six volumes of this work, including this final comprehensive index [ed.].

8:21	28.43	32:6	8.92	5:21	29.44
9:1-2	21.22	32:30	18.88; 24.12	7:1	29.18
9:18-23	20.76	33:1	8.92	8:21	18.68
9:25	26.37	33:14	8.92	8:25	7.53
11:7	2.9	37:1-3	1.56	8:26	10.48
12:1-4	27.17	37:7-9	9.106	10:3	7.53
12:3	4.2	37:7	8.42	10:13-15	31.47
15:11	16.53	37:19-20	9.106	12:10	20.19
15:16	25.23	37:24-25	9.106	12:46	35.13
16:15	20.76	37:28	9.106; 20.76	13:13	27.38
18:1–19:1	2.2	39:1	9.106	13:17	24.29
18:2-8	28.7	39:7-9	27.17	14:15	9.60; 22.43
18:2	9.106; 27.29	39:8-9	30.38	15:18 LXX	16.55
18:16-33	18.46	39:12	2.59	16:8	22.56; 34.53
18:20-21	19.46	39:17	9.106	16:29	18.68
18:20	5.20	41:1-8	11.31	18	7.54
18:27	3.60; 10.49; 18.82; 24.49; 35.3	41:32	35.19	19:3	23.37
		41:41	9.106	19:12-13	6.58
19:1-24	18.46	41:48	9.106	19:18	6.58
21:9	20.76	42:1-2	9.106	20:13-16	28.40
22:6	27.17	42:6	9.106	20:17	28.41
22:9	27.17	46:27	3.22	20:24	3.51
22:10	27.17	49:9	15.69; 18.56	21:24	28.41
22:12	19.13; 21.11; 28.13	49:17	31.43	21:33-34	17.38
		49:18	31.43	22:26	16.6
24:2-9	2.50	49:27	18.25; 33.52	23:11	18.88
24:61	1.21	50:19-21	1.56	24:3	31.45
25:25	20.76			26:7	32.27
25:27	5.20	**Exod**		26:32	28.17
25:33-34	30.60	1:21	18.6	30:34-35	1.55
26:15	16.23	2:11-15	23.37	30:36	1.55
26:18-22	31.53	3:2-4	P.3	32:7	20.14
27:23	35.26	3:3	15.68	32:10	9.23, 60; 20.14
28:12	28.7	3:6	P.3	32:27-28	20.14
28:20	23.49	3:14	4.66; 5.63; 16.45; 18.82	32:30-32	9.23
29:15–31:21	27.17			32:31-32	27.17
30:37	21.2	4:10	35.3, 31	32:32	20.14
30:38-39	21.2	4:13	35.31	33:13	18.88
31:22-30	30.71	4:21	11.13; 29.60	33:14	34.5
31:35	30.71	5:2	34.55	33:20	18.89

33:21	35.13	24:21	31.94	**Josh**	
33:21-23	25.25	25:11	9.23	5:13-16	27.29
33:23	35.13	29:12-34	29.73	5:13	33.44
34:7	15.57	32:4-5	27.25	6:2	27.17
34:14	20.63	32:6-7	27.25	16:10	4.44
34:7 Vulg	16.3	32:13	20.63	**Judg**	
35:21-23	30.23	32:16-17	27.25	2:14	20.63
Lev		**Deut**		3:1	4.44
1:6-13	9.84	6:5	7.28; 10.8; 18.41	3:8	20.63
1:6	1.55	8:3	33.16	13:22-23	5.56
5:6-7	32.4	10:16	28.12	15:16	13.15
6:12	25.15, 16	13:3	19.13; 28.13	16:21	7.37
6:13	25.16	15:19	8.78	**1 Sam**	
15:2	23.28	16:16	7.38	1:13	22.43
19:18	7.28; 18.41	16:20	9.38	1:18	33.43
19:23	8.79	16:21	L.5	2:5	6.5
19:26	8.42	17:11	16.38	2:9	6.39
25:8	1.18	17:16	8.92	2:10	27.38; 29.20
26:12	18.50; 19.22; 27.19	18:9	31.16	2:12-17	30.60
		19:5-6	10.12	3:12-14	30.83
Num		22:10	1.23	6:10-11	7.42
8:7	5.59	22:11	8.87	6:12	7.42
8:24-26	23.21	23:10-11	9.84	8:5-6	27.17
10:2	30.14	24:6	33.24	9:2	32.19
10:5	30.14	25:4	1.23; 35.39	10:1	27.17
11:4-6	20.40	32:1-2	17.35	10:11	27.2
11:16	19.26	32:1	2.51; 29.55	10:24	32.19
11:29	22.54	32:2	9.15; 19.13; 27.45; 29.54	12:23	9.24
12:3	1.3			13:2	8.92
14:3	31.45	32:11	32.7	14:27	30.60
14:6-9	27.17	32:22	18.35; 21.19	15:11	20.63
16:47-48	9.23	32:32-35	25.23	15:17	18.59; 25.35; 34.42
17:1-8	14.68	32:34-35	12.21		
19:15	23.17	32:35	25.23	15:22-23	35.28
20:12	9.23	32:39	6.42	15:30	9.23
22:28	L.2; 27.2	32:40	32.7	16:1	27.17
23:10	33.43	32:42	18.20	16:2	27.17
24:3-4	15.58	33:8-9	8.78	16:7	10.51
24:16	25.25	33:25	34.19	16:10-11	10.51

16:23	18.4	3:16	8.48	4:30-34	9.63
17:48-51	18.24	3:19	21.16	5:11	7.53
17:49	34.22	3:26	21.17	6:4-6	22.9
18	27.17	6:7	34.23	6:5	22.9
18:10	18.4	8:10-11	30.2	13:17	7.4
18:25	6.30	11:4-8	12.23	17:6	22.6
19	27.17	11:4	33.67	19:15-19	8.82
20	27.17	13:1-6	23.54	19:21-22	3.38
21	27.17	13:2	7.53	19:35	8.82
22	27.17	13:4	7.54	20:1	12.2
23	27.17	13:6	7.54	20:6-7	8.82
24	27.17	13:15-22	23.54	20:6	12.2; 16.14
24:15	34.42	17:1	9.23; 11.49;	20:11	8.82
24:17	9.23		19.10	20:17	8.82
25	27.17	17:6	30.60	22:19	18.88
26	27.17	17:17-24	19.10	25:10	30.59
		18:1	19.10		
2 Sam		18:17	7.53	**1 Chr**	
1:21	4.4 (2x)	18:18	7.53	22:8	7.57
4:5-6	1.50	18:27	10.47		
6:20	27.77	18:38	19.10	**Job**	
6:21-22	27.77	18:44	9.23	1:8	11.51; 24.40;
7:2-17	2.89	18:46	7.54		28.0; 35.9
7:23	27.19	19:2-4	9.23	1:11	35.9
11:1-26	12.23	19:3	8.48; 19.10	1:21	2.85, 86, 87
11:1-8	3.55	19:4	19.10	1:22	2.88; 23.1
11:2-4	21.4	19:11-13	5.66	2:3	14.36; 23.30; 28.0
11:2	21.13	19:18	31.107	2:5	14.36
11:11	3.55	21:2	33.67	2:6	32.50
12:7	7.53	21:19-24	19.10	2:9	23.5
12:12	34.25	21:29	25.13	2:20	23.1
12:13	22.31	22:19-22	2.38	3:19	23.46
12:15	9.54			7:1	20.8; 23.41
16:10-12	30.37	**2 Kgs**		7:21	18.10
20:9	15.13	1:9-12	19.10	9:9	27.51
24:25	9.23	1:10	4.2	9:20	18.10
		2:11	20.66	10:13	12.15
1 Kgs		3:13	7.53	12:6	11.1, 2
1:23	7.54	3:14	7.53	12:7-8	11.5
3:5	2.2	4:27	2.89; 7.54	12:9	11.6
3:12	8.48			12:10	11.7

12:11	11.8	13:26	11.51, 61, 62	15:20	12.42, 43
12:12	11.1	13:27	11.63	15:21	12.44
12:13	11.11, 17	13:28	11.64	15:22	12.45
12:14	11.12	14:1-2	12.10	15:23	12.46
12:15	11.14	14:1	11.65	15:24	12.47
12:16-17	11.18	14:2	11.67	15:25	12.48
12:16	11.17	14:3	11.69	15:26	12.48
12:17	11.19, 20	14:4	11.70	15:27	12.50, 51
12:18	11.21	14:5	12.1, 2	15:28	12.52
12:19	11.22	14:6	12.4	15:29	12.53
12:20	11.23	14:7-10	12.5	15:30	12.54–56
12:21	11.25	14:10	12.9	15:31	12.57
12:22	11.26	14:11-12	12.10	15:32	12.58
12:23	11.29	14:12	12.12	15:33-34	12.60
12:24-25	11.30	14:13	12.13–15	15:34	12.62
13:1	11.31	14:14	12.16, 17	15:35	12.64
13:2	11.32	14:15	12.18, 19	16:2	13.2
13:3-4	17.29; 23.3	14:16	12.20	16:3	13.3, 4
13:3	11.33	14:17	11.51; 12.21	16:4-6	13.5
13:4	11.34	14:18-19	12.22	16:4	13.4
13:5	11.35	14:20	12.24, 25; 14.17	16:7	13.8; 14.30
13:6	11.36	14:21	12.26	16:8	13.9
13:7	11.37	14:22	12.27	16:9	13.10, 11
13:8	11.38	15:1-2	12.28	16:10	13.12
13:9	11.39	15:3	12.29	16:11	13.14, 15
13:10-11	11.40	15:4	12.29	16:12	13.16
13:12	11.42, 43	15:5	12.30	16:13	13.17, 18
13:13	11.44	15:6	12.31	16:14	13.19
13:14	11.45	15:7-8	12.32	16:15	13.20, 21
13:15-16	11.48	15:9	12.32	16:16 LXX	13.22
13:15	11.47, 51	15:10	12.33	16:17 LXX	13.23, 24
13:16	11.49	15:11	12.34	16:18 LXX	13.25
13:17	11.50	15:12	12.35	16:19	13.26
13:19	11.52, 53	15:13	12.36	16:20	26.3
13:20	11.54	15:14	12.37	16:20 LXX	13.27
13:21	11.55	15:15	12.38	16:21 LXX	13.29
13:22	11.56	15:16	12.39	16:22 LXX	13.30
13:23	11.57	15:17	12.40	16:23 LXX	13.31
13:24	11.59	15:18	11.51; 12.41	17:1	13.32, 33
13:25	11.60	15:19	12.41	17:2	13.34

17:3	13.35	19:8	14.41	20:23	15.29
17:4	13.36, 37	19:9	14.42	20:24	15.30
17:5	13.38	19:10	14.44	20:25	15.31, 33
17:6	13.40	19:11	14.45	20:26	15.34–36
17:7	13.41	19:12	14.46	20:27	15.37
17:8	13.42	19:13-14	14.47	20:28	15.38
17:9	13.43	19:15	14.48, 49	20:29	15.39
17:10	13.44, 45	19:16	14.50, 51	21:2	15.40
17:11	13.46	19:17	14.52, 53	21:3	15.41
17:12	13.47, 48	19:18	14.54, 55	21:4	15.42
17:13	13.49	19:19	14.56	21:5	15.43
17:14	13.50	19:20	11.7; 14.57, 58	21:6	15.44
17:15	13.51, 52	19:21	14.59	21:7	15.45
17:16	13.53, 55	19:22	14.60	21:8	15.46
18:1-2	14.2	19:23-24	14.62; 18.57	21:9	15.47; 26.33
18:3	14.3	19:25	14.67, 68; 16.41; 23.2	21:10	15.47
18:4	14.4–6			21:11	15.48
18:5	14.8	19:26	14.72, 76; 23.2	21:12	15.48
18:6	14.10	19:27	14.77, 78	21:13	15.49
18:7	14.11, 12	19:28-29	14.79	21:14	15.50, 51
18:8	14.13	20:2	15.1	21:15	15.52, 53; 16.16
18:9	14.13, 14	20:3	15.2	21:16	15.54; 16.17
18:10	14.15	20:4-5	15.3	21:17	15.55
18:11	14.16	20:6-7	15.5	21:18	15.56
18:12	14.17	20:7	15.6	21:19	15.57
18:13	14.19	20:8	15.7	21:20	15.59
18:14	14.20	20:9	15.8	21:21	15.60
18:15	14.22, 23	20:10	15.9, 10	21:22	15.61
18:16	14.24	20:11	15.11	21:23-25	15.62
18:17	14.25	20:12	15.13	21:26	15.62
18:18	14.26, 28	20:13	15.14	21:27-28	15.63
18:19	14.26	20:14	15.15	21:29-30	15.68
18:20	14.27	20:15	15.17	21:31	15.69
18:21	14.28	20:16	15.19	21:32	15.70
19:2	14.29	20:17	15.20	21:33	15.71, 72
19:3	14.30, 31	20:18	15.21, 22	21:34	15.73
19:4	14.32	20:19-20	15.23	22:2	16.1
19:5	14.33, 35	20:20	15.24	22:3	16.2
19:6	14.36, 39	20:21	15.25	22:4	16.3
19:7	14.40	20:22	15.26, 27	22:5	16.4

22:6-8	16.6	24:5	16.60, 61	27:1	18.2
22:9	16.10	24:6	16.62	27:2	18.3
22:10	16.11	24:7	16.63	27:3-4	18.5
22:11	16.11	24:8	16.64	27:5	18.8
22:12-14	16.12	24:9	16.65	27:6	18.8, 9
22:15	16.13	24:10	16.66	27:7	18.12
22:16	16.14	24:11	16.67	27:8	18.13
22:17	16.16	24:12	16.68, 69	27:9	18.15
22:18	16.17	24:13	16.70, 71; 19.4	27:10	18.16, 17
22:19	16.18	24:14	16.72	27:11	18.18
22:20	16.19	24:15	16.74, 75	27:12	18.19
22:21-22	16.20	24:16	16.76	27:13	18.19
22:23	16.21	24:17	16.77, 78	27:14	18.20; 34.17
22:24	16.22	24:18	16.79, 80	27:15	18.22, 23
22:25	16.23	24:19	16.81, 82	27:16-17	18.24
22:26	16.24, 25	24:20	11.1; 16.82, 83; 17.2	27:18	18.27
22:27	16.26			27:19	18.28
22:28	16.27, 28	24:21	17.4	27:20	18.30, 31
22:29	16.29	24:22	17.6–8	27:21	18.32, 34
22:30	16.30	24:23	17.9; 25.6	27:22	18.35, 36
23:1-2	16.31	24:24	17.10–12	27:23	18.37, 38
23:3	16.33	24:25	17.14	28:1	18.39
23:4	16.35	25:2	17.16	28:2	18.44, 45
23:5	16.36	25:3	17.18, 20	28:3	18.46, 47
23:6	16.37	25:4	17.21	28:4	18.50
23:7	16.37; 26.15	25:5	17.22	28:5	18.51
23:8-9	16.38	25:6	16.83; 17.23	28:6	18.52
23:10	16.38, 39	26:1-2	17.26	28:7	18.54
23:11-12	16.40	26:3	17.28	28:8	18.55; 30.25
23:11	16.41, 42	26:4	17.29	28:9	18.57
23:12	16.40, 43, 44	26:5	17.30, 32	28:10	18.58, 59
23:13	16.45, 47	26:6	17.33	28:11	18.60
23:14	16.49	26:7	17.34, 35	28:12-15	18.61
23:15	16.50	26:8	17.36	28:13	18.66
23:16	16.51	26:9	17.39	28:14	18.67, 68
23:17	16.52	26:10	17.41	28:15	18.73, 86
24:1	16.54	26:11	17.42	28:16	18.74, 75, 86
24:2	16.56	26:12	17.45	28:17-18	18.80, 86
24:3	16.57	26:13	17.48, 51	28:17	18.61, 77, 86
24:4	16.59	26:14	17.54	28:18	18.81, 83

28:19	18.84–87	30:10	20.45	31:19-20	21.29
28:20-21	18.88	30:11	20.46, 47; 31.62	31:21	21.32
28:21	19.2	30:12	20.48, 50	31:22	21.33
28:22	19.4	30:13	20.51	31:23	20.6; 21.35
28:23	19.5	30:14	20.53	31:24	22.4
28:24	19.7	30:15	20.55	31:25	22.5
28:25	19.8, 9	30:16	20.56	31:26-28	22.6
28:26-27	19.13	30:17	20.57	31:26	22.11, 14
28:28	19.14	30:18	20.58	31:27	22.18
29:1	19.15	30:19	20.60	31:29	22.22
29:2-3	19.18	30:20	20.61	31:30	22.25
29:2	19.17	30:21	20.62	31:31	22.26
29:4	19.19	30:22	20.65	31:32	22.27
29:5	19.21	30:23	20.66	31:33	22.30
29:6	19.22, 24	30:24	20.67	31:34	22.35
29:7-10	19.25	30:25	20.68	31:35	22.42, 44
29:8	19.26	30:26	20.72	31:36	22.45
29:9-10	19.27	30:27	20.72	31:37	22.46, 51
29:11	19.28	30:28	20.73	31:38-40	22.52
29:12-13	19.29	30:29	20.75	31:39	22.53
29:14	19.32, 35, 38	30:30	20.77	31:40	22.55
29:15-16	19.36, 42	30:31	20.78	32:1	23.8
29:16	19.41	30:21 Vulg	20.62	32:2-3	23.10
29:17	19.47	30:21 LXX	20.62	32:2	23.9
29:18	19.48	31:1	21.4	32:4-5	23.11
29:19	19.51, 52	31:2	21.6	32:6-7	23.12
29:20	19.53	31:3	21.8	32:8	23.13
29:21-23	20.2	31:4	21.9	32:9-11	23.14
29:24	20.6	31:5-6	21.11	32:12-13	23.15
29:25	20.11, 12	31:7	21.12–14	32:14	23.16
30:1	19.15; 20.15	31:8	21.15	32:15	23.16
30:2	20.17	31:9	21.18	32:16	23.17
30:3-4	20.20	31:10	21.19	32:17	23.17
30:3	20.18, 26, 29	31:11-12	21.19	32:18-20	23.18
30:4	20.21, 29, 31	31:13	21.20	32:21-22	23.22
30:5	20.22, 32	31:14	21.21	33:1-2	23.23
30:6	20.23	31:15	21.22	33:3	23.27
30:7	20.24, 38	31:16	21.25	33:4	23.28
30:8	20.25, 41, 43	31:17	21.27	33:5	23.29
30:9	20.44	31:18	21.28	33:6-7	23.29

33:8	23.29	34:22	25.7	36:16	26.65, 68, 70
33:9-11	23.29	34:23	25.12, 18	36:17	26.71
33:12	23.30, 33	34:24	25.19	36:18-21	26.72
33:13-14	23.34	34:25	25.22	36:18	26.79
33:15	23.37	34:26	25.25	36:19	26.75
33:16	23.40	34:27	25.28, 29	36:21	26.77, 85
33:17	23.44	34:28	25.31	36:22	27.3, 9
33:18	23.45	34:29	25.32, 33	36:23	27.5
33:20	23.49, 50	34:30	25.34	36:24	27.6
33:21	23.52	34:31-32	26.2	36:25	27.8
33:22	23.53	34:33	26.3, 4	36:26	27.9, 10
33:23-24	24.2	34:34-35	26.5	36:27	27.12
33:24	24.5	34:36	26.6, 11	36:28	27.15, 16
33:25	24.7	34:37	26.12, 13	36:29-30	27.19
33:26	24.9, 10, 13, 25, 26, 31, 34	35:2	26.15	36:29-31	27.22
		35:3	26.16	36:31	27.22
33:27	24.15, 22	35:4	26.16	36:32	27.24, 26
33:28	24.24–26, 31, 34	35:5-7	26.17	36:33	27.28
		35:8	26.17	37:1	27.31
33:29	24.25	35:9	26.22, 32	37:2	27.33
33:30	24.35	35:10	26.25, 26	37:3	27.35
33:31-33	24.37	35:11	26.27	37:4	27.39, 40, 41
33:32	24.50	35:12	26.32	37:5	27.42, 43
34:1	24.38	35:13	26.34	37:6	27.44
34:2-3	24.39	35:14	25.12	37:7	27.47
34:4	24.40	35:15	26.37	37:8	27.49
34:5-6	24.40	35:16	26.40	37:9	27.51
34:7-8	24.40, 42	36:1-2	26.41	37:10	27.52, 53
34:9	24.43	36:2	26.41	37:11	27.54, 55
34:10-11	24.14	36:3	26.41	37:12	27.56, 57
34:10	24.43	36:4	26.42, 43	37:13	27.58
34:13	24.45, 46	36:5	26.44, 48	37:14	27.59
34:14	24.47	36:6	26.49	37:15	27.60
34:15	24.48, 49	36:7	26.52	37:16	27.61
34:16	24.50	36:8-9	26.55	37:17	27.63
34:17	24.51	36:10	26.56	37:18	27.65
34:18	24.52	36:11-12	26.57	37:19	27.66
34:19	25.2	36:13	26.58, 60	37:20	27.66, 67
34:20	25.3, 5	36:14	26.62, 63	37:21	27.68, 70
34:21	25.6	36:15	26.64	37:22	27.71, 72

37:23	27.74	38:32 Vulg	28.0	39:25	31.69–72, 84–87
37:24	27.75	38:33	29.77		
38:1	28.1	38:34	30.2, 3	39:26	31.92, 93
38:2	23.4; 28.11	38:35	30.6, 8	39:27	31.94, 96, 102
38:3	28.12, 13	38:36	30.9	39:28	31.97–99, 102
38:4-6	28.14	38:37	30.16, 17, 19, 21	39:29	31.100–102
38:4-5	28.15, 21, 26			39:30	31.104, 105
38:6	28.14, 17, 19, 31, 33	38:38	30.18, 22	39:31-32	31.107
		38:39	30.25	39:34	32.2
38:7	28.34, 35	38:40	30.26	39:35	32.3
38:8	28.36, 41, 43	38:41	30.28, 30–32, 35	40:1	32.4
38:9	28.37			40:3	32.5
38:10-11	28.38, 46	39:1	30.36, 41	40:4	32.6, 7, 13
38:10	28.37, 42, 45	39:2	30.44, 46	40:5	32.8
38:11	28.39	39:3	30.47	40:6	32.9, 10, 13
38:12	28.0; 29.2	39:4	30.49	40:7	32.11
38:13	29.5, 20	39:5	30.50, 66, 67	40:8	32.12, 13
38:14-15	29.17	39:6	30.52, 55, 68	40:9	32.14
38:14	29.6, 7, 21	39:7	30.56, 61, 63, 69, 71, 77	40:10	32.16–18
38:15	29.8, 9, 14, 18, 22			40:11	32.20, 21
		39:8	30.64, 65, 78, 80	40:12	32.22, 24, 28, 33, 35, 38
38:16	29.23, 27	39:9	31.2, 3, 30		
38:17	28.0, 25, 29, 30	39:10	31.4–7, 32	40:13	32.29, 31, 40, 44, 45
38:18-20	29.32	39:11	31.8, 33		
38:18-19	29.34	39:12	31.9, 34	40:14	32.47, 50
38:18	29.26, 30, 31	39:13	31.11, 36	40:15	33.2, 4
38:21	29.35, 36	39:14	31.14, 15, 37	40:15 Vulg	29.52
38:22-23	29.37–39	39:15	31.16, 38	40:16	33.5, 8
38:24-25	29.50	39:16	31.17, 21, 39, 40	40:17	33.10, 11
38:24	29.40–42			40:18	33.12–14
38:25	29.47, 49	39:17	31.26, 41	40:19	33.14, 15
38:26	29.50	39:18	31.27, 42	40:20	33.17, 18
38:27	29.50, 51	39:19	31.29, 43	40:21	33.21, 22, 26
38:28	29.54, 62	39:20	31.45, 50–52, 75, 76	40:22	33.27
38:29	29.55, 58, 60, 62			40:23	33.28
		39:21	31.53–56, 60, 77	40:24	33.30, 32
38:30	29.56, 57, 64, 66			40:25	33.33
		39:22	31.61, 80	40:26	33.34
38:31	29.67, 72, 74	39:23	31.62–65, 81	40:27	33.34–36
38:32	29.75	39:24	31.66, 83	40:28	33.37

Comprehensive Scriptural Index 553

41:1-2	33.38, 39	42:9	35.20, 21	7:15	28.36
41:1	33.37	42:10	35.21, 22, 24, 36	8 Vulg	16.67
41:2	33.41			8:3	P.15; 11.39
41:3	33.42, 43	42:11	35.23, 24, 26, 27	8:6	27.29
41:4	33.44, 45			8:8	4.55
41:5	33.46–48	42:12-13	35.36	8:8 LXX	35.36
41:6	33.49–51	42:12	35.35	8:9	11.5
41:7	33.54	42:14	35.43	9:10	20.51; 26.34
41:8	33.55	42:15	35.45, 46	9:11	20.51
41:9	33.56, 57	42:16	35.47	9:15	19.25
41:10	33.58, 59			9:17	18.35
41:11	31.51, 61, 62, 66	**Pss**		9:24	4.51; 12.52
		1:1	29.13	9:26	5.35
41:12	33.67, 68	1:3	19.51	9:28	5.35; 15.13
41:13	34.2, 5–7	1:4	11.42; 30.22; 31.15	9:30	32.25
41:14	34.8, 10			9:38	2.11; 22.43
41:15	34.11	1:4 LXX	28.20	9:10 LXX	27.36
41:16	34.12	1:5	25.25	9:28 Vulg	33.48
41:17	34.17	2:7	32.7	10:2	33.2
41:18	34.19	2:8	30.68	10:3	31.62
41:19	34.21, 22	2:9	7.19	10:5	28.13
41:20	34.23, 24	2:11	5.44; 20.8	10:7	15.55
41:21	34.25, 26	2:12	20.8	11:2	32.27
41:22	34.31, 32	4:2	29.31	11:3	15.13; 20.5; 24.32
41:23	34.33, 34	4:3	14.63; 19.8; 31.11		
41:24-25	17.46			11:7	4.61; 6.6; 16.23; 18.24; 28.17
41:24	34.39, 40	4:5	5.82		
41:25	34.42, 45, 47, 56	5:5	16.72; 23.39	11:9	2.7
		5:5 LXX	8.57	13:1	15.52; 18.3
41:25 Vulg	16.29; 26.44	5:7 LXX	18.5	13:3	18.68
		5:9	35.10	13:5	7.32; 31.21
41:25 LXX	29.15	5:13	33.49	15:2	8.51; 16.2
42:2	35.2	6:6	8.34	15:6	33.18
42:3	35.2, 3	6:7	33.63	15:7	4.24
42:4	35.4	6:8	5.82; 24.8	16:6	35.4
42:5	18.88; 35.5	6:8 LXX	19.53	16:7	32.14
42:6	35.6, 7	6:9-10	5.43	16:8	32.7; 33.5
42:7	14.38; 35.9, 10	7:3	6.49	16:15	18.91; 26.70
42:8	35.11–13, 18, 19	7:5	4.59	17:2	32.14
		7:13-14 Vulg	19.55	17:10-12 LXX	17.39

17:12	4.29; 5.12; 11.28; 17.36; 27.6, 15	28:5	32.22	36:36	15.68
		29:3-4 LXX	18.30	37:6	9.83
		30:2	5.9	37:11	33.63
17:13	29.38	30:2 LXX	6.62	37:12	2.54
17:15	27.20; 30.6	30:8-9	26.66	37:18-19 LXX	9.93
17:28	34.46	30:9	26.66	37:18 LXX	7.21
17:28 LXX	16.29	30:11	34.5	37:19	8.37
17:30	26.24	30:21	4.19	38:2-3	23.18
17:34	26.24	30:23	18.66; 23.41	38:3-4	23.18
17:46 LXX	19.40	30:25	3.40; 15.71; 26.63; 28.12; 30.71	38:6-7	23.41
18:2	9.10; 12.38; 15.37; 17.48; 27.35			38:6	10.15, 20
				38:7	10.21; 22.36
		30:25 LXX	7.24	38:10	23.33
18:5	19.3	31:1	4.27; 16.64; 30.71; 32.2	39:3	29.12
18:6	3.55; 17.4; 34.25			39:6	25.21
		31:4	20.21	40:4	23.46
18:13	11.57	31:9	26.27, 56; 31.43	40:4 LXX	8.41
18:15	19.20	31:7 LXX	26.26	41:2	30.36
20:10 LXX	6.47; 15.35	32:6	17.50	41:3	8.13; 10.13; 18.48; 26.70; 29.4
		32:7	9.11; 19.15		
21:3	20.61; 26.34	32:9	32.7	41:4	5.14
21:7	30.66; 34.55	33:1	35.17	41:5	8.13; 30.20
21:13	7.36	33:2	5.56	41:7	33.13
21:16	3.33	33:11 LXX	15.9	41:8	27.48
21:17-18	34.12	33:6	18.92	41:9	P.6
21:22	31.29	33:17	17.2; 32.10	42:9	23.52
22:1-2	30.49	33:20	15.39	43:20	4.30; 20.56; 26.54; 33.6
22:4	20.14	33:21	23.48		
22:5	17.43; 19.18; 35.26	34:5	3.62	43:22	8.12
		34:6	19.39	44:2	33.7
23:4	7.38	34:10	5.56; 29.18; 34.55	44:3	18.85; 19.3
23:7-8	30.73			44:5	1.16; 9.62
24:2-3	33.4	35:7	27.6; 29.57; 33.2; 34.34	44:6	34.21
24:17	20.28			44:6 LXX	7.4
25:2	2.19; 7.21; 8.20; 22.50	36:10	7.45; 17.10	44:9-10	35.44
		36:23	25.30	44:11	30.71
26:1	14.41; 19.39	36:27	1.3; 13.44; 23.46	44:12	35.45
26:4	4.58; 26.80			44:13	35.34
28:1	30.9	36:35-36	17.10	44:14	8.82; 19.20; 26.42; 35.45
28:3	19.9	36:35	15.68		

44:15	19.20	58:11	33.38	72:18	17.10; 32.11
44:17	4.61; 18.55; 26.75	58:1 LXX	7.24	72:23	10.24
		59:5-6	19.54	72:28	4.59
45:3	9.6; 18.50	61:11	34.53	73:15	33.20
45:10	33.49	62:4	8.51	74:3	10.54
45:11	5.19, 55; 18.68; 33.63	62:6	8.24; 19.24	74:5	31.2
		62:9 LXX	10.13	74:7	33.21
45:11 Vulg	6.57	63:2	6.49	74:8	33.21
47:4	22.46	63:4	19.54	74:9 Vulg	17.43
47:8	4.35	63:8	34.21	75:4	33.49
48:8-9	12.57	65:18	22.6	75:5 Vulg	27.16
48:11	26.32	66:7-8	29.70	75:6	18.28
48:13	26.28	66:8	29.70	75:7	31.43
48:13 LXX	24.15	67:5	19.6; 27.19	75:8 Vulg	11.61
48:19	8.59; 11.47	67:6	34.53	76:2-3 LXX	7.5
49:3	4.11; 9.31; 15.56; 17.54; 18.31	67:8-9	27.19	76:3	18.66
		67:10	29.54	76:4	18.66; 22.46
49:4	15.37	67:11	11.5; 31.3; 35.36	76:11	22.7
49:12	30.66			76:18	29.47
49:16-17	19.13	67:24	20.15	77:13	8.39
49:16	11.23; 15.17	67:25	16.41; 29.28	77:30-31	15.24
50:5 LXX	12.21	67:31	35.14	77:34	11.41
50:7	4.3; 11.7; 18.84	67:32	18.84	77:36	33.12
50:9	27.44; 29.38	67:13 LXX	11.25	77:38-39	9.76
50:16	3.33; 9.58; 13.2	68:2	19.9; 30.3	77:39	4.8; 14.72
50:19 LXX	9.56; 20.73	68:5	3.26	77:49-50	25.23
		68:15	18.78; 34.27	77:57	27.75
51:8-9 LXX	6.48	68:16	26.65	77:61	8.82
53:5	12.41	68:19	26.32	78:2	P.3
54:8	4.60	68:21	17.5; 35.27	78:8	19.31
54:10	34.9	68:24	25.40; 29.8	78:12	22.32
54:16	18.19	68:28	25.23	80 Vulg	16.67
54:24	5.70	71:3	9.6	80:2	33.33
55:7	1.54	71:9	20.26	80:8	26.24
55:8	17.35	72:2-3	6.7	80:13	26.33
56:5	6.35	72:5	5.35	80:16	4.5
57:3	24.32	72:7	15.64	81:6-7	4.25
57:7	19.47	72:7-8	34.55	82:14	16.79
57:11	18.37; 22.23	72:9	12.56	83 Vulg	16.67
57:9 LXX	9.97	72:11	18.3	83:3	4.67; 8.45

83:4	19.48	98:4	25.12	110:6-7	18.14
83:6-7	30.64	99:3	23.9	110:10	19.14
83:8	22.46	100:5	14.6	111:7	11.42
83:11	2.34; 16.54	100:6	16.6	113:3	28.42
85:11	20.8	100:8	16.72	113:11	29.34
85:13	12.13	101:10	25.19	113:13	4.70
85:15	20.63	101:25	16.54	113:16	29.56
86:1	28.14	101:27-28	18.82	114:6	27.24; 34.43
87:4	34.55	101:27	17.11	115:11	22.36
87:5-6	29.24	101:27 LXX	29.13	115:16-17	9.93
87:6	30.66	101:28-29	4.67	116:16-17	4.68
87:9	22.41	101:29	8.35; 26.32	117:1	8.30
87:17 LXX	7.6	102:14-15	23.53	117:7	29.25
87:18	30.3	102:14	13.27; 18.82; 24.49	117:22	28.19
88:2	4.72			117:27	9.43
88:7	18.75, 79	102:15	7.45; 11.67	118:6	18.9
88:9	18.79	102:18	15.17	118:8	20.51
88:11	17.46	103:1-2	32.8	118:15	17.9; 25.30
88:16	24.10	103:3	19.8	118:43	11.23
88:38 LXX	13.27	103:4	11.7	118:57	15.39
88:49	11.61; 20.66	103:6	27.6	118:61	33.18
89:6	29.52	103:8	33.2	118:81	4.67; 8.45
89:11-12	10.15	103:18	30.64	118:85	7.15
89:11	5.16	103:20-21	27.49	118:100	11.24
90:3	6.45	103:22	27.49	118:105	19.18
90:4	32.7	103:24	18.61	118:115	16.23
91:13	32.22	103:29	24.49	118:131	18.83
91:15-16	35.35	103:30	29.53	118:162	18.25
92:1	32.8	104:8	9.3; 35.42	118:164	35.17
92:3	30.8	104:18 LXX	15.3	119:5	4.59; 8.13; 18.48; 23.41
92:4	9.11	106:2	9.29		
93:7	18.3	106:33	29.50	120:1	16.64; 33.2
93:15	26.53	106:35	18.58	124:1	33.2
93:19	35.22	106:40	19.27; 31.72	125:4	27.53
93:20	18.35	108:23	31.48	125:5	30.47
94:2	8.36	108:29	9.68	125:6	7.38; 10.36
94:4	30.78	109:1	8.89	126:1	8.51; 11.12
94:7	30.49; 35.37	109:7	14.68; 33.11	126:2-3	10.35
96:4	30.8	110:2 Vulg	6.33	126:2	8.80
96:5	30.78; 33.2	110:3	18.65	126:2 LXX	30.71

126:6	8.68	146:6	25.20; 32.13	9:2-4	17.43
128:3	13.1	146:8	29.52	9:4	34.43
130:1-2	26.47	146:9	30.28	9:7	10.3
130:1	4.59; 28.25	147:15	29.47	9:8	8.67; 20.47
130:2	34.43	147:18	27.53	9:9	10.3
131:9	14.42	148:5	9.75	9:17	5.45; 16.61; 19.9;
131:15	23.49	148:6	16.46		20.23; 23.49
134:6	6.33	149:1	35.44	10:19	7.58; 10.2
136:2	33.11	149:5	8.41; 23.39	10:25	20.50
136:4	20.47	150:2	9.19	11:21	25.7
136:7	25.27			11:22	31.2, 51
137:6	18.59	**Prov**		11:23	5.79
138:8-10	33.21	1:9	31.44	11:29	20.52
138:11	16.24	1:10	4.51	12:5	19.35; 25.13
138:12	5.2	1:17	16.3	12:21	6.25; 31.55
138:15	5.68	1:20	18.15	12:23	29.55
138:16	4.70	1:22-23	18.15	13:4	20.54
138:17	10.52 (2x)	1:24-25	18.15	14:3	24.40
138:18	10.52	1:26-28	18.15	14:10	5.4; 6.23
138:21-22	4.59	1:26-27	18.31	14:12	5.12
139:8 Vulg	6.44	1:26	9.42	14:24	22.8
139:11	2.28; 13.5	1:32	26.33, 64	14:26	5.33; 12.44
139:12	7.58; 10.2	2:4	5.9	14:30	5.85
140:2	20.5	2:14	6.26; 16.78;	15:1	5.78
140:3	7.61		20.37	15:3	2.4; 17.2
141:4	1.53	3:5	22.7	15:5	14.61
141:4 LXX	7.5	3:16	12.1	15:15	12.44
141:6	12.53	3:18	12.5	15:18	5.78
141:8	8.39	3:26	31.82	15:19	30.51
142:2	18.71; 24.33;	3:28	21.26	16:5	34.53
	29.3, 34	4:23	1.50; 19.33; 25.20	16:18	25.20; 34.48
142:6	18.66; 20.5	5:22	11.21	17:14	5.30; 7.57
143:1	15.43	6:9	8.20	17:15	18.8
143:2	26.84	7:22	1.23; 35.39	17:24	17.9; 20.7
143:5	18.57; 30.48	8:1-2	25.29	17:28	11.35
143:10	15.7; 34.17	8:4	27.6; 28.12	18:3	8.34; 12.44;
144:6	29.38	8:12	1.15		26.69
144:7	29.38	9:1-3	33.32	18:4	7.57; 11.14;
145:4	10.41; 12.1;	9:1	P.17; 17.43;		17.36
	25.8		18.61; 23.6	18:12	16.29; 23.29

18:17	8.36; 22.33; 24.22	30:27	31.46	8:14	6.26; 16.78; 24.14
20:8	19.7; 29.30; 30.78	30:28	6.12	9:1	29.34
		30:29-31	30.9	9:6	12.1
		30:32	30.10		
20:24	29.34	30:33	21.3	9:8	2.82; 9.58
20:27	8.49; 12.64	31:8	15.68	9:10	8.29; 9.104
20:30	23.40	31:18	18.55	9:18	1.3; 19.32
21:11	18.38	31:23	6.9; 10.52; 20.25, 41; 26.51	10:1	18.68
21:16	17.30			10:4	6.40; 14.64
21:20	4.61	31:24	18.55; 33.33	10:7	31.43
21:28	35.28	31:25	8.88; 20.56	10:16	16.72
21:30	6.33	31:27	35.48	11:2	35.17
21:31	31.43	31:31	6.9	11:3	8.30; 12.5
22:6	15.11			11:4	27.15
22:24-25	5.78	**Eccl**		11:8	7.31; 9.92
22:28	16.56	1:2	10.20	11:9	4.1
23:4	20.18	1:4	9.95; 17.11	11:10	4.1
23:20	14.61	1:7	30.8	11:27	13.48
23:21	14.61	1:18	1.34; 18.66	12:5	31.46
24:27	10.26; 31.77	2:2	18.66	12:11	24.41
24:30-31	20.54	2:5	27.6		
24:32	20.54	2:14	17.9; 20.7	**Song**	
24:9 LXX	12.58	2:16	9.40	1:1	14.51; 27.34; 30.48
25:16	16.8; 20.18	2:24	4.1		
25:27	14.32; 20.18	3:7	7.61	1:2	19.19; 24.8
25:28	7.58; 10.2	3:19-20	9.40	1:3	34.32
26:10	7.57	4:12	33.18	1:4	18.49
26:15	22.20	5:2	8.42	1:6	30.79
26:16	23.4	6:8	29.4	1:7	16.56
27:19	15.66	7:3	4.1	1:7 Vulg	30.56
27:21	22.19; 26.62	7:4	5.82	1:11	35.43
28:1	6.25; 10.39; 31.55	7:5	18.66	2:2	1.1; 20.76
		7:9	5.78	2:3	18.32; 33.5
28:9	5.76; 10.27; 16.26; 18.15	7:19	1.3; 19.42	2:5	6.42; 34.21
		7:22-23	22.26	2:9	18.78
28:13	8.36; 22.32	7:24	32.1	2:10-11	27.45; 29.64
28:14	16.51; 20.8; 29.5	7:40	9.92; 13.33	3:1	5.6; 8.41; 27.3
30:13	16.29; 26.44; 34.46	7:14 Vulg	11.12	3:3-4	18.80; 27.3
		8:10	25.25; 29.17; 32.19	3:3	27.3
30:17	18.49			3:6	1.55

3:7	7.24	5:13	1.23; 2.50	18:1-2	13.13
3:8	19.56; 20.8	5:14	26.68	21:11-12	6.34
4:1	9.18	5:18	33.18	21:12	16.72
4:2	11.45; 33.47	5:21	13.45; 18.59;	21:14	23.49
4:3	2.82		26.44; 34.42	23:4	P.5
4:5-6	24.17	6:1-3	35.3	24:16	29.66
4:8	17.52	6:1	18.88	26:1	20.53
4:11	15.13	6:3	29.70	26:9	23.39
4:16	9.17; 27.63	6:5	3.17; 7.60; 35.3	26:10	4.19; 6.47; 6.49
5:2	5.54; 23.38	6:10	29.8	26:10 LXX	20.9
5:6	4.67	7:9	2.71	26:11	2.51; 7.47
5:7	27.3	7:24	19.55	26:14	17.30
5:8	34.21	8:18	19.21	26:20	4.47
5:11	34.26	9:2	4.30; 19.40;	27:1	4.15; 17.51
6:9	4.19; 16.77;		27.68; 29.42	28:19	7.33; 11.41;
	18.46; 29.2	9:4	30.71, 77		15.58
7:4	31.85	9:6	9.48; 24.2	29:13	33.12
7:12	12.6	9:8	2.57	32:13	17.23
8:5	16.24	9:14-15	14.43	32:17	7.58; 10.2
8:5 LXX	18.87	10:22	2.59; 4.4; 20.48	32:20	19.9; 21.15;
8:6	10.39; 29.12	10:22 LXX	9.9; 27.26		31.9; 35.40
8:8	19.19	10:27	19.24	33:7	34.14
8:14	17.39	11:1-3 Vulg	29.74	33:15-16	23.49
		11:3	1.17; 2.43	33:15	9.53; 31.102
Isa		11:7	32.18	33:16-17	31.102
1:3	1.23; 35.39	11:8-9	17.51	33:16	31.102
1:15	9.56	11:15	33.19	33:17	31.102
1:16-18	9.60	12:3	33.20	33:21	18.60
1:16	25.7	13:2	33.2	34:5	32.49
1:17-18	11.33	13:9	20.64	34:13-14	7.36
1:17	19.42	14:1	3.60	34:13	33.10
1:20	27.34	14:13-14	18.32; 19.2;	34:14-15	33.53
2:2	33.2		23.13; 29.15;	34:14	7.36
2:10	31.53		31.43	35:1	30.68
2:22	31.51	14:13	12.5; 17.34;	35:7	29.52; 33.7
3:9	4.51; 14.31		33.66; 34.55	35:9	27.49; 31.16;
3:14	6.9; 10.52; 26.51	14:14	17.46; 24.52;		33.4
3:16	34.2		29.18; 34.40;	37:29	33.21
5:1	19.24		34.55	37:31	8.81; 12.53;
5:6	9.15; 27.15; 29.47	14:29	33.62		18.57

38:1-6	12.58	53:12	26.73	66:23	19.17
38:3	12.36	54:1	5.34	66:24	9.100
40:3	19.6	54:2-3	29.26		
40:6	7.7, 45; 8.68;	54:3	25.21	**Jer**	
	11.67; 17.10;	54:7-8	20.51	1:6	35.3
	32.7, 18; 34.53	54:7	35.22	1:10	18.17
40:9	20.8	54:9	7.21	1:13	18.32; 33.66
40:12	2.20	54:11-13	18.52	2:2	32.7
40:13	14.56	54:11	6.50	2:8	2.52
40:17	17.35	54:12	8.81	2:16	25.27
40:31	7.24; 18.45;	54:13	8.81	2:24	16.6
	19.50; 24.19	55:1	1.29; 6.6; 20.5	3:1	20.13
42:3	33.7	55:2	23.49	3:3	9.8, 15; 27.14;
42:14	9.35; 10.54	55:6	9.104; 18.15, 42		29.54
43:6	27.71	55:8	16.46; 17.54;	3:4	16.71; 20.13
43:19	29.50		32.47	3:12	20.13
43:20	31.11	55:13	18.32	4:14	27.50
43:24	16.62	56:10	20.15; 25.25	4:19	12.64
43:26	25.12	57:1	5.71	4:22	14.63
44:4	33.11	57:17-18	19.8	5:3	2.28; 18.35; 26.57
45:11	30.18	58:14	31.96	5:4	14.54
46:8	19.21; 26.61	59:5	15.19	5:8	24.15; 31.43
47:1	6.24; 14.21	59:8	25.12	5:22	9.11
47:2	6.25 (2x)	59:10	6.34	5:24	20.5
47:8	3.60	60:8	17.36; 18.76;	6:7	16.81; 29.37
49:15	32.7		21.4; 27.15	6:29	18.41
49:18	3.48; 20.58;	60:14	25.3	7:3	21.9
	27.63; 29.13	60:15	13.18	8:6	25.13
51:3	30.68	61:1-2	4.12	8:16	31.43
51:10	29.23	61:7	P.20; 35.25	8:17	34.21
51:23	12.41	61:10	P.14	9:4	3.13
53:1	27.34; 32.7	64:6	11.6	9:5	12.47
53:2	18.85; 19.3	64:7	9.60	9:21	21.4
53:4	1.15; 2.42;	65:20	17.8	10:20	27.19
	17.1; 23.2	65:25	31.15	11:14	9.23
53:5	9.48; 17.1	66:1	2.20; 29.55	11:15	2.54
53:7	3.32; 29.69	66:2	3.34; 5.78;	11:16	20.13
53:8	18.88		18.68; 29.5	11:19	3.28; 12.5
53:9	2.43, 63; 13.25	66:15	28.1	12:1	5.35
53:11	31.100	66:19 Vulg	7.4	12:3	27.45

14:5	30.36	51:7	34.26	3:12-13	24.19
14:6	20.75; 29.52	51:9	26.57	3:19	26.10
14:8	14.49	52:14	30.59	3:26	30.82
15:1	9.23; 20.13	**Lam**		4:1-3	26.9
15:7	26.57	1:1	20.26	5:1	2.56
15:9	6.34	1:2	13.15	6:9	25.20
15:17	4.60 (2x)	1:6	35.14	8:3	31.19
15:19	18.59; 33.33	1:7	5.55	8:8-10	26.7
17:1	14.62	1:11	23.49	8:8	31.53
17:5	4.25	1:12	15.68	9:1	22.44
17:13	25.20	1:20	3.62	9:4	30.74
17:16	4.24; 22.6	2:5	11.25	10:8	6.61
17:18	18.35	2:6	27.19	10:12	19.20
17:9 LXX	9.48	3:1	34.5	13:10	18.8
20:9-10	23.18	3:15	7.25; 20.39	13:18	18.8
20:9	23.18	3:16	11.45	14:14	32.35
20:15	4.4	3:40-41	18.10	14:20	32.35
23:24	2.20	3:44	28.37	16:3	20.13
25:38	32.9	3:51	21.4	16:4	32.20
26:1-2	30.2	3:53	18.30; 26.65	16:42	7.21
26:7-9	30.2	3:64	33.49	16:49	30.60
29:23	9.35	3:65	33.49	16:51	28.41
30:14	P.12; 9.24; 14.45; 18.35	4:1	18.53; 20.77; 27.71; 34.26	17:3-4	31.94
				17:27	12.5
30:15	P.12; 9.24; 18.35; 20.13	4:3	19.27	18:2-4	15.57
		4:4	1.29; 18.51	20:25	28.41
31:19	24.48	4:7-8	32.46	20:32	29.56
31:21	22.35; 31.85	4:8	32.46	22:30	9.60
31:30	11.45	4:19	31.94	23:20	1.23; 7.36; 24.15; 35.40
31:34	30.17, 49				
31:38-39	25.21	**Ezek**		24:7	15.37
32:18-19	21.9	1:9	10.31; 29.71	28:12-13	32.17, 47
36:18	28.2	1:10	31.94	28:13	32.48
38:11-12	25.17	1:14	10.31	28:14	32.48
39:67	7.37	1:18	19.20	29:9	34.55
41:5-7	1.53	1:19	19.36	31:8-9	32.47
48:10	3.24	1:25	35.3	32:19	24.5
48:10 LXX	9.53	2:6	20.76	32:22	9.103; 15.7
48:29-30	23.13	2:9-10	26.26	32:24	9.95
50:23	34.23	3:1	21.24	32:27	9.97

34:4	23.23	4:2	13.2	**Hab**	
34:19	22.56	5:4	26.28	1:16	32.18; 33.13
34:32	24.15	5:5	26.28	2:1	20.8; 22.35; 31.85
36:26	7.26; 10.25;	7:8	11.16; 32.12	2:6	34.27
	18.52	7:9	25.14; 34.6	2:11 LXX	30.66
40:5	30.53	8:4	25.41	3:2	27.33
43:10-11	24.18	8:7	8.70	3:3	33.2
47:3-5	22.50	10:11	20.39	3:4	30.36
		13:8	33.4	3:5-6	35.26
Dan		13:11	25.34	3:5-6 LXX	11.15
1:12	30.39	13:14	12.15	3:10	17.40; 29.27
2:29-31	8.42	14:5	33.38	3:10 LXX	9.39
3:19-25	9.102			3:11	17.22; 30.6
3:19-20	30.59	**Joel**		3:13	22.41
3:46	30.59	1:4-5	33.65	3:15	31.43; 34.27
4:26-27	34.48	1:5	33.66	3:16	22.36
4:27	5.17	1:7	9.82	5:7	18.84
4:28-29	34.48	1:17	24.15		
5:5	11.31	2:1-2	17.54	**Zeph**	
7:8	32.27	2:11	17.54	1:11	18.24
7:10	2.3; 17.18; 18.47			1:14-16	17.54
8:10-12	32.26	**Amos**		3:9	21.33
8:12	26.33; 30.10	2:13	32.7		
8:23-24	32.26	3:8	32.14	**Hag**	
8:24-25	32.26	5:15	21.32	2:7	21.35
8:25	26.33; 32.27;	5:18	4.18	**Zech**	
	34.2	7:4	33.13	1:14	28.9
8:27	4.67	7:14	2.89	2:3-4	28.9
9:21	27.6	7:16-17	2.89	2:3	28.9
9:23	30.39	8:11	6.44; 14.17	2:8	32.7
10:9-12	22.47			2:10	28.1; 34.55
10:11	30.39	**Jonah**		2:34	4.55
10:12-13	17.17	1:3	18.46	3:1	20.48
10:13	4.55; 17.17			3:2-3	20.48
10:20	17.17	**Mic**		3:9	29.74
10:21	17.17	2:1	19.21; 24.32	4:2	29.74
12:4	9.15	**Nah**		5:2-3	15.18
12:7	15.72	1:3	9.31	5:5-8	14.63
Hos		1:9 LXX	18.35	5:9-11	14.63
2:6-7	34.3	1:10	33.55	6:12	1.26; 20.49

Comprehensive Scriptural Index 563

9:15	34.22	13:5	26.17	21:10	33.55
13:7	2.54	17:10	27.48	22:2 LXX	15.5
Mal		17:10 LXX	12.46	22:6	18.2
2:7	5.69; 11.7; 34.14	**Sir**		22:9	24.8
3:1	27.19	1:13	8.88; 10.35;	24:5	2.20
Tob			20.56	27:12	34.25
4:16	6.54; 10.8	1:33	4.62	29:33 Vulg	32.19
		2:1-2	4.42	30:24	19.38
Wis		2:1	24.27	32:1	24.52; 34.53
1:4	15.9	2:5	18.40	32:26	3.13
1:7	2.20	2:11-12	20.51	34:2	11.68; 33.5;
1:11	18.5	2:14	1.36		35.43
1:14	16.45	2:16	1.56	34:7	8.42
2:8-9	34.55	2:16 Vulg	7.45	38:25	18.68
2:12	9.89	3:17	27.53	40:1	2.30; 8.55
2:15	9.89	3:22	16.8; 26.27	41:17	22.7
2:24	5.85; 29.15	4:18-19	20.51	42:14	11.65
3:2	12.6	4:25	4.32	**1 Macc**	
3:5	23.52	5:4	5.35; 19.46; 25.6	6:46	19.34
3:6	23.52	5:6	33.23	**Matt**	
3:7	24.49; 33.7	5:7	29.54; 33.23	1:2	33.17
4:8-9	19.26	7:15 Vulg	10.28	1:11-12	28.19
4:11	5.34	10:4	3.43	1:20	29.36
5:6	8.76; 34.25	10:9	31.2; 34.53	1:25	8.89
5:8-9	18.29	10:13	23.44; 31.87 n.	2:5	35.26
6:6	4.3; 9.98; 24.54	10:15	31.87; 34.47	3:2	23.5
6:8 LXX	9.98	10:15 Vulg	32.11	3:7	3.12; 24.41
6:17	26.17	10:15 LXX	14.19	3:9	18.52; 29.56
7:15	23.31	11:27	3.16	3:12	17.13; 27.54;
7:22	29.24	12:8	7.29		31.9
7:26	5.64	14:5	19.38	3:17	28.8
9:15	4.68; 5.58; 8.40,	15:3	19.9	3:29	2.43
	50; 17.39; 18.71;	15:9	30.74	4:3	2.43; 30.60; 33.16
	20.8; 27.45; 30.53	18:15	21.29	4:4	33.16
10:21	L.2	18:17	21.29	4:7	33.16
11:24	8.31	19:1	10.21	4:8-9	30.71
12:15	3.26	20:7	7.61	5:2	4.1; 14.51
12:18	5.78; 12.14;	20:32	22.7	5:3	2.4, 43; 6.39;
	19.46; 32.9	21:1	4.39		19.31; 21.25; 26.49

5:5	18.66; 20.12	7:13-14	30.56	11:29	34.53
5:6	6.5; 30.55; 31.100	7:13	15.7; 32.46	12:16	4 P.2
		7:14	27.61	12:34-35	11.23
5:8	18.90; 31.100	7:16	15.66; 31.13; 34.56	12:36	7.58; 32.2
5:14	18.81; 32.8			12:43-45	33.8
5:15	30.77	7:21	33.12	12:43	14.64
5:15-16	19.36	7:22-23	8.66; 20.17; 33.13	13:3	31.9
5:16	8.83; 11.46; 22.11; 26.62			13:4	19.2; 26.30
		7:22	8.75; 29.59	13:5-6	34.25
5:19	19.13	7:23	8.75; 11.18; 16.75	13:6	29.41
5:22	21.9			13:17	4.64; 7.7; 9.42
5:25	4.69	7:29	23.24	13:22	1.6
5:27-28	3.59; 21.5; 28.40	8:19-20	28.16	13:28	13.38
		8:21	7.41	13:30	9.98
5:28	21.18	8:29	33.14, 31	13:32	11.5
5:39	27.79; 28.41	8:31	2.16; 32.50; 33.27	13:38	31.16; 33.4
5:40	31.21			13:41	19.13
5:43-44	28.40	9:6	4.61; 8.34	13:47	33.34
5:44-45	16.41	9:9	18.44	13:55-56	11.3
5:44	9.24; 22.25; 34.38; 35.21	9:15	2.48	14:12	11.68
		9:17	23.20	14:16	1.27; 27.22
5:48	29.1	9:25	18.68	14:29	17.45; 27.16
6:1	19.36	9:30	19.36	15:14	31.72
6:2	4.19; 8.69	9:37-38	27.54	15:19	25.20
6:3-4	8.82	10:5	2.48	15:32	1.27
6:6	22.43	10:6	1.2	16:13-14	27.3
6:10	15.37; 27.65	10:22	1.14; 20.13	16:13	18.80
6:12	10.30; 16.6	10:27	11.26; 18.60	16:14	18.80
6:13	3.7; 13.36	10:36	3.13	16:15	18.80
6:15	10.30	11:7	33.7	16:16	18.80; 27.3
6:16	8.72	11:21	35.7	16:17	10.5
6:22-23	28.30	11:25-26	25.32	16:18	35.13
6:22	13.29	11:25	13.45; 27.4, 24; 34.43	16:22-23	3.38
6:23	28.30			16:24	30.74
6:24	5.55	11:26	25.32	16:25	3.46
6:33	15.53; 20.11	11:27	13.27	17:11	9.9; 20.66; 35.24
6:34	9.105	11:28-30	4.66; 30.50		
7:6	35.13	11:28-29	1.24; 18.68; 20.39	17:19	P.6
7:12-22	10.8			17:22	33.27
7:12	6.54; 19.35	11:28	16.8; 21.9	17:23	33.27

18:3	18.42	24:23	20.23	**Mark**	
18:6	6.57	24:24	14.27; 20.13;	1:6	31.45
18:9	6.57		32.24; 33.56,	2:11	23.46
18:10	2.3; 18.91		61; 34.33	3:27	29.49; 33.20
18:32	16.6	24:26-27	20.23	4:26-27	22.46
19:14	18.42	24:28	27.29; 29.4;	4:28	22.46
19:19	19.38		31.105	4:29	22.46
19:21	26.51	24:35	17.11	6:34-44	16.68
19:23	31.2	24:48-50	18.31	6:37	1.27
19:24	35.38	25:1-13	23.17	6:40-41	30.22
19:25	31.2	25:4	26.42	8:33	10.5
19:26	4P.3; 6.9; 31.2	25:8	8.74	9:2	32.8
19:28	4.46; 6.23;	25:11-12	18.15	9:23	10.19; 22.49
	10.52; 11.33;	25:11	33.42	9:24-25	32.34
	20.41; 26.51	25:12	8.85; 20.43;	9:26	10.50
19:29	15.18		33.42; 34.53	9:49	7.8
20:8	35.13	25:13	7.45	11:25	9.24; 10.30;
20:12	8.13	25:27	22.53		35.21
20:13-15	25.32	25:33	11.49	12:40	33.43
20:16	25.21	25:34	6.48; 26.51	13:31	16.46; 17.11
20:22	17.9	25:35-36	6.9, 48;	14:51-52	14.57
20:23	34.55		15.37; 26.51	16:15	6.20; 33.33
20:29-30	19.5	25:40	16.2		
22:13	25.22	25:41	9.97; 15.23;	**Luke**	
22:37	35.42		26.50; 33.37	1:6	35.10
23:2-3	31.36	25:42-43	15.23;	1:35	18.33, 84; 33.5
23:3	6.10; 30.82		26.50	1:38	18.85
23:5-7	15.4	25:46	34.35	1:43	18.85
23:6-7	8.80	26:33	25.28	1:74	9.63
23:15	1.24; 6.4	26:39	12.16	1:76	19.6
23:23	20.20	26:41	20.13	1:79	4.30
23:24	1.21	26:65	2.62	2:13	17.19
23:27-28	18.13;	26:69-72	17.48	2:14	27.29; 28.19, 34
	26.59; 31.11	26:69	25.28	2:16	31.3
24:12	2.2; 16.81;	26:75	9.54; 25.28	2:19	16.44
	29.37; 33.5	27:3-5	25.19	2:29	6.54
24:13	1.14	27:5	11.12; 18.46;	2:35	34.17
24:16	20.20		29.33	3:9	17.3
24:21	32.23	27:19	33.31	3:38	9.3
24:22	32.23	27:32	8.72	4:6	34.55

4:14	3.28	13:18-19	19.3	19:2-4	27.79
4:34	33.27	13:24	11.68	21:3	24.13
5:3	17.37	13:25	25.2; 33.27	21:19	5.33; 21.33
6:17-18	22.27	13:26	1.29 (2x)	21:33	17.11
6:24	18.66	13:27	2.6; 17.2; 23.7;	21:34	20.39
6:30	27.79; 31.21		28.11; 29.59;	22:28	1.56; 27.65
6:37-38	10.30		32.12; 33.27; 34.53	22:53	6.62
6:46	33.12	13:35	8.35	22:56-57	22.46
8:39	6.60; 16.33, 76	14:1-4	14.14	22:61-62	8.30; 30.78;
8:45-46	3.36	14:11	12.5; 16.29		32.10
8:45	20.43	14:26	7.41	23:8	10.53; 22.38
8:46	20.43	14:33	8.45; 31.21	23:9	22.38
9:13	1.27; 8.45	15:2	29.12	23:11	10.53; 22.38
9:23	33.13	15:7	3.34	23:21	6.35
9:29-33	8.92	15:22	12.9	23:31	12.5, 8; 19.51
9:58	19.2	16:9	18.28; 21.30	23:34	13.25
9:59-60	28.16	16:12	8.12	23:40-43	25.19
9:60	4.52; 7.41; 19.42	16:14	14.14	23:40-41	18.64
10:1	35.41	16:19	15.32	23:42	18.64
10:7	1.23	16:23	10.8; 18.29	23:43	20.13; 23.48;
10:17	23.13	16:24	1.11; 12.56;		29.33
10:18	20.13; 23.13		18.30	24:21	14.58
10:20	20.13; 25.20	16:25	5.1; 34.53	24:39	14.72
10:24	4.3; 13.52	16:27-28	8.29	24:46-47	29.26
10:27	7.28; 9.101	16:28	10.8; 15.6	24:49	30.26
10:41-42	6.61	17:5	22.49		
12:17-18	15.26	17:10	17.27; 27.62	**John**	
12:19	8.45; 14.19; 22.4	17:12	18.26	1:1	5.50; 11.11;
12:20	2.2; 8.45; 18.31;	17:13	18.26		27.46; 32.7
	22.4; 25.3	17:21	8.41	1:3-4	27.46
12:31	15.53	17:34	32.35	1:3	12.19; 18.18;
12:32	20.13; 33.33	17:36	32.35		27.34
12:35	22.11; 28.12;	18:2	14.31	1:9	10.53; 18.81
	30.9; 32.20; 33.33	18:8	20.13	1:11	10.53; 14.47;
12:39-40	18.31	18:11-12	19.33		27.46
12:47-48	15.51; 18.19;	18:11	16.18	1:14	14.72; 18.12;
	25.29	18:12	12.36		25.25
12:48	4.3; 22.8; 25.1	18:14	12.5; 23.13	1:18	18.88
12:49	6.56	18:18	1.31	1:29	8.56
13:7	17.3	18:19	9.46	1:33	2.90

1:47	33.32	7:41	14.54	14:2	9.98; 35.46
1:48	18.59	7:48-49	2.51	14:6	29.16, 40
3:5	9.32	8:7	1.16; 14.34	14:10	19.5; 34.55
3:8	10.13; 18.82; 27.41; 29.43	8:12	24.24	14:16-17	5.50
		8:34	20.42; 25.34; 30.66	14:16	5.64
3:13	27.30			14:17	2.90
3:18	26.50	8:36	18.72; 24.5	14:21	18.90
4:13	6.5; 12.6	8:44	13.38; 19.4	14:23	19.6, 21
4:14	21.15	8:47	27.23	14:27	6.53
4:21	21.9	8:55	34.55	14:30	30.9, 71
4:34	30.78	8:58	30.2	15:5	33.38
4:38	9.47	9:2-3	P.12	15:12	10.7
5:14	P.12	9:28	18.72; 23.5	15:14	27.28, 65
5:18	30.3	9:33	11.3; 29.5	15:15	10.52; 27.28; 33.33
5:22	22.44; 28.5	9:39	2.57; 27.4; 29.8		
5:27	30.68	10:1	5.45	15:16	33.38
5:28-29	12.11	10:9	6.4; 7.14; 30.49	15:22	25.28
5:30	34.55; 35.28	10:18	24.3; 35.38	15:24	25.28
5:37	13.27	10:23	2.2	16:2	6.5; 31.39; 34.32
5:43	25.34; 29.75	10:24	6.34; 29.5	16:7	8.41
5:46	7.8	10:27-28	20.13	16:15	27.34
6:15	30.69	10:27	35.32	16:20	6.23; 8.88; 34.55
6:26	23.49	10:30	30.2		
6:27	1.27; 30.78; 31.106; 35.48	11:43	22.31	16:22	6.23; 8.88; 20.12
		11:45-48	27.41		
6:30	11.3	11:47	18.51	16:25	5.52; 30.17, 49
6:37-38	35.28	11:48	29.6; 29.52	16:33	26.26
6:37	30.68	11:50	6.32; 23.5	17:1	28.4
6:41	23.49	12:19	6.32; 18.51; 27.52; 29.5	17:24	27.30; 29.4
6:44	27.23; 33.38			18:4-6	17.54
6:51	6.47; 23.49	12:26	17.9; 34.55	18:4	30.69
6:57	7.7	12:28	28.4	18:6	22.41
6:71-72	20.76	12:31	17.51; 27.49	18:17	17.48
6:71	13.38; 20.13	12:32	12.15	18:18	2.2
7:6	6.62; 10.54	12:35	6.34; 9.96	18:30	29.5
7:12	2.56; 14.54; 29.5	12:43	29.17	18:36	8.12
7:26	14.54	13:3	30.68	19:6	27.49
7:37	1.29; 12.6	13:23	27.16	19:15	29.52
7:38	11.14; 18.58; 19.9	13:30	2.2	19:26	P.3
7:39	11.14; 15.20; 19.9	13:35	20.17; 22.22	19:27	14.57

Comprehensive Scriptural Index 567

20:17	26.53	7:60	7.54; 20.79	14:21	10.36
20:19	30.25	8:1	29.41	15:1-2	28.29
20:22-23	27.22, 34; 28.38	8:20	4.2; 28.38	15:9	6.56
21:5	19.21	8:29	28.2	15:10	29.73
21:10	P.3	9:1-6	29.33	16:3	28.29
21:18	31.69	9:1-5	31.30	16:7	28.15
		9:1-3	11.16	16:9	28.7, 15
		9:1-2	29.41; 31.30	17:18	23.28
Acts		9:2	19.47	17:29	20.41
1:7	34.55	9:3-6	19.11	18:9-10	27.56; 30.83
1:18	9.58	9:3-4	20.9	19:28-31	31.57
1:19	11.12	9:4	3.25; 30.3; 31.43	20:19	20.16; 31.72
2:2-4	17.48	9:5	31.30	20:24	31.58; 35.31
2:2-3	28.2	9:6	18.46; 33.52	20:26-27	26.10
2:2	5.65; 27.34	9:7-18	19.11	20:31	5.25
2:13	23.20	9:13	31.34	21:2	35.31
2:24	29.24; 30.67	9:15-16	12.21	21:13	31.58; 35.31
3:6-8	30.7	9:15	20.9; 29.33	22:8	33.52
3:12-13	30.7	9:16	9.54	23:3	7.53
3:15-16	30.7	9:18	33.52	23:6	34.9
3:15	12.8; 15.69	9:34	23.46	26:14	10.24
3:17-18	7.54	10:1-4	27.72	28:8	27.37
3:19	7.54	10:10-12	28.7		
3:21	10.54	10:11-12	33.33	**Rom**	
4:1-7	17.49	10:13	11.45; 13.15; 14.58; 18.56; 30.26	1:9-11	30.31; 31.17
4:8-10	17.49			1:14	24.39
4:19-20	7.53	10:19	28.2	1:20	26.17
4:20	28.27; 31.67	10:26	21.24; 26.45	1:21	16.71; 25.22
4:32	30.22	10:34	27.72; 28.38	1:24	25.22
4:41	31.55	10:44	2.57	1:26	23.5
5:1-10	26.45	11:1-7	27.72	1:28	16.71
5:28	20.59	11:3	27.71	2:4-5	17.8; 25.5
5:29	17.49; 22.46; 23.52; 28.27; 31.67	11:7	14.58	2:6	16.3; 28.31
		11:18	27.72	2:7	28.31
5:40	17.49; 31.67	12:2-4	20.9	2:12	26.50
5:41	6.16; 17.49; 29.31	13:46	7.11; 9.6; 18.50; 20.47; 29.50; 30.32	2:13	30.74
5:42	17.49			2:15	4.26; 15.38; 24.32
7:49	2.20				
7:51	7.53; 24.41	14:11	23.28	2:16	24.32
7:58	23.25	14:18-21	31.68	3:5	25.21

3:20	29.9	9:20	9.21, 22; 10.7	1:5-6	24.41
3:26	18.81	10:10	18.64; 31.74	1:7	24.41
4:2-3	29.72	11:6	18.62	1:10-11	24.41
5:6	4.66	11:7	4.66	1:10	24.42
5:8	18.62	11:20	16.8	1:21	14.5; 29.1
6:6	19.53	11:25-26	P.20; 2.59;	1:24	1.15, 11;
6:9	14.72		9.9; 18.84;		18.61, 80
6:10	9.41		19.19; 30.32;	1:25	16.37; 20.41;
6:12	14.21; 21.7;		35.24		27.46; 30.9
	31.80	11:30-32	29.56	1:26-27	1.25; 5.73
6:13	9.97	11:33-34	10.7; 28.13	1:27	3.34; 7.53;
6:19	19.49	11:33	29.56, 57		17.6; 18.59; 27.79;
6:21	1.21; 4.32;	11:34	14.56		31.1; 33.32, 34
	28.39; 35.38	11:35	18.63	1:30	16.37; 26.15
7:12-13	7.9	11:36	29.70	2:2	29.54; 31.104
7:18	29.63	12:3	3.45; 16.8, 81;	2:6	30.48
7:19	32.4		18.26; 20.18; 28.23	2:8	9.44; 22.41; 28.37
7:23-24	23.41, 53	12:12	26.26	2:9	4.46; 18.92
7:23	4.54; 6.52; 9.58;	12:14	4.2; 22.25	2:10	18.92
	10.17; 19.12;	12:16	13.45; 26.44;	2:11	15.66; 18.78
	23.21; 29.3; 31.80		34.42	2:13	18.74
7:24	9.58	13:1	20.78	2:16	14.56
8:3	3.33; 33.18	13:2	34.53	3:1-2	17.36; 30.48
8:9	14.72; 15.36	13:4	26.45	3:2	30.48
8:11	9.62	13:10	10.7	3:3	4.25; 6.16;
8:14	22.42	13:11	5.54; 8.20; 30.9		18.92; 24.42
8:15	7.14; 11.55;	13:12-13	18.46	3:4	6.16; 18.92
	14.50; 27.34	13:12	8.48; 29.3; 30.9	3:6-7	27.43
8:18	3.41; 8.14	13:14	9.105; 30.62	3:7	17.27; 27.64;
8:20-22	12.17	14:5	1.28 (2x)		29.49; 30.29
8:20-21	4.68	14:12	26.3	3:9	17.27
8:21	8.13	15:4	30.36	3:11	25.27; 28.14, 31
8:24	15.2; 18.14;	15:9	27.58	3:12	33.68
	31.37	15:18	28.25	3:14	5.27
8:26	2.58	16:18	16.31; 20.20;	3:17	7.56
8:29	20.63		31.35, 72	3:18	13.45; 20.41;
8:34	24.2	16:19	1.1		27.79
8:35	31.61			3:19	2.62; 12.36;
8:38-39	10.39	**1 Cor**			18.67; 20.42
9:11-13	20.76	1:4-5	24.41	4:3-4	5.57

4:4	5.21, 57; 10.15;	11:3	8.49; 20.7; 34.26	**2 Cor**	
	24.33	11:16	8.4	1:8	8.14
4:5	1.13; 18.78	11:31	4.27; 12.2	1:12	8.82; 23.17
4:7	22.20; 23.13	11:32	9.68	1:15	2.59
4:21	24.42	12:8-10	17.50	1:22	16.6
5:3	24.41	12:11	17.50	1:23	26.45
5:5	33.15	12:12	25.12	2:10	33.15
5:6	1.3	12:14-17	28.22	2:11	33.15
6:3	6.24; 26.31	12:19-20	28.22	2:14-15	14.65
6:4	19.42	12:23-24	13.7	2:15-16	29.76
6:5	19.42	12:27	34.8	2:15	24.17; 34.32;
6:7	31.21	13:1	8.76; 32.30		35.43
6:9-10	21.18	13:3	18.41, 42; 20.17	2:16	29.76
6:10	4.2	13:4-6	10.10	2:17	16.74; 22.39
6:12	5.17	13:4	8.2; 22.27	2:29	26.10
7:2	32.39	13:8	30.17	3:3	24.15
7:6	32.39	13:9-10	29.42	3:5	28.13; 33.38
7:28	12.27	13:11	28.44	3:15	9.44; 18.60
7:31	17.11	13:12	5.52; 13.3;	3:17	15.25
7:33	26.44		17.38; 18.89, 90;	4:5	6.24; 7.54;
7:35	26.44		23.41; 28.44;		19.37; 24.42
7:40	1.28; 4.57		31.103	4:7	5.68; 7.19;
8:1	8.72; 16.6; 26.43	13:13	18.64		22.8; 23.20
8:2	27.62; 28.11	13:31	11.48	4:8-9	7.52
8:4	4.13	14:1	19.42	4:16-17	10.35
9:10	31.31	14:20	1.2	4:16	7.19; 31.92
9:20-22	6.54	14:22	27.36	5:1	4.56; 5.68; 6.16;
9:26	30.59	15:9	23.41; 28.13		18.78; 23.41; 29.4
9:27	20.9; 23.41;	15:10	16.3; 18.63;	5:4	31.70
	29.33; 30.59; 31.35		19.52	5:6-7	18.48
10:2-4	23.2	15:14	12.11	5:6	23.41
10:4	3.59; 19.24;	15:20	24.24	5:13	27.44; 30.48
	31.97	15:31	8.12	5:14	27.44
10:7	10.21	15:34	5.54; 8.20; 30.9	5:21	18.81; 26.53;
10:12	25.21	15:36-37	14.73		33.2
10:13	2.19; 9.71;	15:36	6.20	6:2	8.30; 9.104; 18.42
	14.45; 21.7; 24.31;	15:41	17.22; 35.46	6:8	22.17
	28.35; 29.46	15:50	14.72	6:9-10	7.52; 10.35
10:20	4.13	15:51	12.11	6:10	25.25
11:1	31.53	16:5-6	30.31	6:11	26.42; 29.54

Comprehensive Scriptural Index   571

6:13-14	29.30	2:1-2	31.30; 35.31	4:19		31.3
6:16	18.50	2:9	17.42	4:23		22.7; 25.14
7:5	3.40; 14.39; 31.55	2:11-15	29.42	4:26		5.78
8:9	6.35; 18.50; 20.69	2:15	2.56	5:8		17.41; 18.46;
8:10	20.69	2:20	8.44; 24.48			29.32
8:13	20.69	3:1	24.41; 30.47	5:13		4.27; 6.40
8:14	21.30	3:3	30.47	5:14		8.20; 15.65
9:6	20.69	4:4-5	12.15; 29.75	5:16		5.70
10:10	10.51; 27.60	4:4	11.65	5:27		2.55; 13.1;
11	18.13	4:19-20	30.47			20.58; 32.8
11:3	31.16	4:20	30.31	5:31		20.8
11:14-15	33.44	4:29	20.76	6:12		2.38; 13.11
11:14	4.6	5:2	31.32	6:15		34.19
11:20	33.24	5:7	30.47	6:17		19.56; 34.17
11:21-23	19.37	5:13	28.22	6:20		18.50
11:23-25	11.16; 31.80	5:17	29.63			
11:26-28	3.40	5:24	8.73	**Phil**		
11:26-27	19.11	6:2	10.7; 21.33; 30.36	1:8		31.17
11:26	14.39	6:10	9.104	1:12-13		29.31
11:28	31.80	6:14	5.4; 18.89	1:21		8.44; 11.16;
11:29	19.18; 20.77	6:15	30.45			18.48; 29.4;
11:32-33	19.11; 31.58					31.70
12:2-4	17.36; 18.13	**Eph**		1:23		4.68; 8.13, 44;
12:2	31.103	1:9-10	31.99			18.48; 26.55;
12:3-7	33.28	1:11	20.11			29.4; 31.70
12:4	19.11; 29.66;	1:18-19	23.41	2:3		34.43
	31.103	1:18	26.55; 34.5	2:6-7		2.42; 9.63;
12:6	18.13; 29.66	2:3	9.32			34.54, 55
12:7-9	19.11	2:6	3.25; 6.24; 31.95	2:15-16		20.76
12:7	P.21; 19.11	2:8-9	18.63; 23.13;	2:15		1.1; 4.17; 17.22
12:9	19.11, 23.34		33.38	2:19		30.31
12:10	22.13	2:14	28.19	2:21		17.9; 19.56
12:11	24.42	3:13	31.17	3:1		22.1
12:14	30.31	3:18	10.15	3:2		31.16
13:3	P.3	3:20	10.15	3:5-6		8.44
13:4	14.67; 27.3, 46	4:1	5.25	3:7		8.44; 26.55
13:5	31.71	4:14	20.23	3:8-9		8.44
		4:15	P.14; 23.2	3:8		8.44; 20.35
Gal		4:16	28.23	3:12-14		29.33
1:14	31.30	4:18	25.8	3:13-14		26.80

3:13	22.12; 28.13; 31.103; 33.48	5:4	8.17	2:11-12	10.36
3:18-20	26.31	5:4-5	18.31; 25.3	2:19	27.23
3:18-19	31.35	5:5	8.17	2:21	19.42
3:18	31.16	5:7	29.32	2:25-26	34.38
3:19	11.5			3:2	26.62; 33.3
3:20	1.4; 5.69; 6.16; 8.74; 23.9; 31.95	**2 Thess**		3:4	33.3
		1:4-5	5.22	4:6-8	10.38
4:8-9	31.53	2:4	29.18; 32.27	4:6	22.13; 31.52
4:17	19.22	2:6-7	29.15; 34.28	4:7	22.13
4:18	19.22	2:7	23.24	4:8	31.52
		2:8	14.26; 15.69; 29.18; 32.27; 34.10	**Titus**	
Col		2:10-11	25.34	1:6	21.19
1:16	16.33; 32.48	2:10-12	29.75	1:16	4.17; 17.7; 20.43; 25.25; 29.11; 33.12
1:24	P.14; 3.25; 23.2; 29.64; 31.33	3:2	27.23	2:15	23.24
		3:6	31.16	3:10-11	20.47
2:5	30.31	**1 Tim**			
2:8	26.27	1:13	11.16; 18.62; 22.12; 23.13; 31.30	**Phlm**	
3:3	5.9; 6.56; 8.45			7	19.22
3:5	20.78; 26.7, 27; 30.71; 31.80	2:5	3.33; 16.37; 18.85; 24.5	**Heb**	
3:9-10	19.53; 31.92	2:12	3.12	1:3	5.64
3:14	28.46	2:13	12.26	1:14	2.3; 9.26
4:3	29.49	3:16	34.14	2:16	4.12
4:6	7.15	4:3	16.1	4:13	17.33; 19.20; 25.7; 32.2
		4:11	23.24		
1 Thess		5:22-24	5.74	6:7	28.20
2:5-7	19.37	5:23	20.78; 27.37	7:10	32.20
2:6-7	10.51; 24.53	6:10	14.65; 15.22; 20.21	7:19	7.9; 9.63
2:7	26.45; 34.43			8:13	34.34
2:8	33.42	6:16	12.38; 18.92; 25.9	9:23	17.46
2:16	25.23	6:20	18.39	10:25	5.8
2:17	31.17	**2 Tim**		11:1	15.2
2:18	27.56	1:3-4	31.17	11:9	8.92
2:19	11.22; 19.53	1:12	8.12	11:10	16.15
3:2-3	31.17	1:16	19.22	11:13-14	18.48
3:3	3.40; 6.15; 13.18	2:2	30.35	11:27	19.21
3:8	31.17	2:4	5.55; 17.19	11:36-37	25.17
4:13-14	5.54; 12.12	2:9	29.47; 31.65	12:1-2	21.11
5:2	7.45			12:1	25.17; 30.39

12:6	P.5; 6.40; 9.68;	1:4	27.29; 30.80	2:19	12.33; 18.49;
	12.33; 14.35; 15.39;	1:12	18.91		20.15; 23.11
	18.35; 26.37	1:13	13.19; 21.5;	2:27	5.50; 29.49
12:11	6.40		32.20	3:2	5.52; 12.18;
12:12-13	22.50	1:24	17.10		18.79; 25.21
12:12	18.37; 28.12;	2:5	6.50; 8.81; 16.64;	3:4	11.57
	30.74		18.52; 31.97	3:15	16.72
12:17	11.13	2:9	25.15	3:18	21.29
12:20	6.58	2:10	27.58	3:21-22	10.28; 18.9
12:24	13.26	2:21-25	21.11	3:21	9.60; 27.48
13:7	25.17; 30.39	2:21	16.41	4:5	11.23
13:17	34.53	2:22	2.43; 2.62	4:10	33.38
13:22	5.25; 23.29	3:9	22.25	4:18	9.63; 11.55
		3:15	23.24	4:20	7.88
Jas		3:16	23.24	5:16	16.82
1:17	5.63; 12.38;	4:10	28.22		
	25.9; 32.9	4:15	3.41	**3 John**	
1:19	7.58	4:17-18	5.22	11	31.16
1:20	5.78	4:17	5.34; 9.90; 26.37		
1:26	7.58	4:18	13.55; 17.23	**Jude**	
2:10	19.32	5:8-9	19.47; 31.16, 74	5	18.35
2:11	19.32	5:8	5.41		
2:15-16	21.29			**Rev**	
2:20	17.7; 33.12	**2 Pet**		1:4	34.14
2:26	17.7; 29.72	1:19	19.18	1:13	21.5; 34.26
3:1-2	32.2	2:2	31.72	1:20	34.14
3:1	19.22	2:3	31.72	2:13	1.1; 9.89;
3:2	18.71; 19.22;	2:4	8.39; 13.53		20.76; 21.10
	24.33; 29.3	2:7-8	1.1; 20.76	2:14	21.10; 29.15
3:8	7.58; 32.2	2:13	18.66	2:17	19.4
3:14-15	22.53	3:10-12	27.33	2:19-20	21.10
4:3	21.25	3:15-16	24.20	2:20	29.15
4:6	34.53			3:4	9.58
4:9	18.66	**1 John**		3:12	17.42
4:14	7.45; 17.10	1:8	12.38; 18.49, 71;	3:17	34.6
4:17	18.19		21.19; 24.33	3:18	4.61
5:16	22.32	2:1-2	22.42	3:19	6.40; 9.69;
5:20	19.31	2:4	17.7; 33.12		18.35; 26.37
		2:15	18.16	3:21	26.53
1 Pet		2:16-17	18.16	3:22	25.20
1:3-4	6.56	2:18	29.15	3:27	23.13

4:7	31.94	11:2	28.16	17:15	17.31; 19.9
4:10	22.20	11:4	9.10	18:7	9.98
5:5	5.41; 30.9	12:1	34.25	19:10	21.24; 27.29
5:10	25.15	12:4	4.17; 32.25	19:14	31.27
5:12	2.10	12:5	34.12	20:1-3	4.16; 32.22
6:8	4.30; 11.28; 14.20; 18.47; 19.4; 33.6	12:6-7	15.72	20:1-5	18.67
		12:10	2.15	20:6	9.3; 14.19
		12:12	34.1	20:7	4.16; 32.22
6:9-10	2.11	12:14	15.72	20:12	24.16
6:11	2.11; 35.25	13:5	15.72	21:1	17.11
6:12	9.8	13:11	33.59	21:18	18.77; 34.26
7:14	10.36	13:13	33.62	22:9	21.24; 27.29
8:1	30.53	14:14	33.21	22:10	9.15
9:19	33.48	16:8	34.25	22:11	11.18
10:4	9.15	16:15	2.81; 12.9; 16.63	22:12	25.23
10:6	4.5			22:16	29.75